Interviews with M. A. K. Halliday

Also Available From Bloomsbury

Bloomsbury Companion to Systemic Functional Linguistics,
Edited by M. A. K. Halliday and Jonathan J. Webster
Collected Works of M. A. K. Halliday, Edited by Jonathan J. Webster
The Essential Halliday, Edited by Jonathan J. Webster

Interviews with M. A. K. Halliday

Language Turned Back on Himself

Edited by

J. R. Martin

BLOOMSBURY
LONDON • NEW DELHI • NEW YORK • SYDNEY

Bloomsbury Academic
An imprint of Bloomsbury Publishing Plc

50 Bedford Square
London
WC1B 3DP
UK

175 Fifth Avenue
New York
NY 10010
USA

www.bloomsbury.com

First published 2013

© J. R. Martin, 2013

All rights reserved. No part of this publication may be reproduced or transmitted in any form or by any means, electronic or mechanical, including photocopying, recording, or any information storage or retrieval system, without prior permission in writing from the publishers.

J. R. Martin has asserted his right under the Copyright, Designs and Patents Act, 1988, to be identified as Author of this work.

No responsibility for loss caused to any individual or organization acting on or refraining from action as a result of the material in this publication can be accepted by Bloomsbury Academic or the author.

British Library Cataloguing-in-Publication Data
A catalogue record for this book is available from the British Library.

ISBN: HB: 978-1-4411-5487-3
PB: 978-1-4411-9081-9
ePub: 978-1-4411-4585-7
ePDF: 978-1-4411-1031-2

Library of Congress Cataloging-in-Publication Data
Interviews with M.A.K. Halliday : Language Turned Back on Himself / Edited by J.R. Martin.
pages cm
Includes bibliographical references and index.
ISBN 978-1-4411-5487-3 (hardcover)– ISBN 978-1-4411-9081-9 (pbk.)– ISBN (invalid) 978-1-4411-1031-2 (ebook (pdf))– ISBN (invalid) 978-1-4411-4585-7 (ebook (epub)) 1. Halliday, M. A. K. (Michael Alexander Kirkwood), 1925—Interviews. 2. Linguists--England--Interviews. 3. Functional linguistics. I. Martin, J. R., editor of compilation.
P83.H35A5 2013
410.92–dc23
2012041377

Typeset by Fakenham Prepress Solutions, Fakenham, Norfolk NR21 8NN
Printed and bound in India

Contents

Preface	vii
Acknowledgements	ix
Introduction	xi

1	With Herman Parret (1972)	1
2	With Noboru Yamaguchi and Shun'ichi Segawa (1977)	41
3	From *The English Magazine* (1981)	59
4	With M. L. Tickoo (1985)	67
5	With Paul J. Thibault (1985)	73
6	With Ruqaiya Hasan, Gunther Kress and J. R. Martin (1986)	95
7	With Michael O'Toole and Gunther Kress (1989)	135
8	With Caroline Coffin (1998)	143
9	With Manuel A. Hernández (1998)	147
10	With Geoff Thompson and Heloisa Collins (1998)	161
11	With Anne Burns (2006)	179
12	With Hu Zhuanglin and Zhu Yongsheng (2010)	191
13	With Bilal Ibne Rasheed (2010)	203
14	With J. R. Martin and Paul Thibault (2011)	211

Bibliography	257
Index	269

Preface

The idea for this book emerged from conversations between Paul Thibault and Jim Martin when we were colleagues in Hong Kong in the second half of 2010. After discussing the project with Jonathan Webster, we began gathering interviews and arranged for a 'capstone' interview with Michael Halliday, which took place in February 2011. We are much indebted to Cecilia Pun for recording and transcribing that interview, and to Shiwen Chen, Yaegan Doran, Jing Hao and Beatriz Quiroz for help converting a number of pdf files of other interviews to Word format and the awkward tidying up that commutation involved.

Paul's shift from Hong Kong to Norway in 2011 meant that it was left to Jim to push ahead with outstanding transcriptions, alongside editing the interviews, compiling references and writing an introduction. Some of the interviews had not previously been groomed by Halliday, and I am grateful for his painstaking reformulations of the sometimes difficult interview manuscripts themselves. I am also much indebted to the various interviewers who have generously allowed their conversations to be included here, and for previously published material, my thanks to their publishers as well.

The subtitle of the volume adapts a well-known saying of Firth's, which characterises linguistics as language turned back on itself – by way of paying homage here to one of Halliday's main teachers. Those of us lucky enough to have been among Halliday's students or colleagues know first-hand the pleasure of discussing language face-to-face with him. I think I can speak for all involved in this project when I say I hope that these interviews will provide a useful surrogate for those who have not enjoyed the privilege of engaging with Michael in spoken interactions of this kind. We may not have thought to ask everyone's questions, but I think we have managed quite a few!

Sydney May 2012

Acknowledgements

We are grateful to the original publishers and interviewers for permission to reprint the interviews in this volume. Original publication details are provided below:

Chapter 1: 1974 (with Herman Parret, 9 October 1972) M. A. K. Halliday. In Herman Parret. *Discussing Language*. The Hague: Mouton, 81–120.

Chapter 2: 1986 (with Noboru Yamaguchi and Shun'ichi Segawa, 27 September 1977) Discussion with M. A. K. Halliday 1977 (and its Systemic Background Then and Now). *Bulletin of the Faculty of Education (Liberal Arts)* 39, Fukushima University, 83–99.

Chapter 3: 1981 Mark These Linguists: Michael Halliday. *The English Magazine*. Summer 1981, 8–11. Published by the English and Media Centre: London.

Chapter 4: 1985 (with M. L. Tickoo, April 1985) Michael Halliday in Close-up. This text is reproduced here with the kind permission of SEAMEO Regional Language Centre. All rights reserved.

Chapter 5: 1987. (with Paul J. Thibault, September 1985) An Interview with Michael Halliday. In Ross Steele and Terry Threadgold (eds) *Language Topics: Essays in Honour of Michael Halliday*. Vols. 1 and 2. Amsterdam/Philadelphia: John Benjamins, 601–27. Reproduced with kind permission by John Benjamins Publishing Company, Amsterdam/Philadelphia. (www.benjamins.com).

Chapter 6: 1992 (with Gunther Kress, Ruqaiya Hasan and J. R. Martin, May, 1986) Interview – M. A. K. Halliday. May 1986. *Social Semiotics* 2.1, pp.176–195 and 2.2. 58–69. Reprinted by permission of the publisher (Taylor & Francis Ltd: http://www.tandfonline.com).

Chapter 7: 1989 (with Michael O'Toole) Language in Education Conference, Murdoch University: Australia, December 1989.

Chapter 8: 1998 (with Caroline Coffin) Recorded and edited for a masters-level course in Applied Linguistics co-produced by the Open University and Macquarie University. © The Open University. Reproduced here with the kind permission of the Open University. All rights reserved.

Chapter 9: 2000 (with Manuel A. Hernández Hernández, July 1998) An interview with Michael Halliday: The Man and The Linguist. Hernández Hernández, Manuel A. (ed.) *Revista Canaria de Estudios Ingleses*. Servicio de Publicaciones, Universidad de La Laguna, Campus Central, 38200 La Laguna – Tenerife, Spain, 233–43.

Chapter 10: 2001 (with Geoff Thompson and Heloisa Collins, July 1998) An interview with M. A. K. Halliday, Cardiff, July 1998. *D.E.L.T.A*, 17:1: 131–53.

Chapter 11: 2006 (with Anne Burns) Applied Linguistics: thematic pursuits or disciplinary moorings? – a conversation between Michael Halliday and Anne Burns. *Journal of Applied Linguistics* 3.1, 2006, 113–28.

Chapter 12: 2010 (with Hu Zhuanglin, and Zhu Yongsheng, July 2010). Interviewing Professor M. A. K. Halliday by Hu Zhuanglin and Zhu Yongsheng. *Foreign Languages in China* (6): 17–24.

Chapter 13: 2010 (with Bilal Ibne Rasheed, 29 July 2010) An interview with Michael Halliday. Dawn, Books, and Authors.

Introduction

The 14 interviews in this volume span the years 1972 to 2011. Because several of the interviews cover comparable ground, it was not possible to group them thematically; and I was reluctant to disturb the flow of the original interviews by excerpting sections from them. All are in addition contextualised to some degree by the flavour of their times, and so in the end I decided to organise the interviews chronologically, in the sequence in which they were originally conducted.

All of the interviews have been transcribed, and subsequently edited by the interviewers and Halliday, with minor adjustments by myself. In general, the free flowing power of the spoken mode has been preserved, with minimal allowances made for the fact that they will be read in this volume, not heard (although I do allow that Halliday might very well encourage people to read them aloud). Where appropriate below, the theory of language developed by Halliday and his colleagues, Systemic Functional Linguistics, will be abbreviated as SFL.

All of the original references have been compiled at the end of the volume, along with additional references I have added now and again to clarify the discussion. I have not tried to include detailed references to entire bodies of work by Saussure, Whorf, Hjelmslev, Firth, Pike, Lamb, Hymes, Bernstein, Hasan and others when they are mentioned in the discussion, but have simply included references to specific publications where required. Publications by major figures in the field can all be followed up easily on the web by readers who want to further explore their work in relation to the interviews here.

Hasan et al.'s *Continuing Discourse on Language* Volume 2 (2007) includes a complete bibliography of Halliday's works (up to 2007), cross-referenced to the papers in the 10 volumes of Collected Works edited by Jonathan Webster for Continuum (an eleventh volume is currently in preparation) – these lists have not been reproduced here. All of Halliday's papers mentioned in this volume, however, have been cited and cross-referenced to the appropriate volume of his Collected Works. Hasan et al. (2005, 2007) and Halliday and Webster's *Continuum Companion to Systemic Functional Linguistics* (2009) include a comprehensive range of papers by SFL linguists that fully contextualise the discussions reproduced here. Matthiessen et al. (2010) provide a glossary covering nearly all of the SFL terms used in this volume.

I will not tire readers anxious to get on with reading the interviews with a lengthy introduction to each one here, but will simply set each interview in time and place, note the interviewers involved and make a comment highlighting a significant dimension or two of their content. Full details for previously published interviews are included in the Acknowledgements above.

Interview 1 was conducted by Herman Parret in Stanford in 1972, when Halliday was a fellow at the Centre for Advanced Study in the Behavioural Sciences. It forms part of a collection of interviews with leading influential linguists of that time (Chafe, Chomsky, Greimas, Hartmann, Lakoff, Lamb, Martinet, McCawley, Saumjan) – published in 1974 by Mouton as *Discussing Language*. Parret particularly explores the theoretical context of Halliday's theory, drawing out its European heritage and well as North American connections. *Discussing Language* is a fascinating volume and more than repays time spent exploring the company Halliday keeps therein.

Interview 2 was conducted by Noboru Yamaguchi, with the assistance of Shun'ichi Segawa, in 1977 at the University of Sydney, where Yamaguchi was studying as a visiting scholar. Halliday, and to a limited extent the editor, have slightly revised Yamaguchi's transcription and editing of the interview. Yamaguchi particularly probes the relation of Halliday's thinking to various perspectives deriving from Chomskyan formalism, capturing as he does so the way in which this hegemonic tradition positioned others to defend their theoretical ground – in the face of being positioned as misguided 'heretics' standing outside the 'mainstream'. The courage of Halliday's convictions is very much in evidence here.

Interview 3 was published in *The English Magazine* in 1981; it poses a set of questions to three distinguished linguists – Halliday, Chomsky and Hymes. These questions and a short introduction to Halliday preface his response. Halliday's positioning of his work in relation to educational concerns further illuminates the orientation of his theory in relation to the discussion in Interviews 1 and 2. As with the Parret volume, comparing the responses of the linguists involved reveals a great deal about the intellectual climate of those times.

Interview 4 was conducted by Dr M. L. Tickoo in 1985 at the Regional Language Centre, Singapore (as transcribed by Guo Libo) after a Language Across the Curriculum seminar (Tickoo 1985). This interview further explores the language in education themes opened up in Interview 3, particularly language across the curriculum concerns.

Interview 5 was conducted by Paul Thibault in September 1985 and published as an end-piece to the two-volume festschrift *Language Topics*, edited by Ross Steele and Terry Threadgold (Benjamins 1987), prepared for Halliday upon his retirement as founding Professor of the Department of Linguistics at the University of Sydney. This in-depth discussion further clarifies the position of Halliday's thinking within the field, and focuses in detail on several dimensions of the theory itself. This interview nicely complements Parret, with questions formulated by a sympathetic and well-informed insider, rather than a well-read fellow traveller surveying contemporary trends.

Interview 6 was conducted by Ruqaiya Hasan, Gunther Kress and Jim Martin at the University of Sydney in May 1986 and published in two parts in *Social Semiotics* 2.1 and 2.2 in 1992. Alongside picking up on and developing themes introduced in previous interviews (grammatical theory, language in education, language and context), this discussion opens with a section covering biographical details relevant to the development of Halliday's career. This introduces readers, many for the first time I suspect, to Halliday's interest in the development of a Marxist linguistics, and the intellectual backing-off movement he felt was necessary for such a theory to evolve.

Interview 7 was conducted by Michael O'Toole at Murdoch University in Perth in conjunction with the '3D: Discipline-Dialogue-Difference' conference there in 1989.

The conversation includes Gunther Kress, who was also a participant in this language in education meeting. This interview adds the theme of multimodality to the discussions, reflecting Kress and O'Toole's emerging concern with the grammar of semiotic systems other than language – with special reference to language in education issues.

Interview 8 was conducted by Caroline Coffin in 1998 in support of a masters-level course in Applied Linguistics, co-produced by Macquarie University and the Open University. Here Halliday clarifies, for novice readers, the reasons for calling the theory systemic and functional, and comments on the development of work on context in the model.

Interview 9 was conducted by Manuel Hernández during the twenty-fifth International Systemic Functional Congress at Cardiff University in 1998, and published in a special edition of *Revista Canaria de Estudios Ingleses* (alongside interviews with Matthiessen and Martin). It returns to and develops a number of themes introduced in Interviews 1, 5 and 6 in particular. As with interview 6, Halliday's discussion of the influence of his teachers in China and the UK (Wang Li and Firth in particular) and of colleagues Bernstein and Hasan is of particular interest.

Interview 10, with Geoff Thompson and Heloisa Collins, was also conducted during the twenty-fifth International Systemic Functional Congress at Cardiff University in 1998, for publication in Brazil (*DELTA* 17.1). It focuses on the development of the theory, SFL's relation to other schools, critical linguistics, linguistics and cognition, register, practical analysis issues and computer-aided analysis. This interview by Collins, who works in Brazil, and Thompson, who often visits there and regularly hosts Brazilian scholars in Liverpool, reflects the growing internationalisation of Halliday's theory, with Latin America and China (cf. interview 12 below) emerging as key centres of research.

Interview 11 was conducted by Anne Burns for publication in the *Journal of Applied Linguistics* in 2006. It explores Halliday's position in the field of Applied Linguistics, language in education in particular. This affords Halliday another opportunity to articulate his view of SFL as an appliable linguistics, involving a dialectic of theory in practice, and his concern that this dialectic evolve in an expanding range of applied contexts, not just language education.

Interview 12 was conducted by Hu Zhuanglin and Zhu Yongsheng in a plenary session at the 36th International Systemic Functional Congress at Tsinghua University in 2009 and later published in the journal *Foreign Languages in China*. Hu was part of the first group of linguists and literature specialists to leave China to study abroad, at the University of Sydney, after the Cultural Revolution (the 'Gang of Nine' as they refer to themselves) – 1979–80; and Zhu was part of a later group – 1983–85. Their influence in China, alongside that of their colleagues who studied in Sydney, and later in Cardiff (especially Huang Guowen), has been immense – with major university research centres active at Sun Yat-sen University, Xiamen University, Fudan University, Shanghai Jiaotong University, Tongji University, Shandong University, Nanjing International Studies University, Peking University, Tsinghua University, Beijing Normal University and the University of Science and Technology Beijing among others.

Interview 13 was conducted by Bilal Ibne Rasheed (his penname; his actual name – Mushtaq ur Rasool Bilal) in Pakistan in July 2010 and published in *Dawn, Books and*

Authors. Among other themes, it explores further the relationship between Halliday's politics and SFL, including its consequences for his career path, both institutional and theoretical.

The final interview, 14, was conducted by Jim Martin and Paul Thibault (with Cecilia Pun recording) at Halliday's home in Sydney in February 2011, as a capstone chapter for this book. It attempts to fill in bibliographical details missing from previous interviews and to explore, again from an 'insider' perspective, a range of contemporary theoretical and descriptive concerns in SFL. This discussion reflects (as do many others in the volume) Halliday's enduring spirit of generosity as far as alternative points of view are concerned, a generosity not always afforded him by others with respect to either his political beliefs or his evolving model of language and social context.

As a personal comment, there are few in life I can count on as a mentor, colleague, comrade and friend. Halliday is one, and these interviews, collectively, demonstrate for all of us what it takes to be that kind of person too.

With regard to notation, I have adopted standard SFL formatting conventions throughout, with names of systems in small caps (e.g. MOOD, SPEECH FUNCTION, TONE), structural functions written with an initial upper case letter (e.g. Subject, Tonic, Orientation) and class labels in lower case (e.g. noun, imperative, anecdote, procedure).

With Herman Parret (1972)

HP: *Michael Halliday, you are one of the most representative linguists of what one might call the trend of sociolinguistics. You use terms like sociogrammar and sociosemantics; does that imply a very particular view on the scope of linguistics?*

MAKH: I would really prefer to leave out the 'socio', if I had the choice. But we probably have to talk about 'sociolinguistics' these days, because of the shift in the meaning of 'linguistics'. When I was a student, with J. R. Firth, linguistics was the study of language in society; it was assumed that one took into account social factors, so linguists never found it necessary to talk about sociolinguistics. But during the last ten or fifteen years the pendulum has swung in the opposite direction, away from the social context towards the study of language from what I would call an 'intra-organism' point of view, or language as knowledge if you like; so that anyone who is concerned with the other, 'inter-organism' aspect of language, with how people talk to each other, has to prefix 'socio' to what he is doing. Hence you have sociolinguistics; and hence, also, 'sociosemantics' or 'sociogrammar'.

Let me put it this way: these two perspectives – on the one hand the intra-organism perspective, language as what goes on inside the head (language as knowledge), and on the other hand the inter-organism perspective, language as what goes on between people (language as interaction, or simply as behavior) – are complementary and not contradictory. There tend to be fashions in linguistics, as in many other things. I started in a tradition where the perspective was mainly of the inter-organism kind. Then the pendulum swung the other way, largely through the influence of Chomsky who emphasized the philosophical and psychological links of the subject. And so those wanting to talk about language from the point of view not so much that 'people talk' but that 'people talk to each other' have called what they are doing sociolinguistics. I think both Hymes and Labov have pointed out that the 'socio' is really unnecessary, and I rather agree with them.

HP: *You wrote that a good linguist has to go outside linguistics. What do you mean by that?*

MAKH: This is a related point. If you look at the writings of linguists in the 1950s, you find great stress laid on the *autonomy* of linguistics. Linguistics is seeking recognition as a subject in its own right; it has not to be evaluated against other disciplines. Now, as long as you concentrate attention on the core of the linguistic system, on linguistic form (grammar and vocabulary), then the interrelationships that you are studying are – or can be treated as if they were – wholly bounded within language, since their immediate points of reference are also within language: on the one hand the semantic system, and on the other hand the phonological system. But once you become concerned with the linguistic system as a whole, including the semantic system, then you have to look outside language for your criteria of *idealization*.

The essential question at issue is this: what are or are not two instances of the same phenomenon, two tokens of the same type? The moment you include the semantic and phonological systems in your picture, then you are involved in the interfaces between language and something else: in one direction meaning, and in the other direction sound. The two are not symmetrical, of course, because the system is not symmetrical; the classic problem in phonology, the debate over the phoneme, is a debate about the nature of idealization at the 'output' end – in classifying two sounds together as tokens of the same type, do you look 'downwards' and take account of the expression system, or only 'upwards' towards the content? But when we are concerned with the grammatical system our point of reference is clearly 'upwards'. We relate the distinctions that we draw in the grammatical system (grammar and vocabulary) to the semantics. Where then do we find the criteria for distinctions in the semantic system? How do we decide what are or are not instances of the same meaning, tokens of the same semantic type? Only by going outside language. In practice most people, including many linguists, without even really thinking about this issue quite arbitrarily use the orthographic system as their criterion of idealization. They assume that if two things are written the same they are the same, and if they are written differently they are different. (They are reluctant to accept, for example, that differences of intonation may realize distinctions within the semantic system, distinguishing one semantic type from another in just the same way that different words or structures do.) This in the last resort is circular. You cannot find within language criteria for semantic idealization, criteria for deciding whether two things are the same or are not the same in meaning. You have got to go outside language. The accepted way of doing this is to postulate a conceptual system. One says, in effect, we have a system of concepts, two concepts are the same or different, and that is how we decide whether two linguistic elements are the same or different. If we admit that there is a *semantic* system, a semantic level of organization within the linguistic system, then the question we are asking is "What is above that?"; and it is at that point that we move outside language. We are regarding semantics as an interface between language and something else, and it is to that something else that we go for our criteria of idealization. In that sense, the linguistic system is not autonomous. Only, once we admit that, we can then take account of the fact that there is more than one direction that we may go outside language. A conceptual system is not the only form that such a higher-level semiotic can take.

HP: *Do you stress the instrumentality of linguistics rather than its autonomy?*

MAKH: These are not really contradictory. But there are two different issues involved when you talk about autonomy. One is: "To what extent *is* the subject self-sufficient?" My answer is: "It isn't." (But then what subject is?) The second is: "To what extent *are we studying* language for the purpose of throwing light on language or for the purpose of throwing light on something else?" This is a question of goals; it is the question why you are doing it. In this sense the two perspectives are just complementary. Probably most people who have looked at language in functional terms have had a predominantly instrumental approach; they have not been concerned with the nature of language as such so much as with the use of language to explore something else. But I would say that in order to understand the nature of language itself we also have to approach it functionally. So I would have both perspectives at once. It seems to me that we have to recognize different purposes for which language may be studied. An autonomous linguistics is the study of language for the sake of understanding the linguistic system. An instrumental linguistics is the study of language for understanding something else – the social system, for example.

HP: *One needs for a relevant linguistic theory other larger theories, behavioral and sociological theories. One can find in your publications many allusions to Bernstein's sociology. What does Bernstein mean for you?*

MAKH: If you are interested in inter-organism linguistics, in language as interaction, then you are inevitably led to a consideration of language in the perspective of the social system. What interests me about Bernstein is that he is a theoretical sociologist who builds language into his theory not as an optional extra but as an essential component (Bernstein 1971). In Bernstein's view, in order to understand the social system, how it persists and changes in the course of the transmission of culture from one generation to another, you have to understand the key role that language plays in this. He approaches this first of all through the role that language plays in the socialization process; he then moves on towards a much more general social theory of cultural transmission and the maintenance of the social system, still with language playing the key role. To me as a linguist this is crucial for two reasons, one instrumental and one autonomous if you like. Speaking 'instrumentally', it means that you have in Bernstein's work a theory of the social system with language embedded in it, so that anyone who is asking, as I am, questions such as "What is the role of language in the transmission of culture? How is it that the ordinary everyday use of the language, in the home, in the neighborhood and so on, acts as an effective channel for communicating the social system?" finds in Bernstein's work a social theory in the context of which one can ask these questions. In the second place, speaking 'autonomously', this then feeds back into our study of the linguistic system, so that we can use the insights we get from Bernstein's work to answer the question: why is language as it is? Language has evolved in a certain way because of its function in the social system.

HP: *Why this privileged position of language in the socialization process, for Bernstein and for you?*

MAKH: I suppose because, in the processes by which the child becomes a member of society, language does in fact play the central part. Even if you take the most fundamental type of personal relationship, that of the child and its mother, this is largely mediated through language. Bernstein has the notion of *critical socializing contexts;* there are a small number of situation types, like the regulative context (control of the child's behavior by the parent), which are critical in the socialization of the child. The behavior that takes place within these contexts is largely linguistic behavior. It is the linguistic activity which carries the culture with it.

HP: *You and Bernstein mean by language vocalized language and no other systems of signs?*

MAKH: Yes, although we would of course agree on the important role of paralinguistic systems like gesture. Clearly the more that one can bring these into the total picture, the more insight one will gain. But nevertheless language, in the sense of speech, natural language in its spoken form, is the key system.

HP: *Other linguists working in the field of sociolinguistics are Hymes and Labov. Is there again solidarity with these researchers?*

MAKH: Hymes has adopted, in some of his work at least, an intra-organism perspective on what are essentially inter-organism questions (Hymes 1971). This is a complex point. Let me put it this way: suppose you are studying language as interaction, you can still embed this in the perspective of language as knowledge. This is what is lying behind Hymes' notion of *communicative competence,* or competence in use. To link this up with the recent history of the subject, we should mention Chomsky first. The great thing Chomsky achieved was that he was the first to show that natural language could be brought within the scope of formalization; that you could in fact study natural language as a formal system. The cost of this was a very high degree of idealization; obviously, he had to leave out of consideration a great many of those variations and those distinctions that precisely interest those of us who are concerned with the sociological study of language. From this point of view Chomskyan linguistics is a form of reductionism, it is so highly idealized. Now, Chomsky's idealization is expressed in the distinction he draws between competence and performance. Competence (in its original sense) refers to the natural language in its idealized form, performance to everything else – it is a ragbag including physiological side-effects, mental blocks, statistical properties of the system, subtle nuances of meaning and various other things all totally unrelated to each other, as Hymes himself has pointed out. If you are interested in linguistic *interaction,* you don't want the high level of idealization that is involved in the notion of competence; you can't use it, because most of the distinctions that are important to you are idealized out of the picture.

What can you do about this? You can do two things. You can say, in effect "I accept the distinction, but I will study performance"; you then set up "theories of performance", in which case it is necessary to formulate some concept (which is Hymes' communicative competence) to take account of the speaker's ability to use language in ways that are appropriate to the situation. In other words, you say there is a "sociolinguistic competence" as well as a linguistic competence. Or you can do what I would do, which is to reject the distinction altogether on the grounds that we cannot operate with this degree and this *kind* of idealization. We accept a much lower level of formalization; instead of rejecting what is messy, we accept the mess and build it into the theory (as Labov does with variation; Labov 1970). To put it another way, we don't try to draw a distinction between what is grammatical and what is acceptable. So in an inter-organism perspective there is no place for the dichotomy of competence and performance, opposing what the speaker knows to what he does. There is no need to bring in the question of what the speaker knows; the background to what he does is what he could do – a potential, which is objective, not a competence, which is subjective. Now Hymes is taking an intra-organism ticket to what is actually an inter-organism destination; he is doing 'psycho-sociolinguistics', if you like. There's no reason why he shouldn't; but I find it an unnecessary complication.

HP: *That is an interesting point here. What according to you is the role of psychology as a background-theory of linguistic theory? I am thinking here of Saussure's and Chomsky's view that linguistics is a sub-part of psychology.*

MAKH: I would reject that absolutely; not because I would insist on the autonomy of linguistics, nor would I reject the psychological perspective as one of the meaningful perspectives on language, but because this is an arbitrary selection. If someone is interested in certain particular questions, then for him linguistics is a branch of psychology; fine, I accept that as a statement of his own interests and purposes. But if he tries to tell me that all linguistics has to be a branch of psychology, then I would say no. I am not really interested in the boundaries between disciplines; but if you pressed me for one specific answer, I would have to say that for me linguistics is a branch of sociology. Language is a part of the social system, and there is no need to interpose a psychological level of interpretation. I am not saying this is not a relevant perspective, but it is not a necessary one for the exploration of language.

HP: *We are now coming to one of the key points: your opinion about the relation between grammar and semantics, and also about that between behavioral potential, meaning potential and grammar. Can you say that there is a progression between to do, to mean and to say, in your perspective?*

MAKH: Yes. First let me say that I adopt the general perspective on the linguistic system you find in Hjelmslev (1961), in the Prague school (Vachek 1966), with Firth in the London school (Firth 1957, Palmer 1968), with Lamb (Lockwood 1972) and to a certain extent with Pike (1967) – language as a basically tristratal system: semantics, grammar, phonology. (Grammar means lexicogrammar; that is, it includes vocabulary.) Now, it is very important to say that each of these systems, semantics, grammar and phonology, is a system of potential, a range of alternatives, If we take the grammatical (lexicogrammatical) system, this is the system of what the speaker *can say*. This relates back to the previous point we were discussing – it seems to me unnecessary to talk about what the speaker knows; we don't need to be concerned with what is going on in his head, we simply talk about an abstract potential. What the speaker can say, i.e., the lexicogrammatical system as a whole, operates as the realization of the semantic system, which is what the speaker *can mean* – what I refer to as the 'meaning potential'. I see language essentially as a system of meaning potential. Now, once we go outside language, then we see that this semantic system is itself the realization of something beyond, which is what the speaker *can do* – I have referred to that as the 'behavior potential'. I want to insist here that there are many different ways of going outside language; this is only one of them. Perhaps it would be better at this point to talk in terms of a general semiotic level: the semantic system, which is the meaning potential embodied in language, is itself the realization of a higher level semiotic which we may define as a behavioral system or more generally as a social semiotic. So when I say *can do*, I am specifically referring to the behavior potential as a semiotic which can be encoded in language, or of course in other things too.

HP: *One of your statements is that can mean is a form of can do.*

MAKH: Yes and that could be confusing, because it is trying to say two things at once in an abbreviated form. To my mind, the key concept is that of *realization,* language as multiple coding. Just as there is a relation of realization between the semantic system and the lexicogrammatical system, so that *can say* is the *realization* of *can mean,* so also there is a relation of realization between the semantic system and some higher level semiotic which we can represent if you like as a behavioral system. It would be better to say that *can mean* is 'a realization of *can do*', or rather 'is one form of the realization of *can do*'.

Now, in the early sixties those of us who were interested in what people do linguistically were labelled 'taxonomic' by the transformationalists, who criticized us for being data-oriented, for looking at instances, for dealing with corpuses, and so on. To my knowledge, no linguist has ever simply described a corpus; this is a fiction invented for polemic purposes. The question is, what status do you give to instances of language behavior? There are many purposes for which we may be interested in the *text,* in what people actually *do* and *mean* and *say,* in real situations. But in order to make sense of the text, what the speaker actually says, we have to interpret it against the background of what he 'can say'. In other words, we see the text as actualized potential; it is the actual seen against the background of the potential. But note that the actual and the potential are at the same level of abstraction. This is what makes it possible to relate the one to the other. They are at the same level of coding within the system, so that any text represents an actualization (a path through the system) at each level: the level of *meaning,* the level of *saying* (or *wording,* to use the folk linguistic term for the lexicogrammatical system), and of course the level of *sounding* or *writing.*

HP: *The key notion is that of realization, in the Hjelmslevian sense, each level is the realization of the lower level?*

MAKH: Rather of the *higher* level. The earlier tradition usually had the meaning at the top, not at the bottom!

HP: *If you can speak of a teleology of your whole description, can you say that semantics or sociosemantics is the key to the whole system?*

MAKH: Well, yes. If was forced to choose a key, it would be that.

HP: *This semantic level is structured – you use the term network. Can you explain this term 'semantic network' here?*

MAKH: I would use the term *network* for all levels, in fact: semantic network, grammatical network, phonological network. It refers simply to a representation of the potential at that level. A network is a network of options, of choices; so for example the semantic system is regarded as a set of options. If we go back to the Hjelmslevian (originally Saussurean) distinction of paradigmatic and syntagmatic, most of modern linguistic theory has given priority to the syntagmatic form of organization. *Structure* means (abstract) *constituency,* which is a syntagmatic concept. Lamb treats the two axes together: for him a *linguistic stratum* is a network embodying both syntagmatic and paradigmatic relations all mixed up together, in patterns of what he calls AND nodes and OR nodes, I take out the paradigmatic relations (Firth's *system*) and give priority to these; for me the underlying organization at each level is paradigmatic. Each level is a network of paradigmatic relations, of OR's – a range of alternatives, in the sociological sense. This is what I mean by a *potential:* the semantic system is a network of meaning potential. The network consists very simply of a set of interrelated systems, the *system* being used here in the Firthian sense, though perhaps slightly more abstract, and making fuller use of his own 'polysystemic' principle. Let me just define it: a system is a set of options, a set of possibilities 'A, B or C' together with a condition of entry. The entry condition states the environment: 'in the environment X, there is a choice among A, B and C.' The choice is obligatory; if the conditions obtain, a choice must be made. The environment is, in fact, another choice (and here I depart from Firth, for whom the environment of a system was a place in structure – the entry condition was syntagmatic, whereas mine is again paradigmatic). It is equivalent to saying 'if you have selected X (out of X and Y), then you must go on to select either A, B or C'. The 'then' expresses logical dependence – there is no real time here – it is a purely abstract model of language as choice, as sets of interrelated choices. Hudson's recent book gives an excellent account of system networks in grammar (Hudson 1971).

Now this is what is represented in the network. The network is a representation of options, more particularly of the interrelations among options. Hence, a semantic network is a representation of semantic options, or choices in meaning.

HP: *Is there any difference between a semantic structure and a grammatical structure?*

MAKH: We may have some confusion here through the use of the term *structure*. May I use it in the Firthian sense: just as the system is the form of representation of paradigmatic relations, the structure is the form of representation of syntagmatic relations. The output of any path through the network of systems is a structure. In other words, the structure is the expression of a set of choices made in the system network. We know more or less what the nature of grammatical structures is. We know that constituent structure in some form or other is an adequate form of representation of the structures that are the output of the lexicogrammatical level. It is much less clear what is the nature of the structures that are the output of the semantic level. Lamb used to draw a distinction here: he used to say that the semantic structures were networks, while lexicosyntactic structures were trees and morphological structures were strings. I don't think he holds to this any more. If you take the sort of work that Geoffrey Turner has been doing (e.g. 1973), of the investigation of language development in young children, where we have been using the notion of meaning potential in the form of semantic system networks, in this situation it has been possible to bypass the level of semantic structure and go straight into lexicogrammatical constituent structure. That's all right for certain limited purposes. But there is obviously a limitation here, and when we attempt semantic representation for anything other than these highly restricted fields it is almost certainly going to be necessary to build in some concept of semantic structure. But what it will look like exactly I don't know. I don't think we can tell yet. Probably some form of relational network on the lines that Lamb and Peter Reich are working on (Lockwood 1972, Reich 1970).

HP: *The input of the semantic network is sociological and particular, and the output is linguistic and general. What do you mean by 'particular' on the one hand and 'general' on the other hand?*

MAKH: Let me take an example. Suppose you are interested, in a context of cultural transmission, in the way in which a mother controls the behavior of the child. She is expressing, through the use of language, certain abstract behavioral options, which we then characterize in terms which relate them to some model of the social system. In other words, she may be choosing among different forms of control – a simple imperative mode, a positional appeal, a personal appeal or the like, as in Bernstein's work; and when we show how this choice is encoded in language, what we are doing is deriving a set of linguistic categories from options in the social system. Now these will be very general categories, in the linguistic system: forms of transitivity, or forms of modification within the noun phrase, for example. But in order to get to them, we have to go through a network of behavioral options which become highly specific. A linguistic category such as 'clause type: material process, benefactive' appears (among other things) as the expression of some behavioral option that is highly specific in terms of the social theory, such as 'threat of loss of privilege'. The sociological categories which these linguistic ones realize will in relation to the social system be very particular, deriving from particular social contexts. You can relate this to the well-known problem of getting from the 'macro' scale of society to the 'micro' scale of language. This is wrongly posed, in my view; the problem is not one of size, but of level of abstraction. What are for language highly abstract and general categories have to be seen as realizing highly concrete and specific notions in the social structure.

HP: *The whole difficulty is to define the relation on the one hand between the behavioral potential and the meaning potential and on the other hand between the meaning potential and the grammar. These two relations, that is what your linguistic theory has to define. What are the different conditions for a semantic network in connection with the other two levels of the whole theory?*

MAKH: I would see both these relations as defined by the concept of realization. The semantic network is one level in a system of multiple coding. There are two main trends in thinking about language, aren't there? There is the *realizational* view, language seen as one system coded in another and then recoded in another; and the *combinatorial* view, where language is seen as larger units made up of smaller units. Of course both these relations are found in language, but people assign them very varying statuses. If we adopt the first emphasis, which is the Hjelmslevian view, we can extend the realizational concept outside language, so that just as the lexicogrammatical system realizes the semantic system, the semantic system realizes the behavioral system, or the social semiotic. If we then consider any specific part of the semantic system, there are three conditions which our representation must meet. One is that it must associate this part of the system with other parts of the same system on the same level. In other words, we must be able to show what is the total semantic potential within which the particular set of options that we are dealing with operates. But at the same time, we must be able to relate it to the other systems in both directions: both upward and downward. That is, if we claim that we have identified a set of options in meaning, not only do we have to relate these to other sets of options in meaning in a systematic way, but we have also to show, first, how this set of options in meaning realizes an aspect of the social system, and secondly, how it is in turn realized in the lexicogrammatical system. This is a very strong demand, in a sense, because if one says that there is a significant choice in meaning in social control situations between, say, moral disapprobation and other forms of disapprobation, as Geoffrey Turner does, or between imperative and obligative types of rule-giving, then one must be able to specify three things. One, exactly how this relates to the other options in meaning that have been set up. Two, how this expresses higher level behavioral options. Three, how this is in turn realized in the grammar. If we claim that a child can interpret the social system by listening to what his mother says, then presumably a linguist should be able to do the same.

HP: *How can one define the dissimilarity of realization between the semantics and the grammar then? In other words, what is the definition of grammar?*

MAKH: Well, I am not very clear on the boundaries here, between lexicogrammar and semantics. I tend to operate with rather fluid boundaries. But it can be defined theoretically, in that the lexicogrammatical system is the level of internal organization of language, the network of relations of linguistic form. And it is related outside language only indirectly, through an interface. I would also want to define it functionally, in terms of the metafunctions; we haven't come to that yet. Let us just say that it is the purely internal level of organization, the core of the linguistic system.

HP: *With a grammatical and a lexical part?*

MAKH: Yes, but – at least in my perspective; one might conceive differently for other purposes – the two are not really different. The lexical system is not something that is slotted in afterwards to a set of slots defined by the grammar. The lexicon – if I may go back to a definition I used many years ago – is simply the most delicate grammar (cf. Hasan 1978a). In other words, there is only one network of lexicogrammatical options. And as these become more and more specific, they tend more and more to be realized by the choice of a lexical item rather than by the choice of a grammatical structure. But it is all part of a single grammatical system.

HP: *Is syntax also a component of the grammar?*

MAKH: You notice I am avoiding the term *syntax*; only for this reason – that it has come into present-day linguistics from two different sources and so it has two different meanings. On the one hand you have syntax in the context of semantics-syntactics-pragmatics where it is defined in terms of a general theory of signs, on criteria which are drawn from outside language. On the other hand, there is the context in which you have semantics-grammar-phonetics, and then within grammar you have the division into syntax-morphology. This is a different sense of the term, where the criteria are within language itself: syntax is that part of the grammatical system which deals with the combination of words into sentences, or phrases into sentences. But I myself am not convinced of the traditional linguistic distinction between syntax and morphology, at least as a general phenomenon; I think it applies to certain languages only, and not to all of them, and so I don't feel the need to use syntax in that sense. But I am avoiding using it in the other sense because of the confusion between the two meanings of the term.

HP: *I would like to come back to the relation between semantics and grammar. Is it possible that a semantic option has more than one realization in the grammar?*

MAKH: Yes. Well, that's a very good and open question, to my mind. Let me start by saying that I think we must admit theoretically that it is possible. We may have what Lamb calls *diversification* between levels. What this means is that, in addition to one-to-one relations in the coding system, where one element on one level is realized by one element on another level, yon may also have many-to-one and one-to-many. Now here we are talking about one-to-many; in other words, the phenomenon where one element in the semantic system is realized by more than one in the lexicogrammatical system. First, then, we must admit theoretically that this happens, that there is free variation in the grammatical system, with one meaning realized by two or more forms. But then I would add that we should always be suspicious when we find this, because it usually turns out that the distinction in the lexicogrammatical system does in fact express a more delicate distinction in the semantic system that we haven't yet got round to. In other words, let us not go so far as to deny free variation, but let us be highly suspicions of any actual instances of it, because very often it turns out that there is a more subtle or more 'delicate' distinction in the semantic system which is being expressed in this way.

HP: *Can we go so far as to say that the grammatical system is arbitrary in connection with the meaning differences?*

MAKH: What do you mean by arbitrary?

HP: *In the Saussurean sense the relation between signifiant/signifié is arbitrary. There is no isomorphism between the two levels. This seems to be important because in generative semantics each syntactic difference means at the same time a semantic difference. There is no arbitrary relation between syntax and semantics there.*

MAKH: Well, I would tend to agree with this. When we talk about the arbitrariness of the sign, we are referring to the Saussurean content/expression relation. I believe every linguist must agree that there is arbitrariness at this point. But there is I think just this one point in the whole linguistic system where we can talk about arbitrariness – that is, at the line that is drawn by Hjelmslev between content and expression. The relations across this line are arbitrary; this we must accept. But if we are considering the relation between semantics and grammar, which is all within Hjelmslev's content, then I would say it is not arbitrary. Consider a grammatical structure. A grammatical structure is a configuration of roles, or functions if you like, each of which derives from some option in the semantic system – not one to one, but as a whole. Let us take an example from child language. The child says *water on,* meaning "I want the water tap turned on." We relate this to some general meaning or function for which the child is using language: in this case, the satisfaction of a material desire. We can see that the grammatical structure represents this very clearly. It consists of two elements, one identifying the object of the desire, i.e., *water,* and the other specifying the nature of the request, i.e., *on.* We express this by means of structural labels. It is clear that the grammatical structure here is a non-arbitrary configuration of elements which, taken as a whole, represent the function for which language is being used, and each of which constitutes a particular role within that function. Let me say in passing that this was said by Malinowski fifty years ago, when he pointed out that the elementary structures of the child's language represented very clearly the functions that language served for it (Malinowski 1923). I agree with this, but I would go further and say that it is also a property of adult language: if you take a grammatical structure, for example a transitivity structure that we represent in terms of categories like Agent, Process and Goal, or a modal structure, each of these grammatical structures represents a configuration that is derived as a whole from the semantic level of which it is the realization. So, in that sense, I would consider that the linguistic system at that point is non-arbitrary. The arbitrariness comes in simply in the relation between the content and the expression.

HP: *Is it possible to relate all that you said about the scope of linguistics, and about the relationships between behavior, meaning and grammar, to the functional aspect of your theory of language?*

MAKH: Yes. I would accept the label 'functional' and I think the point that we have just been discussing provides an excellent illustration of this. Consider any sentence of the adult language, for example in English *Balbus built a wall*. Taking up what I said just now, this represents a configuration of roles, or syntactic functions, a configuration which is not arbitrary since it represents very clearly the meaning of the sentence as a set of options in the semantic system.

We can now go on to say that this sentence embodies a number of structures all at the same time; there are represented in that sentence at least three – let us confine ourselves to three – different structural configurations, each one of which corresponds to a different function of language. On the one hand, there is a transitivity structure involved in it; we could characterize this as Agent + Process + Goal of result. Now this configuration represents the function of language expressing a content, what I prefer to call the *ideational* function: language as expressing the speaker's experience of the external world, and of his own internal world, that of his own consciousness. But on the other hand that clause has structure also in the modal sense, representing what I would call the *interpersonal* function of language, language as expressing relations among participants in the situation, and the speaker's own intrusion into it. So the clause consists simultaneously of a Modal element plus a Residual element. The Modal element expresses the particular role that the speaker has chosen to adopt in the situation and the role or role options that he has chosen to assign to the hearer. At the same time the clause has a third structural configuration, that in terms of a Theme and a Rheme, which is its structure as a message in relation to the total communication process – expressing its operational relevance, if you like. The point I want to make is this: in my opinion all these three – and I would be prepared to add one or two more – structural configurations are equally semantic; they are all representations of the meaning of that clause in respect of its different functions, the functions which I have referred to as *ideational, interpersonal* and *textual*. So in all these cases the structure is not arbitrary, to link up with what we were saying before.

HP: *Is there any difference between the typology of the uses of language and the typology of the functions of language? I believe that you define the function as a discrete area of formalized meaning potential.*

MAKH: Right. I would like to make a distinction between *function* and *use,* just as you suggest, and somewhat in these terms. As far as the adult language is concerned, it is possible to talk about the 'uses' of language, by which I would understand simply the selection of options within the linguistic system in the context of actual situation types: 'use' in its informal everyday sense. In that sense, *use* is a valuable concept; but we can't really enumerate the uses of language in a very systematic way – the nearest we can come to that is some concept of situation types, of which Bernstein's critical socializing contexts would be an example. Now I would distinguish that from *function,* because the whole of the adult language system is organized around a small number of functional components. The linguistic system, that is to say, is made up of a few very large sets of options, each set having strong internal constraints but weak external constraints. By 'strong internal constraints' I mean that there is strong environmental conditioning on choice: if you make a certain selection in one system within that set of options, this will determine up to a point the selection you make in other systems within the same set. Whereas the external constraints are weak; that is to say, the selection does not affect the choices that you make in the other sets of options.

Take for instance the structure of the clause. There is one set of options in TRANSITIVITY representing the type of process you are talking about, the participant roles in this process and so on. This is a tightly organized set of systems, each one interlocking with all the others. And there is another set of options, those of MOOD, relating to the speaker's assignment of speech roles to himself and to the hearer, and so on; there systems are again tightly organized internally. But there is little mutual constraint between TRANSITIVITY and MOOD. What you select in TRANSITIVITY hardly affects what you select in MOOD, or vice versa. Now what are these components? Fundamentally, they are the components of the language system which correspond to the abstract functions of language – to what I have called 'meta-functions', areas of meaning potential which are inherently involved in all uses of language. These are what I am referring to as ideational, interpersonal, and textual: generalized functions which have as it were become built into language, so that they form the basis of the organization of the entire linguistic system.

HP: *Would you identify the function of language with the structure of language?*

MAKH: May I make a distinction here between two uses of the term *structure*?

'Structure' can be used in a sense which is more or less synonymous with 'system', where 'structure of language' means, in effect, the linguistic system. I have been avoiding using the term 'structure' in that sense, in order to avoid confusion; so let me comment on *function* and *system* first. The linguistic system is functional in origin and in orientation, so that in order to understand the nature of the linguistic system we have to explain it as having evolved in the context of this set of basic functions. System is not identical with function, but rather the linguistic system is organized around the set of abstract functions of language. I think that is true in the phylogenetic sense in the evolution of language; I am sure it is true in the ontogenetic sense, in the development of language by a child. In other words, the nature of the linguistic system is such that it has to be explained in functional terms.

The other sense of structure is the stricter, Firthian sense, where structure is the abstract category for the representation of syntagmatic relations in language. Here I would say that *function* and *structure* are also different *concepts,* and in order to relate them we have to think of function in its other sense of structural functions or roles, like Agent, Actor, Subject, Theme and the rest. A linguistic structure is then a configuration of functions. But this is *function* in a different sense, though the two are ultimately related.

HP: *Isn't it the case that you use an extrinsic definition of function? There is also another definition in the Hjelmslevian sense where function is nothing else than intersystematic relationship. Your definition is an extrinsic definition of function.*

MAKH: Yes; in the first sense I am defining *function* extrinsically. I am not using the term in its technical Hjelmslevian sense. But I think there is an important connection between this extrinsic sense and the second sense I referred to just now, *function* used in the meaning of 'grammatical functions' as distinct from 'grammatical classes or categories'. That notion of function refers to an element of structure considered as a role in the total structural configuration. There is a relationship between this meaning of function and the extrinsic sense in which I am using the term: the grammatical functions, in the sense of roles, are derivable from the extrinsic functions of language. There is determination there.

HP: *The category of function is a very classic one in linguistic theory and has been used since Saussure and Hjelmslev. I assume that the Prague school was inspired and fascinated by Bühler's scheme (1934) of the different functions of language (Vachek 1966). Do you believe that the Bühler scheme is still valuable, or that Bühler's definition of the expressive, cognitive and referential functions of language is still valid?*

MAKH: I think to a certain extent it is; but remember that Bühler is not attempting to explain the nature *of the linguistic system* in functional terms. He is using language to investigate something else. His interest is if you like psycholinguistic; and one might compare for example Malinowski's functional theory of language, which is also aimed outside language although in another direction, ethnographic or sociolinguistic as it would be called now. I would consider both these views entirely valid in terms of their own purposes, but I would want myself to adopt a somewhat different (though related) system of functions in order to direct it inwards to explain the nature of the linguistic system. The definition is still extrinsic but the purpose is an intrinsic one. I can explain very simply the relation between the functional framework that I use and that of Bühler. My own *ideational* corresponds very closely to Bühler's *representational,* except that I want to introduce the further distinction within it between *experiential* and *logical,* which corresponds to a fundamental distinction within language itself. My own *interpersonal* corresponds more or less to the sum of Bühler's *conative* and *expressive,* because in the linguistic system these two are not distinguished. Then I need to add a third function, namely the *textual* function, which you will not find in Malinowski or Bühler or anywhere else, because it is intrinsic to language: it is the function that language has of creating text, of relating itself to the context – to the situation and the preceding text. So we have the *observer* function, the *intruder* function and the *relevance* function, to use another terminological framework that I sometimes find helpful as an explanation. To me the significance of a functional system of this kind is that you can use it to explain the nature of language, because you find that language is in fact structured along these three dimensions. So the system is as it were both extrinsic and intrinsic at the same time. It is designed to explain the internal nature of language in such a way as to relate it to its external environment. [For further discussion see Halliday 1970a.]

HP: *Could you give a brief description of what you mean by the 'logical' and 'experiential' functions of language?*

MAKH: Within the ideational function, the lexicogrammatical system embodies a clear distinction between an experiential and a logical component in terms of the types of structure by which these are realized. The *experiential* function, as the name implies, is the 'content' function of language; it is language as the expression of the processes and other phenomena of the external world, including the world of the speaker's own consciousness, the world of thoughts, feelings, and so on. The *logical* component is distinguished in the linguistic system by the fact that it is expressed through recursive structures whereas all the other functions are expressed through non-recursive structures. In other words, the logical component is that which is represented in the linguistic system in the form of parataxis and hypotaxis, including such relations as coordination, apposition, condition, reported speech and others. These are the relations which constitute the logic of natural language; including those which derive from the nature of language itself – reported speech is obviously one example of this, and another is apposition, the 'namely' relation. I think it is necessary to distinguish logical from the experiential, partly because logical meanings are clearly distinct in their realization, having exclusively this linear recursive mode of expression, and partly because one can show that the logical element in the linguistic system, while it is ideational in origin, in that it derives from the speaker's experience of the external world, once it is built into language becomes neutral with respect to the other functions, such that all structures whatever their functional origin can have built into them inner structures of a logical kind.

HP: *Is the 'ideational' function identical with the 'referential' function of language?*

MAKH: Well, I think it includes the referential function, but it is wider. It depends how widely one is using the term 'referential'. It is certainly wider than the strict definition of referential, but it might be considered as equivalent to referential in the sense in which Hymes uses the term, provided one points out that it has these two sub-components of experiential and logical – I am not sure where Hymes would put the logical element in the linguistic system. Hymes has a basic distinction between referential and socioexpressive; as I understand it, this would correspond pretty closely, his referential to my ideational, noting this query about the logical, and his socioexpressive to my interpersonal (Hymes 1974).

HP: *Is it possible in your linguistic theory to elaborate a hierarchy of functions, or is it sufficient to make up the taxonomy of functions?*

MAKH: Yes the latter. I would not like to impose a hierarchy of functions, because I believe that there can be hierarchy *ad hoc* only for the purpose of given investigations. It is noticeable that those whose orientation is primarily psycholinguistic tend to give priority to the ideational function, whereas for those whose orientation is primarily sociolinguistic the priorities are at least equal and possibly the other way – priority might be given to the interpersonal function. This could be reflected in the direction of derivation. If let us say one was working with a functionally based generative semantics, it might well be that for sociological, or rather 'inter-organism', purposes one's generative component would be the interpersonal function, whereas for a more psychologically oriented, 'intra-organism' semantics the generative component would be, as it usually is in generative semantics, the ideational one.

HP: *I believe that this question of hierarchy of functions is very important in linguistic discussion nowadays. I think for example of the Chomskyan sophistication of the expressive function of language. Chomsky defines language as expression of thought and he wouldn't like to see stressed the more communicative features of the semantic structure of language. What do you think of the stress on the expressive function of language?*

MAKH: I find it unhelpful to isolate any one function as fundamental. I have very much a goal-oriented view, and I can see that for certain types of inquiry it may be useful to single out one function rather than another as prior or fundamental but I don't find this useful myself. It seems to me important to give equal status in the linguistic system to all functions. And I would point out that our traditional approach to grammar is not nearly as one-sidedly oriented towards the ideational function as sometimes seems to be assumed. For instance, the whole of the MOOD system in grammar, the distinction between indicative and imperative and, within indicative, between declarative and interrogative – this whole area of grammar has nothing whatever to do with the ideational component. It is not referential at all; it is purely interpersonal, concerned with the social-interactional function of language. It is the speaker taking on a certain role in the speech situation. This has been built into our interpretation of grammar, and I see no reason for departing from this and treating the social meaning of language as some kind of optional extra.

HP: *It is very peripheral?*

MAKH: I don't think it is peripheral at all. I don't think we can talk about the functions in these terms of 'central' and 'peripheral'. If you want a model of the production of discourse, I would say that meanings in all functions are generated simultaneously and mapped on to one another; not that we first of all decide on a content and then run it through an interaction machine to decide whether to make it a statement or a question. (I avoid using the term 'expressive' in this discussion simply because there is a confusion here between 'expressive' meaning, expression of thought and 'expressive' in the more usual Bühler sense which is non-representational and corresponds to Hymes's use in 'socio-expressive'.)

HP: *Can one say that the communicative function is a kind of super-function or macro-function, and that the other functions that you mentioned are subfunctions of the communicative function?*

MAKH: Again I would be unhappy with that. I would want to insist – though always pointing out that it is simply for the purposes of the kinds of investigation I personally am interested in – on the ideational and interpersonal having equal status. The textual function can be distinguished from these two in that it is an enabling function which is intrinsic to language; but as between the first two, I can't see either being more all-embracing than the other. All three could be called 'metafunctions' – 'meta-' rather than 'macro-', the point being that they are *abstract*; they represent functions of language *as incorporated into the linguistic system*. You notice I am hedging slightly on your question, because I am not quite sure how to relate these to what you are calling 'the communicative function'.

HP: *But that depends on the definition that you give of the nature of language. Do you see language first of all as communication or as an isomorphic system of logical relations?*

MAKH: Certainly not as an isomorphic system of logical relations. I suppose therefore I see it as communication, though I would rather say that I see language as a *meaning potential*. It is a form of *human semiotic,* in fact the main form of human semiotic; and as such I want to characterize it in terms of the part that it plays in the life of social man. Or, what is the same thing in more abstract terms, I see the linguistic system as a component – an essential component – of the social system.

HP: *I believe that it is necessary to say that the speaker and the hearer have a certain knowledge of the functions of language. Can you specify this?*

MAKH: I think that is certainly implied by what I say, but I would make no use of that formulation.

HP: *Why?*

MAKH: Because it is introducing a level of discourse which is unnecessary in this context. It is certainly true that for a speaker and a hearer to interact linguistically they must have this knowledge; but we only know that they have this knowledge because we see them interact. If therefore it is possible to describe the interaction in the form that I mentioned earlier, that is as the actualization of a system of potentials, then it becomes unnecessary to introduce another level, that of knowledge. This would not be true for example in relation to Lamb's work – I mention Lamb because what he does is entirely compatible with my own. We have very much the same premises about language, but we differ precisely in that he is primarily looking at language intra-organistically and I the other way. For Lamb, of course, the whole point is to find out what it is that the speaker has in his head; therefore he is trying to characterize the knowledge that you have just mentioned (Lamb 1970). But I am not. I am trying to characterize human interaction, and it is unnecessary to attempt to interpose a component of what the speaker-hearer knows into the total descriptive framework.

HP: *Is a functional theory of language such of yours a theory of language as 'language system' as the Saussurean 'langue'? I believe that your theory of language is a step against the very classic dichotomies of 'langue'/ 'parole' or 'competence'/'performance' and so on.*

MAKH: Yes. It is true that I find little use for these dichotomies – though I should point out that this thought is far from being original to me. My former teacher, Firth, himself criticized these very cogently in some of his own writings (Firth 1957a, especially Chapter 16). He said that he found it unnecessary to operate with mind/body, mentalism/mechanism, word/idea and 'such dualisms'. I would agree with Firth – again, always saying that it depends on the purpose for which you are looking at language. I mentioned earlier that for what we are going to call sociolinguistic purposes for the moment, it is necessary to minimize the distinction between what is *grammatical* and what is *acceptable*. If I put this another way I think it will clarify the point here. There will always be *idealization* in any study of language, or indeed in any systematic inquiry. The point is here that we need to reduce the level of idealization, to make it as low as possible, in order that we can understand the processes of interaction, the sort of phenomena studied from an ethnomethodological standpoint by Sachs, Schegloff and others (Schegloff 1971). We have to impose as low a degree of idealization on the facts as is compatible with a systematic inquiry. This means, in other words, that what is grammatical is defined as what is acceptable. There is no distinction between these two, from which it also follows that there is no place for a distinction between competence and performance or between *langue* and *parole,* because the only distinction that remains is that between the *actual,* and the *potential* of which it is an actualization.

HP: *What is the meaning of one of your statements: "In order to understand the nature of language, it is necessary to start from considerations of its use"?*

MAKH: Oh, yes, this is a very closely related point, and comes back to what I was saying earlier. I think that the use of language can be defined in precisely these terms, namely as the actualization of a potential. Now we want to understand *language in use*. Why? Partly in order to approach this question of how it is that ordinary everyday language transmits the essential patterns of the culture: systems of knowledge, value systems, the social structure and much else besides. How do we try to understand language in use? By looking at what the speaker says against the background of what he might have said but did not, as an actual in the *environment* of a potential. Hence the environment is defined paradigmatically: using language means making choices in the environment of other choices. I would then take the next step of saying that when we investigate the nature of the linguistic system by looking at how these choices that the speaker makes are interrelated to each other in the system, we find that this internal structure is in its turn determined by the functions for which language is used – hence the functional components we were talking about. We then have to take one more step and ask how is it that the linguistic system has evolved in this way, since as we have seen the abstract functional components are, although related to, yet different from the set of concrete uses of language that we actually find in given situations. This can best be approached through studies of language development, through the study of how it is that the child learns the linguistic system. I think when we look at that from a functional point of view, we find some kind of an answer to the question how it is that the linguistic system evolved in contexts of use.

HP: *What to do with another classic dichotomy, that of 'synchronic' versus 'diachronic'?*

MAKH: Well, these are different perspectives. I think it would be foolish to deny that this is a real difference. For any system one may look either at its internal structure or at the processes by which it evolved and reached that structure. But I personally am very much in sympathy with the trend which puts these two perspectives closely together, in the sense that either can be used to illuminate the other. I would not like to accept the very rigid separation which some linguists at one time tried to maintain. But – if I may put in parenthesis – one must have a historical perspective on the subject. It is very easy to criticize one's predecessors for having drawn artificial boundaries; but if you look at the development of knowledge, knowledge usually advances by the drawing of artificial boundaries in order that one can isolate a certain area for study. It is the next generation which sees that the boundaries were artificial and throws them out. Fine; but they would never have got to that stage if their predecessors had not drawn the boundaries in the first place.

HP: *Is the study of the acquisition of language in the child not a kind of diachronic linguistics?*

MAKH: Yes, I think in a sense it is, though I think one has got to be careful here. I have been interested in language development in the child from a functional point of view, and I think that one gets a great deal of insight here into the nature of the linguistic *system* and how it may have evolved. But I think one has to be careful and say simply how it "may" have evolved. We cannot know for certain that ontogeny reflects phylogeny. All we can say is that when we examine how a child learns the linguistic system from the functional standpoint, we get a picture which *could* be a picture of how human language evolved. One very interesting thing that happens, or at least did in the case of the child I was studying, is that you first of all find him creating his own language on what is presumably the phylogenetic model. Then there comes a very sudden discontinuity – at least a discontinuity in the expression, and, more important, in the nature of the system itself – when the child as it were shrugs his shoulders and says, look, this is just too much work creating the whole of human language again from the start; why don't I settle for the readymade language that I hear around me? And he moves into the adult system.

HP: *Another, the last classic dichotomy that we have to mention here, is the very important distinction between language as system and language as process. This was a very important operational distinction in structural linguistics: language as system, as paradigm, and language as syntagmatic order or discourse. Can you do something with this distinction?*

MAKH: I think you can. Incidentally there is an interesting contrast here between Firth and Hjelmslev. Both of them of course admitted the basic distinction between syntagmatic and paradigmatic relations as formulated (in partly different terms) by Saussure. They then diverged, in that for Firth there was no difference in the level of abstraction between the two; syntagmatic relations were just as abstract as paradigmatic ones. Indeed, in Firth's system the more abstract relations tended to be handled syntagmatically, since Firth was interested not in the potential but in the typical actual, which is rather a different thing (Palmer 1968, especially Chapter 11). Hjelmslev on the other hand made a very clear distinction between the abstract *system*, with paradigmatic relations as the underlying ones, and the *text* as process. Now, I find myself here perhaps somewhat nearer to Hjelmslev than to Firth. The distinction that in practice I find it necessary to operate with – if I may come back again to these terms – is that between the system as a potential, and its actualization. But in considering the system as a potential, I personally find it useful to characterize this entirely in paradigmatic terms, and to regard structure, the structure that underlies the process, as derived from this.

HP: *Is that not a kind of reduction of the specific discursive dimension in human language?*

MAKH: No, I don't think it is. Can I try to answer that in a slightly roundabout way, by talking about the nature of text? There is one view of *text* as a kind of supersentence. This is the notion that text is to be defined by size; a text is something which is bigger than a sentence. I find that rather unhelpful. To me the concept of text is to be defined by level of abstraction, not by size. In other words, *text* is *to semantics* what sentence is to grammar. A sentence is to be defined as a fundamental unit of grammar, and we don't define the sentence as a kind of superphoneme. Now, in the same way, the text is to be defined as a fundamental unit of semantics, and we don't define it as a kind of supersentence. It's exactly the same point: you can't define the sentence as something big on the phonological level, because it isn't abstracted at that level at all; equally, you can't define the text as something big on the lexicogrammatical level: because it isn't abstracted on that level – it's on the semantic level. For any level of linguistic structure, semantic, lexicogrammatical or phonological, there will be certain elements and units which can be isolated from the stream, from the process if you like, and which must be isolated from the process if we are to link them to the linguistic system. So it seems to me there are two stages here. One is the syntagmatic relations within the linguistic units themselves of whatever level, which are part of the linguistic system but derivative from the paradigmatic relations within the system. The second is the discourse relations within the text, which include among other things the options that the speaker selects in the light of earlier stages in the same process; in other words, in the light of what has been said before.

HP: *A very important point seems to me the question of the variation of linguistic units. We have seen in the history of modern linguistics that for instance the morpheme was the privileged unit in structuralism and the sentence in transformational grammar. Do you believe in a privileged position of one of the units?*

MAKH: I don't believe in the privileged position of any unit at any level. It seems to me that for each of the levels of the linguistic system there is a *hierarchy of units*. I am not convinced that these units are universals; there may be some universals among them, like syllable perhaps in phonology, sentence in grammar. But just as in phonology one finds linguistic structure embodied in a hierarchy of units – for one language it might be tone-group, stress-group, syllable, phoneme; for another language something different – similarly in the grammar one finds a hierarchy something like sentence, clause, phrase, word, morpheme. Now I wouldn't pick out any of these as having priority. There may be certain properties which are specific to one or another unit, and it may be that some of them are universals, although I'm not quite sure what that would mean since they're really too concrete to be universals. Equally on the semantic level there may be a hierarchy of units; I suppose there is, in some form or other, but here we are at such an abstract level that at the moment we can only really handle the general concept of text. No, we can go further than that; we can recognize 'discourse units' such as episode, narrative, exchange and so on, which I would locate on the semantic level, but these tend to be specific to particular genres or situation types – I'm thinking for example of Sinclair's work on classroom language (Sinclair & Coulthard 1975).

HP: *Is macro-semantics only a part of sociosemantics or is it the whole of sociosemantics? By macro-semantics, I mean the semantics of units larger than the sentence.*

MAKH: I think it is only a part of it. I am a little worried about the notion of 'macro' because I don't feel that there is any special position to be accorded in semantics to units larger than the sentence. But I would say very definitely that what we are calling 'sociosemantics' involves meaning that is expressed in units smaller than the sentence just as much as that which is expressed in larger units. Note that the sentence in my opinion is not a semantic unit, anyway.

HP: *What we discussed up to now was very theoretical. It is perhaps a good idea to talk now about your more descriptive work in English. And I would like to ask you a few things about your study of* TRANSITIVITY, *as it is a very good example of your functional analysis of some language phenomena (Halliday 1970a). In what sense has your study on* TRANSITIVITY *been a concretion of your options and opinions about language?*

MAKH: In this sense, I think: that one can impose a sort of functional grid on the lexicogrammatical system of any language, by which I mean that one can assign any part of that system to one or another functional point of origin. Now TRANSITIVITY can be defined as the experiential element in the grammar of the clause. Your lexicogrammatical system can be classified according to a function-rank matrix. So, for the rank of the clause, the experiential function is expressed through TRANSITIVITY, the interpersonal function is expressed through MOOD, the textual function is expressed through THEME. So TRANSITIVITY would be an example of what you referred to because it represents a functionally defined component in the grammatical system of the language. Now what does TRANSITIVITY mean? I understand it to mean the grammar of processes; that is to say, the set of options whereby the speaker expresses the whole range of types of process that are recognized in the semantic system of the language – the process type itself, in English material process, mental process, verbal process, relational process and their subcategories; and the participant roles that enter into these processes.

HP: *You study* TRANSITIVITY *as that part of the grammar that is concerned with the expression of processes as integrated phenomena – and the study of* TRANSITIVITY *would lie within the experiential component in the grammar of the clause? Can you possibly explain this a bit?*

MAKH: Yes, perhaps I could illustrate it. I think that in English there are in the system essentially four main types of process, those that I just named: material processes, mental processes, verbal processes and relational processes, and every clause in the language is the expression of one or other of these four. These four types are characterized by different semantic potentials, for instance different sets of options in voice (systems of active, passive, middle and so on). And different configurations of participant roles are associated with each.

Let's take an example of a mental process clause. The main sub-categories of mental process are cognition (thinking, etc.), perception (seeing, etc.) and reaction (liking, etc.) *John heard the music* and *John enjoyed the music* are both mental process clauses, *John enjoyed the music* being reaction and *John heard the music* perception. These are characterized as configurations of three elements: the Process, here represented by *enjoy* or *hear;* the Phenomenon, here *music;* and the element affected by the process, which must be human (or quasi-human) incidentally, which we may call the Cognizant. So the mental process is one type of process recognized by the English language, and it is characterized by having a structure in terms of Process, Cognizant and Phenomenon – of course there may be other, circumstantial elements as well. This is different from the structure of something like *the boys were throwing stones,* which is a material process, not a mental process, and which is a different configuration of participant roles.

HP: *What are in your example now the lexicogrammatical effects of this semantic structure?*

MAKH: Well, let's characterize one of these clauses in *systemic terms,* i.e., in terms of the options that it represents. For instance, *John enjoyed the music* is partially described as mental process, reaction, middle voice, plus domain. (The last means that the Phenomenon is specified.) Each feature that we enumerate in such a list – mental process, reaction, and so on – makes its contribution to the lexicogrammatical structure. So this systemic representation *as a whole* is then represented in the form of a configuration of structural functions, or structural roles, in this case those that I have mentioned: Process, Cognizant, Phenomenon. The way in which we derive these is that each of the features in the systemic network has associated with it a particular realization statement, in terms such as: If the clause has the feature 'mental process', insert the function Cognizant and sub-categorize the Process in a certain way. If the clause has the feature 'middle', then the mental process must be one of the type represented by the verb *enjoy,* as distinct from a non-middle mental process clause which is represented for instance by *please* as in *the music pleased John.* So that each of the features that figures in the description of the clause in systemic terms makes its contribution to the lexicogrammatical structure, either by inserting an element, by ordering the elements, by inserting a lexical item or a member of a set of lexical items, or something or that sort.

HP: *In your semantic representation of the transitivity phenomena you don't speak of participants but of participant roles. Is this because the semantic representation must be very abstract?*

MAKH: Yes, it is. Let us consider again an example such as *John enjoyed the music.* We may describe *John* in terms such as Cognizant, but in fact *John* will be the expression of other roles in other structural configurations at the same time. That is to say, not only will he be Cognizant in a mental process clause, but he may also be Subject in a clause of a certain MOOD, and Theme in a clause of a certain Theme-Rheme structure, so that any element in the structure is in fact a complex of roles. So although we may talk about participants in the special case of TRANSITIVITY structures, it is more accurate to say that what enters into the configuration in question is not a participant as such but a participant role.

HP: *Do you need in your approach to transitivity phenomena the presence of semantic features derived from contextuality?*

MAKH: When you say 'contextuality', do you mean elements which are circumstantial *to the process* like place, manner, and so on, or do you mean features of the situational context of the utterance?

HP: *Of the process.*

MAKH: Yes; the elements of TRANSITIVITY structure include not only the process itself and the participant roles like Actor, Goal, Agent, Cognizant, Phenomenon and so on but also circumstantial elements of Extent, Location, Cause and the like. It is possible to specify the total list.

HP: *And the verbal context, must it be formalized in the semantic representation?*

MAKH: The verbal context, in fact the whole context of the utterance, situational as well as verbal, is not represented in TRANSITIVITY, or indeed in the experiential component at all, but in the textual component. In other words, it enters in through its part in determining the structure that is derived from the textual functions, and that is embodied in structural configurations such as those of Theme and Rheme, and Given and New. These are not part of TRANSITIVITY; they are on a different structural dimension.

HP: *Is there any relationship between the experiential and the textual function of language?*

MAKH: There is a relationship, in the sense that they are both incorporated in the linguistic system and they are both represented simultaneously in the linguistic structure. But I don't think there is any *special* relationship. There's not much mutual determination between them. There is a little: I could give you one example where there is determination between them. In English the system of voice: middle or non-middle, and if non-middle then active or passive, is the expression of meanings derived from the textual function. But the *potential* of any given clause type for options in voice is determined by the TRANSITIVITY features. In other words, TRANSITIVITY determines what are the *possibilities* in terms of active/passive, etc., and the textual function determines which the speaker *actually selects*. For example, in certain types of material process clause you know that there is a system of five voices: middle, active with Goal, active without Goal, passive with Agent and passive without Agent. This is a fact of TRANSITIVITY, deriving from the experiential component. But the difference in meaning among these five resides not in TRANSITIVITY but in THEME and INFORMATION, which derive from the textual component, so that the selection of, say, 'passive without Agent' represents not a more specific *process* type but a specific *message* type. So that is the kind of relationship that you get between the two.

HP: *Another example of function analysis elaborated by you is about nominality. What is the importance of this phenomenon for your functional conception of language?*

MAKH: *Nominality* is another excellent example, because it shows how each of the functions is represented, or rather how meanings derived from each of the functions are represented, in the total structure. If you consider the difference between *John enjoyed the music* and *what John enjoyed was the music*, where you have used the resources of nominality, in this case nominalization, the distinction between these two is derived solely from the textual function; again, it is a distinction relating to the nature of the message. What the speaker wants to make as his Theme is different in the two cases: in the case of *John enjoyed the music* the theme is *John*, while in the case of *what John enjoyed was the music*, the Theme is *what John enjoyed*. Nominalization in English is a device for giving to any particular clause the desired structure in terms of Theme and Rheme.

That of course is only one part of nominality. The whole phenomenon of being a noun, or behaving like a noun, has implications for all functions. In principle the noun *is* a naming element, and naming in general derives from the experiential function, although not entirely, because naming of course embodies connotation as well as denotation: names have an interpersonal component as well as an ideational one, so that in order to derive a particular noun, in the sense of a word of the noun class, we may very well have to go to an origin which is already functionally complex in that it is both ideational and interpersonal. Then, thirdly, there is nominality as a classifying device, which is logical in function. When I build up compound nouns and noun phrases, say I start with *station* and then I add *railway station* and then I add *suburban railway station* and so on, what I am doing every time is introducing a taxonomy, a classification system whose content is experiential but whose form is logical. Hence the structure of these compound noun phrases has a recursive component in it, very well brought out in English by these long strings which are linear recursions. This expresses the fact that the classificatory function of the elements is a logical one, that of forming a taxonomy. But the content of these elements, the meanings 'suburban' as opposed to 'in a city', 'railway' as opposed to 'bus' and so on, are of course experiential. So the noun phrase is a very good example of a complex structure which derives from different functional origins.

HP: *Do you have any idea whether those structures also exist in other languages?*

MAKH: Oh, yes, there is no doubt they do. I would certainly claim that the distinction that I am making between the functions is a universal one; and I would also suggest that the structural uniqueness of the logical component that I mentioned earlier, namely the fact that it is represented by means of recursive structures, is at least a candidate for universality. I don't know, but I think it's a fair guess. Now of course the structures in question will not necessarily have the same form in other languages as they do in English. But I am fairly confident that there is a nominal taxonomy in all languages, and that the expression of this nominal taxonomy includes some recursion. The recursive structure embodies the fact that the taxonomy is open-ended: you could go on sub-classifying.

HP: *That is a very formal universal?*

MAKH: Yes.

HP: *You are one of the few linguists who have elaborated a coherent theory on intonation (Halliday 1967a). It is very difficult to elaborate a theory of intonation within structuralism and transformational grammar. Can you give briefly some characteristics of your conception of linguistic intonation?*

MAKH: Yes. It's very important to remember that distinctions of intonation have quite different roles in different languages. We know for instance the traditional distinction between *tone-languages* and *intonation-languages;* but there's much more to it than that. No doubt all languages use the resource of intonation, but they use it in very different ways. I have examined mainly English intonation, and the point that interests me about it is that it is very clear what the role of intonation in English is in functional terms. We can distinguish here between the two main components of intonation TONE or pitch movement on the one hand and TONICITY, that is to say the location of tonic stress, on the other hand. Now these are clearly distinct in function in English; there are fuzzy edges, as there always are in language, but in general TONE (pitch movement) has an interpersonal function in English – it expresses meanings derived from the interpersonal function, mainly sub-systems of MOOD – whereas TONICITY (the location of tonic stress) has a textual function, that is to say, it expresses meanings derived from the textual component, and more specifically it expresses the information structure. The information structure is that system of the textual component which is concerned with the speaker's distribution of the message into two elements: what he is treating as information that is recoverable to the hearer, which we call the *Given* part, and what he is treating as information that is not recoverable to the hearer, which is the *New* part. We can't make a rule to say that what carries the tonic stress is new and everything else is given, because it is not as simple as that. Nevertheless it is quite clear in English how the tonic stress pattern expresses the information structure. The rules are fairly complex, but they're there. I think myself it is quite impossible to give an adequate account of a language without taking cognizance of those meanings which are expressed through intonation. But we have to find out exactly what these are in each case. There may be a general tendency in intonation languages for TONE to express textual meanings, but I wouldn't go further than that.

HP: *What is the place of the focus in this whole system of intonation rules?*

MAKH: Well, the focus, as I understand it, is simply an element in the information structure. This is what I have been referring to just now. If we say *John enjoyed the music* with the tonic stress on *music*, then the focus of information is on *the music* and the meaning is that either *the music* or *enjoyed the music* or the whole of *John enjoyed the music* may be new information. In other words, at least the final element is New, and, working backwards, any or all of the rest of the clause may be New. If on the other hand we say *John enjoyed the music* with the focus of information on *enjoyed,* then the message is that *the music* is Given, that is to say the speaker is treating it as recoverable to the hearer; *John* may or may not be Given, we can't tell (actually we can tell, by a more subtle distinction within the rhythm); but we know that *enjoy* is New. Now the focus of information is realized by tonic stress; broadly speaking, it is that element in the information unit that the speaker is marking out as being the termination of what is not recoverable to the speaker. Whether or not what precedes it is being specified as not recoverable to the hearer depends on other factors. Anything that follows is always being specified as recoverable. So, as I said, the rules are fairly complex but they're clear; and we can be quite specific about what 'focus of information' means.

Now this is all about English. I do not believe that this is a universal pattern. I am quite sure that all languages have textual structures (that is structures expressing textual meanings, just as they all have ideational structures and interpersonal structures); and probably in some way or other they all make a distinction between the Given and the New. But we cannot just assume that there will be a focus of information expressed by intonation in the same way as in English, and having the same meaning as it has in English, in all other languages.

HP: *Is it possible to identify the focus with some very specific syntactic component of the sentence, or in more logical terms, as some generative semanticists do, with the argument of the sentence?*

MAKH: It is a syntactic element, though not of the sentence. The *information unit* – which is a constituent in textual structure, not in ideational structure like the sentence and the clause – is structured in terms of two elements which we are calling Given and New. The term 'focus' refers to the location of the New element; in English this means specifically its terminal point, since the focus is realized phonologically as tonic prominence and the prominence falls on the item that occurs in final position within the New. Given-New is a syntactic structure just like Actor-Process-Goal, Subject-Predicator-Complement, Modifier-Head and so on. This is what Lakoff apparently failed to understand when he pointed out – claiming to refute me – that the focal element is often one which has been mentioned before (Lakoff 1971). I had pointed this out quite explicitly myself, stating that one of the meanings of 'information being treated by the speaker as non-recoverable to the hearer' (this being the semantic category that is realized grammatically by the New) is precisely something that *has* been mentioned before but is contrastive in the context, for example *Have you seen John and Mary anywhere? I've seen John,* with focus on *John* implying 'but not Mary'. This is what explains how you can have the focus on anaphoric items, which would otherwise be inexplicable. So the focus is a grammatical concept, not a logical one; and it derives from the textual component of the linguistic system.

HP: *One way of studying linguistics could be to see how people learn to mean. "Learning how to mean" is exactly the title of one of your papers (in Halliday 1975). It is a study of the child's language, and language development and acquisition, topics which are very much at stake nowadays. Can you tell me what this study of learning how to mean has to offer to general linguistics?*

MAKH: I see this again from a functional perspective. There has been a great deal of study of language development in the past ten or fifteen years, but mainly on the acquisition of syntax seen from a psycholinguistic point of view – which is complementary, again, to a 'sociosemantic' perspective. To me there seem to be two aspects to be stressed here. One is: what is the *ontogenesis* of the system, in the initial stage before the child takes over the mother tongue? The other is: what are the strategies through which a child moves into the mother tongue and becomes linguistically adult? I would simply make two points here. I think by studying child language you get a very good insight into function and use (which for the very young child, as I said, are synonymous). We can postulate a very small set of uses, or functions, for which the child first creates a semiotic system. I have tried this out in relation to one subject, and you can see the child creating a meaning potential from his own vocal resources in which the meanings relate quite specifically to a certain set of functions which we presume to be general to all cultures. He learns for instance that language can be used in a regulatory function, to get people to do what he wants; and within that function he learns to express a small number of meanings, building up a system of content/expression pairs where the expression is derived entirely from his own resources. He creates a language, in functional terms. Then at a certain point he gives up this trail. In the case that I studied, the child dropped the language-creating process at the stage where he had a potential of about four or five functions with some fifty meanings altogether, roughly fifty elements in the system. Anyway the stage comes when he switches and starts taking over the adult system. So there is a discontinuity in the expression; but there is no discontinuity in the content, because to start with he maps the expressions of the adult system on to his own functional framework. He does this, it seems to me, by a gradual separation of the two notions of function and use; on the one hand the original uses of language go on expanding, as he goes on using language in new and other ways, but at the same time he builds in this functional framework into the linguistic system itself. I have tried to describe how he does this; basically I think he does it through internalizing a fundamental distinction between pragmatic uses of language, those which demand a response, and represent a way of participating in the situation, and what I call 'mathetic' uses of language, those which do not demand a response but represent rather a way of observing and of learning as one observes. Now these two come out of his original set of very concrete functions, but they turn into functional components of the linguistic system itself, the interpersonal and the ideational that we were talking about earlier.

HP: *Are the causes for this change environmental?*

MAKH: I assume them to be environmental with a biological foundation. The biological conditions must be met, the level of maturation must have been reached. Given that level of maturation, then I would look for environmental causes in the social system. I don't want to get into arguments about the psycholinguistic mechanisms involved, because I don't think this assumes any particular psycholinguistic perspective.

HP: *Is your point of view not too behavioristic here?*

MAKH: No, I would say that it is emphatically not behavioristic. It has always seemed to me, and again here I am simply following Firth, that behaviorist models will not account for linguistic interaction or for language development. There is a very curious notion that if you are assigning a significant role to the cultural environment in language learning you are a behaviorist. There is no logical connection here at all. We should perhaps demolish the fallacy of the *unstructured input*. There has been a myth around over the past few years that the child must have a specific innate language learning capacity, a built-in grammar, because the data to which he is exposed are insufficient to account for the result. Now that is not true. The language around him is fantastically rich and highly structured; Labov has said this and he is quite right (Labov 1970). It is quite unnecessary to postulate a learning device having these highly specific linguistic properties. That doesn't mean it is wrong; it means it isn't necessary. I want to distinguish very sharply here between the particular psychological model which you use and the functional conditions on language learning. These do not presuppose each other in any way. What I am doing is simply studying the child's language development in an interactional perspective, and this has got nothing whatever to do with behaviorist theories of psychology.

BH: *How does this viewpoint on language development in the child lead us into a sociosemantic approach to language?*

MAKH: First, it points up the fact that a child who is learning language is learning 'how to mean'; that is, he is developing a semantic potential, in respect of a set of functions in language that are in the last resort social functions. They represent modes of interaction between the child and others. So the child learns how to interact linguistically; and language becomes for him a primary channel of socialization, because these functions are defined by social contexts, in Bernstein's sense as I mentioned earlier. The child's semantics therefore is functionally specific; what he is developing is a 'social semantics' in the sense that it is a meaning potential related to a particular set of primary social functions. And second – though it's a closely related point – it is above all through a developmental approach that we can make concrete the notion of language as part of the social semiotic: the concept of the culture as a system of meaning, with language as one of its realizations.

HP: *Could you explain more concretely your hypothesis about the functional origin of language? What does the system of functions look like in this first phase of the development of language in the child?*

MAKH: In this first phase I suggested that the child learns: the *instrumental* function, which is the 'I want' function of language, language used to satisfy a material need; the *regulatory* function, which is the 'do as I tell you' function, language used to order people about; the *interactional* function, 'me and you', which is language used to interact with other people; the *personal* function, 'here I come', which is language used as the expression of the child's own uniqueness; the *heuristic* function comes a little while behind, and is language as a means of exploring the environment, the 'tell me why' function of language; and finally the *imaginative* function, 'let's pretend', which is really language for the creation of an environment of one's own. In the case of the particular subject I worked with, these six functions had all appeared in his proto-language: he had developed a semiotic system in respect of all these six functions without making any demand on the adult language at all. The elements of the system were entirely his own invention.

Then there came a point at which he switched, and as it were gave up his own special system in favor of that of English. Simultaneously with this switch, he generalized out of his original range of functions this very general functional opposition between what I referred to as the *pragmatic* and the *mathetic*. With this child the distinction was *very* clear, because he developed an interesting strategy of his own, which was absolutely consistent: he used a rising intonation for all pragmatic utterances, and a falling one for all mathetic ones. So he knew exactly what he was doing: either he was using language as an intruder, requiring a response ("I want something", "do something", etc.), which he did on a rising tone; or he was using language as an observer, requiring no response (in the meanings of observation, recall or prediction), and with these there was a falling tone. The pragmatic function evolved here clearly out of the instrumental and regulatory uses of language. The mathetic function evolved in a way that was much less clear; it required a lot of time to trace the history of this, but I think it arises out of the personal and heuristic functions. Language is first used to identify the self, in contra-distinction to the environment; it is then used to explore the environment, and by the same token then to explore the *self*. This child as I say made a beautiful distinction between the rising tone for the pragmatic or 'doing' function and the falling tone for the mathetic or 'learning' function.

Next stage, the adult language, unlike the child's proto-language, gives him the possibility of meaning more than one thing at once. There comes the moment when these functions are incorporated into the linguistic system itself, in the highly abstract form of the meta-functions I mentioned earlier: the pragmatic function into the interpersonal function in the linguistic system and the mathetic function into the ideational function in the linguistic system. Whereas, in the first stage, the functions stand in an 'either ... or' relationship – the child is using language *either* to do this *or* to do that – the beauty of the adult linguistic system is that he can do more than one thing at once. In fact he *must* do more than one thing at once, because now, in the adult stage, every time he opens his mouth he is both observer and intruder at the same time. And this is why human language evolved by putting in between the meaning and the sound a formal level of grammatical structure, because it is the grammatical structure which allows the different functions to be mapped on to one another in a sort of *polyphony*. I use this metaphor because in polyphonic music the different melodies are mapped on to one another so that any particular chord is at one and the same time an element in a number of different melodies. In the same way, in adult language any element in the syntagm – say a word – is at one and the same time filling a role in a number of different structures. Now you can't do this without a grammar. The child's system is a two-level system: it has a content and an expression. The adult system is a three level system, of content, form and expression.

HP: *So this functional plurality makes the difference between adult language and child language?*

MAKH: Yes; this is what I mean by functional plurality – that any utterance in the adult language operates on more than one level of meaning at once. This is the crucial difference between the adult language and the child's language.

HP: *Everything you have said up till now proves that your view of the scope of linguistics differs widely from the views we are acquainted with in various other trends. This is perhaps a good occasion to turn back to our starting-point. I would like to ask you to redefine what you mean by linguistics and by sociolinguistics, and what you mean by saying that a good linguist has to go outside linguistics.*

MAKH: Well, I hope I didn't quite put it that way, that a good linguist *has* to go outside linguistics! Let's go back to the observation that there are two main perspectives on language: one is the intra-organism perspective, the other is the inter-organism perspective. In the intra-organism perspective we see language as what goes on in the head; in the inter-organism perspective it is what goes on between people. Now these two perspectives are complementary, and in my opinion linguistics is in the most healthy state when both are taken seriously. The past ten or fifteen years have been characterized by a very large concentration on intra-organism linguistics, largely under the influence of Chomsky and his 'language as knowledge' or psycho-linguistic perspective. I am personally glad to see that there is now a return to the inter-organism perspective in which we take account of the fact that people not only speak, but that they speak to each other. This is the fact that interests me. People often ask, must you make a choice whether you are going to study intra- or inter-organism linguistics, can't you just study language? I would say, up to a point you can. If you are studying the inner areas of the linguistic system, linguistic form in Hjelmslev's sense – the phonological and lexicogrammatical systems – you can be neutral up to a point; but the moment you go into semantics, your criteria of idealization depend on your making a selection. You either say with Chomsky that linguistics is a branch of theoretical psychology, or – which is equally valid – that linguistics is a branch of theoretical sociology. For that matter you could say that linguistics is a branch of theoretical esthetics.

HP: *What are the implications of your view for the problem of language teaching?*

MAKH: The type of perspective I have on language naturally relates to my own interests. My interests are, primarily, in language and the social system; and then related to this, in the two areas of language and education, and language and literature. All these have something in common. They make it necessary to be interested in what the speaker does; in the *text*. Now in order to make sense of 'what the speaker does', you have to be able to embed this in the context of 'what the speaker can do'. You've got to see the text as an actualized potential; which means that you have got to study the potential. As regards language teaching – could I rather say 'language in education', because I am not so much concerned with pedagogical linguistics as with educational linguistics, and with the kinds of presupposition that are made about language in the educational system at present? – here again you need a functional perspective. Let me take one example. Consider the question of literacy, teaching reading and writing: what is learning to read and to write? Fundamentally it is an extension of the functional potential of language. Those children who don't learn to read and write, by and large, are children to whom it doesn't make sense; to whom the functional extension that these media provide has not been made clear, or does not match up with their own expectations of what language is for. Hence if the child has not been oriented towards the types of meaning which the teacher sees as those which are proper to the writing system, then the learning of writing and reading would be out of context, because fundamentally, as in the history of the human race, reading and writing are an extension of the functions of language. This is what they must be for the child equally well. Here is just one instance of a perspective on language in the context of the educational system.

In stylistics too the emphasis is on the study of the text, and again there is a functional basis to this. We are interested in what a particular writer has written, against the background of what he might have written – including comparatively, against the background of other things he has written, or that other people have written. If we are interested in what it is about the language of a particular work of literature that has its effect on us as readers, then we shall want to look at not simply the effects of linguistic prominence, which by themselves are rather trivial, but the effects of linguistic prominence in respect of those functions of language which are highlighted in the particular work. I am thinking here of Zumthor's point where he has said that the various genres of literature in different epochs are characterized by differences of emphasis on the different functions of language (Zumthor 1972). I think this is very true. It seems to me that you can only understand the linguistic properties of the text in relation to the orientation of the whole of which it is a part to certain patterns of linguistic function. I have tried to illustrate this in my study of the language of Golding's *The Inheritors,* where it is very clearly the TRANSITIVITY system that is at work (Halliday 1971). The whole book is about TRANSITIVITY, in a certain sense. There is a highlighting of man's interpretation of the processes of the external world; and therefore it is no accident that there is a highlighting in the language, in the grammar, of certain aspects of the TRANSITIVITY system. This illustrates once again the same perspective on language. A central position is accorded to the study of the text; no sharp separation is made between competence and performance; the text is seen as an actualization of the total potential, in the context of a functional theory for the interpretation of the potential. I see this as the thread which links the social, the educational and the literary perspectives on language.

HP: *As a conclusion of this dialogue, I would like to ask you two kinds of questions. First I would ask you to thematize your scientific genealogy, if I may call it that. Most people consider you as a representative of the school of English linguistics, namely Firth's London school. Do you agree with this?*

MAKH: I would be quite happy to accept a designation as Firth's pupil. I think he was a great scholar and I have tried to develop some of his ideas. There seems to be a great deal of richness in Firth's work, and much of it still remains to be taken up. But here I have to admit that I find myself having a slightly different interpretation of the recent history of linguistics from that which is perhaps the most generally accepted. It seems to me there are essentially two main traditions in modern linguistics: one represented by Hjelmslev, the Prague school, Firth and the London school, Sydney Lamb and stratificational grammar, and by and large Pike and tagmemics; the other represented by Bloomfield, the structuralist school, and Chomsky; while the later versions of transformation theory, especially generative semantics, Lakoff, McCawley and others, have moved from the latter towards the former.

One symptom of this is the distinction between a *tristratal view of language*, with the key concept of *realization*, of language as a multiple-coding system, which is characteristic of the Hjelmslevian view, contrasted with a bistratal view of language based on a combinatory or compositional conception rather than a realizational one. In other words, language in the Bloomfieldian concept is interpreted as consisting primarily of two levels related by composition: a grammar and a phonology, with grammatical units composed out of phonological units. The Prague school and Hjelmslev see language as having a grammar, a phonology and a semantics, with a realizational or coding relation among them. Chomsky essentially takes over the Bloomfieldian view. One is not denying Chomsky's greatness and originality if one says that he belongs to the Bloomfieldian tradition in linguistics.

So you've got two traditions within linguistics itself: the *combinatorial*, compositional one which is Bloomfield and Chomsky, structuralism and the early transformation theory, and the *realizational* one which is Hjelmslev, Firth, Troubetzkoy and others. In the Bloomfieldian tradition, then, the key concept is that of *constituency*; Chomsky takes this over, he formalizes constituent structure, and then finds it necessary to introduce a 'deep structure' because constituent structure won't handle semantic relations in language. Out of this comes generative semantics, which is again tristratal and basically a realizational concept. Another way of looking at this is from outside linguistics. If we go back to the 'psycho-' versus 'socio-' perspective, fundamentally Chomsky's links are with the philosophical-logical-psychological tradition in the study of language, whereas the other approach is more associated with the ethnographic and sociological study of language. Chomsky for the first time shows that it is possible to formalize natural language. This has opened a whole new era in linguistics; but in doing so Chomsky remained within the Bloomfieldian concept of language and largely within the psychological-philosophical universe of discourse. He imposes a very high degree of idealization, operates with a strong boundary between competence and performance, and so on. The other tradition, which is closer to European structuralism, is more concerned with how people behave, and especially with the *interpretation* of how they behave. My own background is entirely of this kind: an approach to language which is originally ethnographic, Malinowskian in my case; which emphasizes interaction and which operates with a very low degree of idealization – hence much less formalization, and what there is is of a very different kind, best seen in the work of Greimas, with its origins in Levi-Strauss (Greimas 1966a, b). Now, obviously all this is over-simplified. But it may perhaps give some answer to your question.

HP: *This sketch seems very interesting, but still I have some difficulties with it. I would like to formulate two of them here. First of all, I thought that Hjelmslev's linguistics was especially a study of the intrasystematic relations of language, and that is different from the more extrinsic approach to language as in the Prague school and in Martinet. I clearly distinguish between the formalizing structuralism and the substantializing structuralism. These seem to me very opposite directions within structuralism.*

MAKH: I would have said different elements rather than opposite directions. I agree that Hjelmslev is representing the formalizing tradition in structural linguistics; but this is nevertheless within the framework of a basically inter-organism view of language. Hjelmslev is concerned with language as process; process is text, and text is the interorganism instantiation of language. This is why Hjelmslev is so difficult. It looks as though he is formalizing knowledge about language, but he is not. He is formalizing the linguistic system in a context which is really that of text, that of language as process. Lamb in his article on Hjelmslev criticizes him for this (Lamb 1966). I think he's right in showing where Hjelmslev doesn't quite bring it off.

HP: *Don't you think the time has come for a revaluation of the Prague school? What is the importance of the Prague school in linguistics?*

MAKH: I am delighted that so many linguists have now taken up the work of the Prague school. I have always considered this of fundamental importance; primarily because they were the first linguists to attempt to build functional theories into the linguistic system instead of imposing them from outside – they seek to interpret the linguistic system in functional terms. Secondly, because they have a basic concept of the nature of language which is entirely relevant to the sort of problems I am interested in. I would certainly acknowledge the Prague school as a major contributor to modern linguistics.

HP: *My second difficulty then is your analogy between Bloomfield and Chomsky. I agree that from the point of view of the constituent structure they are alike. But don't you agree that Chomsky's notion of creativity is absolutely absent in Bloomfieldian linguistics? Bloomfieldian linguistics is taxonomic and inductive whereas Chomsky's notion of creativity contradicts this.*

MAKH: I doubt this. Of course, I agree that Chomsky has opened a new perspective; but I think he did so in a framework that is Bloomfieldian in its essentials, and not merely from the point of view of constituency. I don't really see that Chomsky was saying anything at all new when he was talking about the creativity of language. This is clearly implicit in Bloomfield, and even more so in Hjelmslev, Firth and others. I think you must look at the thing in a historical perspective. In a sense, Bloomfield was focusing concentration on the surface of language because he saw that linguistics had to become a lot more explicit and that was the only way in which it could do so.

HP: *That is my point; there is no idea in Bloomfield like deep structure.*

MAKH: No, I agree. Deep structure is new in Chomsky; but it is only necessary if you accept the Bloomfieldian position to start with. You don't need 'deep structure' if you are not a 'structuralist'. Chomsky starts with a two-level system: syntax and phonology, no semantics. If you represent language as structure in the Bloomfieldian sense, then you get to the point where it doesn't work. In other words, it is no longer possible to get any 'deeper' than Bloomfield had already got. Harris showed just how far it is possible to get with an essentially combinatorial or compositional view of language; you can get, roughly speaking, as far as the phrase in grammar. Then you stop, because beyond that point language is so complex that it is impossible to construct more abstract units out of combinations of the lower level elements. There is only one thing you can do once you have gone so far: introduce the concept of transformation, that is, invent more abstract structures and rules for transforming the one kind to the other. This is what Harris did and what Chomsky did. But if you haven't started with a combinatorial view, then there is no need to invent deep structures – as the generative semanticists have seen – because you aren't assuming that the whole of the linguistic system can be represented as a combinatorial form. The question is whether, if you keep an IC-type constituent structure, with deep structure as well as surface structure and rules mapping the one on to the other, the deep structure then looks like, or leads on to, a convincing representation of semantics.

HP: *If I understand you well, a very fundamental distinction in the history of linguistics is that between sociologically oriented linguistics and psychologically oriented linguistics.*

MAKH: Yes I think it is significant, and it ties up with the other distinction between the concept of *realization* and that of *composition*.

HP: *Another way of concluding would be by asking you something about the philosophical background of your theory. Two questions here. Could you survey your opinion about the relation between language and experience? And how is experience an operational category in linguistic theory?*

MAKH: As I see it, the individual's experience is mediated through language but in the context of the social structure. When we say that the linguistic system is part of the social system, this implies that what is transmitted to us through language, when we learn it as children, is in fact the social system; and that our experience is codified in language through the intermediary of the social structure – there is no such thing as experience that is independent of the social structure. So when we transmit experience through language what we are transmitting is the social system. You see I would take a view which is Whorfian as modified by Bernstein (Bernstein 1971, Chapter 7).

HP: *Yes, so there is no direct relationship between the individual and language but only a direct relationship between a social structure and language?*

MAKH: That is the direct relationship as I see it, yes. I would like to emphasize that I'm not rejecting the *creativity* of the individual. On the contrary, I am fascinated by it, as anyone interested in *stylistics* must be. But just as an individual's linguistic creativity is defined by linguistic structure, so also at the next level it is defined by the social structure. The individual is a complex of social roles; he derives his individuality from the social structure, and this is what he expresses in language. Some of our most creative acts, linguistically speaking, are repetitions; and let's do away with this notion that nearly every sentence that is uttered is being uttered for the first time – on the contrary, I would say, nearly every sentence that is uttered is *not* being uttered for the first time. Creativity does not consist in creating new sentences. Creativity consists in new interpretations of existing behavior in existing social contexts; in new semiotic patterns, however realized. I am not accustomed to formulating this and therefore I am saying it rather badly; but I think the whole question of the relationship between the individual and language has to be seen as embedded in the social structure. There is confusion here partly because it is assumed that one must posit a direct relation between language and the individual, otherwise one is denying individual creativity. I don't believe this at all. I think the creativity of the individual is a function of the social system.

HP: *My last question: the key problem for a philosopher of language is the problem of the relation between language and world. I would like to know your opinion here. To take an easy formulation: is language the mirror of the world?*

MAKH: Here we come to universals, don't we? There are fashions in linguistics, as I said before. The recent fashion has been to emphasize the biological nature of the human being, bringing out those respects in which we are all alike. This needs to be complemented by reference to the cultural nature of the human being, bringing out those respects in which we may differ. Language expresses both human biology and human culture. It expresses the unity of the human race and it expresses the diversity of human culture. Experience is a product of both, and experience is encoded in language; but it is experience as processed by the culture and by the sub-culture. This is one of the reasons for sub-cultural misunderstandings, failures of communication (including those on a large scale, that we call educational failures) in the community. In a plural society you have sub-cultural differences which lead to different encodings of experience in language. Even when it is the same language, there may be different meaning systems, different orientations in the meaning potential associated with the different sub-cultures. So biology and culture as it were interact in the linguistic system; and since human experience is a product of the two, and is mediated through language, I would agree in seeing a form of dialectic whereby the individual's experience is transmitted to him through language, and then is expressed by him in language, and so transmitted in turn to others. As I said, I would accept Bernstein's modification of Whorf. The weakness in Whorf's hypothesis seems to be that it has no place for the social structure; it is a hypothesis about language, culture, and the individual. I think Bernstein is right in saying that the relation between language and culture is mediated by the social structure. So I would say that in the last analysis language does mirror the world, but it does so only very indirectly, through the mediation of experience which is itself mediated by the social structure. The result is not so much a mirror but – to vary the metaphor – a multiple recoding, an ongoing working *interpretation* of the world as it impinges on social man.

HP: *What are the implications of your opinion about this language-world relation for the problematic issue of universals?*

MAKH: If we start from the distinction Chomsky made between formal and substantive universals – what Firth used to call 'general' categories and 'universal' categories, the latter of which he rejected – then general linguistic theory is a theory of formal universals; there is no dispute about the existence of such universals, however difficult it may be to characterize them at a suitably abstract level. When you come to substantive universals, which are more concrete – sometimes rather too concrete, perhaps, in the form in which they are offered (for example phonological features) – the problem seems to be that the relation between these and the formal universals is quite arbitrary. There is no necessary reason why a system having this particular content should take this particular form. So we interpret the formal universals in biological terms, as given by the structure of the human brain. Now what interests me more are universals of human culture. I should like to know, for example, to what extent we find a universal aspect in the functional origins of the child's linguistic system. After all we know all human groups are biologically endowed with the same brain structure; a few lessons in linguistics have always been enough to demonstrate this. But there is no a priori reason why all human cultures should make identical demands on language. Clearly there is a point up to which they do: as Levi-Strauss has put it, for all cultures "the universe is an object of thought at least as much as it is a means of satisfying needs", and this fact is reflected in language (Levi-Strauss 1966). No doubt we can go further than this before we reach the point of specificity where differences begin to emerge and we find different cultures using language in different ways, but we do reach it sooner or later. These questions may give us something to which to relate the substantive universals if we find them (Greenberg 1963).

HP: *Is grammar that which relativizes the universality of behavior and biological structure, or is it the part which makes universal the particular experiences of the social structure?*

MAKH: I think both can be true. On the one hand, the universals, in one sense of the term, will be found in what Hjelmslev calls the 'purport'; this is simply because we all have the same physiology and we all live on the same planet. These are already relativized in the semantic system, which is the grid imposed on them by the culture, and also simply by the special nature of the language in question; and the grammatical system relativizes them still further. At the same time – and this is where the other kind of universals, the formal universals, come in – the whole of human experience, which is essentially culture-specific in that it is mediated by the social system, is ultimately representable in terms of a linguistic semiotic having certain highly abstract formal properties; and in that sense grammar 'makes universal', by providing a common framework for the interpretation of experience. But this is only at the most general level; I would not like to argue from the formal universals of language to the nature of experience itself. The fact that at a sufficiently abstract level we can represent the internal organization of all human languages in terms of a particular formal system tells us nothing about the conditions of human life.

HP: *I would like to ask you, where is your work leading to?*

MAKH: Since I am probably rather more modest than I may have sounded sometimes when getting excited, I would like to put this in very tentative terms by saying simply what are the fundamental questions that interest me and which I hope linguistics will continue to pursue among other questions that concern it. There are perhaps two fundamental questions lying behind what I do, one intrinsic and one extrinsic. The first one is, why is language as it is? Mankind could have evolved an enormous number of different semiotic systems; why did they evolve a system which has these particular properties that language has? I think that the functional approach is one way of gaining some insight into this question; and it will perhaps allow us to return to an interest in the origins and the evolution of language, which has been somewhat out of fashion for the last hundred years. The second question concerns language and the transmission of culture: how is it that the most ordinary, casual, informal, everyday uses of language, without any kind of instruction and without even any kind of explicit understanding behind them, so efficiently transmit to the child the fundamental patterns of the culture, systems of knowledge, social structure, value systems and the like? I think we have very little understanding of this at the moment, and it is that aspect of language and the social system which interests me a great deal. As a final small parenthesis, I would point out that there is one tremendous gap in our understanding of language which is really fundamental here; that is that we have practically no idea of the nature of children's peer group speech, the kind of language with which young children interact with each other. We've got to find out more about this – among other things, of course – before we can begin to answer the second of these questions, and probably the first as well.

Center for Advanced Study in the Behavioral Sciences
Stanford, CA., U. S. A.
9 October 1972

2

With Noboru Yamaguchi and Shun'ichi Segawa (1977)

Introduction

The work based on M. A. K. Halliday's linguistic theory, Systemic Functional Theory of Grammar, has recently been proliferating to a remarkable extent, both in quality and in quantity. One of the strong pieces of evidence of this may be found in the rapidly growing number of publications within the mould of Hallidayan linguistics.

In the context of the now prospering enterprise of Hallidayan linguistics, it may be of some use to present, as a small contribution to this field, my 'Discussion with M. A. K. Halliday 1977'. The interview reveals some of Halliday's own views about Chomskyan linguistics and its place in the history of the study of language, which may seldom or perhaps never found in his published writings. In addition, the discussion may also clarify aspects of Halliday's general approach to linguistic theorizing, particularly his way of thinking about motivations for setting up a system network and the systemic features in it, which has tended to remain rather obscure in his actual writings. Thirdly, it may let us know something very illuminating, which has again been not very explicit, about Halliday's pioneering work on child language development, *Learning How to Mean* (Halliday 1975), and its interesting background, as well as its significant relevance to his work on adult language. These, though the most important and intriguing, are only some the very informative remarks in the discussion.[1]

NY: *I want to go back to the argument you raised about linguistic universals in the lecture this morning.[2] I thought that your criticism was only about substantive universals, but not about formal universals. But Chomsky's idea about linguistic universals is centering not so much around substantive universals as around formal universals, such as possible forms of grammar, possible transformations and so on. For him, substantive universals are minor things, while formal universals are much more important.*

MAKH: You may be right in saying that, for Chomsky, the important things are the formal universals, that is, theoretical categories. And of course I am happy with that. I mean, when it comes to those, the discussion then is essentially metalinguistic and even metatheoretical to a certain extent. That's a different point. But in practice, work deriving from Chomsky does operate very strongly with substantive universals. Now some things are borderline. I mean, the old business about the PS rule, S →NP + VP, and what you mean by that. But I am thinking of things like, say, Fillmore (e.g. 1968) setting up essentially case frames which are claimed to be universal or basic categories like the one I used this morning – like definiteness for example. Now all the literature based on the Chomskyan approach assumes that definiteness is a universal category.

NY: *But if you analyse other languages like Japanese where you may not find such categories, you can possibly get rid of those substantive categories. This may not cause any change of formal universals.*

MAKH: Right. But in practice what happens is that people don't get rid of those substantive categories. They impose them on other languages because of the conviction that they must be there. This distorts the descriptions of the other languages. They may know that a substantive universal is subject to empirical verification; but in practice people don't behave like that. What they actually do is to start with this built-in assumption, just as the medieval grammarians started in Europe with the built-in assumption that the syntactic categories of Latin were universal. Of course you will find such categories by looking for them; but it does distort your description of different languages.

NY: *But if you criticise other theories like Transformational grammar, or any other contemporary theories of grammar, I don't think you can use those substantive categories as a point for criticising them.*

MAKH: Of course you can. The fundamental issue is that the theory generates the substantive descriptions. They are not two separate things. That's a fair criticism of the theory.

NY: *I think it's important, but the first thing you have to do is to compare competing theories in terms of formal universals.*

MAKH: No, you can't. Theories are not comparable. I don't think theories are comparable.

NY: *There is something in common between theories, which may be comparable.*

MAKH: Something so abstract and metatheoretical that you can't really use It. I don't believe you can compare theories. I don't think theories are comparable. And certainly I don't see how you can compare theories that are based on such different conceptions of the nature of what a theory is.

NY: *But criticism usually comes from comparison.*

MAKH: Yes, all right. But the sort of criticism I make, which is not a metatheoretical one (it's a theoretical one in the sense that it's a criticism of the work that is actually done in the terms of this theory) doesn't in the last resort depend on comparison. I don't think it does. Even if I didn't think I could do better I'd still be entitled to say I do not agree ... I think that a theory which leads to what I would call ethnocentrism is to be criticised in those terms.

NY: *I am under the impression that you are against the Transformationalist way of looking at language as a formal system. But what do you think of those people in the Systemic school, such as Richard Hudson (e.g. 1971), Robin Fawcett (e.g. 1980) or other people, who are trying to develop Systemic counterparts of generative grammar?*

MAKH: I am not against the goal of representing language as a formal system. I am against the price that they pay. I criticise Transformational theory not for trying to represent languages as formal systems, but for the cost, which is this very high degree of idealization. Now why I like, say, Hudson's work, or that of Winograd (e.g. 1983), is that they are trying in different ways to achieve this goal without paying that price. So it's not the goal of representing languages as formal systems that I criticise. That's a perfectly valid goal. It's not one I place high in my own priorities, but that's a different thing.

NY: *Do you think that the theories the Systemicists are developing are better than those of the Transformationalists?*

MAKH: I think that they have more promise.

NY: *If you limit your attention to the formal analyses of grammar, not to the other aspects like functions or social contexts ...*

MAKH: I find that difficult to do – that is to say, to evaluate a theory in terms of what is only one part of its own declared goals. But let us try and do this, then it seems to me that Hudson's work, though he hasn't got there yet, holds up the promise of getting further. But I think it is artificial to try to separate that aspect from its other concerns, because to me the importance of the theory is that it's going this way without sacrificing what seem to me to be both essential insights into languages and essential concerns of linguistic theory.

NY: *Even if you regard Systemic theory as better than Transformational theory, you can't ignore the fact of those Transformationalist insights into language and languages, that is to say, the enormous number of insights which have come out of the work by them. You cannot ignore the fact. If it had been not for the Transformational theory, I don't think those insights into language and languages would have come out.*

MAKH: Well, this is, of course, something that neither you nor I can ever know, a question of 'what would have happened if.' Yes, of course I agree. I do not ignore the very important things that have come out of the work done by so many people in this field. But I think it's still worth making two points. Most of it could equally well have come out within the framework of other theories. And if I may go back to my illustrations of this morning, there are certain things which are simply historical accidents. Why, for example, did Saussure, rather than Mathesius (e.g. 1964), become the father or mother of linguistics? In fact, there is every bit as much insight in Mathesius' work as there is in Saussure's. But it did not become mainstream until very recently. It could have done. All the insights that came from the Saussurean standpoint could equally well have come out of the standpoint of Mathesius. But for various, in the long run irrelevant, reasons, it was Saussure's work that became known, but not Mathesius'.

I think there was a similar effect with Chomsky. Chomsky happened to come out in a context in which he was in a position to have a great deal of influence. To start with, he was a pupil of the greatest teachers of the American Structuralist school. He therefore took off from a point where people were already. Moreover, he came in just at the moment when they have reached an impasse, when Harris' work had hit the high point, and it was clear that no one would get any further. In addition, he came at the point when there was tremendous expansion in American scholarship, and indeed in Western scholarship and world scholarship generally. And there was money flowing up with all lots of people coming in and looking for fields in which to study. He also matched the permanent interest of Western thinking in formal logic and dogmatic philosophy. Chomsky combined a whole lot of these features at just the right historical moment. This is the sort of thing which creates a poet: there are many possible poems around, but only one or two actually emerge if the historical conditions are right. That is in no way to detract from his genius, but I still think that if other factors had been there to release this kind of energy, without Chomsky it would still have had the same effect in advancing ideas in linguistics. People could have taken up Hjelmslev or other ideas of quite a different kind. I wouldn't like to say that if it had not been for Chomsky these things could not have happened, because you never know.

NY: *But they actually happened. There have been lots of insights coming out of this work. And even Systemicists are absorbing these insights so as to elaborate their theories.*

MAKH: Oh yes. But also it's equally true that the Transformationalists themselves had to work their own way through the history of linguistics; and a great deal of what they presented as new was not new at all. They started with things everybody knew about language, which they simply rewrote in their own terms. And a great deal of the problems that they dealt with were purely internal housekeeping problems, problems created by their own theory. So when you peel off all this, the total is not so great as you think. But of course, what is genuine there, anyone, I hope, would take. But equally, they refuse to take insights from other theories; they just ignore them. Things have been said in Transformational theory, which have been said earlier by other people; but they get credit for them, because they set them within the terms of their own establishment. And it was a very brutal establishment. This is a political issue as much as anything, because under the banner of being great revolutionaries, which they are not, in terms of European ideas ... many of their fundamental ideas were normal things that we were taught as students. I don't mean advanced theoretical notions, but basic notions about linguistics, such as the fact you can't base the theory on procedures. And most of their polemics were totally irrelevant to European linguistics. They were arguing against behaviourists; but none of us ever were behaviourists. There was no trace of behaviourism in European linguistics, and yet so much of Chomsky's reputation in the early days depended on his demolishing Skinner, on his rejecting behaviourist psychology's basis for linguistics. But we never held those ideas. Firth himself was explicitly anti-behaviourist – he said in a number of his writings that he just cannot accept this behaviourist notion; but Chomsky is the one who gains credit for this. Much of his thinking comes out of American Structuralism – for example what to do when constituency theory lets you down. He did, of course, take the metatheoretical step of rejecting procedural approaches, which nobody in Europe held anyway, to introduce a new kind of theory from outside linguistics – from philosophy and logic, and I'm not denying the value of this achievement. But then, the distinction that Chomsky makes between "generative" and "taxonomic", I think is false – I think it's a non-distinction. This should have been just an academic argument; but what happens instead is that Chomsky makes it into a political movement. He introduces himself as a great revolutionary, demolishing the whole of preceding linguistics and much of psychology. He has a message, and in the process, he makes it impossible for other linguists to get along with their work. We did massive studies of text linguistics in the 1960's, which simply could not be published – people couldn't get jobs if they went along this line. Precisely the thing that Chomsky was complaining against in the preceding generation – which didn't happen in Europe; whether it happened in America or not, I don't know – happened in his own name in the 1960's. And it was a very uncomfortable time to work. Those who were not in his mould could not afford to teach students our own ideas. In the whole of the 1960's, I never taught students my own ideas, because they would not have got a job. I had to have people to teach Transformational theory. And this is not good enough. Now Transformation grammar happens to be, in my view, also a rather elitist theory; but that's a different issue – it's something which one can have opinions about, and other people may not think this. But the way in which transformationalists behaved as an establishment in linguistics was very harmful. People are still suffering for this; today there are generations of linguists in America who are trained to do nothing else except to work within the framework of Transformational theory. Now that people are moving away from it, they are the ones who are suffering.

NY: *One of the interesting things about the Systemicists is that Huddleston has left the Systemic arena (cf. Huddleston 1971). Why has he left?*

MAKH: I don't see that it is an arena. It seems to me that if you could remove the tone of violence from it and simply consider that knowledge advances through people having different ideas and different theories, then you take what you want according to what you want to do. Now Huddleston was interested in formal representations of certain things he found out using Systemic theory. He chose to present them in Transformational terms perhaps because he considered that this was the area where the main frontiers of the field were located. If someone says that 'for my purposes I consider that this theory has got more to offer,' that's fine. I will never complain about that.

NY: *What do you think of the trend of those young Systemicists trying to motivate the features in a system network (e.g. Martin 1987)? You could introduce whatever features you like into a system network. But I think it is necessary to motivate them in one way or the other. You must give some good reasons when you set up features. One of the possible motivations may be that they can be formally realized by means of realizations.*

MAKH: I agree it's very desirable. I think that Jim Martin has been the one who has perhaps most satisfactorily stated what he would consider to be the criteria for motivating features. I have tended to leave this rather loose, because I believe that a theory should have more apparatus in it than you actually need for any one task. And this was again opposite to the Chomskyan notion of economy. I think theories should be extravagant. I would not use a theory of language, as Chomsky does, to make conclusions about the nature of the human brain. I have left a whole lot of rather open-ended conditions under which one may set up a system network. But I am fully in sympathy with the attempt to take a step to tighten this up, now that we have got some experience in this kind of thing. I don't think there's any point in doing it in advance. It's a waste of time.

NY: *Is it not contradictory to your notion of delicacy?*

MAKH: No. Because ...right, that's a good point. But no. In no way does it run counter to the notion of delicacy. Martin is not at all saying that you reach a limit of delicacy. All he is saying is that there should be a way of choosing among alternative representations. This can be achieved by making explicit a limited set of criteria which are required if a particular feature is to be recognized. Now, on the whole, I think I would be right in saying that it tends to be at the earlier stages in delicacy, rather than the later ones, that this question tends to arise. For example, the question such as whether one identifies the feature simply because, although it contributes nothing to the realization, it is defined as having a common potential in terms of the later systems. Now this tends to happen earlier rather than later. So I don't think it's in any way conflictive with the notion of delicacy.

NY: *People like Jim Martin (1987) or Robin Fawcett (1988a, b) seem to believe it is preferable for systemic features to be realized formally. For example, Fawcett tried to get rid of the feature of case out of his pronoun or deictic system network, because case is not an inherent property of pronouns (Fawcett 1988a). It may be an extrinsic* *feature, which arises in relation to structural environment. Now, in this connection, I want to proceed to your system networks in child language development. In these systems, formally realized expressions are what the child actually utters or voices, not real words or a sequence of words like those of an adult's language, but simply certain sounds or perhaps sometimes postural expressions. When you set up relevant features in a child's linguistic system, how do you motivate them? There doesn't seem any motivation there.*

MAKH: In the children's language, in the protolanguage, you have rather a special case, because since there is no grammar in it, it's just a set of signs, content-expression pairs. You could treat these, of course, as a simple list. But there are two or three reasons for introducing more system than that. One is that on extrinsic or external grounds; we do gain in our interpretation if we relate them to some initial set of functions. The major reason is, I think, that there are semantic generalizations to be made. Now normally with system networks, we are to be involved in two adjacent levels or strata. In other words, we look for motivations both in semantics and in grammar, or both in grammar and in phonology. We haven't got that kind of stratal organization in the child's protolanguage. But we can say that, in the case of protolanguage, for example let us say, two elements in the language may have in common the fact that they are used as responses, not as an initiation. Now, I would regard this as justification for saying that there is a feature [response] in that network, which constitutes the generalization about the two signs one of which is a response to call and one of which is a response to something else. It's that kind of thing which is the main motive.

NY: *I'm sure that you have already read John Dore's review of your Learning How to Mean (Dore 1976). Towards the end of that review, Dore is saying as a sort of criticism, 'The paradox is highlighted by Halliday's glossing practices. Every theory of language relies on the glossing of meanings, but the theoretical motivation for the glosses varies widely. Halliday's glossing reflects, to use Roger Brown's phrase (Brown 1973), a very "rich interpretation."' What do you think of his opinion about your interpretations of Nigel's utterances? Are they too rich?*

MAKH: I think he is wrong. It's a very fair review. I am pleased. But I don't agree with that. Of course, as I tried to make it clear with the gloss, it's only a gloss. It's an attempt to give a translation into adult language, if you like. I do try to say that the meanings are not those of adult language, so that it's not a semantic interpretation. It is a gloss – a translation. In Malinowski's sense (1923, 1935). But I think that they are justified. I'm not arguing for this particular formulation rather than another. But they were very carefully filled out. And I think that the point I want to make is that if you watch the mother interacting with the child, and the way she responds to what he says such that he accepts that response as satisfactory, then you have to say that some meaning like that is embedded in what he is saying, something which was there if she was to translate it into her own language. Of course, she doesn't do, because typically the mother is not conscious of reacting in this way. But if she was to translate it into her own language, she would, I think, be forced to put into something like that meaning. So I don't think they are too rich.

Of course, I'm not saying that there could not have been better formulations. When I write these glosses, partly I do it for humorous effect.

NY: *But parents sometimes misunderstand what their children mean, I suppose.*

MAKH: Sure they do. But the child makes it very clear when parents misunderstand. One of the few things I am sure of is that we knew what the child meant and that he made it very clear when we didn't. If he got a wrong response, then he went on trying. He is a very obstinate child to this day. He will go on and on until he gets his meaning over. I am quite confident in my interpretation, that it is right in a sufficiently high proportion of the time, which could be anything up to 99 per cent. But don't forget that these signs are being used hundreds of times every week. They are not just odd occurrences. The child is using them all the time. If you could be wrong the first time, the first ten times, you are not wrong the first hundred times. You are wrong the first few times. That is true. I'm not saying that we got them right the first time. And this is my worry about the sort of studies of child language which people do in a more experimental framework. Sampling observations are much more difficult, because you are not with the child long enough to be sure that you've got the meaning right.

NY: *The sort of research that you have done in child language, on Nigel's language, seems to be very difficult for ordinary students of language to follow. You are very lucky, I should say, because you are already well-informed about language and have a good framework within which to work. You can observe the child successfully in a proper way. But nobody can follow it up. The point I want to make is that it seems to me that nobody can justify or corroborate your study.*

MAKH: No, they can't justify this particular piece of work on this particular child. But people now are beginning to do this kind of work on other children. And the results are turning out to be very similar.[3] The protolanguages are of a very similar kind, having a similar range of functions. We are getting one or two or three other pieces of evidence. Now I agree that you can't go back and test this, by its nature, on this child. But anyone who has a real training as a linguist, and by that I mean who is really able to listen to what people are saying – it might be that a whole lot of linguists are not able to do that, especially the philosophical ones – philosophers are not really able to listen to what people are saying! But true linguists properly trained in linguistics – and if it also happens to be parents or uncles or aunts who are right in the family – they can do this.

NY: *But one of the dangers about that is that those who try to do a similar sort of research may be affected by your observations as a kind of established truth. They may try to pick up something out of your work, from what you have already said, as their starting point.*

MAKH: Yes, once it's published. But if you know human nature, they are trying their best to demolish it. While we are trying to support it, they are trying to disprove it. Susan Ervin-Tripp told me that she came out of a very similar picture. She was doing this simultaneously with my work (see Ervin-Tripp 1973). She didn't know about me. I agree you are right. But in the last resort, not everybody is going to try and find the same scheme. I think that it is perfectly possible to distance yourself from it without either trying to support it or to demolish it, but simply, as a linguist, trying to be objective. The important thing in any of this kind of work is don't pretend you don't know. You are doing the job. You are the linguist. It's up to you to say what language means. And it's just the same, whether you are working on adult language or child language. It's up to you to say what it means. And I think now people are taking pre-speech and infant speech seriously. They weren't before. They didn't treat them seriously at all. But now they are treating them seriously. I think you'll get other descriptions, and no doubt the picture will be modified. I am not presenting this as universal. I am totally convinced that my interpretation of Nigel's acts of meaning is largely correct. But that doesn't mean that my interpretation of the process by which he got from infant to adult language is necessarily correct, even for him. And even if it is correct for him, we have no idea to what extent his own strategies would turn to be general or universal.

NY: *I could agree to your argument you are making, in Learning How to Mean, against the Transformationalist view of language acquisition, that children learn or acquire structures of a language or rather rules by means of which those structures are generated. You say in the book, agreeing with Roger Brown, 'if language development is primarily the acquisition of structure, why does the child learn one set of structures in order to discard them in favour of another?' The main point you are making is, I think, that it is nonsensical or at least hard to understand why children learn structures or rules which they must reorganize later in their life. I also think that this process is rather strange. But even if I admit this argument, I am still wondering why, when children make errors in their speech, they do so systematically and regularly. This seems to me to provide a sort of evidence that there should be some rules acquired in the process of their linguistic development.*

MAKH: I don't mind if you want to call these rules. As I say, I don't use that term. But there is nothing wrong with the traditional notion of analogy. If you want to call these analogical processes rules, that's OK. Sure, the child is looking for generalizations. And he gets some wrong, so he has to replace them by another one. That, I think, is different. That is to say, a generalization which turns out empirically to be wrong is a different thing from the notion of creating a rule system, and then, without it being tested against any empirical evidence, it's simply proved not to work – replacing the whole thing with another one, and that being the basis of the developmental process. I don't think it is. It is a rather different thing.

But what I am mainly concerned with is not whether we want to state the process in terms of developmental rules. It is rather two points: on the one hand, the narrower point – by that I mean, say, ten years ago, the orthodox

Transformationalist view that came to be known as nativism, in which you assume that in fact the child is genetically programmed with some, at least, basic rule schemata for language. I think not many people accept this now anyway, so we don't need to flog a dead horse. But, essentially, the arguments put in favour of it are false. In other words, the notion that the child is not surrounded by a rich enough resource on which to build is simply false. It's based on misunderstanding of the nature of language in contexts to which the child is exposed. I mean, ordinary speech is very highly structured. It's very fluent. It's very closely related to the context. So that I think that argument is false.

The broader point is that I think that, once you take the protolanguage seriously, the nativist point of view was only tenable in so far as you assume that the whole process begins with the mother tongue. But once you find that there is this protolinguistic stage, which has nothing whatever to do with grammar or any of the formal properties of human language, then the issue becomes rather meaningless. What I am much more concerned about is to say that what is really false – and it's common to the Transformationalist and behaviorist views, which are really variants the same thing in this respect – is that they are both individualist. They are both the products of extreme Western philosophical individualism. That is, the child is treated as an isolate bound by his skin and the rest of the world is out there. And his job is to go and get it. It's readymade. It's a construct. It exists in some sense. And the child has to, in some sense, acquire it. I don't believe this at all. I think that the child is in fact – if you like, you could use the word 'creating', but the word 'creating' has so many overtones in English. Let me use the term 'construing' rather, because it implies mental construction – the child is construing language, that is to say. But the child is not doing it as an individual. He is doing it as an intersubjective process together with the mother. And it is a process that cannot happen in the individual. It can happen only as a social interactive or intersubjective process. And it's this that constitutes my main philosophical objection to both the Transformationalist and behaviourist models of language learning. And until people like Trevarthen (e.g. 1974) came along I didn't ... I am not a psychologist, as you know, but I wasn't aware of psychological theories which seemed to me to be saying what I wanted. It seems to me that that kind of work does. He has the very much same idea, not about language but about the whole of what you call psychological acts. Now, I see that as being a very good model of language learning.

NY: *Your emphasis on the interactive aspects of language learning, I mean, the importance of interactive relations between the child and the mother or other people around him when the child develops his language seems to lead to your consideration of the interactive aspects of adult language in a social context. Am I right?*

MAKH: Right.

NY: *Reading your recent studies, I am under the impression that most of them are putting a good deal of emphasis on the consideration of these social interactive aspects of a language. I've read, for example, your 'Anti-languages' paper (1976a) which I find very interesting in this connection.*

MAKH: I do agree. I see this as very much part of the same picture. I do take very seriously the view that in the last resort we will only understand language and the linguistic system if we interpret it in relation to its functions in social contexts. I think there are two points to make here. One is, I do think that, for some people some of the time, language must be an object in the Saussurean sense. In other words, we call ourselves linguists ... I don't care what we call ourselves. I don't care whether what we are doing is linguistics or whatever. What does concern me is that it is an important part of human intellectual endeavour to try and explain language. We may call that linguistics. Then, why does language take the shape it does? The human brain could have constructed millions of different types of symbolic system. Why this one? And this, I think, we will only get at by looking at it in a functional context. So part of my motivation here is a purely linguistic one, simply wanting to explain the nature of language. But also secondly, the other point, I'm also interested in the nature of society or social relationships. Therefore, I also want to focus outwards and look at language in this context. Now obviously, the main impetus to work in this field in the modern period has been Labov, his insights into social structure, or rather into linguistic structure acquired through looking at language in its social context. I think it is important to say that what you have in Labov (e.g. 1972a), and the work which derives from him, Sankoff (e.g. 1978) for example, is brilliant original linguistics. But I wouldn't call it sociolinguistics, in the sense that it doesn't tell us anything about the relation between language and social structure or language and social systems. What Labov has done is simply to put language back into a social context and use his original, very simple model of social class plus style scale, in order to build up these matrices which then enable us to say something about language variation. From this, they've gone on to do brilliant work on history of language, you know, showing how we can really increase our insight into historical processes in language through a variation model. And perhaps, I think, it's a much more important contribution to linguistics than Chomsky. Labov has a place in the ... he'll have a place in the history of ideas about language in a sense more central than that of Chomsky. However, what is lacking there is that there is no component of insight into society. This is why it's regrettable in a way that this came to be labelled sociolinguistics, because people think this means that it actually tells us something about language and social structure. No it doesn't. It tells us something about language, a great deal, but there is nothing about society in it. We cannot derive from it any conception, any new ideas about the nature of society. It's not of interest to sociologists, because it has nothing in it for them in terms of insights into social structure. Now I think that ... In a sense, you can see the way forward ... This is the sort of thing I've been trying to do with little pieces in the 'Anti-languages' paper and in the paper for Quasthoff (Halliday 1978a), where we try and say ... All right, in what sense can we see that language is functional with respect to the social structure?

Now let's take this point about diversity. Labov studied New York speech (1968), and then he did it in Detroit and Washington and so on (1970). And we get a very good picture not only of the present state, but also we get very good evidence for thinking that diversity is increasing. Now why, why is it that in the situation where you would think there was a strong pressure on people to speak more and more alike, in fact the evidence is the opposite? In these big cities, the diversity tends to increase. This could only be explained in terms of the functions that such variation has in respect to the social structure. So we look at the way language varies in dialect and register. And we look at these, but separately, and then as they interact, and try and see in what ways they are functional, with respect to the individual in his creation of reality, in his social construction of reality, and with respect to the community in the way in which they set up and transmit all the patterns of social hierarchy there and there and there – a social class system or caste or whatever it is. And if we look at these rather closely and then try and see ... What I was then trying to do in the 'Anti-languages' paper was to set this out on a single scale, wherever you looked at the extremes – from what you call pathological, if you like, on one end to the so-called normal on the other end. Then I think you begin to see the ways in which these features of language represent primary symbolic means by which people maintain, transmit and therefore, in a sense, create the social structure. They use language as an active symbolism in this sense. Now, so my interest ... this links up therefore ... both on the one hand, the developmental point of view we started from ... namely the fact that we can only understand the child's construction of language as an interactive social process, and on the other the notion that we can only explain the nature of language by looking at its functions with respect to social structure and social process.

NY: *I understand that there is a close link recognized between your study of child language and that of adult language, in that both of the languages are products of interactive social process. Now, it seems to me that in your thinking the study of child language has come from or has been affected by the study of adult language.*

MAKH: Yes, true, in my thinking. This is certainly true. That was a later development. In fact, I started working on child language much more in an educational context. That's a result of the work that I was doing on curriculum development in London in 1960's. We began producing these materials, *Language In Use* (Doughty et al.1971) and *Breakthrough to Literacy* (Mackay et al. 1970). This was for the teaching of English as a mother tongue, for using them in city schools in those areas with children that were likely to fail. And in the course of that work we used to do a lot of work with teachers – in in-service courses for teachers who were trying out our materials in the classroom, the *Breakthrough to Literacy* materials and the *Language in Use* materials. And constantly we were being called on to discuss questions of the pre-school child. The primary school teachers, when they got interested in our reading materials, they wanted to use these and they started studying the linguistic background to these. And they would all say, 'What happens to the child before he comes to us? What is the history of the individual being before he reaches school?' And I had really done very little in child language at that time and I started reading it. This was in the mid-1960's. I started reading around so that I could contribute to this. And that was an age, of course, where the dominant theory was the Transformational one and the dominant notion of child language was the acquisition of syntax. So it was the acquisition of syntactic structures. And this didn't really have much for us. There wasn't much for educators, in that there wasn't much to learn from it. They wanted much more to know about the child's resources in language by that age: how he got where he was. And this was the time when my wife had a baby. It naturally happened that she didn't see me making notes; she was focussed on the child. And it was also very neat, in a sense, that in that particular year I had taken a job in Canada. I'd decided to leave London, because the financial conditions were very stringent and I was fed up with trying to build a department with no money. Well, the Canadian government wouldn't let us in. They wouldn't give us a visa to enter Canada, so that for most of the year, I was unemployed. This was very lucky, because it meant that I spent a lot of time at home, just when that child was small. So I was able to interact with him a great deal and learn a great deal from him. If I had been in normal process of employment, you know, coming home at the end of the day worn out, and only wanting to put the child out of the way, (laugh) I would never have been able to do it. So I always feel that I really ought to put in that book *Learning How to Mean* (1975), at the beginning, as an acknowledgment, I should've put, 'My thanks are due to the Canadian government for refusing my wife and myself admission to Canada' (big laugh).

SS: *I am very much interested in the discussion between Professor Halliday and Mr. Yamaguchi. I myself haven't prepared any questions relevant to your work. So I would like to ask something about your lecture this morning. In that lecture, you seem to have said that the Transformational grammar is a sort of rearrangement of historically foregoing views of language. Do you mean that the Transformational grammar is a sort of newly revised version of the Port Royal grammar or any such grammars?*

MAKH: I don't know whether I used the word 'rearrangement', but I wouldn't want to put it that way. I think what I was trying to do was simply to place Chomsky's own origin, as well as his own work, in historical context. There are, as I was saying this morning, two main streams in the history of Western linguistics. I know that's an oversimplification. But by and large, it's true, I think. The dominant one, most of the time, has been the philosophical one, essentially Aristotelian, which tries to explain linguistic structures not in linguistic but in logical terms. Now this was the ideological background to medieval syntax. So the greatest scholarship of the Modistae in medieval Europe was essentially of this kind. And their work is carried on very directly in the Port Royal school. Their grammars are essentially medieval in conception, in that their goals are those of medieval syntacticians. They introduce new ideas, but it's essentially in the same ideological framework. And it is this tradition that is then taken up again by Chomsky, as he rightly claims that his own antecedents are there in what I'm calling philosophical linguistics. Now this defines, to a certain extent, their goals, because it does mean that Chomsky, like his predecessors in this respect, does want to interpret language in terms of logical relations – not in the sense, of course, that he thinks that there's a necessarily pre-existing scheme of logic to be imposed on language but rather in the sense that language is such that it should be able to be represented by means of a formal system. And of course what is new in that respect, which Chomsky refers to as generative, is the notion that one can actually set up a formal system which will specify language in the sense of turning out sentences, as it were, but more importantly, of course, in the sense of ... in the old formulation they used to talk about the generation of grammatical sentences with associated structural descriptions.

NY: *You say there have been two main streams in the history of Western linguistics. You belong to one of them (Halliday 1977a). Chomskyan linguists belong to the other. Do you think that Chomskyans have to make a good excuse, namely justify their standpoint, because they are sort of newcomers.*

MAKH: I don't agree with that at all. I would say that throughout Western history the dominant stream of Western thinking about language has always been the philosophical one. It is the ones who have tried to look at language as an object in its own terms and in a social context that have had to justify their position rather than the other way round. Look at what happened in the classical period. The early insights into language, the rhetorical ones, are lost. And what remains to us from classical Greek is essentially the learning of the establishment, and the establishment is of course Aristotelian. The Stoic material is lost. The Stoics, who very clearly defined language as an object, who developed a theory of the sign, who departed from Aristotle's view of language as the expression of logical relations, they were just lost. It was never the dominant trend in the classical period, and the same in the medieval period. We don't know what there was other than formal syntax. There may have been, as part of the more underground trend in the medieval thinking, which is very strong of course in Europe – there may have been work on language there, too. We don't know. Maybe not. In the modern period, after the Renaissance, the two came to be more on a par, in the sense that you can say that the sort of work that has been done by the 17th century linguists in England is out on the side, because what they were trying to do was to create a universal language of science, a universal system for the representation of human knowledge, which was also a very medieval preoccupation that belongs to the other strand in medieval thinking, the strand which produces great cosmic constructs and which is closely related to the mysticism, and so forth. Now, if you go into the modern period, then in the 19th and 20th centuries you see these two coming side by side. And it is true that, in the first part of the 20th century, if you look at certain European schools, including Hjelmslev ... this is one of the reasons why people find Hjelmslev so difficult, because the Chomskyans assume that he has their view of language, but he hasn't. He belongs much more on the other side. He's much more concerned with language in a social ethnographic functional context. But he's trying to express this in terms of mathematical theory. OK, that is true. But on the other hand, you've got the American Structuralist school, which is very much in the philosophical mould ... I'm picking out certain things and ignoring other things, you can't help it in a sketch like this. But I think that essentially it's true that, if you take the two streams in America, there is Boas-Sapir-Whorf (Hymes & Fought 1975), which is my angle, which deals with functional aspects, and there is Bloomfield-Harris-Chomsky, which is the other. Now they were roughly equal in strength. If anything, it was the Bloomfieldians that were the dominant group, and they were very much indeed in the formal philosophical mould. Their goals, I mean; their methods were not ... I mean, their notion of a linguistic theory as definable in terms of operations may seem to us very odd. But it was definitely an attempt to construct a formal theory. That's what it was. So, really, even in the 20th century, it has been the tradition represented by the Transformationalists which has remained the dominant one. And this is, I think, because of the enormous strength of dogmatic philosophy in Western thinking that has tended to assume that theories must in some sense relate to a mould that can be expressed in terms of symbolic logic or formal logic. It's the Aristotelian influence in Western thinking, I think. That combined with this very very strong individualism, which has been the humanist contribution, which is what produces the Chomskyan type of ideology. So, the two do go side by side. But, if anything, I would say, on the whole, that most of Western linguistics has been philosophers looking at language rather than linguists.

SS: *This is a rather fanciful question, but how do you think future linguists will look back retrospectively on the present situation of linguistics?*

MAKH: I don't know that I can add much to what is implied in what I've been saying. I think they will see this sort of shift of emphasis. They will see the explicit definition of goals characteristic of Chomsky's work very clearly. They will see to what extent the achievements measured up to the early claims and the early goals that they defined. They will certainly look, with great interest, on the way in which, say, the Generative Semanticists hived off from the Chomskyan mould, without apparently realizing that what they were doing was radically changing the ideological premises of the theory. In other words, if I was trying to do what they are trying to do, I wouldn't start from there, because it's a kind of inherent contradiction. And I think they would certainly see, as you have said, the impact in the sense of the tremendous energies that were released in 1950's and 60's by all that. But I hope that they will also see that most of the polemics of the early Transformational work were irrelevant, that they were aimed at views most people never held. They were positions created in order to be knocked down. I suppose obviously the other point I've made already about Labov ... I think that variation theory does constitute a major step forward, and, in an interesting way, that it is perhaps due to variation theory people, more than anyone else, that we have really begun to accumulate new facts about language. But I suspect that they will see, as the main ideological struggle in 20th century linguistics, none of all this, but the old battle of cultural centrism or ethnocentrism – in other words, the old struggle of human beings to stand outside their own cultures and not try and impose on their interpretation of others the patterns that belong to their own way of life. In other words, Whorf (1956) will remain, I think, the major figure in this century ... perhaps more than any of the others.

But we need time to think over a question like that. I never really thought of it in those terms. And I suspect again that it's like other fields of scholarship. The point is that we are very much at the end of the era. As far as the West is concerned, we are at the end of what we could call humanist period and at the beginning of another one. But I don't know what the next one is going to be like. But I do know that this one is coming to an end, and many of the features that characterise the thoughts of the end of an era can be found now. The tendency, for example, to retreat inside the individual – this is the tendency in linguistics to concentrate on what the speaker knows. This kind of inward looking ideology is very characteristic of the end of an era. A new era always begins by looking outward. So it is to this extent that there will be a shift of focus, in which we don't express things so much in terms of what the speaker knows about it, but in, no doubt new terms of what we can't even think of. I'm also sure that this is going to come about largely through a great deal of actual fact-finding about non-European languages by speakers of non-European languages working in their own languages and developing their own linguistics for that purpose. I'm sure that that is going to be ... again we are beginning to get a new period of actual accumulation of knowledge, genuine knowledge about different languages, not really rewriting them in terms of English. This is a very hard struggle and may be the most important single thing, just as in the wider world, in a way, the most important ideological battles people are fighting at the moment are race prejudice and cultural prejudice. And linguistics should be playing a central part in getting around this.

SS: *This is our last question. Will the main trend in linguistics become a more text-oriented one? Will at least one of the main trends tend to go towards textual analyses of languages in the near future?*

MAKH: Well, textual ... let me not overstate this. There's a lot of interest in discourse, in text linguistics. This is partly simply because linguists have become dissatisfied with idea that you can explain language as sentences, and they understand that what is important is text, that is, meanings in contexts of situation. So, I think, that is certainly something we can expect to continue. A lot more insight into text structure of various kinds, including variations of register and so forth, this is one thing. I think we can expect much more work in the direction of language and social structure, and structure also in the sense of social construction of reality, if you like – the notion of ... how do children actually construct, through language, their models of culture? We are really going to begin to know how this happens. I think we can expect to know a lot more about social interaction of various kinds, for example young children's peer group. We know very little about how young children exchange meanings among themselves. I hope we shall see more developments in language education, where we genuinely begin to put all these things together in a focus on how people learn language and learn through language, in an educational context, as well as in an out of school context, and take account of the sociology of education, the relationships between educational knowledge and everyday knowledge, and how these are coded in language. Well, I am in no way predicting what is going to come from outside, in terms of, say, advances in neurophysiology, which lead us to a lot more insight into how the brain processes all these things; or in the whole field of what has become computational linguistics, whether it's in the formal machine translation or the form of parsing programmes or abstracting programmes or now artificial intelligence.

Clearly, all these will continue to feed in as we are able to process more of the data. And the notion that Winograd (1983) has, for example, of trying to build into all this some representation of linguistic functions, using a functional interpretation of semantics, this sort of thing interests me, whether this can be built into the sort of representation which has been used in these contexts. This is another direction in which I'm sure we shall have to go. So I think the picture will continue to be messy, much as it is at the moment.

University of Sydney
27 September 1977

Notes

1 This discussion was undertaken on 27 September 1977, when I was studying at University of Sydney. I am most grateful to Professor Halliday for having kindly shared time for the discussion and allowing it to be made public. I am also very much indebted to Mr. Shun'ichi Segawa for his encouragement and cooperation through arranging, participating and tape-recording the interview. The text of the discussion is mostly written down as it is spoken, except for some minor textual modifications, in order to keep intact the spontaneous discoursal nature of Halliday's thinking and speaking. It is indeed very regrettable to be obliged to leave out the Discussion's phonetic component which carries a great deal of no less important interpersonal and emotional information than its graphic component. Spoken texts should be, by nature, heard rather than read.
2 'Linguistics: Past, Present and Future' (transcribed by Shun'ichi Segawa), a special lecture given to students in the Faculty of Education's TEFL programme.
3 For a review of subsequent research see Painter 2009.

With *The English Magazine* (1981)

In a previous issue of *The English Magazine* we put the same set of questions on Literature and Criticism to four well-known critics. We've used the same device in this issue with three distinguished linguists. Linguistics is a complex and wide ranging discipline. Some people have assumed it to be remote from the central concerns of English teaching, while others have sought from linguistics instant guidance for classroom practice. Our questions were designed to illuminate the ways that linguists view the possibilities of their subject.

1. How far do you think the analytical methods of linguistics have really done justice to the richness and inventiveness of language use. What kinds of work are still to be done?
2. Many people would say that linguistics ought to be interesting and yet appears to be arid. Have these people got it wrong?
3. Linguistics on the whole has paid relatively little attention to texts. How much would you say linguists have contributed to our understanding of the production and reception of written texts?
4. Educationalists have attempted to draw from the work of linguists implications for educational practice. What is your experience of this process, particularly with reference to your own work?
5. Teachers have turned to linguists for help in understanding why working class children and ethnic minorities have failed in school. It has become something of a growth industry. How would you assess their contribution? Can linguists contribute to a more just society?
6. The study of language has recently become an explicit part of the curriculum in some schools. What aspects of language do you feel it is particularly important for people to understand?

Michael Halliday

Very few eminent linguists commit themselves wholeheartedly to language issues in education while maintaining a consistent contribution to major advances in their discipline. Many teachers in London and elsewhere have reason to be grateful that Michael Halliday is one of the very small band. He espouses totally that language is rooted in social meaning, that a child learning his language is learning the significant social meanings of his society (social semiotic, as he calls it). This means he is engaged in a most ambitious project, which is to show a systematic relationship between language use and social structure. It is characteristic of his work that it moves to and fro between the most abstract concepts of language structure and detailed analyses of language in use (young children, literature, dialogue etc.) always pushing towards a more coherent and comprehensive theory. He has collaborated closely with Bernstein giving the latter's work his own interpretation.

Good news. Halliday wrote a most accessible short work (63 pages) explicitly for teachers (Halliday 1974). A full exposition of his ideas is found in Halliday 1978b.

What linguistics is

Isn't the first question slightly off the mark? It seems to me rather like asking whether the analytical methods of acoustics have done justice to the richness and inventiveness of musical composition – or even whether mathematical astronomy does justice to the beauty of the heavens. I'm trying to make clear to myself what 'have really done justice to' means, and to imagine what kind of analytical methods would lead someone to answer 'yes' to this question; but I find it difficult.

Precisely for that reason, perhaps, it is a good question to ask. It shows up, I think, a mismatch (not really anything to do with linguistics) between the notion of 'analytic methods' and the evaluative concepts of 'richness and inventiveness' – between the process of understanding a thing, and the value that thing has in someone's mind, or in the value system of the culture.

Let me relate this to the study of discourse, or 'text' as linguists call it. Suppose we analyse a text in linguistic terms, which means in such a way as to relate it to the system of the language. What are we trying to do? We are trying to explain why it means what it does. (This is not the same thing as saying what it means; that, in general, is not a technical linguistic exercise, although the linguist's search for explanation often does, in fact, suggest new meanings which had not been obvious before.) How the text comes to mean what it does – that is the primary goal. There is a further goal, more difficult to achieve, which relates to the question being asked here: namely, why is the text valued as it is in the culture? This is obviously important in stylistics (the linguistic study of literature); we would like to be able to explain why one work is more highly valued than another. Now, if the question means, can we, by the analytic methods of linguistics, explain not only why a text means what it does but also why it is valued as it is, then I think it is a very clear question, and I would answer it by saying – no, not yet; that is a very high goal to aim at; but we are trying hard, and we think we have some ideas and partial results.

However, linguistics is much more than a body of analytic method. Linguistics is often defined as the systematic study of language; that is all right, provided we point out that a discipline is defined not by its terrain but by its quest – by what it is trying to find out, rather than by what phenomena it is looking at. So whereas lots of people other than linguists – nearly everybody, these days – are engaged in studying language, for them language is an instrument, which they use for asking questions about something else, such as culture, or the brain, or why children fail in school. For linguists, on the other hand, language is an object. To say you are doing linguistics means that language is your object of study; the questions you are asking are questions about language itself. In order to answer those questions, of course, you have to investigate a lot of other things over and beyond language; so here the boot is on the other foot – what is 'object' for an anthropologist, say non-linguistic semiotic systems in a culture, for us become 'instrument', additional evidence we can use to shed light on the nature and functions of language.

The critical step

Naturally (glancing for a moment at question 2) linguistics isn't everyone's cup of tea; what I find interesting is not what someone else may find interesting. There have always been people fascinated by the study of language – linguistics is one of the oldest sciences; you find it in ancient China, India, Greece and Babylon – and others who find it arid. Personally, I have always found it very exciting; whereas when I tried to take up psychology many years ago, I found it boring and arid, and had to give it up. But I take that to be a fact about me, not about psychology; and of interest to no one but myself. The reason for taking up this point, however, is that I think there are special problems that some people have with the study of language; connected, I think, with the fact of its unconscious nature, stressed by the great American linguists Boas and Sapir. Some people find it threatening to have to bring language to the level of consciousness; and many others, though they may not feel threatened by it, find it extraordinarily difficult. And I think until you have taken that critical step the study of language may tend to seem rather arid. Once you have taken it (and you'll know when you begin to be able to listen to grammar, and words, and sounds, as well as to meanings), you are likely to find it fascinating.

One of the things that has always struck me since I started working on texts, back in the early fifties, is how much a linguistic analysis (actually I would prefer to say a linguistic interpretation of a text, since explaining a text is a work of interpretation) adds to my enjoyment of the text. The process of discovering why it means what it does reveals so much of the covert patterning in the text (presumably this is the 'richness' referred to in question 1) that by the end one's appreciation of it is immensely heightened. So although the analytic methods of linguistics have not yet done full justice to the richness of language use, they certainly help us to appreciate it. And I hope it is clear that I am not just talking about the study of literature. It tends to be in the most unconscious uses of language – ordinary everyday spontaneous dialogue – that the richness of language is most fully developed and displayed.

But the methods of linguistics are not designed only to explain texts. They are aimed at establishing the system that lies behind the text. In my view one of the great weaknesses of twentieth century linguistics has been its sharp separation of system and process. Saussure made the distinction very clear, back in the 1900s: the *process* that we observe, as speech or writing, is the outward manifestation of a *system* (what I have called a 'meaning potential'); and we use our observations of the process, or rather of the product, in the form of text, as evidence for construing the system. But, as Hjelmslev (who I would say is the greatest theoretical linguist of this century) always insisted, system and process have to be interpreted as one; whereas linguists have tended to study the system in isolation from the process, describing it in ways such that it is hard to see how it could ever engender a real text. (Likewise many people who study the product – text – do so in ways that make it impossible to conceive that it could ever have been engendered by any system.) But text is only understood by being referred to the system that generated it. (This is why it is very hard to learn a foreign language by the old 'literature' method, which is based on the assumption that a learner can construe the system from a very few instances of highly valued text, mapped onto the conception of a linguistic system that he brings from his own mother tongue. It is an interesting notion, and it does seem to work with a few people, but I think they are rather exceptional.) You appreciate poetry in a language because you have been talking and listening in that language for a long time; you can relate it to the whole of the rest of your experience – not piecemeal, but as that experience has been incorporated and 'coded' into the system of the language as you control it.

If I may be allowed to invert Chomsky's dictum, I would say that language is an infinite system that generates a finite body of text. This means that we can never do full justice to the system. But we can do justice to its nature as a system, as a resource for living and meaning. (That last sounds like a slogan, but it is intended to be taken seriously. Language is a resource for meaning, and meaning is, for human beings, an essential component of living.) Linguistic theories have mostly been theories of linguistic structure: inventories of sentence formulae, with devices for relating one sentence to another. There, 'a sentence' is one thing, and its 'relatedness' to other sentences is another thing, distinct from the sentence itself. In a theory of the system there are not two phenomena here but one; a sentence, or any other linguistic entity, is simply a set of relationships, a complex process of choice, or of choosing let us say, within an intricate web of meaning potential. This is what I understand by the richness of language; and the inventiveness of language use I take to refer to the way in which speakers and writers explore, exploit and expand that potential in the process of creating text.

Can linguists help?

Can linguists contribute to a more just society? Linguists are a cross-section of the human race, and obviously differ in the weight they would give to this question, and in their understanding of what it means. Personally I set store by the social accountability of theories in general; at the same time I don't always expect an immediate pay-off. (This is the great problem for teachers, which I'll come to in a moment.) I do feel committed to the usefulness of linguistics, and have tried to organize work in the subject, where this has been my responsibility, in such a way that those who are researching, teaching and studying it maintain strong links with the community and an interest in community problems. For me this has meant that a lot of my work has had an educational focus; and I have tried to work with teachers on problems of literacy and language development, language in the classroom, mother tongue and foreign language teaching and so on. In London in the sixties I was able to bring together the Nuffield/Schools Council team of primary, secondary and tertiary language educators who produced *Breakthrough to Literacy* (Mackay et al.

1970) and *Language in Use* (Doughty et al. 1971), and subsequently *Language and Communication* (Forsyth & Wood 1977). In Sydney we have built up a Department of Linguistics all of whose members are involved in community language problems and language education: language problems of multicultural education, and the 'language profile' of the community; the language of school texts, and their difficulties for the migrant learner; the development of children's writing in different registers; and the place of linguistics in language teaching. We recently held a week-long 'Working Conference on Language in Education', with nine simultaneous workshops examining different aspects of language education in the Australian context. And I myself have been active from the start in the 'Language Development Project' of the Curriculum Development Centre in Canberra, which focuses particularly on language development in the middle school years (see also Halliday 2007a).

Now, in one sense none of this has to do with educational failure. That is to say, we're not producing remedial language materials for the disadvantaged or devising tests for predicting children's performance in school. In common with most linguists, I think, we hold the view that the underlying causes of educational failure are social, not linguistic; but there are obvious linguistic links in the causal chain, and it is reasonable – indeed necessary, if only to get the picture straight – to look to linguistics as a contributory source of ideas and practice. The point I would make is that, given the nature of the problem (and of language), the contribution of linguistics will be indirect and global rather than direct and local. In other words, it is by trying to raise the general level of community discussion of language, and the general efficacy of language education in school, more than by specific language-stimulating projects aimed at particular groups, that linguistics can be most help in the cause of education for a just society.

This is not to belittle the importance of special programmes designed to help those who are at risk. It is simply that here the guiding considerations are pedagogical rather than linguistic. Linguistics comes in, once again, as background knowledge and ideology, providing descriptions of languages, and of varieties – dialects and registers – within languages; and, in the process, helping to raise the status of those languages and varieties that are part of the symbol-package by which a particular group is marked off, and marked out, for discrimination and abuse.

Implications for practice

With any academic discipline (turning to question 4), there is always a problem of 'implications for educational practice': what do you teach, out of the huge accumulation of knowledge, and how does your teaching relate to the theorizing of the practitioner in the field? Experience in science education, and maths education, shows how big a problem this is even in those subjects.

The relationship is even more complex in the human sciences, and especially in the sciences of human behaviour. What implications does one draw from sociology, psychology and linguistics? Whatever else, you don't draw your content from them. Traditionally (that is, the past hundred years or so), the answer has been from psychology you get the basic theory and practice of education, and from sociology and linguistics you get nothing. This dominance of psychology over sociology in the theory of education reflects western obsession with the individual, and the conviction that learning is an individual rather than a social process. It would help if we had a more balanced contribution from these two disciplines – especially in countries where different cultures mix (which means all English-speaking countries, now).

From linguistics, of course, it is not true that nothing has been drawn; there is a long tradition of taking content from linguistics, in the form of 'school grammar', the version of classical and medieval linguistic scholarship that went into the making of humanist descriptive grammars. It is not a bad grammar, but it is not very useful in school. It is formal; rigid; based on the notion of rule; syntactic in focus; and oriented towards the sentence. A more useful grammar would be one which is functional; flexible; based on the notion of resource; semantic in focus; and oriented towards the text. Hence the recurrent cycle of love and hate for it: 'we thought it would help children to write; it doesn't so we abandon it; they still can't write, so we take it up again', and so on.

When I say that no implications have been drawn from linguistics, I'm not intending to denigrate classroom grammar, where linguistics has supplied the content of the teaching. But by 'educational implications' I understand not the content but the theory and practice of the educational process. I think linguistics is of central importance here, and yet this aspect of its value is still very largely ignored.

In working with our Language Development Project (cf. Maling-Keepes & Keepes 1979) I have suggested that language development is three things: learning language, learning through language, and learning about language. Again, perhaps, by making it sound like a slogan I may stop people from listening to what it means; but, again, I mean it to be taken seriously. Let me take up the last part first.

Learning about language is, of course, linguistics; this refers to the importance of the study of language (as an 'object') in school. This does not have to be grammar; when *Language in Use* was written, at a time when grammar was 'out', the authors found no difficulty in devising 110 units for work on language in secondary school without any reference to grammar at all. Now, I think, we are reopening the question of a 'grammar for schools'. I think it will be possible to develop a school grammar that is interesting and useful; I have some ideas of what it might be like, but I don't think we have one yet. But even given an ideal grammar, it would only be one part of the 'learning about language' that needs to go on in school.

Learning through language refers to the fact that almost all educational learning (as well as much learning outside school) takes place through language, written and spoken. This notion comes into educational parlance as 'Language Across the Curriculum'. A child doesn't need to know any linguistics in order to use language to learn; but a teacher needs to know some linguistics if he wants to understand how the process takes place – or what is going wrong when it doesn't. Here therefore linguistics has the role of a background discipline, like psychology and sociology. I think it is probably as important as they are and needing about the same emphasis in teacher education; however not all branches of linguistics are equally important (this is true of any background subject); but it is not too difficult to identify those that matter.

Learning language means construing the mother tongue – and before that the 'child tongue', the protolanguage with which an infant first exchanges meanings with those around him. There is a special branch of linguistics – child language studies, or developmental linguistics – that is concerned with how children learn their mother tongue; it has made enormous strides in the past twenty years, probably more than any other branch of the subject; and its findings are of tremendous importance for education. For one thing it has shown that children take certain steps in their semantic development – that is, control certain meanings and meaning relationships – well before they have been thought to do in cognitive-psychological representations of the learning process. Since, presumably a child's semantic system does not run ahead of his cognitive system (I don't even know what that would mean; I suspect they are simply two different ways of looking at the same thing), we may have to revise some of the prevalent notions about cognitive development. More important: by supplementing the cognitive model with a semantic one (which relates meaning to its 'output' in words and structures, sounds, and writing), we get a much more rounded picture of the nature of learning, and the relation of learning to environment.

I have always been an 'applied linguist': my interest lies in linguistics ... in what you can do with it. But there must be something to apply. Applied linguistics is not a separate domain; it is the principles and practice that come from an understanding of language. Adopting these principles and practices provides, in turn, a way in to understanding language. In this perspective, you look for models of language that neutralize the difference between theory and application; in the light of which, research and development in language education become one process rather than two. But this means selecting, refining, adapting; and being prepared to hasten slowly. The one difficulty I have always had in working with teachers is that they so often want immediate results; the latest findings translated there and then into effective, not to say magical, curriculum design, classroom processes. Now, I think we can often make intelligent research applications of our latest findings right there, on the spot (partly because no-one will get hurt if they turn out not to work). But for shaping what we do, with children, and adult learners, I think we have to depend more on the indirect and oblique and thoughtful application of the accumulated wisdom of the past. I get worried by the fashions of language teaching, which are sometimes only half-baked application of ideas about language which themselves were only half-baked in the first place.

Knowledge about language

There are lots of 'customers' for linguistics. But the questions are about 'aspects of linguistics and education'; and educational applications are perhaps predominant, certainly in terms of the number of people affected. What aspects of language are most important for people to understand (your question 6)? I think we have to balance two things: (i) those aspects of language that people are already interested in, and (ii) those aspects of language that you have to follow in order to understand the rest. (Linguists tend to ignore the first and everyone else tends to ignore the second.)

Senior students are likely to be interested already in such questions as translation and its problems; language policy and planning; dialect and accent; language and power structure; language and the media; ambiguity and failures of communication; language and literature; rhetoric and the writing process. All of these are valuable topics to explore. (I am not suggesting one should explore all of them in one course!) But I do think that, in order to understand any of these properly, and to derive benefit from exploring them, you need to have some fundamental grasp of the nature, functions, and ontogenesis of language. This means knowing something about speech sounds and sound systems, including the rhythm and melody of language; about grammar and vocabulary; about meaning; about language variation; about writing systems; about language development of children; about language and social context; and about language universals and variables – what all languages have in common, and what may vary from one language to another. If you don't know something of the topics listed under these second headings, your appreciation of those listed under the first headings may be superficial, or even distorted. But again, it is often not so much the content of what is studied as the level of understanding brought to it by the teacher that determines the value of the work.

People know quite a lot about language simply by virtue of the fact that they listen and talk – that they have been listening and talking, in real situations with real purposes to be achieved, since the very first year of life. This is gut knowledge, not head knowledge; it is very difficult to bring it to the level of consciousness. I have found it quite useful sometimes to begin with a kind of folk linguistics, discussing the concepts which are the very earliest of the linguistic concepts mastered by a child: things like 'say' and 'mean' and 'call', 'make up' and 'tell' and 'rhyme' (usually expressed by verbs rather than nouns). You can build up a very perceptive account of language without any formidable technical apparatus. This may be the best way for those whose feelings about linguistics lie behind the two questions posed at the beginning of the list!

The English Magazine
Summer 1981

4
With M. L. Tickoo (1985)

[Transcribed by Guo Libo]

MLT: *Professor Halliday, I first thought I'd tell you how happy we feel in having you here and in the fact that you really started the thing off with your highly informative as well as highly exciting plenary speech. And I thought it might be useful for the people in the region to know the way in which the ideas you gave us at that time could become helpful either to researchers or to teachers in classrooms here and elsewhere to carry forward the ideas on language across the curriculum.*

MAKH: Well, I was very happy to be here. Thank you. And I found it a very stimulating and rewarding occasion. I suppose the task of the speaker in the first session is to try and bridge the gap from the ceremonial opening to the point where you move in to the more technical aspect of the seminar. And in a way what I was trying to do was to anticipate what might be some of the main concerns. There is always an element of uncertainty that you can be very wrong. I think that perhaps it wasn't too far out in the sense that the whole conception of language across the curriculum is one that we were trying to review, looking at what's happened in the ten or more years since the term has been used – and of course use that review as a way of looking forward into the future. That I think certainly happened. My feeling is that it's been a very positive experience. I don't share the view of those who feel that nothing much has been attained. One can always be dissatisfied. I hope we always will be dissatisfied because if not, that will be an end to progress.

But it seems to me that important things have happened in the field. The speakers and the discussants, and those giving workshops, did collectively I think focus on in a sense the key area which is the notion of language education – the idea that all learning is learning language and learning through language. And you know I had used, not on this occasion, but elsewhere (I don't want it to be a slogan), a way of expressing what I feel to be the unifying notion in language across the curriculum, which is that of learning language, learning through language and learning about language. I think these are all important aspects of language development as an educational process. You could say that when you are focusing on language across the curriculum then you are kind of highlighting the second of those three, you are highlighting the notion of learning through language, that is, using language essentially as a tool for growth, for development, and for learning other things – learning the things that we define in the school as subjects in the curriculum.

MLT: *Yeah. I am also thinking that this idea of language in learning and language for learning takes us back to someone like George Sampson in 1921, who said that every* *teacher is a teacher of English because every teacher is a teacher in English. If one looks back on a thing like that, it would perhaps trigger off many ideas; one would then say that there is a lot of similarity between what has been happening in Britain from the days that Language for Life (Bullock 1975) came out and what has been happening in Australia. I find a number of case studies in the classroom that may have a lot of relevance to what could be happening in countries like Singapore or even other countries where English is not the only language but is certainly a language towards life and learning. So in this context I thought it might be useful for people here to get something from what you contributed to language in schools in England, and tell us a little about what that is doing to work in England.*

MAKH: Well, as you know, I am a little out of date with what's going on in England. I left in 1970 and haven't spent much time there since. But I think it's useful to be reminded that there were people saying very similar things in their reports in the 1920s. We could probably find some of these even earlier – for example the notion that every teacher is an English teacher or every teacher a language teacher in a more general sense. But in the Singapore context I think one would focus that on English. It enables us to say, as I would certainly say, that in the training of teachers it is very important that all teachers should have some exposure to the study of language and its place in education. That is the notion of language in education. I think everyone needs that. I would say in passing that it's probably in the in-service context that you can do most. You can do something in the pre-service training but at that time the intending teacher is not really prepared for it in the sense that he or she doesn't yet know why it is relevant. Once you've been in the classroom and you've been faced with the real problems then you start asking questions which turn out to be questions about language. We find certainly that it's really very much in in-service workshops and things of this kind that teachers are really ready to focus on language, asking questions about it and so on. Now the corollary has been or can be sometimes that if every teacher is in some sense, I won't say a language specialist, but at least knowledgeable about language ...

MLT: *aware of language ...*

MAKH: aware of language, does that mean that you no longer need a specialist in language? I don't think it does. I think you must still have somebody who has an overall vision. Now the science teacher can be expected to know about the language of science, and the history teacher about the use of language in the study of history, but they cannot have an across-the-curriculum view; so you come back to the English teacher. And I know that sometimes our colleagues in English teaching have said, well fine, language is everybody's business, so I can go back to teaching literature [laugh]. And I think you have to say 'No, look, no. You, the English teacher (I don't mean every single one) ... language must remain a concern of the English teaching profession.' I think that you train your specialists in the sense of those who have this broad conception of language in education we have been trying to talk about this week.

MLT: *Yeah, I am also thinking about this whole idea some people are putting forward now that language across the curriculum is a matter of methodology rather than of work on language. I think it relates to teacher attitudes, and also the management of the classroom. I'm thinking in this connection that it might be useful to know the kind of work that was done on language that children use or teachers use or language that gets used in the classroom by Basil Bernstein; I think you had an important share in that, that has something to tell us here.*

MAKH: Yes. Can I comment on the point about methodology? Because of course there is always a component of methodology, in whatever you are doing as a teacher. Obviously you are using certain practices in the classroom which you have learned or developed and these can be studied or usefully discussed. But I think it's quite wrong to suggest that language across the curriculum is solely or even primarily a matter of methodology. I don't believe it is. I think that it covers the whole range from theory to practice. I should say in passing that I don't really believe in the distance between theory and practice. I see these are the same thing. There's no real difference between theory and practice. You could focus on one angle, if you like, trying to make generalizations, to develop principles; you can focus on the other, which is looking at classroom practices. But there isn't really any difference between the two. I think what we are talking about here is something which is very much a focusing on language, 'how people use language in life' to take from the *Bullock Report* a famous expression. But specifically in school life this means using language as a means of learning in classroom situations. Now, OK, the second point is that this to my mind is essentially an interactive process. We have tended to kind of seal up the individual as a kind of island. There's the child, there's the learner, and here's all this input from the outside. I don't believe in input. I believe in interaction. The child is a learner interacting with other learners and with the teacher and with discourse – with texts. What people I think have tried to do since that period, originally just from an educational standpoint, and subsequently from a linguistic and sociolinguistic standpoint, has been to focus on what actually goes on in the classroom. And of course now we can record it – we can make audio, we can make video records, what we are doing now. You can actually focus on this. And teachers can observe how they themselves have behaved. They will always be surprised by this.

Now I think in those studies, going back to the sixties of course in England, what Bernstein and his colleagues were concerned with was the problem of educational failure.

MLT: *Yes.*

MAKH: You know; you were there at the time. The question was 'Why?' – why children who apparently had perfectly adequate home circumstances (I mean it wasn't the problem of poverty) were still failing in schools. And he came up with this idea that there was a gap, a mismatch between the way in which the child had developed and used language in the home background and the sort of demands that were being made on language in school by the teacher. And depending very much on the social class background of the child, you might get a greater or lesser gap. The greater the gap, the more likely the child is to fail. And if the teacher is not prepared, if they are not trained to recognize the problem, to diagnose it, then of course she has no way of trying to solve it. In Singapore of course you've got the additional problem that there's a language gap in the sense that you've also got to show not only that the child knows how to use language as a means of learning but specifically how to use the English language as a means of learning. That's the other side of it.

MLT: *Could I also take you for a little while to the ideas you have given to the communicative teaching of languages, where people like Christopher Brumfit and Henry Widdowson and others have taken your ideas, or even Wilkins has taken ideas, as he says, into the language curriculum for you? Do you see anything uniting these two things, language across the curriculum and the communicative teaching of languages?*

MAKH: Yes, I think they are very closely connected. And you see, you know very well that we've seen lots of fads and fashions in language teaching. Somebody gets a good idea, and it gets overplayed because people think it's the solution to all problems. It isn't, so they get disillusioned. This is happening and it will go on happening. There's nothing we can do about it. But in my opinion, the notions that the colleagues you've mentioned have been developing in what can be called communicative teaching are in fact very positive and have made a very important contribution. I would say it seems to me that they match our understanding of the nature of language and language use. That is important because a lot of the more traditional conceptions and approaches to language teaching in particular have tended to conflict with what we know as linguists about language, the nature of language today. That one doesn't; it is very much in harmony with it. And secondly, it seems to me that it also corresponds very well with what we know about the nature of learning. There are theories of learning, models of learning, that come from educational psychology, but in my opinion we don't have any really adequate theory or model of learning which looks at it as a linguistic process. I think this is very important work that needs to be done, a kind of language-based theory of learning (cf. Halliday 1993). Meanwhile it seems to me that what I understand by communicative approaches or methods is that they represent if you like the specifically linguistic component, or a way of coping with the specifically language tasks in the context of language across the curriculum.

MLT: *You see a deep kind of relationship between the two.*

MAKH: Yeah an important relationship.

MLT: *You said that work needs to be done on the psychology of learning and how it can be made more useful to language teaching. Is there any work being done on this front?*

MAKH: I'm no psychologist as you know and I'm not up to date in what my colleagues in learning theory and psychology are doing. I know all the time progress is being made and certainly in the context of educational theory and practice ... cognitive development ...

MLT: *Breakthroughs there ...*

MAKH: Yes, since Piaget and obviously Vygotsky, there have been important advances in our understandings there. But I still feel that this is not yet been integrated with linguistic theories which look at language development – not trying to fit in with some pre-existing conceptions from outside but rather saying 'No, let's look at this now starting from linguistics', or let me say rather, 'Let's look at the whole process of language development as something which takes place from birth and even before birth, as I was saying in my paper, but certainly from birth, through home, then the neighborhood, the school... see the school as a partner in this process, but try to understand it and set it up in terms of language growth. I'm not saying that is the whole truth; what I'm saying is that it's part of the truth that has been lacking. We have been focusing from psychology, looking at learning as a cognitive process; we haven't yet really been complementing this with a view from language. It's that view from language that I think we need. And that's got to be something which is a cooperative effort of linguists and teachers, very much the sort of thing we were doing back in London, University College. You remember down in that hall of the basement there which you visited occasionally [laugh], we had a splendid team of ourselves, university teachers, secondary teachers and primary teachers, all working towards materials of this kind. I think something came out of that.

MLT: *Lastly I thought it might be useful to ask you, now we are at the end of the seminar, is there anything you are looking forward to in the field in the next few years – one or two things that ought to happen or that could really happen here or elsewhere?*

MAKH: Well you've put me on the spot because I've always been very cautious about making predictions. I know you are not asking what would ...

MLT: *future gazing ...*

MAKH: I don't know, but I do feel you know very strongly that the conception of language education is a very powerful one, and I think there is no doubt we will see advances on this front. You mentioned earlier what was going on in different countries I think we have a very distinctive group in and associated with our own department in Australia ...

MLT: *Sydney ...*

MAKH: Sydney, yes, where for example my colleagues Jim Martin, Joan Rothery (Martin 1993, 2000) and others have been working on development of children's writing. I don't mean handwriting I mean the ability to use written language ...

MLT: *expressive language ...*

MAKH: yeah. And how children can learn to control the registers, the genres to use a word that was mainly used in this conference – things like narrative, expository writing, personal narrative, descriptive, and so on. And how they can learn to do this in a way which makes full use of their own linguistic resources and extend these resources at the same time. That's just one little bit of it. But I think there is a lot of work going on around the world, in different places, looking at different aspects of this process. And I think we'll see quite a lot coming out of this. And I'm very interested to see your next seminar here is going to focus on language in the classroom in the Southeast Asian region. And I think that whole conception of classroom interaction, classroom discourse, it sees learning as an interactive process, that's terribly important – to focus on that in relation to educational policy and educational practice, in the countries of this region, I think that itself is going to be a very important step in the direction that we want to go.

MLT: *Well, thank you very much. Let's look forward to having you here again, well 86, 87. Have a good weekend.*

MAKH: Sometime, I very much hope so. Thank you.

Regional Language Centre, Singapore
April 1985

5

With Paul J. Thibault (1985)

Introduction

Michael Halliday is the founder and principal architect of the systemic-functional school of linguistics, which has its historical basis in the earlier work of Malinowski, Firth, Hjelmslev, and Whorf. However, the present interview does not attempt to trace in any detail the "origins" and historical developments of Halliday's work. An excellent sketch of this is to be found in the Introduction to Halliday (1976b), by its editor Gunther Kress. It is also inappropriate to suggest that systemic-functional linguistics embodies a single, necessarily coherent epistemology through which its theoretical practices can be assessed. Indeed, the theoretical practice of systemic-functional linguistics produces a number of theoretically constructed and defined "objects" which range from the critical, materialist sociolinguistics of Kress and Hodge (1979), to Fawcett's (1980) cognitive model of a "communicating mind", Mann's (1984) non-finalistic teleological interpretation of the metaphor of "choice" in terms of "intentionality", and Halliday's own "social semiotic" and "functional" emphasis on the relations between the "internal" paradigmatic functional organization of the linguistic system and the patterns of social use of its linguistic resources.

The present interview thematizes the systemic, the functional, and the social semiotic bases of Halliday's work. It attempts to explore and clarify the epistemological and theoretical criteria on which these are based. This involves some re-exploring of the development of the conceptual basis of the model. However, it also provides the opportunity to situate Halliday's thinking in relation to other contemporary theoretical positions in linguistics and semiotics. A further aspect of this interview concerns recent developments of the systemic-functional model, which are taking place in Sydney and elsewhere.

It is now some ten years since the first appearance of the previous interview with Herman Parret (1974; Interview 1 this volume). Michael Halliday's contribution to linguistics and semiotic studies has long been recognized as a leading and central one. Further, it seems to the present interviewer that Michael Halliday has always refused a Kuhnian positivistic conception of a linguistic science, whereby scientific activity is analogous to the increasingly specialized study of specific problems seen independently of their social and cultural contexts. The present interview attempts to give "voice" to the social conditions and epistemological foundations in which the specialist knowledges and techniques of systemic-functional linguistics are now being recognized as playing a key role in the so-called New Dialogue between the humanities, the social sciences and the biological and life sciences. This is now beginning to be "voiced" as a unified theory and praxis of human social meaning making. This is witnessed, for example, by the success of the first two International Systemic Workshops held in North America: at Glendon College, York University (Toronto) in

August 1982 and at the University of Michigan, Ann Arbor in August 1985. Not to mention the course "A Social-Semiotics of Grammar" which Michael Halliday taught in June 1985 at the International Summer Institute for Semiotic and Structural Studies at Indiana University, Bloomington.

This interview took place in the Department of Linguistics in the University of Sydney (Australia) on 4th September, 1985. Paul J. Thibault completed his Ph.D. thesis under Michael Halliday's supervision in the Department of Linguistics at the University of Sydney in 1984.

PJT: *You relate your work quite explicitly to the principal European functional schools of linguistics: the Prague school (Vachek 1966), the French functionalists (e.g. Greimas 1966a), the London (Firth 1957a, Palmer 1968) and Copenhagen (Hjelmslev 1961) schools. How would you describe the relations of your work to these various schools of linguistics?*

MAKH: I would see my work as falling clearly within this tradition. As you know, I was taught by Firth, and so the Malinowski-Firth or the so-called "London school" is the closest, and I accept a lot of the basic concepts that come from there. But in two aspects in particular I've taken ideas from other European functional schools: from Hjelmslev, or the "Copenhagen school", a particular theoretical orientation, especially in relation to system and text – Hjelmslev's interpretation of the Saussurean position, which I find most helpful; and then from the Prague school, their interest in what we would call register variation, in the text as an object, and, of course, in the theory of verbal art.

PJT: *Anything about the French in particular?*

MAKH: I'm less aware of this as a specific component, but I would of course regard it as a central element in European functionalism.

PJT: *The focus of much of your work has been on the relations between system and text – or system and process in Hjelmslev's terms. What does this distinction mean in the systemic-functional perspective?*

MAKH: I think the notion of system and process in Hjelmslev's sense is a good starting point. I would see text as instantiation of the system; the two must be mutually determining. Hjelmslev says that you could, in principle, have a system without process – a system without it generating any text, but you couldn't have the process without the system; he presents it as a one-way determination. I prefer to think of these as a single complex phenomenon: the system only "exists" as a potential for the process, and the process is the actualization of that potential. Since this is a *language* potential the "process" takes the form of what we call text.

PJT: *The Saussurean discussion of this relation has tended to disjoin system from text so that the ontological status of the system is privileged. The systemic-functional model,* as well as the earlier work of Firth and Hjelmslev, has quite a different view of this relation. The systemic-functional model is oriented to both "meaning" and "text". Can you explain this relation?

MAKH: I've always felt it was rather a distraction in Saussure that he defined linguistics as the study of *la langue*, with *parole* being simply the evidence that you use and then throw away. I don't see it that way. Firth, of course, was at the other end of the scale, in that for him the phenomenon was the text. He wasn't interested in the potential, but rather, as I think I put it in one of my papers, in the generalized actual, so that it was the typical texts that he was interested in. Firth tended to privilege the text as against the system. I don't want to privilege either.

PJT: *Actually, that's new to me – the notion of "generalized actual". Is that, perhaps, where the notion of register comes from – i.e. the typical semantic choices made in social situation-types.*

MAKH: Yes, I think it is. Firth himself had the concept, as you know, of restricted languages, and this derived from his concern with "typical texts in their context of situation", to use his own wording.

PJT: *The systemic aspect of the theory, like Saussure's, is defined relationally in terms of the oppositional values among the terms in a given system, i.e. that these relations are neither contingent nor external, but are defined only by internal criteria. How do you account for the work – i.e. the formal and institutional conditions – which must be performed on the system to produce text?*

MAKH: Can we put it this way? You have to express the system in some form of discourse which is obviously going to be metaphorical, and I tend to use the notion of "choice" . That does raise problems of possible misunderstanding. As you know, the way that I think of this is that the system at any one level is a set of interrelated options and the selection of any one option at any one point becomes the environment for a further set of selections. So if, in the situation where you have options x, y, and z, you choose x, this means that, in turn, you are in a position where you choose in another set of options a/b; and so forth. Remember that it is a synoptic representation: the "movement" is in delicacy, or progressive approximation, not in time. That's something which you can think of in various ways. You can think of it as something which you switch on and operate randomly; and there are some forms of pathological discourse which could be modelled in that way, as being random passes through the system. In most discourse, the operation of the system is part of a total activity set: the selections are motivated in some way, from a higher level semiotic.

PJT: *Is it an abstract potential then, or is it something more concrete?*

MAKH: No, it is an abstract potential. Let's say human beings engage in social processes, in various social activities; and we can represent any of these in terms of general semiotic concepts. These are the systems which represent the meaning potential of the culture as a whole, and some of these are activated through language. That's Hjelmslev's sense of the connotative semiotic – language as being the semiotic system which is the expression plane of other semiotic systems, which are not language. This means it is an abstract potential, but one which is called upon as a form of social action. Language is not only a *part* of the social process – it is also an *expression* of it; and that is why it is organized in a way which makes it a *metaphor* for social processes at the same time. In that sense, there's a concrete aspect to the system: language as a form of social activity.

PJT: *You make a careful theoretical distinction between system and structure (e.g. Halliday 1981a), calling structure the output or instantiation of some pathway through the system networks. Does this mean that "structure" is a transformation of the systemic "meaning potential" into something which is necessarily complete?*

MAKH: Well, obviously, the basis of this is the original Saussurean-Hjelmslevian paradigmatic-syntagmatic generalization, which will apply to any semiotic systems, any systematic form of behaviour. Firth made a clear distinction between system and structure as the organizing concepts for these two axes respectively: system is the organizing concept for interpreting relations on the paradigmatic axis, and structure that for interpreting those on the syntagmatic axis. His interpretation of text was as the interplay of these two, so that typically the structure – if you like, the deep syntagm – defined environments within which then the systems – i.e. the deep paradigms – were operating. The environment for any system was a specific place in the structure.

Now, I found it helpful in the work that I was doing to re-order this system-structure distinction so that I could represent the whole system (in the Hjelmslevian sense) entirely in paradigmatic terms as a series of system networks, which are formally equivalent to one huge system network. That meant that the structure became the output of the network; it became the work that you had to do in order to translate a path through the network into an actualization. The structure then becomes the way in which systemic choices are realized. Whether the structure is always "complete" depends on how you are using the network – and on how you define "complete", of course.

PJT: *Is there, perhaps, a non-finalistic teleology implicit in your notion of structure as the output of a pathway through a system network?*

MAKH: If I understand what you mean by that, then I think the answer is "no", because there is no implicit teleology at all. Let's start from the notion of exponence, or realization: the "output" is simply what you do in realizing a particular choice. This is talking about the network as a generative device; if we think of "parsing" then of course the direction is reversed. The thing itself is entirely neutral; but there is no way of talking about it that is neutral – no metalanguage that detaches it from some particular way of using the network. The system-structure model says nothing at all about any decision-making process, or any intentionality on the part of speakers, or listeners. We model a semiotic system as a set of sets of alternatives; and a structure is simply the realization of some choice among these alternatives – of a "selection expression", as we call it. The notion of structure as output is also neutral as between a propositional form, which says "the selection of option *a* is realized by structure $x + y + z$", and an instructional form, where you say "in order to select option *a*, then perform operation, $p + q + r$". But remember that it's the system network, not the structure, that embodies the theoretical interpretation; so if you want to build any teleological implications they would relate to the notion of system rather than to that of structure.

PJT: *I should like to explore your use of the notion of "function". You claim (Halliday 1970) that language structure is as it is because of the social functions it serves. This seems quite close to Durkheim's notion of "function" as the correspondence between social structure and its needs (besoins) or "necessary conditions of existence" in Radcliffe-Brown's later modification of this term. Isn't there the risk of a tautological connection between the two? Does this presume a necessary functional unity of the social system?*

MAKH: Yes, I take this point. There is a risk of this being seen in terms of some rather naive social functionalism. What I would say here is that it does seem to me we're looking for explanations of the nature of language – why it is as it is. I do not believe that representing something as a formal system is in itself any explanation of it. An explanation is something which shows correspondence with other things we know about human cultures, about human societies. If you observe language in contexts of situation, especially in what Bernstein (1975) called "critical socializing contexts", where language is being worked hard to construe the social system (unconsciously of course), you can make generalizations from this, and the most important single generalization you can make is that language is being used, in the Lévi-Straussian sense, both to act with and to think with. Now, when you come to interpret the grammar – and this was part of my own personal history, because I had never thought of grammar in this way at first – when you start representing the grammar of an actual language in these systemic (paradigmatic) terms, then you find these clusters in its organization; one tightly organized network of options here, and another one here, but with relatively sparse interconnections between them. So you say, well, what are these clusters doing? Are these purely arbitrary features of the syntax? Clearly they're not. It turns out that there's a dense grouping of options which relate to language as reflection – language to think with – and these are centred around the TRANSITIVITY systems; and another group that relates to language as action, with the MOOD systems at the heart of it.

PJT: *These are the metafunctions.*

MAKH: Yes, these are the metafunctions, exactly. Now, the notion of metafunctions is simply an attempt to capture this relationship between the internal forms of the language and its use in contexts of social action.

PJT: *You have suggested (Halliday 1977b: esp. p. 25) that a means-end, goal-oriented conception of the speaker helps to explain the functional "choices" which are made. Doesn't this suggest an empirical, rationalist conception of the speaking subject in your theory?*

MAKH: Have I? What do you see as the alternative to this? What are you opposing the empirical, rationalist conception of the speaking subject to?

PJT: *What I'm thinking of really goes back to this issue in relation to the notion of "choice", which, of course, we move on to later on. What does it imply epistemologically? What kind of speaker – is it one who makes ready-made rational decisions, or not? I see the possible danger that the rational, goal-oriented subject is seen as the starting point for rational choices and so on. Personally, I don't think so.*

MAKH: Not if you put it that way; that's why I was asking you how far you are pushing this. I think of the speaker-listener – the semiotic "subject", the one who engages in acts of meaning – as an active participant in social processes. But semiotic actions, especially those that are central to the subject's construal of reality (including himself) are largely unconscious. Especially acts of language: I agree with Boas, if we may go back that far, that language is unique among cultural processes in the extent to which it remains below the level of consciousness. If you want to understand the nature of semiotic acts, and particularly semantic acts – the "linguistic" ones, you have to pay attention to the most unconscious uses of language. It is there, interestingly enough, where you see not only language at work, but also language *expanding*, both within the individual and also within the culture, phylogenetically and ontogenetically. The frontier of language, where new meanings are created, is located in its most unconscious uses.

PJT: *Systemic theory is said to be functional in much more than the sense that items in structure are functionally related. This would be a structural account of linguistic function. In what other senses is the theory a functional one?*

MAKH: I see it as three interrelated senses. One is in the technical, grammatical sense: a grammar is interpreted in terms of functions rather than classes. There's a reason for that, of course: it has to be a *functional* grammar to get you from the system to the text. So there we're talking about the low-level sense of grammatical functions; using notions like Theme, Actor, Medium, and so on. That in turn relates to the second sense of function, which is the metafunctional one. What this means is that the whole paradigmatic organization of the grammar is functional, as seen in the way the systems are interrelated: they fall into the broad metafunctional categories of what I call the ideational, the interpersonal, and the textual. That is what relates language to what is outside language, to other semiotic systems.

PJT: *So, the metafunctional level is the interface between language and the outside.*

MAKH: Exactly. There's been a lot of confusion about this, and I suspect I'm responsible! Let me say clearly that I see the metafunctional organization as belonging to that interface which is what we mean by semantics. But for that very reason it also determines the form of the grammar. The relation between the grammar and the semantics is non-arbitrary. People have said to me: sometimes you say the metafunctions are in the semantics, sometimes you say they're in the grammar; where are they? They're in both. The metafunctions are the theoretical concepts that enable us to understand the interface between language and what is outside language – and it is this interfacing that has shaped the form of the grammar. Then there is the third sense of function, again related to these two, but which is more like a commonsense use of the term, where function equals use. This is the sense in which you have the traditional non-linguistic functional theories of language, like those of Malinowski, and Bühler, which were taken up by the linguists and built into their own systems: Malinowski by the London school, Bühler by the Prague school. Jakobson is on the fringe here (cf. Halliday 1970a). You remember the arguments that the Prague linguists had over the years about whether the functions were functions of the utterance or functions of the system, and they never got fully built into the system.

PJT: *Yes, and that seems to me to be a flaw in Jakobson's theory.*

MAKH: I agree.

PJT: *What distinguishes a systemic-functional interpretation of language from other, more syntagmatically based functional interpretations?*

MAKH: Well, I think you've given what I would give as the answer: it's the paradigmatic basis of systemic grammar which I think is the distinguishing factor between this and other functional grammars. Now, I don't believe in an all-purpose grammar; I have in mind, rather, a grammar for the sort of purposes that I have been interested in, and those people that I have worked with. Grammars vary in their delicacy of focus. You may need for certain purpose a very delicated grammar, one that's only going to do one job, and that job will totally determine the form of the grammar that you choose. At the other end of the scale, you have the notion – as is traditional in linguistics – of an all-purpose grammar, one which is the best for every job, which I really don't believe in. I've tried to move in at a midpoint on this scale – aiming at a grammar that will do a number of different jobs. It won't be totally dedicated, but nor will it be the reverse: it's not designed to do all possible jobs. So for the sort of questions that I have been interested in, this paradigmatic orientation has helped, in a number of different ways of which I'll just mention one. When you write a grammar this way, then the question "what is the description (or – I prefer – the interpretation) of this item, this clause, or whatever you're looking at?" and the question "how is this item related to other items?" become one question and not two. In other words, if you have a syntagmatic grammar, then the question "what is the nature of phenomenon *a*?" and the question "how does phenomenon *a* relate to phenomenon *b*?" are discrete questions. In a paradigmatic grammar they're not. They're the same question; you can't ask one without the other.

PJT: *This question relates, in part, to the third aspect of functionalism, which we talked about before. The systemic-functional approach adopts a functional interpretation of the internal, paradigmatic (systemic) organization of meaning relations. But what are its wider implications – in relating the linguistic system to the social system, for instance? How does systemic functional theory interpret this relation?*

MAKH: This is one direction we're trying to explore. One of the ways that I see the two relating is probabilistically. Jay Lemke (1985) put this very clearly in his discussion of the need for intermediate level generalizations between the macro- and the micro- that you're familiar with (except that it shouldn't be represented as size: it should be "meta-" rather than "macro-"). Let's discuss these in terms of Malinowski's notion of the context of situation. The context of situation is a generalized semiotic construct deriving from the culture – something that is recognized by the members as a form of social activity that they engage in. Now any given instance of a situation-type can be defined in terms of three factors that we call the field, tenor, and mode: what's going on, who's taking part, and what part the particular semiotic system (in this case language) is playing. What happens is that the interactants in any given situation access certain aspects of their semiotic potential: they get them ready so they can be brought into play. What is the nature of this operation? As I see it, it is not a cutting off device. It is not that I switch on this bit and switch off that bit. It is, rather, that I re-order the probabilities among them. So I think you must see language as a probabilistic system. I would represent language in terms of a global set of probabilities. There's good evidence that speakers of a language are sensitive to relative frequency – to this being more, or less, frequent than that. Register variation is analogous in many ways to dialect variation; but it is functionally based and it can be interpreted, therefore, as a re-alignment of the probabilities in relation to the particular contextual configuration – in particular, the context of situation. We're trying to find ways of modelling this at the moment.

PJT: *Register, it seems to me then, is another interface notion; in this case, between the semantics and the social situation.*

MAKH: I welcome the opportunity to clarify this, because I know I've often been misunderstood – again, it's my own fault. I would see the notion of "register" as being *at* the semantic level, not above it. Shifting in register means re-ordering the probabilities at the semantic level ...

PJT: *... which way they're skewed in that situation-type.*

MAKH: ... whereas the categories of field, mode, and tenor belong one level up. These are the features of the context of situation; and this *is* an interface. But the register itself I see as being linguistic; it is a setting of probabilities in the semantics.

PJT: *Speech act theory proposes an autonomous "pragmatic" component to account for language use. You make no such distinction between the "pragmatic" and "semantic" dimensions of meaning. Why?*

MAKH: I've never seen that it's necessary. It seems to me that in the grammar – that is, at the lexicogramamtical level – we don't need to make a distinction between the *system* and its instantiation in *text*. Our theory of "grammar" is at one and the same time an interpretation of the system and an interpretation of the texts that are engendered by that system. Now, it seems to me that pragmatics is simply the name of the semantics of the text. I'm not making a terminological point. It seems to me that a theory of semantics must encompass both the system and the process in exactly the same way that the grammar encompasses both the system and the process. We don't want a separate thing called pragmatics.

PJT: *In any case, it seems to me that most of so-called linguistic pragmatics has a very impoverished view of grammar.*

MAKH: I couldn't agree more.

PJT: *You say that the organizing principle of meaning is its internal, paradigmatic organization. Can you explain this? How does this relate to the grammar of the clause, for instance?*

MAKH: The clause, I think, is the gateway, the main gateway between the semantics and the grammar, just as the syllable is the main gateway between the content and the expression. The clause is where the meanings are all organized together. So I see the clause as being the primary grammatical unit in the sense that it is there that the options relating to the different kinds of meaning – the different metafunctions – are brought together so that they get mapped on to one another into this single output. I sometimes use the metaphor of polyphonic music: that, in a sense, you have one unfolding melodic line from the experiential, another melodic line from the interpersonal, and another from the textual component. These operate through three: major systems at the clause rank: the TRANSITIVITY, the MOOD, and the THEME.

PJT: *Systemic-functional theory proposes, as we have just seen, that at the grammatical level of the clause, meanings are organized into three simultaneous sets of options. These relate to distinct kinds of metafunctional components in the semantic organization of the language. What is the relation between the semantics and the grammar in a "metafunctional" account? What do you consider to be its principal advantages over other accounts of language structure?*

MAKH: It's a hypothesis, obviously; but one which can be tested. Not simply; we won't get a formal test – but then the problem in the human sciences is that anything that can be subjected to formal tests of the kind that we have available at the moment lends to be rather trivial, so that doesn't worry me very much. But over the longer term it's something that can be inspected and tested.

The hypothesis – as embodied in the term "metafunction" – is that there is this relationship between the form of the grammar and the semiotic construction of the culture as instantiated in particular situations. I don't think any other linguistic theory has suggested an interface organization of this kind. This leads to a further hypothesis, which is that these different metafunctions, are typically represented by different *kinds* of grammatical organization. Specifically: (1) experiential meaning is typically represented in constituent-like, particulate structures. Most people who've worked on language have been largely taken up with experiential meaning; and this means that they view language in terms of constituency, which is a very partial consideration. (2) Interpersonal meanings are typically prosodic, with field-like manifestations. (3) Textual meanings typically give you the periodic movement which is so characteristic of discourse at all levels; everything from the very smallest waves to the very large ones. In other words, there is a hierarchy of periodicity, and that comes from the textual metafunction. So not only can you build this bridge systematically between the language and the situation, but you can also say that the different patterns of realization taken by the linguistic system relate to these metafunctional distinctions.

PJT: *The distinction between the ideational and interpersonal metafunctions helps to overcome the classical dichotomy in the western cultural tradition between language as "thought" and language as "action". Wittgenstein's notion of "language-game" is one attempt to integrate both language and the social actions it performs into an integral whole. How do you conceive of the relationship between language and social action?*

MAKH: If I can say this without it sounding as if it's just a clever slogan: language is both a part of and a metaphor for social action. Actually there is a threefold relationship. First, language is the *realization* of social action: in other words, it stands to social action in the same way that, within language, the phonology stands to the grammar. That's Hjelmslev's connotative semiotic. Secondly, language is a *part* of social action: one component of any instance of social action is the verbal action that takes place within it. In some type of situation the two are very closely interrelated – instructions, games, and things of this kind; in others there is more distance. Thirdly, language is also a *metaphor* for social action: the forms of the language itself give us a metaphoric representation of the forms of social action. This can be seen, for example, in the facts of register variation and dialect variation, which represent metaphorically variation in social processes, on the one hand, and in the social structure on the other.

PJT: *What kind of distinction would you make between text and discourse in this regard?*

MAKH: I've not been consistent in making any clearcut distinction between the two. I started with the term "text" because it's the traditional term in linguistics; certainly among the functional schools. So I was simply adopting their terminological practice. In contemporary usage 1 think we can talk about either discourse analysis or text analysis – it doesn't make much difference. But it has become useful in recent work to have "discourse" as a separate term in order to be able to use it to refer to heteroglossic notions (Bakhtin 1981) – the "discourse of" something or other; and also (as you use it yourself) to the way in which text functions to embody or enact an ideology. We're accustomed now to using the term "discourse" to focus on these aspects, and "text" to focus on the more linguistic aspects.

PJT: *Is it perhaps discourse in the sense of the social practices in which texts are embedded and which, in some sense, they are the realization of (viz. the first of the three kinds of relationships between language and social action)?*

MAKH: Yes, right.

PJT: *The systemic-functional model assumes a tri-stratal organization of language, consisting of a phonology, a lexicogrammar, and a semantics. What particular assumptions concerning meaning are made in this model?*

MAKH: Maybe two things. One is that the tri-stratal model embodies, initially, the Saussurean line of arbitrariness, at the frontier between lexicogrammar and phonology. Of course, one has tended to exaggerate the extent to which this line is solid: there are a great many non-arbitrary aspects of the relation between the expression and the content (though that's a separate point, I think it is a very interesting and important one). So the first cut, if you like, is that between the content plane and the expression plane; and you see that kind of bi-stratal organization in children's protolanguage (Halliday 1975). As you know, I think the ontogenesis of language shows very clearly the beginning of language as a bi-stratal system, which then evolves into a tri-stratal one. Presumably that's how language evolved in the human race. It makes it sound very concrete if I put it this way, but it has to be read in the light of everything we said before: what happens is that in moving from the protolanguage to the mother tongue the child slots in a grammar in between the meaning and the expression, so that the content plane now splits into two and becomes a semantics and a grammar. We can see both how it happens and why it happens. The new interstratal line that is created in this process, however, is definitely nonarbitrary; this is important. I'm not sure to what extent Saussure was also referring to that stratal boundary; Ruqaiya Hasan certainly thinks that his discussion encompasses that line as well as the other one. Anyway, there is a different relationship between the semantics and the lexicogrammar, which is non-arbitrary, from the one between that "content" block and the phonology, which is basically arbitrary. Now the second point is this: as you know, Firth always insisted that each level is itself meaning-creating, and he didn't like the term "meaning" to be siphoned off to refer only to what I am calling semantic patterns.

PJT: *Indeed, because you can have foregrounded patternings on any given level.*

MAKH: Exactly – I agree with that. Jim Martin has pulled me up for obscuring that aspect and making too close a tie-up between "meaning" and this notion of a specifically "semantic" level. I admit I have done that, and I think it's wrong; the whole system is meaning-creating. Meaning is the product of the interrelations among the parts. This is well brought out by the foregrounding you referred to: the kind of "de-automatization" whereby meaning is being created at the phonological level, and at the grammatical level, as well as in the "automatized" process of the realization of semantic features.

PJT: *More recent developments in the Department of Linguistics here of the tri-stratal model propose a stronger orientation to discourse. Here the concern is with the relations among the levels of discourse, lexicogrammar, and phonology. Why has this shift in emphasis taken place?*

MAKH: This is a part of the discussion with Jim Martin (cf. Martin 1992). He is making two points. One is that moving above the lexicogrammar essentially has to be a move on the "size" scale as well. In other words, what he's locating there are conjunctive relations and so on which enable the grammatical system to be used for the construction of larger units. This he sees as a necessary step in order to get from the grammar, through this interface, to the register and the genre, and eventually up to the ideological system. Secondly, he's not convinced that you need to have a separate semantic representation of all the features that are there in the grammar. He considers that you don't need a semantic cycle for the TRANSITIVITY system over and above the TRANSITIVITY system itself as represented in the grammar. I think you do (cf. Halliday & Mattheissen 1999).

PJT: *Does he say then that that cycle in the transitivity system is its own semantics?*

MAKH: Yes. He's saying that you can handle the whole thing in terms of TRANSITIVITY itself.

PJT: *...when in fact it's easier in the case of the interpersonal component to put above that role relations and so on.*

MAKH: He sees the need for a semantic of the interpersonal component, but not for a general semantic stratum. I think that one phenomenon we've been working on a lot lately, that of grammatical metaphor, demonstrates that we do need this.

PJT: *Your theory is also described as a "social semiotic" one (Halliday 1978b). What is the relation between the social semiotic and the linguistic system? How do you position your use of the term "social semiotic" in relation to the principal European schools of semiotics – the Greimasians in Paris, Eco in Bologna, for instance?*

MAKH: When I used the term "social semantic" in the first place what I was trying to say was something like this. We need an interpretation of language which does not treat language as a thing in itself, but as part of a wider set of phenomena which we call the social system (or the culture, in American parlance). It doesn't make sense to me to try and interpret language except in a context of this kind. That was the "social" part. I wanted to say, furthermore, that we can represent the culture as a whole as an assembly of semiotic systems, of which language is one. It was those two things that I was trying to say in one move. I think it was Greimas, in fact, who used that same term in the International Days of Sociolinguistics Conference in Rome in the late 1960s (Greimas 1969). I wasn't there, but I think it was in Greimas's paper that you find the term "social semiotic".

PJT: *Yes, I've seen the term even in more recent work of his as well (Greimas 1983).*

MAKH: It seemed to me we were talking about the same thing and that what I was trying to say fell naturally within the scope of European semiotics. I see certain points of difference; one difference would be that I am still working as a linguist – a grammarian, in fact. What I'm seeking to do is primarily to interpret language, rather than using language to interpret other things, which is the perspective of most semioticians. But to make sense of grammar you had to relate it to society.

PJT: *Greimas is a linguist with a Hjelmslevian basis, which can be traced right back to his earlier work (Greimas 1966a).*

MAKH: Right; I would also differ in that I'm trying to interpret language in relation to other processes (for example, those of learning), rather than by attempting a formal representation of semiotic systems – as, say, Eco does.

PJT: *What is the status of "grammar" in both the systemic-functional and social semiotic perspectives?*

MAKH: I gave a course in Bloomington this year called "Grammar and Daily Life" (cf. Halliday 1998) and there I was saying two things. First, insofar as language plays a part in the total array of social semiotics, the central processing unit of language is grammar. We have to understand that, in order to get any kind of sensible interpretation of the whole. Secondly, referring back to the foregrounding notion we mentioned earlier, the grammatical system takes on a life of its own – as symbolic systems always can do. We see this at work in a lot of spheres of social action. Now, when we focus on the grammar in its relation to various aspects of daily life, we can see how the grammar itself – the grammatical system – in addition to functioning as the automatized realization of the semantics, and through that of the context of situation, is also functioning directly as a form of social action in its own right.

PJT: *There is a Whorfian dimension to your theory, which seems relevant here. Much confusion has been created – not by Whorf, but by others – concerning*

Whorf's conception of the relation between "grammar" and so-called "world view" or "metaphysics". Could you comment on this in relation to your own theory?

MAKH: Yes, there has been a lot of confusion here. People are still disproving Whorf; there's been another round just recently, and yet he pops up again because he's not been disproved at all. These efforts have very little to do with what he was on about. I think that the great merit of Whorf was to point out the essential dialectic relationship between language and the social semiotic systems within which language functions as a realization. In other words, there is no one-way determinism. Now Whorf concerned himself only with the system; but what he was saying applies both to the system and to the text. Text creates the situation as well as the situation creating the text; just as the linguistic system creates the other semiotic systems of the culture as well as their creating it. But Whorf did not go over to the other extreme. He didn't replace one form of determinism by the other. He insisted on this rather complex form of dialectic: that between a symbol and what it symbolizes – between the two sides of the sign, if you like. This has an enormous importance, for example, in the process by which a child grows up as a member of a culture – being given, in Whorf's terms, a "recept". Children are given this through the linguistic system, and that becomes the grid, to use Sapir's old metaphor, through which they interpret their experience. But what Whorf was able to show is, I think, a necessary part of our explanations of how we, in turn, can use semiotic systems in order to change the things that generated them in the first place. This is a major to factor which people who "reject" Whorf totally fail to explain – how by working on the language you can have such an influence on the other systems in the culture.

PJT: *Yes, indeed. The Chomskyan concept of "creativity", which is not set within any notion of either linguistic or social practice, is just so badly off the mark, in my opinion. What you're saying there really embodies a much richer, more effective notion of creativity itself.*

MAKH: Yes, that is an important sense of creativity. I agree with that. At one end of the scale, there's the interesting case of the highly valued text – the great poem or whatever – through which an individual, or the discourse of an individual, can actually innovate: the writer as creator of new meanings. These are rare, but they're not non-existent. And then there is the more general sense, which is that whereby the social processes as a whole – people engaging in these forms of activity – create, bring about change: change at every level of semiosis.

PJT: *Transformational-generative approaches to grammar are primarily concerned with form-form relations. Systemic-functional theory is concerned with the relations between grammatical forms and their patterns of social use. How would you characterize this relation?*

MAKH: I'm not sure that I want to say much more than what has already been said; except perhaps just one small point, since you refer here to grammatical forms.

As you know, I don't argue at all from the form of the grammar to the structure of the human brain or to any kind of psychological processes. I think that we can, however, use some of our insights into the forms of the grammar to help us towards an understanding of how people construct social realities; and an obvious example would be TRANSITIVITY. It seems to me that TRANSITIVITY systems in all languages – I think this is a universal feature – embody a tension between the ergative and the transitive modes of interpretation. Now, these are not, to my mind, simply formal alternatives. I think they represent different, complementary ways of interpreting experience. They're complementary because they're mutually contradictory. That's what enables the tension between them to create this very vital, unstable interpretation which we live with: we see our processes both in terms of an ergative-type, cause and effect model and in terms of a transitive-type, mechanical transmission model. I think that by looking at the grammar – by understanding the nature of the system – we can get quite a lot of insight into our social construction of reality.

PJT: *Yes, expressed more metaphorically or, perhaps, more accurately, in terms of the contemporary epistemological confrontation between dynamics and thermodynamics in the physical and life sciences, we can say that in our social construction of reality there's a constant tension between the mechanistic and deterministic Newtonian model, which is seen as embodying a fundamental level of description and, hence, of reality, and there is the dynamic quantum model which introduces both instability and probabilistic features into our interpretations.*

MAKH: I see these as embodied in every clause in English, and no doubt in every other natural language. But taking your formulation seriously; this is where it gets more complicated. I don't think Newton's picture was mechanistic, though it's been interpreted that way (Hill 1974). What the grammar provides is the two sides, two complementary components, of Newton's universe: the technological (transitive: process as the *transmission* of force) and the scientific (ergative: process as the *explanation* of force). The dynamic, quantum model is represented, I think, not by either one of these, nor by some third interpretation – I don't see any third interpretation in the grammar; but rather by the tension between the two. This is an aspect of its nature as a dynamic open system, as Lemke (e.g. 1995) has shown it to be.

PJT: *That's very encouraging, for most linguistics is still at the Newtonian stage in its epistemology. We have to get both.*
  Register theory is one of the intermediate levels of analysis proposed for cutting up the social semiotic system into different social situation-types. How do you define the social situation?

MAKH: I find it useful to talk in terms of the three concepts of field, tenor, and mode. As you know, I started many years ago trying to re-interpret the Malinowski-Firth concept of the context of situation, and arrived at these notions from above, so to speak. It was only later on that I saw them to be motivated also from below – from the grammar, in the form of the metafunctional hypothesis. That seemed to suggest an independent reason for using this kind of model: it shows just *how* the context of situation "redounds with" (construes, and is construed by) the semantic system.

PJT: *The concept of "register" relates typical co-patternings of discourse and lexicogrammatical options to their social situation-types. As we have seen, it is an intermediate level of analysis, which can relate texts to the social formations which produce and re-produce them. How do you see "register" as a possible analytic construct for relating texts to social institutions as sites for the production of particular kinds of social meanings?*

MAKH: As I was saying earlier, I see the "register" as essentially the clustering of semantic probabilities: it's a linguistic category. The context of situation is "above" the register. The context of situation is what is modeled in terms of field, mode, and tenor. Just to add one point: Jim Martin (e.g. 1992) and Ruqaiya Hasan (see Chapters 4–6 of Halliday & Hasan 1985) are both working in this area, asking how one can refine this notion and get more insight into it. Jim is operating with the notion of a stratal distinction between what he calls register (my field, mode and tenor if you will) and genre. He feels it's necessary to have another level above his register, a level which in a sense is a development out of field, and which specifies the nature of the activity, but in terms of purpose or intentionality. He says this is what engenders the structure of a particular genre. And this higher level construct is then represented through the register. So he has two levels here. Ruqaiya does it in a single level, using what she calls the "contextual configuration", the specific values of the context of situation in terms of the variables of field, mode, and tenor. It is this contextual configuration which determines the structure *potential* for the text.

PJT: *In the system-functional model, "structure" is the realization of a configuration of systemic choices, which are then mapped on to the resulting syntagm. In what sense do you intend the notion of "choice"? Does it perhaps imply individual voluntary actions in the sense of the early Parsons (1964), or something more like his later notion of functional requisites or functional imperatives?*

MAKH: No, certainly not – I've not guarded enough, I realize, against that sort of interpretation. What it implies is simply an OR relationship, a set of alternatives. We can define the "system" as a set of alternatives with an entry condition. Now there are instances where the activation of a system of that kind can be seen to involve a conscious choice. But those are special cases. There is no suggestion of intentionality – voluntary action – or of functional imperatives, in the theoretical concept of a system, or system network.

PJT: *The concept of register itself suggests a constrained skewing of the probabilities of the meaning system, as we saw before, according to the situation- type. Is there a danger that this overemphasizes the normative or consensus basis of social power relations? How would you characterize differences of power among discourse interactants?*

MAKH: I wouldn't see it as normative. I would interpret the power relations in a particular situation, when we represent that situation in terms of field, tenor, and mode, by building in to our representation the fact that the situation may be different thing for different interactants. The total picture is obviously going to bring in all angles; but in any typical context of situation in which there is a power relationship of inequality, then the configuration embodied in that situation is different from the way it is seen from either end. This means, of course, that the register that is being operated by the interactants will be bifurcated, although we may choose to characterize the register of the situation as a whole by building in both strands. I wouldn't call this normative, if that implies, as you say, a kind of consensus basis.

PJT: *... which is the structural-functionalist model in a sociological interpretation of, for example, Talcott Parsons (1964).*

MAKH: But again with that view you would not be able to explain the way that the interactants can manipulate this in order to try and change the power relation. Often they don't, and they may not succeed when they try; but it is a permeable frontier.

PJT: *The interpersonal metafunction, which is concerned in part with the social rule relations among interactants, suggests the principle of exchange structuralism in the sense that a given society is maintained by the reciprocal exchange of information and goods-and-services, i.e. by a general norm of reciprocity, which helps to explain social behaviour. Is the emphasis here on the structured patterns of social relations or on the processes of social interaction?*

MAKH: You can set up – we haven't dealt with this – a kind of system-structure cycle at this level also (e.g. Halliday 1984). If you do this, then what you're emphasizing, as the underlying representation, is processes of social interaction, and these can also be seen as interrelated sets of alternatives. Then the patterns of social relations are set up as the manifestation of these social processes via the statuses and roles of the interactions.

PJT: *Could the role notion which is built into the interpersonal component help to bridge that gap?*

MAKH: Yes, I think it could. I think that it can be a link in the total interpretative chain. How much part it would play I don't know. I think Jim Martin might say that there would be a danger of reifying it, where his view of the interpersonal tenor relationships is rather in terms of power and distance – as relations, rather than as terms in the relations (e.g. Martin 1992). I think one can avoid that danger if one keeps both perspectives in mind.

PJT: *Most linguistic theory is speaker oriented. Do you have a corresponding conception of the hearer?*

MAKH: You're right, of course; most linguistic theory is speaker-oriented. I would accept this has also been true of my own work, although I try to emphasize the notion of speaker-listener – this is why I prefer the term " listener" to "hearer", because the listener is the active role. The text, the discourse itself, is a creation of both speaker and listener; I see this as a single unity, the speaker-listener complex, if you like.

PJT: *I think you've called it an "interact" (Halliday 1977b).*

MAKH: Yes, an interact. And similarly with constructions that the text creates in its turn. This is very important in child language: in the protolanguage stage. There is a sense in which the speaker is privileged, because the parents don't speak the protolanguage – only the child does. But one has to look behind that and recognize that even there the protolanguage is very clearly the creation of child and parents together. The parents, or other caregivers, have to be creating the language along with the child. The fact that they are speaking English or some other adult language, not the child's protolanguage – may distract attention from the fact that they are, as listeners, also creating the protolanguage. Even here the text is very much the creation of listener and speaker together.

PJT: *You have written (Halliday 1975) an extensive and important body of work on the process of language development in the first years of a child's life. This involves the process of inserting the child into a symbolic order of the socio-cultural meanings of a given community. How would you characterize in general terms the model of "man" and "woman" which informs this thinking?*

MAKH: You could start from a kind of socialization model, in which "man" and "woman" are the human being who has been through this kind of process – through the stages of child language and all the other "socializing" processes of the culture. But that seems to me to imply a rather too deterministic approach. It's as if there is something given "out there" and in some sense this reality moulds the human being to fit itself. There is an element of this in the process, but I think it's one-sided, put like that. This relates perhaps to what I was saying before; that the child, in the process of becoming "man" or "woman", is taking part in the creation of that socio-cultural reality. The language is as much a means whereby the child construes the culture as it is a means whereby the culture constructs the child.

PJT: *How would you position systemic-functional linguistics in relation to contemporary social theory?*

MAKH: It seems to me that social theories tend to have a big hole in the middle where language should be and I would hope to see systemic-functional linguistics as, in a sense, filling the hole. That's the context in which I've always thought of it. As you know, one of the reasons why I was always interested in Bernstein's work is that he seemed to me to be unique among social theorists in not merely paying lip service to language, as everyone does – saying yes, of course, language is important – but actually building it into his interpretative framework and seeing it as an essential part of the process of cultural transmissions. In linguistics we've now had a generation of work that has been called "sociolinguistics", stemming mainly from Labov and Fishman, which has been significant for the theory of language (variation theory, for example). This makes explicit that there is a social context to language: but it hasn't aroused much interest among social theorists because it has still been largely a theory of language: of language in its social context, yes; but not really a theory of language in society. Excepting the later work of Dell Hymes, it lacks the conception of a social semiotic. Language and society haven't really met yet, but I would like to think that systemic-functional linguistics could have something to say about that.

PJT: *Does a specific social programme inform your work? If so, how would you describe this?*

MAKH: I've always been interested in applications of linguistics, and never seen any real gap between theory and practice, or theory and application. On the other hand, I've been interested in a number of different applications of linguistic theory, ranging from research applications, at least what are in the immediate sense research applications like the study of literature, to more immediately practical ones particularly in education. I suppose the context in which I myself have worked most – and I think this is probably true of people working in systemic theory generally – has been educational. Not in the specific sense of language pedagogy, although there often are implications for what a teacher would do in a classroom, but more in the broader sense of language as the main resource through which the human being develops and gains knowledge. So I do see linguistics as part of a programme which is concerned with the development of human beings in the social context, with language and language development as the primary resource.

PJT: *Most of Western linguistics is founded on a narrow range of culturally and ideologically dominant notions concerning language, society, and the individual. You have had extensive experience throughout your career with non-Western linguistic and cultural traditions. What can these offer to a Western social science of language?*

MAKH: I'd have to answer on two levels. One, in the specific sense of non-Western traditions in the study of language itself, I think there is a great deal to be learnt from these. Linguists are now familiar, of course, with the Indian tradition, which was in many ways more fruitful than the Western one in that it was clearer about the nature of language as a phenomenon. It was able to objectify – to identify language as object – in the way the Western tradition found extremely hard.[1] Then from the Chinese tradition, I think there's a great deal to be learnt towards prosodic interpretations of language; both directly at the phonological level – Chinese phonology was very Firthian in its prosodic approach – but also in its implications for other levels of language, which can be seen as not being constituent-like. The

Chinese, who were of course highly theoretical thinkers, were able to create a totally abstract model of phonology – the only people who did. That's at the more specific, technical linguistic level. If you then move on to, as you put it, a "Western social science of language", then I don't know enough about other aspects of these major traditions to be able to say whether or not there was a relationship set up there between language and society – language and the social order – in the way that we need. I'm not aware of it, but that doesn't mean it wasn't there. Of course if we move up to other aspects of these traditions, I mean Chinese thought as a whole, clearly we have another way in to the whole question; but not through language. I'm not aware how far language was linked with society in those traditions.

PJT: *The social semiotic orientation of your work assumes no specific psychological or biological models of language. Yet, cognitive and psychological theories of language have frequently dominated Western linguistic theory. Why have you so consistently refused such a position?*

MAKH: Partly, I suppose, that I am just obstinate. If everyone does a thing one way, I tend to think it ought to be done the other way, if only to redress the balance. But also partly my own personal inclinations. I tend to believe in social explanations for phenomena where I find it hard to believe in psychological ones. But this is because I can't see the sort of psychological explanations we are familiar with as a basis for modes of action. Do you see what I mean? – as something you can use when you're facing particular problems in an educational context. Educational practice has tended to be dominated by the theoretical stance that has come in from psychology, and it has tended to neglect both the sociological and the linguistic. At a deeper level this has to be explained as Bruce McKellar has done (e.g. 1987), in terms of the history of ideas in the West, especially the constant conviction of a separate order of existence called "mind", or "soul". In recent centuries – I've said this often enough – this has led to our Western obsession with the individual. Using cognitive instead of semantic interpretations – talking about "thought" instead of about "meaning" – is another way of elevating the individual at the expense of the collective.

PJT: *Systemic-functional linguistics is currently involved in computer models of text-generation; in particular, the NIGEL Project at the Information Sciences Institute in the: University of Southern California (Matthiessen & Bateman 1991). Does the human-computer interface underscore any major shift in the predominantly human-istic epistemological assumptions in linguistics concerning the production of meaning and of knowledge itself?*

MAKH: I hope not; I certainly don't see it that way. Let me say first that I have been in and out of computational linguistics twice in my life before this; first back in the 1950s, in the early days of machine translation (Halliday 1962), and then again in the mid-sixties when we were doing our research in London in the scientific English project (Huddleston et al. 1968). In those early stages the technology simply hadn't caught up; there was no way that you could do computational research on language. (You could build dictionaries, and so forth, which was important, but it didn't address the questions that I was interested in.) When we came into the second round, we were able to get as far as using the computer to form a paradigm from a system network, to test simple forms of output and so on (later published as Henrici 1981). I was surprised, then, to find myself back in again a third time in the 1980s; but the reason is that in the meantime the technology has changed so drastically that we are now learning fundamental things about language by modelling it in the computer, for example through text generation projects (Mann 1984). It used to be linguistically trivial – it was a purely internal housekeeping matter – what form the system had to take in the computer. We didn't learn anything from it. Now we're beginning to learn something from the way in which grammars have to be written – how they are represented in the text-generation or parsing process. But the most important point is that, in the study of a language like English, which has been reasonably well worked over – we're about to pass from pre-history to history in the linguistics of English, and the interpretation of the grammar has now got to the point where you can no longer test it manually: it's just too big. You have to put it in a computer in order to be able to test it. That's looking at the question from the point of view of the contribution to our understanding of language. There are, secondly, a number of applications of this work, which will be important for human life. Going back to the early days, the reason I got interested in machine translation in the first place was because I was convinced of the value of people being educated in the mother tongue. Now, people can't be educated in the mother tongue if there aren't any textbooks. There are not enough human translators; but maybe a machine could do the job. Thirdly, then, we come to the question of the effect of the man-machine dialogue on forms of meaning and of knowledge. This is a huge question, which we haven't time for here. I see three levels at which the impact is taking place, those of the channel (new forms of text), the register (new semantic patterns) and the ideology. The last is where we will see linguistics developing as the new "science of sciences", replacing physics, to cope with the interpretation of the universe in terms of exchange of information, rather than of cause and effect.

PJT: *How would you define the role of the academic discipline of linguistics in relation to the current historical phase of technological, mass consumer, and increasingly information based capitalist society?*

MAKH: I think that anything which increases our understanding of ourselves as human beings, and of the nature of human social processes, is valuable. It has a practical value in helping to protect the consumer from the massive pressures of high tech selling, whether what is being sold is goods-and-services or information. And like any other scientific knowledge it can be used and it can be abused. You can use linguistics to help you sell information, or goods-and-services, to people just as much as you can use linguistics to protect people against having these things sold to them. This is the familiar ethical dilemma of the sciences and I think it's very clear that linguistics is a science in this sense. It is capable of being used in all kinds of ways. I hope, of course, that we're constructing a kind of linguistics which is able to be used in the ways that I would see as humanistic, progressive, forward looking – such as defending the individual against the excesses of this kind of society. Let's take our notion of grammatical metaphor as a case in point. I think the sort of work that we' re trying to do in this area is enabling us to see much more clearly the linguistic processes and, therefore, the underlying semiotic processes that are going into mass consumer discourse, or bureaucratic (Hardaker 1982) or political or militaristic discourse. Grammar is the most powerful tool we have for understanding and therefore for controlling these things. It shouldn't be seen just as a form of defence, though. With a grammar derived from a social semiotic it should be possible to *shape* the kind of technological, information-based society you're talking about, to ensure that it is not dehumanized in the ways we see happening today. By "grammar" here of course I mean a theory of grammar – it is a curse of English to use the same term both for a phenomenon and for the study of that phenomenon. Would you let me coin the term "grammatics" to refer to grammar in this second sense? We need a grammatics to account for, and hence enable us to control, the languages that are now construing this information-based society (and the information-based universe of the physicists that I was referring to just now, since we model nature on ourselves). I hope our systemic linguistics can make some contribution to that.

University of Sydney
September 1985

Note

1. Halliday makes the distinction between language as "object" and language as "instrument". In the first perspective, the focus is on the nature of the linguistic phenomenon itself, that is language as object. The second perspective is concerned with using language to ask questions about something else as is the case in speech act theory or propositional analysis. See Halliday and Martin (1981: 15–16) for further discussion of this. The Indian tradition referred to here is exemplified, for example, by Panini's Sanskrit grammar of around the fifth century B.C.

6

With Ruqaiya Hasan, Gunther Kress and J. R. Martin (1986)

Edited by Ruqaiya Hasan and J. R. Martin[1]

Semogenesis

GK: *Well Michael, the first question is why linguistics? We've heard you say that you first turned to linguistics because of frustrations you felt with the way people talked about language in literature classes. What actually frustrated you about literature teaching and why kinds of answers did you find were available in linguistics at that time?*

MAKH: That was at school where I was trapped in a system which, in a way, I still find unbelievable. It was so over-specialised that from the age of about fourteen I was doing nothing but classics, twenty seven hours a week out of thirty three, and the others were in English. The English part I liked because it was literature and I enjoyed it very much, except when they started telling me something about language in literature. It just made no contact with what was actually there. And this worried me just as it used to worry me when people made folk observations about phonetics; I mean the kind of attitudes Barbara Horvath[2] (1985) observed in her studies of Australian English – for example, that Australians are nasal. It is absolutely wrong, of course, but it takes time to see through these popular beliefs. You asked what was available in linguistics: the answer is – nothing. I didn't find any linguistics, as such; I just went to the library and found a book by someone called Bloomfield on language and tried to read it.

JRM: *What, even in a high school?*

MAKH: Yes, it was in the library. But I didn't get very far with it. I could write the critical essays when I found out what attitudes you were supposed to have, but I always thought there must be something else – some other way of talking about literature. I felt that there was more to it than what I was hearing.

JRM: *Did you think that language might provide a key or perhaps some kind of objective way of getting access to what literature was about?*

MAKH: I doubt whether I could have formulated it in those terms, but I felt that literature was made of language so it ought to be possible to talk about that language. After all, my father was enough of a grammarian for me to know there were ways of talking about language. He was also a literary scholar although he didn't particularly combine the two in so far as I am aware. I certainly wasn't far enough into it to be able to be more explicit – I think it was more prompted by trying to be more explicit, but as Jim says, I was trying to interpret some of the comments about the language of the work.

RH: *But when did you make your real contact with linguistics, Michael? When is it that you actually began to feel that linguistics has a possibility for providing answers?*

MAKH: Well, it was through language teaching. When I left school, it was to take the services' language training course. They took us out of school about eighteen months before we were due for national service, to be trained in languages. I was just seventeen when I left school and joined this program. Now those courses were being run at SOAS.[3] During those eighteen months we certainly heard the name of Firth and we heard that there was such a thing as linguistics. But I don't think I learned anything about it. The initiative had originally come from Firth at the beginning of the war, who said that there was obviously going to be a war in the Far East and in Asia and it was time that they trained some people in Asian languages. They shelved this for a while but eventually they got the thing going. The first thing I encountered was a language aptitude test designed by Firth. So when we went from school we were all called up to London for two or three days and we were given these tests and interviews. This test had two parts: one was a general language aptitude, to find out if you could decode made-up languages and it was very, very good. Then, there was part of it which was language specific. There were four languages in the program: Chinese, Japanese, Turkish and Persian. I remember one of the things you had to do was to recite from memory an increasingly long list of monosyllables on different tones.

Now I had in fact wanted to do Chinese anyway and I came out alright on the ones which favoured Chinese so I got my choice. But I presume that if somebody had put Chinese first and it turned out that they couldn't hear a falling tone from a rising tone, they'd have switched them into Persian or some other language.

JRM: *And that was how you really got into Chinese?*

MAKH: Yes.

JRM: *Before that, you hadn't studied it anywhere?*

MAKH: No. Apparently for some reason – I have absolutely no idea why – I had always wanted to go to China, from the age of about four.

JRM: *Oh really.*

MAKH: So I'm told. Apparently I wrote a story when I was about four-years-old about a little boy who went to China.

RH: Yes, that story is really very, very fascinating. Michael's mother showed me. It has parts of India in it. It has China in it. Nearly all the places that you visited, you had already forecast that you were going to visit – at the age of four.

MAKH: I hadn't studied Chinese at all. I really wanted to do Chinese to get out of classics; that was the main motive. I just hated classics at school and I wanted to get out.

GK: *So you must have been very good at languages to have been called up for this test?*

MAKH: Well, I don't think you had to be very good. It was just that you had to show that there was some chance you might possibly learn a language. So anyway, they gave us this eighteen months training and we then joined up with the services and I served a year and a half training and then about a year and a half overseas in India. After that year and a half, a small number of us, four out of the whole group that had learned Chinese, were pulled back to London to teach in the subsequent Chinese classes.

This was 1945 and they thought that there were years of war ahead against the Japanese. And so they increased the number of people being trained for the three services. But they needed more teachers; so what they did was to bring back four of us who had done well in the first batch. So John Chinnery, who is now head of the department in Edinburgh, Cyril Birch who is at Berkeley, Harry Simon who is at Melbourne, and myself were brought back. And so for my last two years in the army I was teaching Chinese. The relevance of this is that this course was also at SOAS, although, because of bombing and everything SOAS was not a unit – it was scattered around London. But again we heard more about Firth then. I saw him but I don't know whether I ever actually met him at that time. I remember very well the first class that I had to teach in Chinese; it was a dictation I had to give to a group of very high-powered airforce officers.

Anyway, even at that time I still wasn't studying linguistics, but I was becoming aware that something like linguistics existed and that there was rather a good department of linguistics just down the street.

GK: *We've got two questions that follow up your comments – one is about language teaching and how that led into questions about linguistics, and one is about Chinese. First Michael, you've characterised yourself on numerous occasions as essentially an applied linguist who pursued linguistic theory in search of answers to questions posed by language teaching: teaching Chinese to English speakers and later in China teaching Russian and English to Chinese. Initially what was the nature of these questions and the teaching problems that posed them?*

MAKH: Well, I was brought back to England, actually on VE day. The first two years I was teaching Chinese. So the problems first arose in that and again I doubt whether I could have formulated them terribly clearly except for the need simply to understand the grammar and the structure of the language that I was teaching.

RH: *It was more like a realisation ""these things that I thought would work didn't work"".*

MAKH: Yes. I had to explain things and I had the advantage of teaching a language which isn't your own and which you've only fairly recently learned; so at least you've formulated some of these problems for yourself – some questions about the structure. I think I began with very straight-forward questions about the grammar because there were so many things in Chinese grammar which just simply weren't described at all and we had been told nothing about them because they just weren't within the scope of traditional grammars and existing grammars of Chinese. We just had to discover them for ourselves. Now I felt very well aware of these and wanted some way of studying them. So this was the first attraction to linguistics, before any other kind – the attraction of educational or pedagogical questions which arose in my mind.

GK: *Where did you get this consciousness about the problems of Chinese from? Had you been with Chinese people in India?*

MAKH: Well, I had just under two years as a student of Chinese. So first of all I got aware of the problems simply as a learner, making mistakes, and asking in the usual way, "why didn't this work?" – making the wrong generalisations the way that a learner does. But then during the time that I'd served in India, which was about twelve months, I was with the Chinese Intelligence Wing. It was largely counter-intelligence and most of the time it was working on Chinese with Chinese people, reading Chinese and talking quite a bit of it. We had been plunged into it, so we knew very well what we'd failed to learn.

GK: *Well perhaps we can go to the next question which is about China. Are we right in thinking that your first degree was in Chinese and your first linguistic work explored Mandarin? What was the nature of your work in China itself and how do you feel this influenced your early thinking about language?*

MAKH: This continues from what we were just talking about. I taught Chinese then for those two years while still in the army. It was particularly during that time that I became interested in Chinese studies generally. Then what happened was that Eve Edwards, who was the Professor of the Chinese department, and Walter Simon, who was then the Reader, felt they had these people who might be interested in studying the language properly. So they organised it in such a way that we taught our courses in the morning and we studied Chinese in the afternoon: all the Chinese courses given by the department for its students were scheduled in the afternoon.

Now at that time, you could specialise in either modern or classical Chinese. I was obviously interested in modern Chinese, so we did a lot of modern Chinese literature and what we could by way of conversation. When I came out of the army in 1947, I decided that I wanted to go on and study the language and the sensible thing to do seemed to be to go and do it in China. I didn't have a degree of course, because having been in the army you couldn't actually take the degree; but I'd done a lot of the work. Walter Simon happened to know the man who was acting as President of Peking University. Simon wrote to him to ask if he would take me on as a student and find me some way of earning a living – I thought I could go and teach English in a high school. In order to support myself I took my F.E.T.S.[4] grant. This was a grant for people whose education was interrupted by the war. Normally it meant you got your fees paid at university but I went to the Ministry of Education and applied to be given the grant so I could buy a ticket to China, which saved them a lot of money. So they accepted my request. I bought a ticket to China, turned up at Peking University and Simon's friend said, "Oh great, you start teaching next week in our English department". Of course, you know, I'd never taught any English before; but they were very desperate for speakers of English because, of course, English had been totally banned under the Japanese and most of their students were pretty well beginners. So, in 1947 I enrolled as a student in Peking University in the Chinese department and taught English in the English department. And in the Chinese department I went to everything that I could find – literature, classical Chinese and all – still not knowing what I wanted to do afterwards, except my idea was to prepare myself for the external London degree, because you could take the London degree anywhere in the world. You don't have to actually study there; you could take it as an external degree. So after one year in China I flew down to Nanking where the British Council was operating.

JRM: *What year was this?*

MAKH: 1948. They administered the London degree. It was exactly the same examination papers as the internal; it simply means that you don't have to have been enrolled. And so I took that degree after one year in China. It was in Modern Chinese – a combination of language and literature, including History of Chinese Literature from the year 1500 BC to the present day – that was in **one** paper. And there was one question that you knew you were going to get about a particular modern author, and you knew you were going to get one question which was 'Write about the author of your choice'. I'd in fact been to see my author, who was living and working in Shanghai at the time, and spent a couple of days with him; so I was very well prepared for that. At the time I had no idea whatever of going on to postgraduate studies. I took a job in China working for the Chinese Industrial Cooperative. It meant going up to a very remote part of northwest China where there were these little village cooperatives that were a kind of industrial base during the Second World War. These were about the only industrial production centres, because all the cities of course had been occupied by the Japanese. They were pretty well defunct by that time, killed off by inflation and civil war and so forth; but about three hundred and fifty of them were still going. They wanted publicity written for them in English in order to collect money in Australia, Britain and New Zealand.

So I went around with a young Chinese who was an accountant helping them to keep the books and I wrote publicity. I did this for about six months and then, in some very very small village up in northwest China, a letter arrived which had been chasing me around for about three months, saying I'd been given a scholarship for post-graduate study. I had not applied for it, but Professor Eve Edwards had seen my results and said "Let's apply for him". So she had applied for me for this government scholarship because they were very keen on making sure they had a few people qualified in these languages.

So anyway the letter said "Proceed back to Peking immediately", and the conditions were that I could spend two more years in China studying and then had to go back to England and do a higher degree. And I thought "Well, do I do this?" I thought that they probably won't ask me again if I turn it down, so I took it. And that meant getting back to Peking. This was difficult because I was way up in a little village miles outside any city in northwest China. I finally found a bus and it took me about five days to get to Lanzhou. Then I found an aeroplane and it got me back to Peking just before the communists occupied the airport; otherwise I would never have got back in.

So I re-enrolled at Peking University rather late, about the middle of November. Now it was really in that time that I decided to do linguistics. It was really a choice of language or literature in Chinese studies, so I said "Right, I want to do the language". I went to see the Professor of Linguistics at Peking University, who I had met before because I'd been to one of his courses. I had done a little bit on language. He took me on and started training me in historical linguistics and Sino-Tibetan studies. He was a marvellous man.

RH: *What was his name?*

MAKH: Luo Changpei, Professor Luo; he died in about 1957. He took me on and I really appreciated this. I wrote essays for him and studied with him. I also went to other seminars.

GK: *Small tutorials?*

MAKH: Yes, they were. I can't remember that there was anything like a graduate course; it was more tutorial type of work with groups.

JRM: *Had you done some linguistics back at SOAS?*

MAKH: No, actually not, none at all.

JRM: *This was the beginning?*

MAKH: This was absolutely the beginning of it, this study with Luo Changpei.

GK: *Was there an indigenous Chinese linguistics?*

MAKH: Yes there was. He knew it very well and it had a very strong tradition going back to the third or fourth centuries BC. However it didn't deal with grammar.

Since there's no morphology in Chinese, traditional Chinese linguists never go into grammar. There was a very strong and very abstract phonological tradition which goes back about two thousand years, and as well there was a lexicographical and encyclopedic tradition. There were these two traditions, yes, but not a grammatical one.

JRM: *What was the linguistic background of your teacher?*

MAKH: He had been trained in comparative historical linguistics.

JRM: *In China?*

MAKH: I can't remember exactly. I think it very likely that he would have been in Europe at some stage, but I can't remember where. Probably in Germany. Wang Li, my other teacher, had been trained in France; but I'm not sure about Luo Changpei. He certainly knew very well the comparative method as worked out in Historical Linguistics; but his own specialisation was in Sino-Tibetan studies. In fact, he was one of those that had worked on the reconstruction of early Chinese.

JRM: *Was there any influence of Sapir and the other American linguistics?*

MAKH: With Luo Changpei I didn't get into this at all; but it became clear to him after six months or so that I really wanted to work more in modern studies. My **own** idea had been to work on Chinese dialects. I was very interested in Chinese dialects and was beginning to know something about them. So he said "Well then you need to go and work in synchronic studies; you should go and work with my friend Wang Li". So I said "All right, thank you". I assumed he was across the street, but in fact, he was in Canton, a long way from Peking. What's worse, by that time Peking had been liberated because the Communists came in January 1949. This was about May and he was saying "You should go down to Canton". Canton had not yet been liberated and we didn't know how long it would take. But I decided to try to get into there because he'd told me about Wang Li's work; not only was he a grammarian but he was also trained at working on dialect research. He was doing a dialect survey of South China.

This was in May '49. So I did altogether about seven months with Luo Changpei. You couldn't travel down the country of course because there was very heavy fighting; actually the last big battles were in that very month. So I took a boat out to Korea and then another one down to Hong Kong and then got back in again to Canton which was still Nationalist. That got liberated again about two or three weeks after I got there. Anyway I went to see Wang Li.

Wang Li at that time was the Dean of the Faculty of Arts in Lingnan, which was a private university. He took me on and that was really where I got into linguistics, through dialect studies. We did basic dialectology, field work methods, and a lot of phonetics, thank goodness. I am deeply indebted to Wang Li for having really made me work at the phonetics and phonology and also sociolinguistics – the whole notion of language in social and cultural context. All those were his contributions.

JRM: *What kind of linguist was he? Did he have a more modern, synchronic background?*

MAKH: Yes, he had actually been trained in France. His phonetics was very good. He had been trained by very fine French phoneticians, but his background in grammar was essentially Jespersen. He was very interested in Jespersen's work and had applied Jespersen's notions to Chinese. In fact his first grammar of Chinese was very strongly influenced by Jespersen's ideas.

GK: *You said just now that the linguistics you studied with Wang Li included sociolinguistics. Can you say something about how he talked about the area of language and social context?*

MAKH: There was an input from different places by this time. During this period I had become gradually and indirectly aware of some of Firth's notions and while in Canton, I think, I had actually read something of his – what finally came out as his paper 'Personality and Language in Society' (Firth 1950). I can't remember how I'd got hold of it. It might have been through Wang Li. Some way or other I'd got some of Firth's ideas and I think Wang Li himself knew some of Firth's work. That was one input. Then secondly, of course, for political reasons, I had become very interested in Russian scholarship. Again, this had started already in London between 1945 and 1947, when I went to study Russian. I had also heard of the Marr school of linguistics. I had read quite a bit of that as well as Prague Linguistics looking at the development of national languages, language policy and development of standard languages.

Slavonic linguistics generally has always interested itself in issues such as the development of literary languages and national languages. So that was the second input. So there was the Firthian input and there was that one; and then Wang Li himself as a dialectologist was interested primarily in regional dialects, but was also interested in changing dialect patterns and the social background to these, the spread of the standard language in China, areas of contact between different dialects and the social patterns that went with them. So there were those three parts to it.

GK: *So although you got your first interest in linguistics in China, as you have just described, it was largely a kind of European linguistics, although perhaps inflected in particular ways?*

MAKH: Well it was fairly mixed because of all the Chinese linguists, Wang Li was the one who knew most about the Chinese tradition. One of the things that I read and was very much influenced by at the time was his own *History of Chinese Phonology*, which is a marvellous book. It was so simple, but so very scholarly. He showed how Chinese phonology had developed from the first century of the era through to the tenth century and how it had developed as an indigenous science and then been influenced by the Indian scholarship which came into China round about the seventh century AD. So there **was** very much a Chinese and even an Indian input. Of course Firth then continued that interest later on – he was very interested in Indian linguistics. But through Wang Li I knew something about Indian phonology and quite a lot about the origins of Chinese phonology and a little bit about the Chinese lexicographic tradition. Then on the European side there was the historical linguistics that I got from Luo Changpei and the Marrist stuff that I was reading myself. I remember in fact writing a long essay for Wang Li that year about convergence versus divergence as a model of linguistic history, because the Marrist position was that the traditional view of the history of languages as essentially divergence from a common ancestor was totally wrong. He argued that the processes should be seen much more as one of convergence.

JRM: *How long were you in Canton?*

MAKH: A year – well, I arrived in September and left the following May, so essentially a sort of academic year.

JRM: *Was your own research taking some sort of direction at that time?*

MAKH: Yes, it was actually dialect field work because Wang Li was doing a survey of the dialects of the Pearl River delta, which are essentially varieties of Cantonese. He had a little group of research students, working on this. Now I used it as a way of getting training in dialect field work in phonology; but I wrote my own questionnaire for a grammar survey because I was more interested in the grammar. I don't know if I've still got it but it concerned a large number of sentences in standard Cantonese because that was the local regional standard. Wang Li couldn't go out and do this survey work in the villages because there was just too much chaos all around; so he had to work with students who were natives of all the small towns and villages in the different areas. They had their own village dialect as well as city Cantonese. So we got their phonology, and he got me to do the tones. He said I was the best of the group on actually hearing the tones. Apart from that I wasn't doing phonology.

I wrote this questionnaire with a large number of sentences and I got them to give me the versions of these sentences in their own local dialects. When I went back to England I tried to get that accepted as a Ph.D. subject but they wouldn't have it – it was too modern. I was very cut up about that.

RH: *So what happened to all that data?*

MAKH: It's lying around somewhere; but I couldn't interpret it now I don't think. It's all written in local characters.

JRM: *So you were already a grammarian even by that stage.*

MAKH: I was really very fascinated by the differences between Mandarin and Cantonese grammar and then how these very local dialects differed in their grammar from the Cantonese. It was very interesting.

GK: *Do you think your interest in lexis and grammar comes in some way from Chinese traditions in linguistic scholarship?*

MAKH: I don't think so, because in those days, there **wasn't** a tradition unless you want to say that I was interested precisely because there wasn't anything there and therefore it had to be filled. But I don't think so. I think I was always basically interested in grammar.

GK: *What about the lexical part?*

MAKH: Well, there is one point which hadn't occurred to me before. The earliest Chinese work of lexical scholarship is in fact a word list from about 250 BC, which is a thesaurus, and I was always interested in the thesaurus as a tool of lexicography. I have no idea whether there is any connection between those two. It had nineteen different topic headings and lists the difficult words under those headings.

That year with Wang Li was just marvellous. He died recently, just in May – just within the last month. I saw him a couple of years ago – he was a marvellous man and very kind.

Now the terms of the scholarship then were that I went back to England to take the degree and I assumed that I was going to be in London and would be able to study with Firth. So I finished what I could do with Wang Li, collected all this stuff that I'd got from the dialect work, which I was hoping to work on for a Ph.D. I was hoping to do this under Firth while teaching in the Chinese department at SOAS, which was laid on. But I got witch-hunted out of that.

GK: *Out of where?*

MAKH: Out of the SOAS, totally – both the Chinese department and the linguistics department.

RH: *Why?*

MAKH: Well that's another story. I had left England in 1947 before the Berlin Wall; I came back to England in 1950 at the height of McCarthyism, which was very strong in England.

They asked me when I went for the job at SOAS whether I was a member of the Communist Party. I said "No", which I wasn't. Then they asked would I undertake that I would not become a member of the Communist Party. I said "No, I wouldn't"[5]. So I didn't get the job. When I then asked the person who had questioned me about that afterwards whether that was the reason, he said "Political considerations were not absent". I thought this was the classic answer of all time. So the point is that I got shunted off to Cambridge.

Cambridge luckily always resisted any McCarthyist pressures. The great advantage of being a medieval foundation of that kind is that you can get away with a lot more. SOAS was always in any case a very political institution because that's where the Foreign Office trained its diplomats. So I suppose SOAS was probably one of the sensitive places that was particularly hit by McCarthyism. The point is that I had the scholarship and what they did was to transfer it to Cambridge.

JRM: *Chinese?*

MAKH: The Chinese department at Cambridge. Now that was alright in one sense; the man in charge was a very nice man, a Czech, Gustav Haloun, who was a philologist of the old school. But there was no modern Chinese at Cambridge at all; it was all classical. I said "Well, look, I wouldn't mind going to Cambridge but I'm not going to do classical Chinese".

JRM: *How disappointing was this for you? You had particularly wanted to study with Firth.*

MAKH: It was very disappointing because I wanted to study with Firth and I wanted to work on my dialect material. The price of going to Cambridge was that we agreed on the *Secret History*[6] as a compromise. The text and that idea came from Haloun. He said, "Well all right, you want to work in Mandarin. This is the earliest text in the Mandarin dialect: *The Secret History of the Mongols.*" It's a traditional Mongolian biography of Genghis Khan with mythological origins. The reason it was in Mandarin was that it was translated into Chinese to be used as a textbook for Chinese civil servants who had to learn Mongolian. When the Mongols occupied China they insisted that all the civil service was done in Mongolian, which the Chinese of course hated. And so the Mongols did this as a textbook, which is the reason why the text is not in literary Chinese. It wasn't meant to be a work of literature. It was meant as a textbook for learning Mongolian. This meant that it gives you insight into the origin of modern Mandarin, so it was a reasonable compromise.

My supervisor was Haloun but I was negotiating with him to be allowed to go up to London to study with Firth, who had agreed to take me on for a casual supervision. Then Haloun died quite suddenly, so I had to go on negotiating myself. I think I just went to see Firth at that time, and asked if he would accept to be my supervisor. So what happened then was that Firth became my total supervisor, although the degree was still in Cambridge. So I had a season ticket on the train from Cambridge to London. And then, of course, was able to get into –

JRM: *Devious ways he finds to ride on trains!*

MAKH: Yes, that's when I started finding you could work on trains.

RH: *But this is extraordinary. They didn't allow you to stay at SOAS because you wouldn't give an undertaking not to enlist in the Communist Party; and then you still came back, and you were still on the premises.*

MAKH: Yes, but I wasn't teaching. That's what they were scared of! I was not in a position to subvert.

GK: *So your first contact with Firth had been fortuitous but when you returned from China you actually chose to study with him in London. What prompted your interest in his framework and how did you go about extending his ideas so that they could be applied to Chinese, and later to English, grammar?*

RH: *That's asking the entire history.*

MAKH: "Interested in his framework". Okay. From the start when I became gradually aware of his ideas, particularly I think during that year with Wang Li, I felt very sympathetic. It seemed to me that he was saying things about language that made sense in terms of my own experience and my own interests, and I just wanted to explore those ideas further. My main concern was just to learn from him and I managed to organise it so that he took me on officially as a student. What I got of course from him was enormous, both in terms of general philosophical background and insight into language. But I didn't get a model of grammar because, as you know, Firth himself was interested in the phonology, semantics and context. He had very little to say about grammar, although he certainly considered his basic system/structure approach was as valid in grammar as it was in phonology[7]. My problem then, as it seemed to me, was how to develop system/structure theory so that it became a way of talking about the language of the *Secret History*. Now the text was a corpus – for Firth it was a text and that was fine. That meant it had its own history and had to be contextualised and recontextualised and so forth. It was also **closed**, in the sense that you couldn't go out and get anymore. This was 14th century Mandarin and that was it. There wasn't any more. So you treated it as it was. I was not yet, of course, aware enough to be able to ask questions about what it meant to consider it just as a text as distinct from considering it as an instance of some underlying system. But I tried to work out the notions of system and structure on the basis of what I read and what I got from Firth in phonology.

JRM: *Was W. S. Allen working on applying Firth's ideas to grammar in this period too?*

MAKH: Yes, although I didn't actually get to know him very well. The person who helped me most other than Firth at that stage was Robins. In fact Firth got Robins to do some of the supervisions for him. I used to write essays for Robins and so forth. Robins was terribly nice and very helpful. But I didn't know Allen very well.

JRM: *Robins was on staff there?*

MAKH: Yes.

JRM: *Allen was also?*

MAKH: Allen was, yes. All that generation was there. Of course some were still students.

JRM: *When did you have a chance to see 'System and Structure in the Abaza verbal complex' (Allen 1956)?*

MAKH: That was not until after I finished my thesis.

JRM: *So you really had to do this all on your own?*

MAKH: Yes.

RH: *When **did** you finish the thesis?*

MAKH: At four o'clock on the last day after the last extension, I can tell you that. It was an hour before they closed the offices and it was the 31st of December. I can remember that, and it would have been in 1954.

JRM: *So you spent three years in Cambridge.*

MAKH: Four years, because it was 1950 when I moved to Cambridge.

JRM: *And Robins, had he been thinking of applying system/structure theory to grammar?*

MAKH: No, I don't think so. He was more interested in phonological applications. I was very much on my own at that. It wasn't that there wasn't any place for the grammar for Firth. He would introduce examples in his lectures – for instance working through the forms of the German definite article as a way into raising a whole lot of interesting grammatical problems. And he was developing, at that time, the notion of colligation, which actually Harry Simon labelled for him. But it was never very much developed so that it's not terribly clear what Firth was ever planning to do with it; but it was the beginnings of thinking about grammar.

GK: *Who were the other students at that time?*

MAKH: I'm not sure which year different ones were there but certainly listening to Firth lectures at different times during this period were, for example, Frank Palmer and Bill Jones who were themselves just getting onto the staff of that department, Bursill-Hall who then went to Canada. Mitchell was already on the staff, as were Robins, Allen, Cornochan and Eileen Whiteley. I also went to other lectures when I could – to Eileen Whitely for example and to Eugenie Henderson. I got a lot of phonetics from them as well as other things. Eileen Whitely never wrote anything, but she just had a fantastically broad range of interests. She was one of the people who really could have developed Firth's notions, especially in the direction of text – in a semantic direction. She was very very good.

GK: *Could we return to that question about how you went about extending Firth's ideas so that they could be applied to the grammar of a language?*

MAKH: I tried to understand, not always very successfully, the key notions that could be interpreted at a general enough level so that they could be applied to grammar as well as to phonology. For example the concept of prosody – the notion that syntagmatic relations pervaded items of differing extent. Firth as you know was concerned that you didn't start and end with phonemes, and so forth. Rather you looked over the larger patterns and then residual effects, so to speak, were handled at the smaller segments. Now I tried to apply that idea to grammar, so I began at the top. That's one very clear example, using a kind of top-down approach, beginning with what I could recognise as the highest clearly defined unit in the text, a clause, and then gradually working down. Then another basic concept, of course, was the system/structure notion, which I found very difficult – especially expressions like systems giving value to the elements of structure.

I tried to set up structures in a framework that was formal in the sense that you were not relying on some kind of vague conceptual label. For example, it was possible in Chinese grammar to set up categories of noun and verb on distributional grounds. These then gave you a basis for labelling elements in the structure of the clause.

RH: *How important was the idea of exponence for Firth?*

MAKH: Well, it was very important. You see, there are a number of ways in which I built on his ideas that he certainly wouldn't have followed, as he made clear to me. I got on well with him and he didn't like people who weren't prepared to argue with him. But of course the cost of this was that I would often be seizing on things that he'd done and, from his point of view, **mis**interpreting them in some ways, in order to try and do something with them. Exponence would be one example of this. Firth had a long running argument with Allen in 1954–1956 about the nature of exponence and about the relation between the levels and exponence. As far as Firth was concerned the levels (the phonetics, the phonology, the morphology, and the grammar or whatever) were not stratified but were rather side-by-side, each directly relatable to its exponence. So you didn't go through phonology, so to speak, to get to the grammar. On this point Allen disagreed about the nature of this pattern. As far as Firth was concerned, there was absolutely nothing wrong with using the same bit of datum over again in setting up patterns of different strata, whereas Allen seemed to say "Well, if you'd built this particular feature in to your phonetic interpretation, you couldn't use it again in the phonology". So there were differences of this kind in the way they worked out this notion, and Allen's, in fact, was the more stratified view, although I don't think he expressed it like that. I did **not** follow Firth on that because I just couldn't see any way that you could get the notion of realisation into the grammar except by stratifying (although I didn't use the term realisation then).

So exponence for me became this kind of chained relationship, which it was not for Firth.

Grammatical theory

GK: *We would like to ask you about the grammar and our first question is about the focus on system. We think you are a great relativist and unusually modest about the claims you make for systemic theory. Your theory gives greater prominence to paradigmatic relations than any other. What are the strengths and weaknesses of this focus?*

MAKH: Well, I didn't start out that way of course. Because that links back to what we were saying about Firth. As you know, for Firth, there was no priority between system and structure – they were mutually defining. Indeed, if anything, in the context of linguistics of the time, his emphasis was on the importance of syntagmatic relations.

So in a sense, I'm going against Firth. Now why was this? Firth himself didn't really believe in "The System" in the large sense at all. His interest was not in the potential but in the typical actual. Now this meant that for him, in fact, the priority was to structure over system – not in the structuralist sense of language as an inventory of structures, but in the sense that, as he put it, the system is defined by its environment and its environment is essentially structural.

So in a sense, the larger environment is the syntagmatic one. Now trying to work this out in Chinese grammar generally, I felt that I needed to be able to create the environment that was needed. The environment had to be set up in order for the general framework of the grammatical categories to make sense. But this environment seemed to me ultimately to have to be a paradigmatic one. That took a lot of steps – say 1962 when I was writing 'Syntax and the Consumer' (Halliday 1964), or 1963, when I was doing the 'laundry card grammars'[8] in Edinburgh. It was certainly influenced by other considerations as well. For example, I always had the feeling that I was never happy with what I could say about one little bit of the grammar if I didn't see how it fitted in with the whole picture. So I was quite different from Firth for whom there was no whole picture. I mean he just wasn't interested. Now I couldn't work in that framework. I wanted a kind of comprehensive notion of the grammar. And this was the time when I was first struggling with Hjelmslev, trying to build that in.

By various steps, I came to feel that the only way to do this was to represent the whole thing as potential – as a set of options. And this was certainly influenced by my own gut feeling of what I call 'language as a resource' – in other words, language was a mode of life, if you like, which could be represented **best** as a huge network of options. So that kind of came together with the notion that it had to be the system rather than the structure that was given priority.

GK: *How do you see that now?*

MAKH: Well, in an important sense I would think that there are a lot of purposes now for which it's important. Just to mention one of them, I think that in order to crack the code, as a probabilistic system, we have to start with a paradigmatic model. It doesn't make sense otherwise. But, of course, it does beg a number of questions in a sense – this is something we often talk about. The great problem with the system is that it is a very static form of representation. It freezes the whole thing, and then you have to introduce the dynamic in the form of paths through the system. Your problem then is to show how the actual process of making paths through the system changes the system.

This is crucial to the understanding of ontogenesis, phylogenesis – any kind of history. So I think I shall continue within that framework because that's the one I'm familiar with and I've not enough time to start re-thinking it.

GK: *In the era of post-structuralism Firth seems more contemporary than you. I mean I already have problems with post-structuralism and the dissolution of system, but that is the contemporary flavour of thinking about things.*

MAKH: I often get the feeling that all these -isms, wherever they raise their head, want to go too far either in this direction or in the other direction. In practice it is just not possible to have systems without the product of those systems, which are the structures; which means that the structures must be there to deduce the system. How far do we go back in this kind of argument? Either you're forced to the point where you say the entire system **is, was, has always been,** or you have to say that in some sense, structure, which is a constraining name for process, is where it all begins. Because otherwise you can't have systems.

I would comment that these things obviously switch between extremes. There is an important sense in which you can deconstruct the system, as it were; you can remove it from your bag of tools. But you have to get it back again, if only because you can't deconstruct something if it isn't there; so there's no meaning in doing so. I think we are now at a stage where we are realising that the models we have to look at for systems are not solely in the areas this kind of post-structuralist thinking is reacting to. Their critique has almost become irrelevant, I think, in the light of much more general developments in modern scientific thinking, which really transcend the differences between human and non-human systems. Once you start looking at systems in this sense, you have to have the concepts. Take for example Jay Lemke's work (e.g. 1995) in dynamic open systems. This is the sort of thing that I find interesting as a way of looking at language. And the sort of work that's being done in physics as well is totally annihilating the difference between human systems and sub-atomic systems.

GK: *We wanted to ask you about strengths **and** weaknesses. Do you see any weaknesses in that greater focus on system rather than structure?*

MAKH: Well, one I've mentioned is that it's overly synoptic[9]. I mean it's static. Also there is the danger of its pushing the system too far apart from process/text. I mean I've tried to avoid doing that. It's one of the things that Firth so strongly objected to in Saussure – the dichotomy of langue and parole which prevents you from seeing that langue is simply a construct of parole. I would agree with that and I think that there is a danger of using system as a tool for thinking with and forcing a kind of dichotomy between the system and the text. I think those two are dangers really.

GK: *We've got a question about function: since the late sixties, systemic grammar has always been for you "systemic **functional** grammar". What is the relationship between different concepts of function (for instance 'grammatical function', 'meta-functional' component, and the natural relation you propose between metafunction and register) that you use? And just how critical is their place in your model?*

MAKH: I think they're important and I think they're closely related. I have usually felt that the best way of demonstrating this relationship is developmentally because you can actually see, if you follow through the development of a mother tongue (Halliday 1975), how the system evolves in functional terms. In the beginning, function equals use, so that there is a little set of signs which relate to a simple theory, on the part of the infant, that semiosis does certain things in life. You can then watch language evolving in the child in this context.

So the metafunctions are in my view, simply, the initial functions which have been reinterpreted through two steps. The first involves generalisation: initial functions become macro-functions, which are groupings which determine structure. Then macro-functions become metafunctions: modes whereby the linguistic semiotic interfaces with contexts. So I see this as very much homogeneous. The notion of the context plane as something natural is part of the same picture.

GK: *Can you just expand on that last phrase?*

MAKH: If language is evolved as a way of constructing reality – then it is to be predicted that the forms of organisation of language will in themselves carry a model of that reality. This means that as well as being a tool, language will also be metaphor for reality. In other words, the patterns of language will themselves carry this image, if you like. This is what I would understand by talking about a 'natural' grammar.

RH: *Would you say that's another way of saying that reality is the product of semiosis?*

MAKH: Yes.

RH: *And in that sense the question of a 'natural' relation between the grammar and the reality that it constructs has to be either answered 'yes' or it becomes a meaningless question?*

MAKH: Okay. Right. I mean that reality has to be constructed, so it's another level of semiosis. So it's inevitable, in a sense, that the semiotic that you use to construct it will, in some sense, replicate that which you are constructing with it, since it's all part of the same process. I want to be rather cautious on this. I think we're in a phase at the moment where we are emphasizing this point. We've gone against naive realisms which assume that there is something out there that is given and that what we have to do is to mirror it in some sense, which is certainly where I started from. And we've kind of moved into a phase of thinking again, the opposite extreme so to speak. We are now emphasising, as you were saying, the fact that it all has to be constructed. It is, in fact, a many levelled semiotic process. And that, in a sense, is an important corrective to naive realism.

JRM: *I was interested in the grammatical functions themselves, Subject, Theme and so on. You use functions and class labels in your model. How crucial is that to this functionalism idea, and this idea of a natural grammar.*

MAKH: It's part of the picture. In order for the system to work with some kind of output, in other words to end up as speech sounds, signals or writing on whatever, there has to be this re-coding involved in it. The fact that there has to be this re-coding means that there must be a non-identity between functions and classes; otherwise you wouldn't need to re-code: you could do the lot at one level. So somewhere or another you've got to be able to talk about this. Now it seems to me then you have to decide in finding ways of interpreting language how you're going to do this. An obvious example would be formal systems. If the main priority is representing language as a formal system, then presumably you'll prefer a kind of labelling in which you have class labels and conventions for deriving functions from them. For my own part, I prefer theories to be extravagant and labelling systems to be extravagant. As a tool for thinking with, I've always found it useful to separate function and class and build that amount of redundancy into the discourse about language. It then becomes possible to operate with sets of functional labels in the grammar, things like Theme and Subject and so forth which, in turn, enable you to make the links outside. So I think it is a useful and important part of the whole process. There is a reason for wanting to separate these two, although if you focused on any one specific goal, as distinct from trying to keep it all into focus at the same time, you could do without it. And I think I would say this as a general truth. There's very little in what I've done, or what is done in systemic theory if you like, that couldn't be done more economically in some other way if that was all you were interested in doing; and, I suppose, what I've always been concerned with is to work on little bits in a way which I then don't have to abandon and re-work when I want to build them into some general picture.

GK: *I think this relates a bit to what we were saying earlier where you were talking about system and structure. The question is: In your model the relation between various components, between strata, between ranks, between function and class, between grammar and lexis, is handled through the concept of realisation. This involves, in English at least, setting up a Token/Value structure with the component closer to expression substance as Token and the component closer to content substance as Value. This gives the Value component a meaning of temporal priority, apparent agentivity, greater abstraction, greater depth and so forth. Is what English does to this concept, in fact, what you mean by it?*

RH: *In raising this question we were trying to build in the informal kind of discussions we've been having recently on realisation. You've argued very strongly that when we say 'x realises y' then, in some sense, because of the structure or whatever, you get a pre-existence postulate there which you would like to deny. This seems to me a very important point. To my way of thinking it also links ultimately to system and structure, to the langue and parole question, and is altogether the most central concept in the whole theory.*

MAKH: I'm with you. It is absolutely fundamental. Maybe we could have a workshop, an International Systemic Workshop, just on realisation. That would be nice.

You know, the problem is you can't talk about it in English. Not only the temporal priority but of course the agentive priority gets in the way. I mean the Agent **is** the Token. According to the grammar of English it's the Token that does the work so to speak. I started with a fairly simple notion of something 'out there' to be realised through the code. It's, again I think, something that we have to think of in the light of recent thinking about the universe we live in as an information system. And what English does to the concept, I think, is a very important clue. I mean, what any language does to the concept has to be taken as a very important clue, a way of thinking about it. And again it's at this point that the grammar as a tool for thinking about other things becomes crucial. I think linguistics has got to accept its responsibility now, as being **the** core science. In a sense it has to replace physics as the leading science[10].

RH: *There is another problem here. If you think in terms of languages that in their structure are very very different from Indo-European languages, well then you might expand this discussion. So in some sense to me the problem becomes circular. We perceive that there is this problem for expressing the relation of realisation of structure of English, and yet we cannot yet bring evidence from any other language that it could be otherwise, because by our way of talking, we will impose a pattern on that language.*

MAKH: In a sense it's one of these things that probably has to be done before it's too late. What happens in practice is that people tend to borrow English (or whatever the international language is) ways of talking about things, and you want to know how they would develop otherwise.

GK: *We have a question which is around that point of grammar and linguistics and the language shaping both the linguistics and the theory – what you think of as grammar symbolising reality. Following from the point about realisation that we made in our earlier question, to what extent have the meanings available in English or Chinese consciously or unconsciously shaped your model of language?*

MAKH: Let me answer that quite quickly. I'm sure they have and I've tried to make it conscious. It's impossible that they couldn't so I have tried to be conscious that they **are** shaping it when thinking about it. One of the things I regret most is never having been able to learn another totally different language. I made two attempts to come to Australia in my life, one in 1954 and one in 1964, and these were with a plan to work on Australian Aboriginal languages. I wish that I knew enough to get under the skin of a language which is very much more different in its construction of reality.

JRM: *Chinese and English weren't different enough?*

MAKH: Not really. They are different in interesting and important ways but they both have a long written tradition.

GK: *In terms of that question about realisation, it would be nice to have a language that was far more verbal and not written, to understand how people might think about that.*

RH: *Yes. I think if one did this kind of study one would find that writing does another thing – it objectifies in a way that the oral tradition doesn't so that what you would get would be more like myths as metaphor for certain sorts of beliefs, certain sorts of perceptions, instead of this explicit analysis where the concepts are defined, placed in relation to each other clearly, and then you go and talk about their interrelations. That's the way it happens in languages that don't have a literary tradition.*

MAKH: That's also why we're still stuck with Whorf. I don't mean by that that I want to give up Whorf, as you know; but what I mean by that is we've got nothing else yet. It's easy enough to get the mythologies, the things at that semiotic level, if you like. Now as you move into the grammar what happens is that nearly everyone working on the grammar in these languages is a universalist. So of course, they're interested in making them all look alike; and so you're left with Whorf. And it's in the grammar, you see, that I want to find new models.

JRM: *What about, say, between English and Chinese. I mean, can you point to the parts of your model where it would have been different if you hadn't known Chinese?*

MAKH: It's very hard to say of course. I suppose that one of the things that is absolutely critical has been that for me grammar has always been syntax, since Chinese has no morphology. I cracked the Chinese code first. There are other things, yes, for example temporal categories.

GK: *What about that point you made earlier about prosody?*

MAKH: Yes – that, of course, could have come from Firthian phonology without necessarily going through Chinese, although the Chinese helped. But it was Chinese phonology at the time of course.

GK: *And tone?*

MAKH: That's true. That's certainly true. Then there's the point of syntax. Then I think there are certain special features about Chinese grammar which **did** affect my thinking. There was something that Jeff Ellis and I wrote many years ago, which I must see if I still have, because it wasn't a bad article. It was on temporal categories in the modern Chinese verb. It was important because, you see, it was a non-tense language. Jeff was extremely well informed about aspect as he had started off in Slavonic and he had studied aspect systems round the world. So Chinese helped me to think about time relations in a non-tense sort of a way – the Chinese system of phases has a clear grammatical distinction between a kind of conative and the successive; the verb essentially doesn't mean you do something so much as you try to do it. It does not necessarily imply that you succeed. Now I don't read a naive cultural interpretation into that but it forces you to think differently about the grammar.

JRM: *Would the lack of morphology in Chinese have been something that pushed into paradigmatics?*

MAKH: Okay, yes. That's a good point. I mean your paradigms have to be syntactic. You can't start with a word and paradigm approach. There are no word paradigms and one of my main strategies in working on Chinese was setting up syntactic paradigms. They were there already in that article in 1956 on Chinese grammar.

GK: *A question about choice. Although you model language in terms of choice, in many respects this choice is almost never free. What is the place of your position on the probabilistic nature of linguistic systems in modelling these constraints?*

MAKH: I have always thought of language, the language system, as essentially probabilistic. You have no idea how that has been characterised as absolutely absurd, and publicly ridiculed by Chomsky in that famous lecture in 1964[11]. In any case, one point at a very simple level is that nobody is ever upset by being told that they are going to use the word *the* more often than they're going to use the word *noun*. But they get terribly upset by being told that they're going to use the active more often than the passive. Now **why** is that? We know of course that we have well developed intuitions about the frequencies of a word – and can bring those to the surface. But we can't bring them to the surface about grammar; and in fact all that is doing is just showing that, as always, the grammatical end of the lexicogrammar continuum is very much deeper in the (gut) and it's much more threatening to have to bring it out. But it's there. The question then of what this actually means in terms of the nature of the system is extraordinarily complex and it really does need a lot of thinking and writing up, exploring what it means in terms of real understanding of the nature of probability and statistical systems and so on. Again, what **I** want to do is try to bring probability into the context of a general conception of systems[12], dynamic open systems, of what this means in terms of physical systems. It has to be seen in that light as I was saying before.

JRM: *This seems to be something quite critical in your theory, this idea of probabilistic systems, especially in terms of not losing sight of the text and the way in which the text feeds back into the system. You have to view text as passes through the systems which are facilitating.*

MAKH: I would agree with this and you **have** to have this notion in order to show how the system shapes the text anyway. The pass through the system in fact changes the system just as every morning if you turn on your radio they will tell you that the temperature is ten degrees and that's one below average so to speak; but **that** has changed the average. So everytime you talk, everytime you produce a text, you have of course changed the system.

Language in education

GK: *The next section is on language development and education. Our first question is about language in education. You've been the driving force behind language education movements in both Britain and Australia. What is it about language and education that makes their integration so important to you?*

MAKH: Well, I come from a family of teachers so I suppose that the whole educational process has always been of interest; and I had my own time as a language teacher. I've always been, if you like, motivated in working on language by the conviction that this had some practical value, and that education was the most accessible in a sense. There are a lot of other applications. Obviously an important one is clinical. But I don't know anything about that, and in any case we were a long way[13] from actually getting linguists working together with pathologists. But it seemed in the late fifties that people were ready to think about language in education.

My first position in linguistics was in the English department at Edinburgh; so my students were mainly graduates in English. Most of them went out to be teachers in the Scottish system. We would encourage them to come back and talk about their experiences in schools after leaving the department. In large measure, once we'd built in the linguistics, they came back and said: "That was what was interesting. That was what we found useful." So we set up this interaction with the teachers: Ian Catford, John Sinclair, Peter Strevens and myself used to work with groups of teachers. I used to go over to Glasgow every Saturday and spend the day with two groups of teachers.

Each of us had different groups of teachers that we used to work with. Now this was when I came in to mother-tongue education, because these were English teachers in the Scottish schools. It kind of reinforced my feeling that we really needed an input from linguistics.

Then when I moved to London in 1963, the first thing I did was to set up this project with Nuffield money, which became the School Council Project in Linguistics in English Teaching[14], which was producing *Breakthrough to Literacy* (see Mackay et al. 1970).

RH: *But behind this, at a deeper level, didn't you have a feeling that linguistics is a mode of action, that linguistics is for doing rather than just intellectualising?*

MAKH: Yes, very much. I don't really separate the two in any sense at all. I've always seen it like this. My problem has always been that teachers want results too quickly. In fact the reason why we have to work in this field as academics is that we have a longer term perspective. We can say: "You've got to go back and do so much more fundamental work. You've got to back off for a bit. You can't expect results by next Tuesday". And that's where linguistics comes in. It's a mode of action but it's a mode of longer term action, if you like. You **have** to have the luxury of being able to look further into the future.

GK: *We have a question about applied linguistics as a mode of action. Our question asks whether this is an expression of your political beliefs. We have a little aside here which asks whether, like Chomsky, you see linguistics and politics as unrelated spheres and, if not, how it is that you are able to make as much use as you have of Firth's ideas when your politics and his were far apart.*

MAKH: That is an absolutely fascinating question. You'll have to stop me because I'd love to go for two hours about that. No, I do not see my linguistics and politics as separate. I see them as very closely related. To me it's very much been part of this backing-off movement. In other words, I started off when I got back to Cambridge being very politically active and trying to combine the role of being a graduate student in linguistics with being active in the local Communist Party, setting up a Britain-China Friendship Association and all that. But even then there were only 24 hours in the day, and the two came to clash. I had to decide which I was better at, and I thought: "Well, I don't know. Probably there are more people who can do the political spade-work". But there's a more important point than that. What worried me at the time was the search for a Marxist linguistics.

There was a lot of things going on at the time. There was the Marrist school; there was the Pravda bust-up in 1950; there were current developments in English Marxism and things of this kind. Later on came the New Left, of course. But it seemed to me that any attempts to think politically about language and develop a Marxist linguistics were far too crude. They involved almost closing your eyes to what you actually knew about language in order to say things. My feeling was we should not. Of course the cost of doing this is that you may have to cease to be a Marxist, at least in a sense in which anyone would recognise you as one, in order to go away for fifty years and to really do some work and do some thinking. But you're not really abandoning the political perspective. You're simply saying that in order to think politically about something as complicated as language, you've got to take a lot longer. You've got to do a lot of work. And you've got to run the risk of forgetting that what you are doing is political. Because if you force that too much to the forefront your work will always remain at the surface; it will always be something for which you expect to have an immediate application in terms of struggle. You **can't** do that in the long run. You're going to pay the price that you may achieve something that's going to be useful for two weeks or two years and then it'll be forgotten.

I always wanted to see what I was going towards as, in the **long** run, a Marxist linguistics – towards working on language in the political context. But I felt that, in order to **do** that, you really had to back off and go far more deeply into the nature of language.

JRM: *You were ready then for teachers' reactions to your ideas? It's the same problem of distancing.*

MAKH: Yes, it is. Now with Firth, you see, it is very interesting because Firth was right at the other end of the political spectrum. There was in fact another interesting occasion when I went to be interviewed by him for a job at SOAS (not the same as the first one, different in a very interesting way, although with exactly the same result).

It was after this interview in fact that Firth said: "Of course you'd label me a bourgeois linguist". And I said: "I think you're a Marxist", and he laughed at me. It seemed to me that, in fact, the ways in which Firth was looking at language, putting it in its social context, were in no way in conflict with what seemed to me to be a political approach. So that it seemed to me that in taking what I did from Firth, I was not separating the linguistic from the political. It seemed to me rather that most of his thinking was such that I could see it perfectly compatible with, indeed a rather necessary step towards, what I understand as a Marxist linguistics.

GK: *So Firth must have been, at some level, confused – to have contradictions in...*

MAKH: Does that necessarily follow?

RH: *I don't think people's ideologies are coherent.*

MAKH: No, that's certainly true.

RH: *I don't think they are. I think Firth had this ideology about language, its role in society, about its role in forming people and all that. On the other hand he also had this very strong authoritarian attitude towards institutions and their maintenance and things.*

GK: *A question which relates to all of that – theory out of practice. To what extent has your commitment to applied linguistics influenced your model? And how has it influenced the research that you've pursued?*

MAKH: Well it's influenced it, of course, in one sense by making sure that I never had time to do much thinking about it. Yes, I think it's influenced it. It's hard to say exactly how. I mean, I've always **consciously** tried to feed back into thinking about language what came from, say, the experience of working with teachers. The

Breakthrough materials would be one case in point. I have always tried consciously to build teachers' resources into my own thinking about language; David Mackay for example, made an input with observations on children's language learning in an educational context. Then, of course, through Basil Bernstein's[15] research and Ruqaiya's part in his unit, there was another source of input from what, in the broadest sense, is a kind of applied linguistics.

RH: *Can I stray from the point here? It seems to me that talking to the teachers and the need of making your linguistics accessible to the pedagogical circle had a different influence on your work from that which say, for instance, contact with Bernstein's unit might have had. The first one forced you to write in a way that would make your material accessible. In other words, I do not see that the shape of the theory, the categories as such, got terribly shaped by that, (though it is always a bit doubtful to make these kind of divisions). On the other hand I feel that contact with Bernstein's work had an effect of a slightly different kind in that it really fed right into theoretical thinking.*

MAKH: That is definitely true. I wasn't prepared to shift because of teachers in what seemed to me to be short term directions just because it seemed to be something that would be a payoff in class and so on. So it was more in the form of presentation. But I think there was some input from educational applications.

GK: *Most of your work has been in mother-tongue teaching and we were wondering how much of this was historical accident, how much by design?*

MAKH: My first publications relevant to language teaching had a strong E.S.L. focus (Halliday et al. 1964). In Edinburgh the leading institutional base was the School of Applied Linguistics where Ian Catford was the director. Although I wasn't in it, I did a lot of teaching for them. There would be another reason of course, and that is that on the whole, E.S.L. was ahead of both mother-tongue education and foreign language teaching in the English context, in its applications of linguistics.

GK: *That's true now isn't it, in lots of ways?*

MAKH: It's true in lots of ways although there are some ways now in which I think mother-tongue teaching is taking over.

GK: *You've been centrally involved in two major mother-tongue research programs, the Nuffield Schools Council and the Language Development Project[16] work in Canberra, and are currently an active participant in Australia's Language in Education network[17]. Could you comment on what has been achieved in the past twenty-five years of language in education work and where you think things should be heading now?*

MAKH: I suppose what has been achieved is a number of fads and fashions, some of which will remain. In the English Language Teaching context it seems to me there are two developments which were applied linguistic developments which were important. One is the notion of language for specific purposes, which came quite squarely out of Firth's restricted languages and concept of register. And so I think that's been an important part. I think in the mother-tongue area, two things have been important. One is the awareness of the child as a human being who has been learning language essentially from birth so that the learning in school becomes continuous from that. And related to that perhaps, the notion of language as a process in education. Things **have** changed. The very concept of language education didn't exist twenty-five years ago, or even fifteen years ago. So I think that most of the achievements have been based on gradually raising the level of awareness of language among educators. One has to remember this sort of thing has to go on, over and over and over again. It doesn't suddenly happen.

GK: *But are there things now that you don't any longer have to say very strongly that you might have had to say twenty years ago?*

MAKH: Well, there are some I think, but not very many. I think you have to go on and on and on saying them every year, to each new group of students. I suppose we don't any longer have to fight the old fashioned views of correctness and language as table-manners (again we can't be complacent about these things). And we don't have to fight the notion of standard and dialect, and dialects as being inferior. I think people have moved quite a lot on that. There's a more complicated history as far as relations between spoken and written language are concerned. At one time I would have said we no longer have to fight the battle for recognition of spoken language in education. But I'm not sure about that now. I think we're going to have to gear up for a new battle there, though on a different plane certainly.

Even where one doesn't feel there has been much progress, the discussion may have moved onto a different plane. I think we've always been aware, and it's certainly true now in Australia and elsewhere, that teacher education, which is where the action has to be, really hasn't changed that much. So that most of what we've done with teachers in pre-service education, it's not been effective education. In-service and workshops and this kind of thing is where we've had the effect and I hope we'll continue to do so. But it's still minor. This is not at all to minimise what's been happening. I think what's been happening in Australia is tremendous over these years. But I think it's still got to be recognised that it's only hitting a small fraction of the profession. So a large part of what has to happen is simply just more work, more dissemination, more spreading around and more developments of people on the spot. I mean, we need more people like Brian Gray for example (Gray 1985, 1986, 1987, 1990), developing programs which are really based on insights into language in relation to a particular problem, in a particular context, like the program in Traeger Park.

GK: *We've got a question which follows that up a little bit. Your theory has been designed to solve problems or at least to play an active apart in solving them. Which parts of it do you think have been most effective and what are you most proud of in terms of what has been achieved?*

MAKH: I suppose it ties up with this section generally. I feel that it's been in the educational area. I think I'm a little bit proud of that, and have that feeling on various levels. For example, I first started intervening myself when David Abercrombie said to me, "Will you teach on my summer school, the British Council Summer School for the Phonetics of English for Foreign Students." This was in 1959. And I said: "Certainly. What do you want me to teach?" He said "Well, you know Chinese. Teach intonation". I knew nothing about English intonation, so I started studying it (Halliday 1967, 1970b, Halliday & Greaves 2008), trying to describe English in such a way that the description was useful to those who were going to be working on language in the classroom, in an educational context. The fact that we are now getting to the point when people are saying: "I can use this grammar for working on language in the classroom." is an achievement. When I went to the Nuffield Foundation in 1963 I said: "I want some money for working on language in this sense, but I don't want to see any teachers for years because we're not ready for them, so to speak". And they said, "If you put the teachers in right away, we'll double your money". You can't refuse that kind of thing. Of course they were quite right. What this meant was that we used to have those weekly seminars, when we had David Mackay and Peter Doughty working on grammar, from the point of view of where it was going to be used. Now at that time you didn't dare put it into the program because, certainly in Britain, no teacher would stand it for a moment if you said you had to teach any grammar. It was out and that was it. When we did *Language in Use* (Doughty et al. 1971), there was not a single unit on grammar in those 110 units. Our point at the time being to say: "No, you can work on language. Working on language doesn't mean that you're having to be working on grammar". But I like to think that the grammar is something which can be turned into a tool. I think what's been tremendously impressive is going around to places and finding people with bits of texts they've recorded in the classroom and saying: "I want to analyse this". This is a change. Certainly that could not have happened in England in the sixties.

One of the things I feel most happy about is the developmental interpretation that I tried to put on early language development and the importance of that for later work on language in education. That again, came out of teachers. When *Language in Use* was taken up in the 'Approved Schools', that is the schools run by the Home Office for children who had been before the courts, the teachers came to Geoffrey Thornton and Peter Doughty and said: "We want to use these materials. Would you lay on a workshop for us". And they asked me to go and talk. At the same time David Mackay and Brian Thompson, who were the *Breakthrough* team, set up a workshop for primary school teachers. Both groups asked me the same question which was: "Tell us something about the language experience of children before they come into school at all". I hadn't done anything of course at that time but I read around on what there was. Not much of it was terribly useful. Ruth Weir's was one of the best in those days. But it started me thinking on early language development. That was the time when our son was born and when the Canadian Government wouldn't let us into Canada. This meant that I had a whole year at home with no job and so I was able to listen to Nigel's developing language.

RH: *Those were difficult, perhaps fortuitously difficult times in more than one respect. In some sense the rise of Chomsky's linguistics must have impinged on your work in the sixties and the early seventies. Why did you hold back, in spite of general acceptance of the TG framework, and how did you see yourself in relation to that whole movement?*

MAKH: Chomsky's work quickly became a new establishment, and in many ways a rather brutal establishment actually. At University College London one great problem was whether it was fair on students to give them anything except establishment transformation theory because they wouldn't get a job. Now it was not as bad in England as it was in the United States, where the whole thing was polarised much more. But I certainly found it difficult in the sense that there was a lot of excitement generated in the early sixties, in relation to applications of linguistics in the School of Applied Linguistics in Edinburgh, and one or two other centres. Then this tidal wave of Chomskian linguistics washed over the United States and then England and other places. It became a very rigid establishment using all the tactics that one expects: those of ridiculing the opposition, setting up a straw man in order to knock them down and so on. "Why didn't I sort of fall in with it?" Because I found it in every way quite unacceptable. I thought that intellectually it was unacceptable.

The way the goals of linguistics were defined at the time, the notions embodied in all the slogans that were around, 'competence' and 'performance' and things of this kind, I just found quite unacceptable. Intellectually I thought they were simply misguided and in practical terms I thought they were no use. So that I thought that if one is really interested in developing a linguistics that has social and educational and other relevance **that** wasn't going to help. We just had to keep going and hope that it would wash over and we should be able to get people listening again to the kind of linguistics I thought was relevant.

RH: *And it happened.*

MAKH: Yes, it happened, and now we know it'll all disappear into the history of the subject eventually.

Language and context

GK: *We've got a set of questions on language, linguistics and context. Our first question is on politics. You are someone whose career has been disrupted more than once because of your political beliefs. Have these experiences affected your approach to linguistics, especially linguistics as doing?*

MAKH: No, I don't think so. I mean, yes, okay, I **was** witch-hunted out of a couple of jobs for political reasons. And the British Council refused to send me anywhere at all during that time, however much people asked. But I don't think that this has affected my approach to linguistics. Linguistics as doing is part of a political approach and I didn't suffer in the way that a lot of people suffered. Of course I've no doubt that I would have gone in very different directions had this not happened. For example, if I had been taken on and kept on in the Chinese department at SOAS I might well have stayed principally in Chinese studies and worked on Chinese rather than moving into linguistics generally. And secondly, of course, the thing that I really wanted was the job on Chinese linguistics in Firth's department. It was for purely political reasons that I didn't get that. I wish that I had that interview on tape because it would be one of the most marvellous documents **ever**. It would be fantastic, absolutely fantastic.

RH: *For the analysis of ideology!*

MAKH: Yes, it really would be. It was absolutely incredible. In any case if I'd got that, I think, I would have remained much more closely a Firthian. I wanted to get into Firth's department. If I **had** got into Firth's department, I would have quite definitely have worked much more within a Firthian framework. You have to remember that to the extent that I have departed from Firth, certainly initially it was simply because I wasn't there in the group in any sense and therefore I wasn't able to get answers to questions, and, in some ways, to correct misunderstandings.

This meant that, in a sense, I was pushed out to working on my own in two instances where in either case, if this hadn't happened, I might well have continued to work in the pre-existing frameworks, both institutional and intellectual frameworks. I'm not sorry.

GK: *Our second question is about language and social reality. You are one of the few linguists who have followed Whorf in arguing that language realises, and is at the same time a metaphor for reality. How Whorfian is your conception of language and what part has Bernstein's theory played in shaping your views?*

MAKH: Well, I think it's Whorfian (cf. Halliday 1990a). Partly this is because you can make Whorf mean anything you want. When I say I think my conception of language is Whorfian, **you** know what I mean; but for a lot of people who would interpret Whorf differently that might not be the case. I certainly follow some aspects of Whorf's work, which I think are absolutely fundamental. One is the relation of language to habitual thought and behaviour. Another one, perhaps less taken up, but which I think is fundamental, is the notion of the 'cryptotype' where it seems to me that Whorf (and of course in this he was simply following the Boas-Sapir tradition) was so right in the seeing the action at the most unconscious levels. The whole point is that the Whorfian effect takes place precisely because of what is going on at the most unconscious level. And, one might add to that, it's going on in what is an evolved human system and not, as sometimes represented, an artificial system. Language is a natural system. In fact, it is these two things, the naturalness and the unconsciousness which make these effects possible.

I was arguing this with an economist about two years ago. He was saying in effect that it is only through the most conscious forms of human activity that ideologies are transmitted and that social structure and social system is maintained. And he was therefore defending sociological and economic models of research. In other words you go and study how people plan their budgets or do their shopping or whatever. And I was arguing the opposite case. He was saying: "How can you claim that language can have any influence on this because it's all so unconscious". He wasn't disputing that the processes were unconscious but saying that **because** they were unconscious they could have no effect on ideology. And my view is exactly the opposite – that it's at the most unconscious level that we essentially construct reality. And that, I think, is Whorfian. Therefore, particularly in terms of the grammar, it's the notion of the cryptotype that I would see as absolutely essential.

JRM: *I wondered if Chinese comes in here again in the sense that a grammar of Chinese could only be a grammar of covert categories, because there are no overt ones.*

MAKH: It never occurred to me but it may well be true. I've never thought of that. Now as far as Bernstein is concerned, he himself, as he often acknowledged, also took a great deal from Whorf. He makes the entirely valid point that Whorf is leaving out the component of the social structure. Whorf essentially went straight at the ideational level, from the language into the culture, so to speak. Bernstein has pointed out that there has to be, at least in any general theory of cultural transmission, the intermediary of the social structure. I think this is actually right. Bernstein is still, uniquely as a sociologist, someone who has built language in as an essential component to his theory, both as a theory of cultural transmissions and as a general sociological and a deep philosophical theory. He convinced me that this was possible. Perhaps this hasn't come out clearly from what went before because we talked more about the **applied** context, educational and other applications. But I think it's important also to say that a representation of language has to be able to interpret language in the context of more general theories of social structure, social processes and so on, and ultimately of the whole environment that we live in. In general that had never been done. In fact, the problem has always been in linguistics that linguists have always shouted loudly for the autonomy of the subject, and that always seems to me to be of very little interest. Linguistics is interesting because it's not autonomous. It has to be part of something else. Now Bernstein was the first person that made it part of something else and so the way in which he did this was obviously important.

I used to argue with Bernstein when he was doing it the wrong way. Early on he was looking for syntactic interpretations of elaborated and restricted codes; I always said, "That's not where you should be looking". And he gradually moved into a much more semantic interpretation.

JRM: *What did Bernstein have that you didn't have from Malinowski or Firth? They both have context, haven't they?*

MAKH: I think he added a coherent theory of social structure. I know he himself has now disclaimed some aspects of this but at the time, as it influenced me, he added a whole interpretative framework which enabled you to show not only the Whorfian effect, but also why patterns of educational failure were essentially class linked. In a society like the current western societies with their very strong hierarchical structures of class primarily and all the others, he asked "How were these, in fact, transmitted, maintained? What essentially is the nature of these hierarchies as semiotic constructs?" Bernstein put that in. I don't think that was there before. At the time there was all this stupid argument – Labov was trying to demolish him. But, if there was one person that needed Bernstein to give him theoretical underpinning, it was Labov[18]. I mean, Labov doesn't make sense unless you've got something like Bernstein behind him.

GK: *We have a question about semiotics and systemics. Your model of language has connections to the work of Saussure and Hjelmslev alongside Firth. How would you position yourself in respect to continental structuralism and what role do you see for systemic theory in relation to post-structuralism and semiotics?*

MAKH: We need another seminar on this one. I mean, it's a good thing we didn't start with this question.

Firth, as you know, was very critical of Saussure on a number of points and regarded him as somebody who was perpetuating certain ideas in the history of Western thought which he didn't like, certain basic dualities. Now Ruqaiya would say (e.g. Hasan 1985a, 1987b), I think, that he was misrepresenting Saussure in a number of these ways, and maybe he was. In any case it seems to me that the world after Saussure was different from the world before. That's a fact and I certainly belong to the world after, although certainly there were things in Saussure, when I first read him as a student many years ago, and re-reading subsequently, that I wouldn't accept. I **do** think I share Firth's suspicion of langue/parole, although from a somewhat different standpoint.

As I see it, if you take the Saussurean view then you find it very difficult to show how systems evolve. But, it seemed to me that Hjelmslev had, to a certain extent, built on Saussure and also corrected that point of his; Hjelmslev's notions were much more adequate. To the extent that Hjelmslev differed from Firth, there are two important respects in which I would follow Hjelmslev. One is that Hjelmslev did have a very strong concept of a linguistic system, but a non-universalist one. This lies between the Firthian extreme which is: "There's no such thing as a language; there's only text and language events.", over to the other extreme of the universalists. Hjelmslev lies in the sort of middle position, which I think I would share. And then, of course, Hjelmslev constructed a fairly clear, useful, stratificational model. I haven't used it in the Hjelmslevian form and there are certain parallels built in between the different planes which I certainly wouldn't follow.

Certainly in the attempts to construct an overall pattern at the time when I was first doing this, I was very much influenced by Hjelmslev, and that's something which Firth just didn't have[19]. In the last five to seven years I just haven't kept up with all semiotic and post-structuralist literature, so I've got a very partial picture. I was in Urbino for two or three summers in the early seventies, late sixties. That was when I first interacted with semiotics in the continental sense. It seemed to me that the general concept embodied in semiotics was a very valuable one because it enabled me to say: "Here is a context within which to study language". Partly it's simply saying: "OK. We can look at language as one among a number of semiotic systems". That's valuable and important in itself. That then let's us look at its special features. We can then ask questions about its special status – the old questions about what extent language is unique because of the connotative semiotic notion – because it is the expression through which other semiotic systems are realised. And then thirdly at a deeper plane, semiotics provided a model for representing human phenomena in general, cultures and all social phenomena as information systems. This, of course, is really a development in line with technologies it seems to me. It goes with an age in which most people are now employed in exchanging information rather than goods and services.

Technology has become information technology. So our interpretations of the culture are interpretations as an assembly of information systems. This is what semiotics tried to interpret and increasingly, as I've mentioned, the physical sciences are interpreting the universe as an information system. So semiotics should provide a good home within which linguistics can flourish in this particular age, it seems to me. Now there are certain respects, of course, in which it's gone off in directions that I don't find so congenial.

JRM: *If you have a well-articulated comprehensive Halliday/Bernstein model, would that be an alternative to what the Europeans have in mind? With respect to the language and ideology conference last year[20] and the way people were talking about ideology and language, it struck me as another way of talking about things that that Halliday-Bernstein model would be interested in. It's not doing something else. Gunther should really follow this up.*

GK: *I feel that systemic theory provides the most worked out model for thinking about semiosis. And semiotics on the other hand has the ability to ask certain kinds of questions, or have a slightly different view point to look at language again. I think that's the formula of the relationship.*

RH: *One of the problems of course is what is one thinking of as an example of post-structuralism.*

MAKH: Exactly.

RH: *If you're thinking of Derrida, that raises a different question which, at the deepest level, is really a question of realisation – the signifier and the signified and the relation between them. If you look at Bourdieu then that is a different question again and that question is the question of langue and parole, the sorts of relations that there are.*

MAKH: Bourdieu would be much more compatible with what Jim is referring to as the Halliday/Bernstein thing.

RH: *Yes. Greimas is yet another voice. He's not exactly what you would call a post-structuralist. But it is really very difficult with Barthes and Greimas to say exactly at what point they cease to be seen as structuralist. I myself find it very difficult to define the term structuralism. And that's what makes that question a little bit difficult to answer in one go.*

MAKH: We need another seminar on this one too. It seems to me, that in so far as post-structuralism has become a literary theory, then some of the ideas that are used in discussions of literature and are ascribed to structuralists by people working in the general semiotic and post-structuralist field really aren't there at all. I mean they're quite different from what these people are actually saying.

RH: *That's generated a very interesting point: how it is that a discipline retains its old assumptions while using new names, and resists any innovations. Literary criticism is one of the disciplines that is a prime example of this kind of thing. One should study that for how to retain ideology and not to change it.*

GK: *It seems to me, just to make two comments, that structuralism and post-structuralism ask questions of linguistic theory which are important to ask. Derrida's work, for instance, really sharpens up the question about system, because it in itself is a model that works without system. It works only with the surface effects of structures. So it asks really important questions about system. But the thing that interests me most is that post-structuralism asks questions about the constitution of language uses, in linguistic terms, which linguistics, because of its concerns with the system itself, hasn't I think addressed as fully as it might. That seems to me important.*

Anyway, we have a question on speech and writing. Is there an implied valuation of speech over writing in your descriptive work? The second part of the question which is: How does your recent work on grammatical metaphor relate to this issue (Halliday 1985a, b)?

MAKH: In a sense there **is** an implied valuation of speech over writing in relation to this notion of levels of consciousness, if you like. It seems to me there's a very important sense in which our whole ability to mean is constructed and developed through speech, and that this is inevitably so. In other words speech is where the semantic frontiers are enlarged and the potential is basically increased. I know that one of the problems here is that there's a risk in this being interpreted like the old, early twentieth century structural linguists, who insisted on the primacy of speech over writing for other reasons. But there are things I want to say about natural spontaneous speech which do, in a sense, give it a priority.

This has been partly of course political because I feel that it is essential to give speech a place alongside writing in human learning and therefore in the educational process. I still feel very strongly about that. Now the work on grammatical metaphor is partly an attempt to explore the nature of the complementarity between the speech and writing. There are modes of action and modes of learning which are more spoken, speech-like and which are more naturally associated with spoken language, and others which are more naturally associated with written language. This is something which needs to be explored. I'm always asking teachers if they feel that there are certain things in what they do which are more naturally approached through the spoken. At a deeper level differences between speech and writing have to be explored in the wider semiotic context that we're working with.

We need to ask about writing as a medium, the development of the written language, and the development of technical discourse, exploring a technicalisation that is part and parcel of the process of writing and which involves grammatical metaphor. We need to ask what the nature of the realationship among these things is and between all of these and the underlying sorts of phenomena that they've used to describe[21].

Beyond this it's the whole question of how far can we use notions of grammatical metaphor, and indeed the whole systemic approach to language, to try and understand the nature of knowledge itself. It relates to what we've been talking about in some of these seminars on a language-based theory of learning.

When I started in the E.S.L. area I remember going to Beth Ingram, the psychologist at the School of Applied Linguistics. This was in about 1959 when I started teaching there. And I said to her: "Can you give me a bibliography on the psychology of second language learning?" And she handed me a blank piece of paper. Now I have never been temperamentally one who's been really able to feel at home in psychology! I find it very hard to read. But we were criticised more than once both in England and even more here in Australia in the Language Development Project for not offering any general theory of learning. And of course this was true. To start with at least, I didn't think it was our job to offer one. I had hoped to be able to take over some learning theory and use this in the context of educational linguistics. Then it just seemed to me that there wasn't one.

We had a lot of useful ideas but nothing that could be thought of as a general learning theory into which this our work could be fitted. So it seems to me we have to ask the question "Well, can we build one out of language?" I mean "Don't we by now know a lot more?" I am obviously influenced by Jim here[22] who's been pointing out all along that linguistics should in fact simply take over a lot of these things and see what it can say from a language point of view. And I certainly think that we have to work towards a much more language-based theory of learning and language-based theory of knowledge. And in that, notions like grammatical metaphor, and the difference between spoken and written language, are obviously fundamental.

GK: *Our next question in a sense addresses that in a somewhat broader way. Your work has paved the way for a radically larger role for linguistics in the humanities and social sciences and perhaps beyond than has been possible in the past. What, to your mind, are the limits of semiosis? Just how far can a language-based model be pursued before turning over to other disciplines?*

MAKH: I think that we've drawn disciplinary boundaries on the whole far too much. We had to have them of course. I think Mary Douglas[23] sorted that one out many years ago very very well. The discourse, so to speak, had to be created in definable circumscribed realms. But the cost of this was defining these far too much in terms of the object that was being studied. Thus linguistics is the study of language, and so on. Now that is really not what disciplines are about. A discipline is really defined by the questions you are asking. And in order to answer those questions you may be studying thousands of different things. Linguists start by asking questions about language. And if you ask "Well how far do questions about language take us?", then the answer is "They take us way beyond anywhere that we are yet operating in." The frontiers are well beyond. I don't know where they **are**, but they're certainly well beyond where we are at the moment. They certainly take us into a lot of questions that have been traditionally questions of philosophy, which has always been about language to the extent it's been about anything and into questions of general science. I mean, this is why I've become increasingly interested in scientific language and general problems of science.

It has become increasingly clear that you can ask questions about language which turn out to take you into and even way beyond human systems. So I don't know where the frontiers are but they're certainly a great deal further than I think we've been able to push them. And, in a sense, I've tried to have this kind of perspective in view all along; I wanted a linguistics which is not defined by object language as object but rather by questions. These questions began by being questions about language but eventually expand into areas that we don't expect. I certainly think that we should be fighting a lot more for the centrality of linguistics, not only in the human sciences but in science generally, at least for the foreseeable future.

GK: *In what way do you mean that? As a means of elucidating what scientific disciplines are doing?*

MAKH: Yes. Current thinking has been emphasising the similarities among human, and between human and non-human systems, between human and physical systems if you like. Take first of all Lemke's work, which I think is tremendously important, on dynamic open systems (e.g. Lemke 1995). He's taken over the social semiotic notion, which he's characterised in these essentially physical terms. Language fits in, but then becomes a way of looking at other human semiotic systems, which are language-like in this respect and for which language serves as both the semiotic which realises them (the connotative semiotic sense) and also a model and a metaphor in a very important sense. I think you can go beyond that now into physical systems. The universe in modern physics is being thought of as one, whole, indivisible and conscious. In other words the present generation of physicists is adding consciousness to the universe, talking about exchange of information.

That came originally out of quantum physics. Now my point is I want to say not "one, whole, indivisible and conscious" but rather "one, whole, indivisible and communicative". In other words I want to say the universe, in an important sense, is made of language, or at least made of something of which human language is a special case. Taking the notion of a natural grammar, one step further is to say that language is as it is because it not only models human semiotic systems (realities we construct in a very important sense); it also models natural systems. Obviously, talking like that is talking in a very abstract way; but on the other hand, I think that there is an important sense in which the situation has been reversed. Instead of modelling all our thinking in some respects on physics, as in the classical period (and from physics via biology it got into linguistics), I think there's an important sense in which in the next period the thing is going the other way round. We are going to start from the notion of the universe as a kind of language if you like, and therefore move outwards from linguistics. Towards human and then biological and then physical systems.

GK: *A materialist linguistics.*

MAKH: Yes.

GK: *We have one last question which is about linguistics and machines. Very early in your career you worked on machine translation and since then your work has played a central part in a number of artificial intelligence projects. Is this because of or in spite of your socio-functional orientation? How has your recent involvement in I.S.I.[24] influenced your thinking about language, linguistics and machines?*

MAKH: I don't see the interest as in any sense conflicting. As you know I have never thought of either the machine or the linguistic theory as in any sense a model of human psychological processes, so there's no question of seeing some model of the brain as a common base.

Now I've had one concern throughout which is that it seemed to me right from the beginning when I first tried to learn about this back in the late fifties in the Cambridge Language Research Unit that the machine was, in principle, a valuable research tool. Now that was the nature of my first interest. By seeing if we could translate Italian sentences into Chinese, which we were doing at that time, we learned more about language. I've been in and out three times now. First of all, while in the very early stages, we had some fascinating discussions and it was all great fun; but it was obvious that the technology itself was still so primitive that we were constrained by the hardware, the internal housekeeping rules so that we weren't actually learning anything about language in the process.

I had another interest in it which is that I felt that machine translation[25] had an important political role to play. There were lots of cultures around the world where people were beginning to be educated in a mother tongue and if you could possibly have a machine to translate a lot of text books at least it would help the process. So there are practical concerns like that. Then in the late sixties I came back again with the project on the Linguistic Properties of Scientific English that Rodney Huddleston and Dick Hudson, Eugene Winter and Alec Henrici[26] were working on. Henrici was the programmer and at that time we used the machine to do one or two things in systemic theory. For example he had a program for generating paradigms from a network. So you could test out a network that way. And he could even run little realisations through it. But again there were tremendous limits in the technology. At that time I started being interested in generalising and parsing programs.

I wanted to **test** the theory and of course, I **was** responding to external pressure. At that time in the sixties unless you could show that your theory was totally formalisable it was of no interest and I was responding to these pressures. This was why I was interested in Henrici actually generalising clauses by the computer.

But my real interest in that was that I was beginning to realise that you could no longer test grammars except with a machine, in the sense that they were too big. If you really had delicate networks, the paradigms were just huge; you had to have some way of testing this.

There was still a limit on the technology then. I wanted to write the grammar in metafunctional terms. I wanted to say "I don't like the sort of transformational model where you have a deep structure and then obligatory transformations and then optional transformations on top of them. I want to be able to represent things as being simultaneous and unordered". And the answer was "Well, we can't compute this and therefore it must be wrong". I never accepted that answer. It always seemed to me to be incredibly arrogant to say that if our logic or our hardware cannot do something at this stage therefore it must be wrong. So I just backed off again and I never thought I would come back into it at all.

I thought that was it until Bill Mann came along when we were in Irvine; he turned up at one of my seminars and said "Will you come and talk to us. We're going to use systemic grammar for our text generation". This was very exciting. I talked to Bill right away about the background and why I had got out of it before and the things which I was told you couldn't do. And he just laughed. He said "What do you want to do now? Of course. No problem". There had been of course, dramatic changes. At I.S.I. it seemed to me that we really had for the first time the possibility of setting up the grammar in such a way that it was testable in the computer. And that was, of course, what interested me about this. I'm not the slightest bit interested in the particular things that their sponsors want them to do the grammar for. But it does seem to me that we are now in a stage where we can learn. And if we get people like Christian Matthiessen, who really knows the grammar, and also knows how to put it on a machine and test it, this is tremendously valuable. And I get the impression that there's really only one last frontier in the technology that hasn't been crossed for our purposes. And that is the integrated parallel processing system whereby the computer can do 'n' number of things at once.

Parallel processing is not a problem but there are still constraints on the extent to which each of these processes can consult all the others as it's going along and modify its own behaviour in the light of that consultation. It seems to me that if you can get that kind of thing available then we really can learn a lot by constructing parsing and generating programs and using them to test the grammar. It's been as a research tool mainly that I have been interested in this, although there obviously are practical applications that are useful.

RH: *Where is the point where systemics needs more growth? Which direction is it going? What is your hope that systemicists would develop?*

MAKH: Well, more of what they are doing I think. I mean we just need more people, more time, more resources, the usual thing. One of the things that we have been very weak on is any kind of clinical applications and the underlying theory that goes with those. Bruce McKellar (1987) is the one who has certainly done most that I find interesting, but he hasn't written up much of it yet on that side. I mean, he's written an enormous amount of background material, but less about the neurolinguistics. McKellar's notion is that systemic theory is likely to be useful, more so than others he thinks, in developing neurolinguistics. He doesn't believe that there is such a thing yet, but he sees ways of doing it. And the interesting thing is that he sees this not so much in relation to the particular representations of the grammar or the linguistic system, as in the social semiotic background to it. Now that's one development I think is very important – towards a neurolinguistics and towards clinical applications. Again we will in turn learn from these things. So I would like to see it far more used in context of aphasiology and all kinds of studies of developmental disorders (cf. Armstrong et al. 2005, Fine 2006).

RH: *Let's go back to the machines and how they can be used for testing the grammar. At the present moment all they can do is test the grammar of a clause or with luck, clause complex; but they are not able to do anything yet on what constitutes a normal natural sequence of people's sayings in any context of situation without going up and building in context of situation. That was the context in which I had raised that question of probability because it seems to me that the only way that probability is going to link up with text is in some way through context.*

MAKH: Well, there has to be some sort of register model, as part of it. But I don't know that in principle there's any reason why this can't be built in, given that point that I was saying about the remaining limitations on the technology. The environment, as they call it in the I.S.I. project, which means the knowledge base and the text planner, are still very primitive. But they're primitive because we just haven't had enough people doing enough work on them. I think that given a research effort in that area then it should be possible to represent these things in such a way that they can be part of the text generation.

University of Sydney
May 1986

Notes

1 The questions in the interview schedule were designed by Hasan, Kress and Martin and given to Halliday a few days prior to the interview. Hasan and Martin subsequently edited the interview into its present form.
2 Horvath, a Labovian sociolinguist, was Halliday's first appointment to the Department of Linguistics he founded at the University of Sydney in 1975.
3 The School of Oriental and African Studies in London.

4 Further Education and Training Scheme.
5 Halliday did in fact join the Communist Party, and was a member until 1957 when he left over the party's failure to condemn or even to properly discuss condemning Russia's invasion of Hungary. While a member he met regularly with the party's 'Linguistics Group', which included Jeff Ellis and Jean Ure. SFL register theory was first developed in these discussions.
6 Halliday's Ph.D. thesis was published as Halliday 1959.
7 For an overview of Firth's theory see Firth 1957b.
8 Halliday's first scale and category grammar of English was written on the cardboard inserts he received inside his shirts from Edinburgh laundries. [A great-uncle of mine in Toronto preferred to use his for plates! – JRM]
9 For a summary of the discussions on synoptic and dynamic representations referred to here, see Martin 1985.
10 For further discussion see Halliday 1987.
11 See Chomsky 1964a for a dismissal of corpus evidence.
12 For a summary article see Halliday 1991.
13 See however Armstrong et al. 2005.
14 For a retrospective overview of this initiative, which produced the *Breakthrough to Literacy* and *Language in Use* materials, see Pearce et al. 1989.
15 See Bernstein, B. 1971, 1973, 1975, 1990; Bernstein 1973 is particularly relevant to the discussion here.
16 During the late 1970s the Curriculum Development Centre in Canberra funded the Language Development Project, a national language in education initiative with Halliday as a key consultant. See Maling-Keepes & Keepes 1979.
17 This is a fluid network of linguists and educators (anchored by Fran Christie and initiated by Halliday in 1979) which has held several conferences on language in education issues around Australia.
18 For discussion of these debates see Atkinson 1985 and Gerot et al. 1988.
19 For a recent statement on levels see Halliday 1992a.
20 For the proceedings of this conference see Threadgold et al. 1986.
21 See Halliday & Martin 1993 for work in this arena.
22 See for example Rose & Martin 2012.
23 See Fardon 1999.
24 The Information Sciences Institute in Los Angeles, California; for an overview of this research see Matthiessen & Bateman 1991.
25 See Halliday 1962.
26 See Huddleston et al. 1968; Henrici 1981.

With Michael O'Toole and Gunther Kress (1989)

The School of Humanities and the School of Education at Murdoch University are hosting a workshop on language in education, with the overall title '3D: Discipline – Dialogue – Difference' (Giblett & O'Carroll 1990). This is one of a series of workshops on that topic, language in education, which was started by Professor Michael Halliday at the University of Sydney in 1979. Our two main speakers for the first day are Michael Halliday and Gunther Kress, who also works in Sydney. Michael Halliday is the founder of the Department of Linguistics at Sydney University and now Emeritus Professor of Linguistics at Sydney. Gunther Kress is the Professor of Communication at the University of Technology in Sydney. Both of them have been extremely active in the world of linguistics, describing language, giving us the tools for analysing linguistic texts, but are also both very interested in texts other than ones that are purely in language; and I'm quite sure that discussion of those kinds of texts will arise as well.

The title of the program, 'Discipline–Dialogue–Difference', really starts from the notion that a lot of the debate about the teaching of languages in schools assumes that language has to be taught as a discipline: one must instil grammar into pupils. But we're raising questions about whether it shouldn't just be the instilling of a discipline but it should be much more of a dialogue. In other words, that the linguistic experience of pupils themselves is an important factor in the whole process of learning about language; and in a way, that's the way we're trying to shift the focus this week.

And then the question of difference in a sense raises all sorts of issues about the different kinds of language which people speak – the different kinds of language that's spoken by teachers and their pupils, by different kinds of pupils, who come from different social classes, who are of different sexes, or different races, and so on. And so in a way the whole conference is devoted to exploring some of these issues, both in keynote papers such as we've had today, and also workshop sessions where there's intensive discussion for about seven hours in each case (with gaps for coffee) of the kind of concerns that come under the general heading of language in education.

MO'T: *So I'll start by asking Michael Halliday whether he thinks that we've reached a point in discussions of language in education where this kind of broadening of the agenda is appropriate?*

MAKH: Yes I think we have. Since I started working, a long way back in history now, with teachers at different levels in this area that we now call language education, there has been a very interesting move – not anything that is neat and clearly defined but nevertheless something which has been constantly broadening its scope. You yourself referred to the traditional concept of language in schools; indeed it used not to be called language. You did some grammar, which meant that you learned to parse sentences and a little bit of formal analysis, which was then never used for the rest of your educational career. The teachers never used it to help you to write better compositions or whatever. You had no real sense of a reader for your writing; and then when you got into secondary school, you had to write essays and maybe develop some kind of sense of how to produce a good composition. You had subject English, which by and large meant literature. OK, what have we, if we move on to cover, say forty years since then?

Over that time we've seen a broadening of the interest in different kinds of texts, so it's no longer just literature. First of all people became interested in language in non-literary contexts of various kinds; it was recognised that spoken language had a place and was worth developing and worth looking at. We've had attempts to look at what the child's language experience was before coming into school, so that language development became a kind of continuous process from the home, and then the neighbourhood, and into the school. We've had the notion of language across the curriculum, where we recognised that language wasn't just a thing you studied but that it was part of all your learning experience – language of science, language of history, and so on. Then we had an even broader notion of something sometimes referred to as the role of language in learning; that phrasing was used for example during the Language Development Project here in Australia at the Curriculum Development Centre, characterising language as the basis of all learning; so that all learning is in some sense, at least in part, mediated through language. And perhaps most recently in the last ten to fifteen years we've broadened that still further to what is now sometimes now called constructivist models in education, where we recognise that the learner is not simply reproducing some given construct from outside but is actively constructing knowledge, and constructing social relationships, and again primarily through language. So in a sense all these I think represent a gradual broadening of the context in which we talk about language in education.

GK: *Just to make a comment on Michael's use of the term grammar, for people who may have terrible memories of what grammar in school had meant – when we come back to talking about grammar now I think we don't mean at all what grammar meant twenty, thirty years ago but rather, particularly in systemic linguistics, grammar has at least a double meaning: one of its meanings being the kind of… well, let me start at a different point … Language is seen in systemic linguistics as a storehouse of cultural meanings, a repository, a resource for making meaning. I think that's a fundamental point – it's a resource for making meaning, rather than being a means for transmitting meanings – so a means for constructing, for producing meanings. And grammar is the term that refers to the kinds of categories, the inventory, the means of producing those meanings. So in that sense everybody has access to grammar. Everybody knows grammar, everybody uses grammar all the time, particularly once one is a fully functioning member of the culture. And when there is now debate about the role of grammar in education, or in language in education, that I think this is taken for granted; everybody involved in learning in education has access to that grammar. What isn't perhaps quite settled is the issue to what extent it's productive to formalise the kind of knowledge that everyone has – to make it overt, to make it explicit, to bring it into consciousness rather than leaving it somewhat beyond consciousness, and* whether knowledge of that kind can help, let's say first of all, the teacher, who's charged with the responsibility of advancing the skills and knowledge of students, and secondly perhaps whether it can even be of use in helping students change their skills – their command and mastery of language.

MO'T: *Something that hasn't come up at the conference so far today is the actual grammatical interest and experience of the young children. You and I happen to have rather young children, Gunther; Michael happens to have done a study of his own child, from the earliest stage of language development, and one of his most well known and exciting books has been Learning How to Mean, which is about language development in the child (Halliday 1975). What strikes me watching my own child, Janek, who is only twenty months old, is the fascination with language as such, even in a kind of formal sense. Of course they don't articulate formally what is going on and yet they play with formal patterns. They seem to know what formality is, for the purposes of play. And it seems to me that in many ways we ought to build on this notion of play, and very often what gets lost in the grammar school grind of the secondary school, which has such a bad press, and we keep running down, is the very notion of play, and the very natural curiosity people have and the spontaneous excitement with patterning in language, which comes from the early stages of language learning.*

MAKH: The first point that I would make, going back to my own direct experience with this, and trying to observe a child pretty well from birth building up the language, is how hard they work at it. Now they don't draw a great distinction between work and play of course, in that sense, but they are really putting energy into it – rehearsing sounds, trying out words, then trying out their own constructions, checking whether when they point to something and say "Green bus" and somebody answers them and says "Yeah, that's a green bus" or else they say "No, that's blue" and all the time they're both learning language and learning through language. That's I think one way of looking at it. Now, at the same time, as you say, they're also playing with it and you can see that play function in there very early – I can remember instances of my child playing with sounds, playing almost with metaphors, even at about twenty, twenty-two months – of changing the meaning of their own noises in a kind of game context. And I very much agree that's something that plays a very fundamental part. I think you have to watch out, of course –once you try to build play into the school curriculum, then it's no longer play. So, I mean, one wants to value this, but one has to be careful not to try and somehow simulate it in the formal learning process.

GK: *This is an area where most of what we say are anecdotes. But the inventiveness of children and their response to the kinds of information that are given to them by parents is a nice metaphor perhaps for the process of education generally. So on the one hand children are constantly testing out kinds of things, in the context of information given to them by people who know more, and coming to a kind of approximation, a kind of compromise perhaps … and that seems to me a very important thing that might perhaps be carried on in the school. In other words, a certain encouragement of children to be active.*

MAKH: It's dialogic, isn't it? That's the critical thing about it. It's interactive.

GK: *Dialogic, yes, that's the crucial thing about it. We need children to remain active in the school, acknowledging that there are people who have more knowledge with respect to a number of things and yet also acknowledging that to be active is an essential part.*

MO'T: *So is it the power structures of the school as an institution which tend to inhibit this dialogue?*

GK: *I don't actually know because when you look at, as Michael has done much more than I have, in the few cases that I've looked at where parents or friends of parents interact with children or perhaps texts from a play school, what you see quite clearly there is the kinds of structures that are normally said to be characteristic of the school, and perhaps to be inhibiting in the school, are there. I mean the school isn't a weird place which is marked by a great distortion of differences in power between children and adults. The school is a place where perhaps that's slightly heightened; but I think children come fully prepared to school in relation to that. What is in the school that discourages the child's activity may be the mere institutionality of the school, in the sense that there is a curriculum to be gotten through and there are forty or thirty or twenty children in the room and one adult to interact with as against a house or a home where there may be one adult and perhaps two children.*

MAKH: I think there's something more to it than that although in a sense that's one way of saying it. I think it's something to do with bringing processes to consciousness. You can use the term inhibiting if you like. I mean how is it that we all learn to succeed as language users. We did it by processing at a very early age, through the head as it were, and lodging what we could do firmly down in the gut, so we no longer had to think about it. So in other words in order to be successful with language you've got to stop thinking about language. That is the experience of the 18-month-old, the 2-year-old child, and it's our experience in everything else that involves a kind of control – like you know learning to ride a bicycle, a standard example; once you start thinking about it you fall off. Now, what the school requires is for you to bring language back to consciousness. There's no way to avoid this, partly because you have to do this in learning to read and write. Becoming literate means reflecting consciously on your language, and some people find this very threatening. We know this. We teach linguistics. Don't our own students often find this threatening, having to reflect on something which is buried below the level of awareness? And we see it for example in the way in which switching between spoken and written language in early classrooms, infant classrooms, the early years of primary school – having to focus on the mechanics of actually writing the written language, and on the new ways of making meaning that this involves – how this switching has the effect of slowing the process down, of tying the tongue if you like. Kids become tongue-tied, but not because they feel threatened – most teachers these days are highly interactive and very ready to let children talk. If the children don't talk I think it's partly that they are being required to bring the language learning process back to consciousness. And what's tied in with this is that in doing so one thing that teachers sometimes don't do so successfully is make them aware of why they're doing it. This is particularly true for written language.

GK: *I think that is an important point – that what is being focused on is making knowledge overt again and conscious; and yet on the teacher's part there is perhaps a lack of knowledge about the very process that is being brought into consciousness. And so I think there is a real problem, because the teacher in a sense is a bit hampered in what he or she is doing and you can see that quite often in looking at the kinds of comments teachers can make on children's writing, which show a limited understanding of the processes that have to be made conscious and have to be brought into overt knowledge for the child. And I suppose that's where knowledge of grammar would be enormously enabling for the teacher and I think enormously helpful therefore for the child.*

MO'T: *I think all of us who teach English using systemic functional grammar, the model of language that you developed Michael, and that many people around the world are developing further now, is precisely of course the notion of functions – the fact that it enables one to look at language in different ways, one at a time and simultaneously; so instead of the overriding assumption of a lot of teaching about language that language is all about propositions, that language is all about statements of fact, of course it's also about reflections of social relationships and so on and it's also about the making of texts. And so it seems to me the debate is enriched in the school very much by children becoming aware that they can be looking at different facets. It's all one text in a sense and yet by drawing attention to particular facets of any text at all it's going to have much more to do with their personal experience, either because it's propositional or because it's interpersonal and about the social relationships that language is expressing or because it's about generic texts – about types of texts that they know out there in society, recognise and again maybe get some kind of purchase on. They get some kind of purchase on the power behind the text in a sense by recognising its textuality.*

MAKH: Well yes it's always seemed to me you have to look at language functionally; as you said, we refer to it as a functional grammar rather than a formal grammar and this implies various things of course. It implies certain things about the actual technical apparatus of the grammar itself – how you see these clauses and phrases as being constructed and so on; but also on a broader scale it implies something about the place of the text in social processes, and the way in which the forms of the language when you do focus on them turn out to be motivated. Because the problem with the old teaching was that they treated the whole thing as so arbitrary – a set of rules you had to learn and of course language is not like that; it's not arbitrary. The forms are by and large … I have to say this, there are arbitrary features in language; it's a coding system, to use one metaphor, and certain parts of the total pattern of the language are in a technical sense arbitrary. That's a technical term which is often misleading in a way. But insofar as you're looking at the way in which texts are constructed, the way in which sentences are organised, and so on, it's not arbitrary. A functional grammar will show you that language, as I put it once in writing, is as it is because of what it has to do.

Now I think that is something which you have to share as it were with the learner. Jenny Hammond for example in her work has been struck by the fact that if the children who have discussed some topic in a very animated way with very elaborated use of language, very colourful and rich and so on, have to write about the same topic, then they tend to produce something very simplistic and dull; and you say well it's because of the difficulty they have with the medium. Well that may be part of the picture. But she's pointed out, and I think she's quite right, that a lot of the difficulty is that they don't see the purpose of writing it down having already talked about it; so that if you've already had a long discussion about what you did at the zoo, then what's the point of sitting down and writing about it. We expect that if you produce a new text, it's because it's got a different function. And I think that's something which can be built in to the learning/teaching process. Just give a context for these writing tasks which is different from the context of speech – because that after all is how writing evolved. It didn't evolve to do the same things as spoken language. And then I think it will make much more sense for them.

GK: *That goes back in a sense to an earlier question you asked. Why is it children become inarticulate in school? It may be that when children are asked to do odd kinds of things they recognise the oddness and don't respond in the way that we would want them to. In my own experience children are enormously aware of the significance of change in form and its social implications. To be anecdotal, my children made a clear distinction between calling me Gunther, and Daddy or Dad, which I could always trace to a particular change in the social variable.*

But to pick up that point about function, what is interesting about the functional theory of language and something that is happening more and more now is that the functional theory of language, and I don't need to tell you (directed at MO'T) because you've worked in that very area, is now being applied to areas other than language. I mean your work in relation to art, architecture, other people's work in relation to say music, or performance, or theatre studies, shows that other semiotic modes seem to be organised in quite the same kind of way – that they have to respond to particular social demands: they have to represent relations between people, they have to represent states of affairs in the world, they have to be able to construct coherent texts. And I think that's a nice justification for the design of that linguistic theory, or that grammar, that we're working with.

MO'T: *Yes I think so; and the excitement of working in this area now precisely is that we seem to be dealing with a general semiotic model. Studies in semiotics always seem to have started from linguistic models, some of which seemed to be too rigid or too, I don't know, too set in a mould to give much flexibility for expansion and development through other semiotic codes; but now I think quite a number of us feel that we have*

a model which isn't ... although it starts with language, probably the richest of our codes, it actually has potential for exploring all of the codes.
   Is there anything you wanted to say to wind up?

GK: Well, yes, just to wind up, I think that in the past language has been used as a metaphor to discover other semiotic modes, and I think that's been a real hindrance, because people have looked for nouns and verbs and phonemes or whatever, sounds – in film or in painting or in architecture. I think we have a much better understanding now that there is a more fundamental organisation of meaning in culture. And I think the kinds of translations that are being made now are at that level and therefore more productive that the kind of translations that were being made before, which were too direct and therefore always bound to fall down in the end.

MAKH: Just two comments on that. I think, yes, I strongly agree here and I think that it's useful not to forget what might be called the kind of hinge areas of verbal art – literature and drama, which are on both modes at once, as it were. I mean they are made of language and at the same time they have their own semiotic structure. So they are in a sense intermediate between these and forms of semiotic which are not mediated through language.

   The only other comment to make is that I think that looking at it as a linguist, there's a lot in what's in it for me, in the sense that we can then feed back into our understanding of the grammar precisely what we learn by applying these to other forms of semiotic.

MO'T: Good. Thank you very much indeed Michael. Thank-you Gunther.

Language in Education Conference
Murdoch University, Australia
December 1989

8

With Caroline Coffin (1998)

CC: *In this next section, we look at systemic functional theory. This is a theory that considers how language is used in different cultural and social contexts. One of its chief developers is Professor Michael Halliday. Here he outlines some of the key concepts of systemic functional theory. He begins by explaining how the theory came to be called systemic functional.*

MAKH: The systemic is really concerned with representing language as a resource. I have always tried to make this distinction between the notion of language as rules and the notion of language as a resource. And the concept of the system is really set up to kind of capture the potential at any point – what are the meanings that are available to the speaker or the writer and what are the possible ways of expressing these and linking them up with what's around. So the systemic part is, as I say, really the notion of language as resource.

Let me try and pick up on this notion of language as resource and choice. What that means really is that as you speak or write you are ongoingly making selections among this vast potential. And what I want to say is: to understand the meaning of what anyone chooses to say, you've got to put it in the context of what he or she might have chosen to say but didn't – what were the actual alternatives at this point. And this is what the system network is trying to capture.

Now it is not saying at all of course that the choosing is a kind of conscious process. You can bring it to consciousness, and we all do at certain times. I mean, you know, well obviously say writers do. Say a poet has to think about rhymes, writers are selecting words or appropriate expression.

The functional part is really kind of itself multi-functional – that is there are three different senses. There's the basic notion of simply function in the sense of use – how people use language, what they do with it, what they expect it to do for them if you like.

So the second sense is the way we actually represent the grammar. So, of course, we talk about basic word classes – nouns and verbs and adjectives, you can't have any grammar without that; but as the main way of representing let's say a structure we use functional concepts. So we tend to talk about things like the Process, the Actor in the process, the Goal, the Circumstances. Or then we may switch to notions like Subject, which is a meaningful functional concept; it's not just a formal label. Or to things like Theme and Rheme. So the second sense is the kind of analysis that we do.

And the third sense is perhaps a more abstract one, which because it is more abstract I labelled as metafunctions, where what we're saying is the whole architecture of language is in fact functional in origin. So it has evolved really around these three basic concepts of language as a way of representing our ... I would rather have a more active word. We sometimes use the word construing, that is actually constructing the individual's model of reality – of the world that they live in and what goes on inside them. We refer to this as ideational. And then secondly, as a way of what we call enacting, of actually taking part in social processes – building social relationships and so on. We call that the interpersonal. And then thirdly, in the sense of as part of doing all this, the construing bit, the enacting bit, you have to have a text. You have to have a sense in which you construct a discourse, which is continuous, which relates to the environment. This we call the textual. And what I'm trying to say here is that these three very fundamental functions are actually intrinsic, are inherent in the whole way that language has evolved, the way it is learnt by children and so on.

CC: *Professor Halliday then continued by explaining what is meant by context, which is a central concept in systemic functional theory. He refers to Firth, who was his teacher at London University in the 1940s and 50s. In turn Professor Firth drew on the work of Malinowski, the British anthropologist, who studied Pacific Islanders and their communities in the second decade of the 20th century.*

MAKH: The notion of context was quite central to Firth's work and he in turn had built it up on the basis of what he had done together with Malinowski, the anthropologist. What Firth was saying was that if you are interested in real language as what he often referred to as typical texts in their contexts of situation – what he meant by this was that his interest was in the way people used language, spoken or written, as it might be, and the situations, the environments in which they used it, because that was really the only way in which you could look at language from a functional point of view. And he defined meaning at one point as function in context (e.g. Firth 1957b).

So this was an attempt to model the situation in which language was used and in a way which enabled us so to speak to look at it from the linguistic point of view – so that we were actually using the same tools that we were using for the grammar. Now an interesting question arises whether you want to sort of set up some kind of determination from one to the other and people often ask this question: does the context cause the text or does the text cause the context. I think that you have to get away from this causal notion and use rather this concept of realisation, where what you're saying is "No, these are different aspects of a single process. You could look at it from either end." And whichever end you look at it from you can say that it is in a certain sense constructing or construing – I use that term because I want to think of these rather as processes of meaning. So construing.

Now, you can sort of construe from either end. So think for example of playing games, some kind of game in which the language is an important part. Now if you see four people sitting around a table with a pack of cards you can make certain predictions about what they're going to say. If you can see the layout, it's a game of bridge, or it's a game of whatever, you can predict the sort of discourse that goes on. But equally if you just heard this discourse on tape, you could reconstruct the situation. So we in fact as speakers, users of language, we're all the time construing from one end or the other. Or typically of course from both, if both are accessible to us.

Those are simply features that can illustrate what is in fact a process that is always taking place, whether it's written or spoken, whatever kind of language is being used, there is always a context and there is always this possibility of a kind of two-way movement from one to the other.

CC: *Prof Halliday went on to explain how the concept of context was further developed within systemic functional theory.*

MAKH: We came to a sort of model, which was in terms of really three variables: the kind of social action, what you might think of as the activity that was going on but in terms that would be recognised in the culture as a form of social action, so that it could be described; then, secondly, the participants, the interactants, let's say those who were actually involved in this situation and their relationships to each other in terms of statuses and roles; and then thirdly, in the broadest sense, the role that language was being required to play in the situation, and this included at the most obvious level the channel, I mean was it spoken or written – but obviously there's a lot more than that, there's a whole lot of rhetorical aspects about how language was being used, and these I put together. So we had three headings in fact for these: the first, the social activity, we called the field; the second, the interactants, interpersonal relationships we called the tenor (I at first called it style); and the third one we called the mode, which was fairly obvious.

So this was an attempt to model the situation in which language was used, and in a way which enabled us so to speak to look at it from the linguistic point of view.

Open University
2005

With Manuel A. Hernández (1998)

Introduction

The transcriptions of the oral interviews that follow have the purpose of providing a current perspective on some central topics of Systemic Functional Linguistics by leading thinkers in the Australian context. Needless to say, Michael Alexander Kirkwood Halliday is also the founder of the theory and the inspiration for numerous recent developments of the systemic functional model. J. R. Martin and Christian Matthiessen have worked and continue to work "close to the master" – 'the boss', as M. Gregory commented in Cardiff – and have brilliantly explored and developed some important threads of the theory. The interview with M. A. K. Halliday took place in the context of "the 25th International Systemic Functional Institute and Congress", July 1998, at Cardiff University, U.K. The ones with Christian Matthiessen and J. R. Martin took place during "The Tenth Euro-International Systemic Functional Workshop", July 1998, at the University of Liverpool, U.K.

The first time I met M. A. K. Halliday was at a summer course in systemics given by Ruqaiya Hasan and himself, in the summer of 1994, at the University of Leuven (Belgium), where he approached me on one occasion and asked me the usual questions that every teacher asks students the first time they come to class. From then onwards I have admired the linguist and the man. During this brief encounter I asked him whether his theories have been applied to systems other than language and his immediate response was citing the title of a book published that same year: Michael O´Toole's (1994) *The Language of Displayed Art* (that I read afterwards almost at one sitting).

During that course, while he was outlining the main elements of his theory, I thought to myself: "This man is a philosopher rather than a linguist or a semiotician." Today some six years on from that time I realise I was wrong: he is all three things – linguist, semiotician *and* philosopher, although we all know that his contribution to linguistics and semiotics has been recognised as the central one. Starting from a social perspective of language, which has its roots in Malinowski and J.R. Firth among others, M. A. K. Halliday developed a comprehensive theory of linguistics which resulted in the creation of a new school called Systemic Functional Linguistics and he continues today to lead and inspire new developments even as we stand at the threshold of the twenty-first Century. If I were asked about M. A. K. Halliday´s importance as a linguist, I would mention first – as a kind of exercise – his conceptualising of language as social semiotic system, his consistent interest in education, his respect for all languages, the applicability of his theoretical conceptions to multiple areas of knowledge, and his penetrating analysis on the antecedents to language (origins of the metafunctional description). Secondly, and focusing now on the characterisation of his theory, I would point out the relevant role of the grammatical system of language at all ranks organised in terms of the three metafunctional meanings, the structural multilayered descriptions (polyphony), and the descriptions of the contexts categorising varieties of language.

It occurred to me that *Arms and the Man*, the famous play by G. B. Shaw, could have served as the title to Hallidays's interview in various ways and for different reasons: First, because of his courageous independence against the prescriptive tendencies of linguistic transformational generative models led by Chomsky in the 1960s and 1970s, and his alignment with richer social linguistic traditions (Halliday 1978b: 4; Hodge 1998: 144). Second, because although Halliday hasn't ever had the intention of universalising his theory, I think that nowadays we can affirm that his influence on today´s scientific thought is all pervasive, a fact that is not always recognised by some scholars under the influence of generativist schools. Third, because of the applicability of his language theories to the description of many languages other than English, without privileging the English code: as Halliday himself puts it: "... there is a tendency to foist the English code on others. Modern English linguistics, with its universalist ideology, has been distressingly ethnocentric, making all other languages look like imperfect copies of English" (M. A. K. Halliday 1985a: xxxi). Fourth, because nowadays the man and the linguist is not alone any more as the number of important linguists working on and reworking Halliday´s theories is demonstrating, so much as the success of courses and conferences gathering lots of like-minded people from all over the world – from different language cultures, and from a variety of fields such as linguistics, education, sociology, psychology, computing, neurology, etc. – around a thinker of that stature.

The questions I put to Halliday follow this general pattern: Questions about the genesis of his theory of language, his beginnings in the hands of J. R. Firth, the people who influenced his thinking, the origins of the metafunctional description, and future perspectives of the theory. His words still resound in my ears and I discovered that his voice and his profound and lively conversation resemble the tones and repetitions that characterise some of his writings, in which it is sometimes difficult to know where 'the hare' is going to jump – this is the impression I had when I first read *Learning How to Mean* (1975) or *Language as Social Semiotic* (1978b). While writing this introduction to the interview I was surprised on finding a similar impression in a perceptive paper written by Hodge, when he says that "the series of restatements form a polyphony, not a mere repetition" and that Halliday can combine new ideas with change "in such subtle proportions that it is often difficult to specify them" (Hodge 1998: 156).

Martin's and Matthiessen's responses raise important issues related to Systemic Functional Linguistics' theoretical core and to its present and future perspectives and developments. At one point Martin says that "the (systemic) functional linguistics will thrive because it can be valued by the community and can contribute to the community." I can only hope that his words become all the truer as we move into the twenty-first Century.

Finally, I would like to publicly acknowledge my gratitude to M. A. K. Halliday, and also J.R. Martin and Christian Matthiessen for their generosity and trust in agreeing to be interviewed for the *Revista Canaria de Estudios Ingleses*.

Acknowledgements

I wish to thank the authors for the corrections on the draft version of the interviews. I would like also to thank to Eija Ventola and Ana Mª. Martín Uriz for their valuable help with these interviews, and to Rachel and Daisy Pérez Brennan for their help in the transcription of the tapes.

An interview with Michael Halliday: The man and the linguist

MAH: *I am very interested in the genesis of your theory of language. So, going back to the '60s and '70s, what do you remember of those days when you worked with Firth? How was it that you decided to begin exploring new roads out of the generativism and structuralism of those times? Do you think that you were yourself an enfant terrible, 'a rebel' in a sense?*

MAKH: No. I do not think I am a rebel in the sense I would understand the term! I would rather emphasize the continuity between my thinking and what I learnt from those who went before me and those who were around me. But I would like to push the beginnings a little further back, because, in fact, I began as a language teacher. I was instructed in Chinese by the British Army, on one of the many language courses that were required during the Second World War. I worked for some time in counterintelligence, using my knowledge of Chinese; and then I was made an instructor in the language. So I was already beginning to teach a foreign language at a very early age – in 1945, when I was just 20 years old; and for 13 years thereafter I was mainly a teacher of languages. So my way into linguistics was very much with the experience of someone whose questions had arisen in the course of learning, and then of teaching a foreign language.

I was first taught linguistics in China, by two very distinguished Chinese scholars, one of whom in particular taught me the foundations of modern linguistics and phonetics. This was Wang Li. He had himself been trained in Europe, first of all as a phonetician; he was also very much influenced by Jespersen. He taught me a whole range of things including – this was very important – the tradition of Chinese linguistics. So that was my first input. Then when I came back to Britain I went to study with Firth, so Firth was the second major source. Firth placed himself very strongly within the European tradition.

MAH: *Can you add something more about the Chinese source influencing on your thought?*

MAKH: There were two aspects to it: One was work in the history of Chinese linguistics, which goes back about two thousand years. The early Chinese scholars mainly were phonologists, and after about a thousand years they in turn borrowed many ideas from the Indians, who were also great phonologists but with a totally different orientation, because the Indian phonology was based in phonetics, whereas Chinese phonology was a highly abstract system with no phonetics at all. So what was interesting was what happened when the two came together. This was my way in, as it were, from the historical end. Simultaneously with that, the second aspect was through my teacher Wang Li, who was himself both a grammarian and a phonologist and phonetician, and also a dialectologist. He taught me dialect methods, which I found extraordinarily valuable. I worked on Chinese dialects with informants, and learnt to record their language and study both the phonology and the grammar, so that involved the field methods as well as the underlying theory which Wang Li himself was developing.

MAH: *What are then the main sources of your own theory of language? Why did you pick up the notions of context and text studied by Firth?*

MAKH: Well, I was always convinced of the importance of, so to speak, looking in to language from the top, from the higher units, and the higher levels; and during the 1950's, as well as studying with Firth, I worked a great deal with some close colleagues at the time: Jeffrey Ellis, Trevor Hill, Dennis Berg, Jean Ure, Peter Wexler, and others. What we shared was a Marxist view of language. We were trying to understand and build up a theory of language which would be – as I put it the other day – giving value to languages and language varieties which at that time were not valued either politically or academically: so, non-standard dialects, spoken as opposed to written language, unwritten languages, colonial languages, some of which were struggling to become national languages, and languages of lower social classes – all the varieties of language whose value had not formed the basis of linguistic theory. We were trying to bring these in, working for example, on the emergence of national languages in ex-colonies. That's where the theory of register became important.

There were two sources for this. The first was Firth's notion of a restricted language, which had been very important during the 2nd World War. What Firth said was that any typical discourse – he wouldn't have used the term 'discourse' but, rather, 'text' – belongs to some restricted language, so that the meanings that are expressed are not, as it were, selected from within the totality of the language, they are selected from within some fairly special subset. A critical example of this was taken from the war against Japan: the Japanese pilots would communicate with each other in plain language, not in code, because they assumed nobody else spoke Japanese. So Firth said, "We can train our people in the restricted language used by the Japanese aircrew to communicate with each other and with those on the ground." And they did this very successfully and in very short time. So that was one source of the notion of register. The other was our own work in the evolution of 'standard' national languages, when we said, "Right, there are dialectal varieties, originally regional and now also social; but there are also functional varieties." We had debated a long time what to call these, and we got the term 'register' from T.B.W. Reid (1956), the professor of Romance Philology at Oxford. From these two sources together, we were able to derive the notion of 'register' in the sense of functional variation. Michael Gregory, who did a lot of work in this area, introduced the term 'diatypic' varieties. Now, the notion of context, how you actually investigate it, and how you bring it in to the domain of linguistics, that was from Firth. Firth himself, of course, had based his own ideas on the work of Malinowski, who was an anthropologist.

MAH: *I have a question connected to that: "What do you think makes your theory so attractive to people from so many different linguistic and cultural backgrounds?"*

MAKH: I hope that it does show its multiple origins. To follow up with my own history: when in 1958 I moved from teaching Chinese to teaching linguistics, I was immediately very closely involved with teachers, first in Edinburgh (Scotland) and then in London, and these, of course, were teachers in British schools, therefore with medium English. And they were not mainly foreign language teachers, but rather either teachers of literature, teachers of the mother tongue, or teachers of other fields, such as science, or history, or whatever. So my orientation naturally shifted: I had to work on English. And it is true that, as you noticed from here, in the meeting, the majority of the people in this group for one reason or another have concentrated on English, either in educational contexts or computational linguistics and so on. So we have to work always both to extend the domains so that the model is used for languages other than English and also to keep the doors open so that ideas are coming in from outside, not just from the Anglo-American world but also from other traditions. I don't say we always succeed! – but we are at least aware of this problem, and certainly we are aware of the problem of being Anglo-centric which so much recent linguistics has suffered from.

MAH: *Retrospectively speaking, do you feel that you could have worked more effectively to expand your theory in the way that other approaches to linguistics have done, such as generativism, pragmatics, etc.?*

MAKH: Coming back to Firth. He required that his postgraduate students should read around in all schools of linguistics. His own orientation was primarily European, so we tended to know more about Hjelmslev and the Danish school, about the Prague phonology, about Martinet and the French linguists, and so on. So this was our main background. We also read American structuralism (Firth was not very keen on the work of the American structuralists; he was more impressed by Pike), and of course, we read the background in Bloomfield and Sapir ... When Chomsky came along, I spent a lot of time reading Chomsky's early work and that of those who worked with him, but I found they didn't answer the questions I was interested in, so I continued to develop my own ideas and to look for others who shared the same concerns – such as my very good American friend Sydney Lamb, whose ideas were very close to mine. I worked with him.

Now, I'm not a missionary. I'm obviously very pleased if people take up what I've done. But it is not my aim to try to spread it around. If people find it useful, that is good, and I learn from them; but it was never part of my thinking to try to promote my ideas. Somebody once said to me, a few years ago, "Don't you feel very distressed about being so much out of fashion?," and I said, "Look, there is one thing that would worry me more than being out of fashion and that is being *in* fashion!" But of course, the theory has expanded into all kinds of new domains – through the work of other people. Look at the topics covered in this Congress!

MAH: *The next question is also related to your beginnings. Did you meet Whorf?*

MAKH: No, he died very young. I think he died in 1943.

MAH: *Your notion that language does not reflect, but creates reality reminds me of B.L. Whorf's hypothesis. Can you please explain this for a minute? How was it that you came to think about this?*

MAKH: I did read Whorf very early, relatively early; and in the '60s, when I was teaching at University College London, I gave one course over two or three years using Malinowski and Whorf, as a way in to functional theories of meaning, Now, what I took from Whorf, particularly at that time, was the notion that different languages hold different semantic schemata. The notion of constructing or constituting reality, as opposed to reflecting it, took me longer to work through – with the help of Bernstein, and also Berger and Luckmann (1967). My early views were more attuned to classical Marxism, where in Marxist theory priority is given to the technological – to the material rather than to what we would now call the semiotic. Let me use a generalization and say that human history is essentially the interplay of two broad types of process, the material and the semiotic. 'Semiotic' includes language, but of course it includes lots of other things as well; it covers all processes of meaning. Now, classical Marxism always gave priority to the material – it was 'technology driven', or whatever you want to call it; in my early thinking I had accepted that perspective, and it took me a long time to reappraise it. You get involved in all kinds of details, trying to construct the model rather than reflecting on the underlying assumptions. But after working, through the '60s and '70s, with new groups of colleagues, like Michael Gregory, then Bob Dixon, Rodney Huddleston and Richard Hudson, then Ruqaiya Hasan, then Robin Fawcett, and in the '80s with Jim Martin and Christian Matthiessen, and many others ... (I can't mention everybody that mattered!), naturally my thinking evolved. I had never taken language as a thing in itself, but only as part of human history; and I tried to reflect on it from the standpoint of the work of the British Marxist historians – Christopher Hill, E.P. Thompson and others, which I greatly admire. This gives a perspective within which you can integrate the two, the material and the semiotic. Some people in the '70s and '80s jumped to the opposite extreme, they overplayed the semiotic as if everything in human history had been and was being determined discursively, as if there was nothing but discourse. I gave this view a label, I called it 'naïve discursivism'. What you need is a balance between the two. There is a dialectic relation, a dialectic in which the semiotic and the material are constantly interpenetrating, and what happens is the result of the tension between them. Given that perspective, then, you see the constituting effect of the semiotic, the extent to which reality is in fact constituted by language just as it is constituted by our material practices and the material processes that go on around us.

MAH: *I think that your reflections have made me understand much better why you call language a social semiotic system ...*

MAKH: In the '60s, when I was very much concerned with developing systemic notions of grammar within the system-structure framework set up by Firth and others, almost all the interest in grammar among linguists was in formal grammars. But these were not relevant to scholars looking at language from the outside – notably Basil Bernstein. A lot of the pressure to continue working within a functional semantic orientation came from Bernstein, and the linguists in his unit; then Ruqaiya Hasan started working in his group in the late '60s. But the main stream in linguistics was so strongly focused on formal models in grammar, all based on structure, that I felt that, for a while, I had to back away from trying to study the grammar systemically; and so for about ten years I concentrated much more on the social aspects of language. Most of my work in the '70s was directed towards this notion of the social semiotic. The term and the basic concept, by the way, come from Greimas.

MAH: *You have mentioned Basil Bernstein, and I think that his theory of educational development and social class had an important influence on your description of congruent and metaphorical language and in your approach to educational problems. Since you said in one of your lectures that he had been misunderstood, can you please explain just for a couple of minutes what you really meant?*

MAKH: I got to know Bernstein in 1961, or so. In Edinburgh we read some of his early work and we invited him to come and give us a seminar. He had been a teacher in London and had faced the problem of children failing in school; and he was trying to understand why this educational failure was so obviously linked to social class. He worked through various theoretical models; but language, he saw from the start, played an essential part. He started to make a distinction between what he initially called 'public language' and 'formal language'; this gradually evolved into a theory of codes, recognizing that educational knowledge was construed (whether or not it had to be was a different issue; but in fact it was) in new linguistic forms – new, that is to say, in terms of the prior history of the child before the child comes into school. But if you then look at the family background of the children before they come to school, you find that there tends to be a significant difference according to social class, so that middle class children typically had already gained entry to the language of educational knowledge in their homes; therefore, they were all ready to go. As soon as the first day they got into school, they knew what was happening, they recognized the forms of discourse. The typical working class family, which at that time Bernstein related to the notion of personal and positional family structures – there were different types of role system in the family, in the way the child creates an identity – typically, had largely used what he first called the public language, later 'restricted code', and therefore there was a disjunction, there was a big gulf to be crossed when they had to move into the language of education; the problem being, not that it can't be crossed, but that the teachers had no way of knowing this; they disvalued these children's language anyway, and had no conception of how to help them to build upwards from it. This was all totally misunderstood, particularly by American colleagues because they were … partly, I think, it was a panic reaction to the notion of social class, which rather frightened them. But, in any case, Bernstein was vilified and attacked as if he was denigrating the working class and saying that their language was inferior and they were inferior – which, of course, he wasn't. Mary Douglas,[1] one of the British anthropologists who understood him very well, understood that, in fact, he was much more critical of the middle class than he was of the working class, but you have to read him with some intelligence. So, in any case, Bernstein was conducting this project throughout the 1960s, gathering data of different kinds, partly dialogue, partly narrative, trying to investigate this situation from different angles; and we were … I myself, early colleagues I've already mentioned, and the teachers in the curriculum development project that I had initiated, such as David Mackay and Peter Doughty – we tried to work towards a grammar that would be relevant for educational purposes. But we still had a long way to go, and so we really weren't yet able to provide the kind of resources that Bernstein needed, although we got some way, and one or two of the people here now, like Bernard Mohan and Geoffrey Turner, were working as linguists in Basil's team. This was where my wife, Ruqaiya Hasan, got into it. She started working with Basil Bernstein in 1968, and there she began to develop her own ideas first in relation to the analysis of children's texts (stories told by children were some of her main data at the time) to see what could be done to bring out the underlying grammatical and semantic patterns so that one could test whether there were significant differences between different groups.

MAH: *To finish this first part, I would like you to talk a little bit about Ruqaiya Hasan's contributions and mutual influences.*

MAKH: You know she was one of my students. She came to Edinburgh in 1960, starting from a background in literature. She had been teaching English literature in Pakistan, and she was at first very sceptical about the relevance of grammar and linguistics towards what she did, but she went deeply into it and wrote a brilliant thesis on the language of literature, using two modern novels as the basis. Then she worked for some time in our (Nuffield / Schools Council) Programme in Linguistics and English Teaching, as one of the linguists working along with the teachers; she started specializing there in the area of cohesion, which she was able to develop when she joined Bernstein's unit, and we worked on this together when we wrote the book *Cohesion in English* (1976). She backed off for a little while because she had a baby and she was looking after the child; then when she got back to work she contributed substantially to the 'core' levels of grammar and semantics and to sociolinguistics as well. What she's particularly brought to the work has been an immensely wide reading in areas around language and linguistics, in philosophy for example, and especially in sociology. Recently for example she has written some very good critical work about Pierre Bourdieu's ideas on language (see section 3 of Hasan 2005). She has always had this sort of perspective where she has been able to work on the inside of language but to look at it from round about; and I have certainly learnt a great deal from her.

In the 1980s Ruqaiya set up a research project, at Macquarie University in Sydney, with research colleagues David Butt, Carmel Cloran, and Rhondda Fahey – a very well designed project, in which she identified 24 mother-child pairs, where the child was always between three and a half and four – well advanced linguistically but still just before schooling; and structured according to sex of child and social class, so the four sets were: middle-class boys – middle-class girls – working-class boys – working-class girls. She did a detailed analysis of many hours of spontaneous conversations between these mothers and their children. She explored the semantic variation; that is to say, what she was interested in was the systematic variation in the meanings that were preferred, the semantic options that were taken up in the various situations in which the mothers and the children were involved. She subjected the results to a particular kind of factor analysis, 'principal components' analysis – derived from Labov's methods but which she modified in certain ways to suit this kind of material. What came out of this were some very remarkable findings. When she looked at particular domains within the total material, for example the way that mothers answered their children's questions, or the way that mothers gave reasons for instructions they were giving to the child on how to behave or how not to behave, she found that these mother-child pairs fell out into very clearly defined groups, and these groups were defined on two dimensions. In some cases, the difference arose between the mothers of boys and the mothers of girls, so the mothers of boys were talking to their sons in very different ways from the ways the other mothers were talking to their daughters. The other dimension was social class, so that the mothers in what she called the 'higher autonomy profession' families, the middle-class group, were talking with their children in very different ways from the mothers in families of the 'lower autonomy profession'. This was something that simply emerged from the analysis: the groups were part of the design of the original sample, of course; but they were not present at all in the analysis – they simply emerged through the principal components analysis in the computer and turned out to be statistically highly significant. What she was doing, you see, was essentially testing the basic theoretical hypothesis that had been developed by Bernstein, but using data which were much richer than those available to Bernstein in the '60s, because the techniques were not available in the '60s for doing very large scale recordings of spontaneous conversations. By the '80s they were; and furthermore our grammar and our semantics had developed immensely during that time; so, on the one hand, the resources for structuring the sample and collecting the data had improved, and, on the other hand, the grammar and the semantics had advanced to the point where she was able to set up a semantic model for actually investigating this sort of data. This has been a very major contribution (consolidated as Hasan 2009).

MAH: *Referring to your description of the metafunctions, when did you realize that a good theory of language had to begin by studying language functions? I am referring to your brilliant research on Nigel (Halliday 1975), which implied a substantial modification of the well-known Bühler's and Jakobson's functions (Halliday 1970a).*

MAKH: I knew that work, and indeed I used to compare different concepts of linguistic functions, those of Malinowski, Bühler and others, but looking at them from another perspective – from the perspective of the internal organization of language. I always thought that these were important in helping us to understand the context of situation and the context of culture; but I was also not happy with the way they were interpreted only as functions of the utterance. It was Scalička, one of the leading Prague scholars, who actually raised that question – I didn't see the paper till much later – in relation to Mathesius's work, the question whether the functions should be regarded as functions of the utterance or whether they have some place in the linguistic system; in other words, did they belong just to *parole* or were they, in some sense, present in the *langue*? Now, I was unhappy with their assignment to *parole*, to the utterance, because when you actually looked at texts you could never say ... well occasionally you could cite utterances which were clearly one thing or another, but most of the time all functions were going along side by side. So I thought they must in some sense be located in the system – I didn't know how. But, from a different standpoint, when I started using system networks, when I decided that for the questions that I was asking I needed to be able to model the total resource – what I called the meaning potential – as some kind of network of options, then I found – first of all on a small scale grammar of a particular Chinese text but then on a much larger scale when I came to be working on English – then I found ... well: imagine a large piece of paper like this, on which you're representing the grammar of the English clause by writing networks for it: you stand back, and you find that there is a whole bunch of systems here that are closely related and then there is a kind of gap, not a total gap, with a little bit of wiring across it but much less dense, and then you have another big block here, and then you have another gap and another big block. And I thought, "Why? What is happening?", and then I realized that these blocks were, in fact, very closely related to the notions of function that have come from outside linguistics. Remember that Bühler and others were looking at language from the outside; they weren't grammarians. My grammar networks matched up closely with their concept of functions. There was clearly one component which was, let's say, *Darstellung*, 'representational' in Bühler's sense – this is what I called 'ideational'; then there was another component which combined what in the English translation are called the expressive and the conative. The grammar did not in fact separate these two. This is not saying that there is no meaning to the distinction between expressive and conative; but if you look at them from inside the system they are aspects of the same thing. For example, if I set up an interrogative MOOD, you can think of that in the expressive sense 'I want to know something', but you can also think of it in the conative sense, 'you tell me something'; the grammar had what I called the 'interpersonal' function. But then there was another component in the grammar which didn't correspond to anything in Bühler: this was the function of creating discourse, which I then referred to as the 'textual'. This included all the sort of things that create discourse, like cohesive patterns, texture, thematic and information structure ... and they formed another block. These three functions were intrinsic to the system of a language.

Then, around that time (mid '60s) the primary school teachers had been asking me about early language development; and very conveniently just at that time we had our own baby. I thought, "Right, I'm going to do a detailed study of the one child, so I can do it very intensively." So for three and a half years I studied this child's language. It was clear that he started off with what I called the 'microfunctions', as he built up a protolanguage before moving into his mother tongue. There were three or four distinct functional domains from about ten months onwards. So what I was interested in was how these get mapped into the functions that are present in the adult linguistic system. A lot of my book *Learning How to Mean* (1975) is about this mapping. So the functional model comes from these two sources: one, as a grammarian, trying to model the grammar and then matching it up with the functions proposed by others from the outside; and the second, working with teachers on early language development and trying to model the way that a child constructed the grammar.

MAH: Why didn't you write a book like the Introduction to Functional Grammar before 1985? I was very surprised when I began reading it and learned a lot. I have read "Notes on Transitivity and Theme" (1967b, c; 1968), Explorations in the Functions of Language (1973), Language as a Social Semiotics (1978a), and others, but it was not until 1985 that I became really convinced that your theory of language was powerful and really applicable.

MAKH: Well, as you know, in the 1960s I wrote "Notes on transitivity and theme", which contains many of those ideas. But I'm not very good at writing books; and also I tend to write in response to people who ask me. I tend to respond to the context rather than initiate it; people would ask me to give them a talk, and then to write it up as a paper, so I usually wrote little bits all over the place and it took me a very long time to get that *Introduction to Functional Grammar* written. It wasn't that I hadn't thought of it ... it just took me a very long time, because I was doing too many things at once. I liked teaching, but I spent a lot of time preparing classes; and when I became the head of a department, I was very taken up with administration. Most of that book was written on the train going to and from work. This is why to me it was so important always to have a train trip – yes, seriously! But there is another reason also: as I said, I did back off during the '70s in order to work more in the area of the context of language, trying to get a sense of the relationship between language and society, linguistic structure and social structure ... and moving from (as I was putting it earlier) the more classical Marxist position in which language was merely a reflection of material reality, towards a view that is perhaps more 'neo-Marxist'. One person that I was exchanging ideas with was Jim Martin, who has developed a powerful model relating language to its social context (Martin 1992).

MAH: *About Jim Martin. In 1997, he wrote, together with Christian Matthiessen and Clare Painter, a wonderful book with exercises 'explaining', in a certain sense, your Introduction... (Martin et al. 1997/2010).*

MAKH: Yes – it is an excellent book. Jim Martin was always pushing more towards the constructivist viewpoint ... I was already convinced of this, but I was also always aware of the danger of going too far, and you can go too far in this respect. The thing that was always important to me was to maintain a comprehensive viewpoint. The problem these days is that the subject (linguistics) has evolved so far that you cannot be a generalist any more. You have to specialize in this field or another ... My mind was always saying, "Well, if I look at this bit of language in this way, how will it seem when I jump over to look at it from here, or from here, or from here?" It seemed obvious to me that whatever I did I had to keep in mind all the other aspects, I mean, if one looked at something in a certain way in adult language, could one still explain how children had learnt it? Could one still explain how it had evolved that way? This means that it takes a long time to sort out the major perspectives, but I think it is very important. Those who are very much leaders in the field, and have been all along, have tended both to share his view and also to complement each other in the aspects of language that they were primarily foregrounding. Jim Martin, for example, is an outstanding grammarian, working in the core of language; he has also done an enormous amount of work in language education, collaborating over many years with school teachers in Australia. Christian Matthiessen, also a brilliant grammarian, has done fundamental work in computational linguistics; Robin Fawcett is another leading theorist with expertise in this field. They can tell us what the grammar looks like when we're trying to operate it on a computer. I've already talked about Ruqaiya Hasan's work in the relationship of language to society. I could give lots of other examples. To me it is important that all these ideas feed back into our notion of language. So we are not just asking questions from the inside, the sort of questions set up by linguists, but we're asking questions that are set up by people around about, who are interested in language from other angles. That's what I've tried to bring about.

MAH: *Something you want to add? Are you asking yourself any new questions?*

MAKH: I think I'm too old to be asking any new questions!

MAH: *I don't think so! You can yet inspire a lot of new questions to all people around the world!*

MAKH: Well, new questions will come up. I think that if the theory that has come to be known as 'Systemic Functional Linguistics', if it is still a living organism, as it were – and I think it is – this is partly because we are not simply going over the same ground. We are always asking new questions, and new people are always coming in with questions of their own. So it's not so much whether I myself ask new questions but whether there are people who do; there are, and they do. And this is why it is so important what's going on in a conference like this, because a lot of people around have new questions to ask of each other. There is another point that I just want to add here. We have had two plenary sessions now: by Erich Steiner, and by Michael Gregory. Erich is another major formative thinker in these areas, someone with a very strong sense of social accountability.

MAH: *Do you agree with Steiner's perspectives on Systemic Functional Linguistics in philology, technological fields, education, cultural studies ...?*

MAKH: Indeed. I agree with his perspective very much. I'm not sure I would divide it up in the same way, and there are one or two specific points that he made where I would want to say, "Well, actually, it wasn't quite like that." Just to give you an example: Erich talked about where systemics, or maybe scale and category, met up with strata and levels. But, in fact, it wasn't a meeting: the strata and the levels were always part of the theory from the start. So there I would say, "Well, look, no, that was not the order of things; this was part of the original architecture." But the basic picture is as he set it out.

I think the only final thing I want to say is this. For a lot of people who are coming across our work now, this may look to them as if it is some huge edifice that was suddenly spontaneously created. But, of course, it wasn't. It evolved very slowly; it evolved over a very long time; it continues to evolve and there is nothing fixed about it. We have worked towards certain concepts, certain methodologies which seem to us to be useful in taking on certain tasks and in addressing certain questions. But it has always been part of a much wider setting: others' functional approaches to language, and beyond these the whole field of linguistics. All these are permeable, and I very much agree with Michael Gregory that one should be all the time interacting with what is going on outside. This sets up a tension, because if you are running a linguistics programme you are taking students through a course, through one, two, three or four years, and most of those students are not going to be professional linguists. They are going to be any number of things: teachers, computer scientists, specialists in law or in medicine, information technologists, journalists, librarians ... What they want is to be able to engage with language. Some people would say, "Right; you've got to tell them a little bit about everything that's going on: a little bit about government and binding, a little bit about West Coast functionalism, a little bit about mainstream European linguistics, a little bit about pragmatics, a little bit about systemics, and so on." And, of course, one can agree with this: it is a good liberal principle! However, that doesn't teach the students to engage with language. What it means is that a course in linguistics, instead of being a course about how to study language, becomes a course about how to study linguistics. It becomes a totally meta-operation ... Now, that is fine for those who are going on to become linguistics specialists; by the time they get, say, to third or fourth year, you can start doing all this. But to my first and second year students I want to give them tools, resources to work with. That is how I came to work towards this kind of model: I just had to work out something to meet my own needs. I wasn't thinking at all of being a theorist, or an innovator, or a rebel as you suggested at the start. I tried to find out what theory and methods were available. But there were certain gaps, resources I couldn't find ... so I started to develop my own ideas because I needed to engage with language. Now, if we choose to say, "Right, to begin with, we're going to teach you one particular model," this is not because we think that we have the monopoly of truth, but because we want to give them tools. You can start analysing texts; you can start looking at your own language; you can apply this to whatever you teach in the classroom: literature, English as a foreign language, or whatever. I think it is only fair to the students to do that. Of course, it has its dangers: they may then go away and think that there is only one truth. One way to get around this, in my view, is to teach it historically. You can't range over every particular model that's around today; that's too much. But you can say, "We're selecting this way of doing it, so you can engage with language; but I want you to know where it came from, and why." And that will give them the perspective. That's all I wanted to add!

MAH: *Thank you very much, Dr Halliday.*

Cardiff University
July 1998

Note

1 See the comments by Douglas in Bernstein's obituary in the Guardian: http://www.guardian.co.uk/news/2000/sep/27/guardianobituaries.education [accessed 3 September 2012].

10

With Geoff Thompson and Heloisa Collins (1998)

The development of the theory

HC: *Can I ask you first about how you see your own work as fitting into the development of linguistics as a whole, and especially language as social practice?*

MAKH: I see it as part of the development of the field. I would always emphasize how much I share with other linguists: I've never either felt particularly distinct or wanted to be distinct. I never saw myself as a theorist; I only became interested in theory, in the first place, because, in the theoretical approaches that I had access to, I didn't find certain areas developed enough to enable me to explore the questions that I was interested in. For example, in Firth's work – obviously, the main influence on me was my teacher, J. R. Firth – there was a sort of hole in the middle. He did a lot of work at the phonology-phonetics end, and he did a lot of work at the context of situation end, but he didn't work with grammar. So I felt I had to develop that. But, essentially, I took his basic notions of systems and structures. And in the broader sense, I've always felt that what I was doing was very much part of the tradition – well, I should say, perhaps, part of the European tradition, because we didn't take very much from American structuralism. I did, though, draw on the Sapir-Whorf tradition in the United States – but not so much the post-Bloomfield school, which seemed more remote. And also when I came to know of Pike's work, I found that it was much more compatible with what I was doing. And then, bringing in another aspect, I was also very much influenced by my study in China, where I had been taught both traditional Chinese phonological theory, and also modern theory but as applied to Chinese linguistics. For example, I did my historical linguistics in relation to Sino-Tibetan, not in relation to Indo-European; and my dialectology in Chinese dialects and so on.

Now as regards the social practice, again I would feel that what I've explored has been a development of these interests. Again, it goes back to Firth, whose view was – and I think he said it in so many words – that the important direction for the future lay in the sociology of language. In the sixties, the name and the concept of sociolinguistics came into being. It was defined by somebody in the United States – I've forgotten now if this was Labov's formulation or Fishman's (e.g. 1970), or whose – as inter-relations between linguistic structure and social structure. I suppose my own thinking was a bit different from the main-stream sociolinguistics as that evolved and developed; indeed I was quite critical of it in some respects. My influence came more from Bernstein. I generally accepted his view of cultural transmissions and the framework he was using at the time: family role systems and their effect on language. He struck me as the one leading sociologist who really built language into his theory. So there was a lot of influence there, and that provided the context for my thinking on these issues.

HC: *I remember that in one of the lectures during the institute you told us about why it was that Bernstein for a while suffered all sorts of criticism: the way he put across his ideas at the time was not completely well-received.*

MAKH: He was totally brutalized (cf. discussion in Atkinson 1985, Halliday 1995, Labov 1969, 1972b): it drove him right out of the field. I think it was mainly in the United States that his work was misunderstood,[1] although that meant the picture got transmitted back across the Atlantic and his work was misunderstood over here as well, and in many other places – although not quite universally. At that time, Ruqaiya Hasan had got interested in Bernstein's work and Bernstein invited her to join in his project along with another linguist, Geoffrey Turner, who is here at this congress; and Bernie Mohan (now in Vancouver) worked with him for a while as well. Bernstein was at the Institute of Education in London while I was at University College, so it was very easy to meet and to interact.

GT: *You've talked about some of the main people that influenced you. What about the way your theory developed? What kind of stages would you see in your thinking?*

MAKH: From the late fifties onwards, and particularly when I started working with teachers, I felt that I needed to get a much more secure grounding both in an overall theory, an overall model of language, and also specifically in grammar and semantics. We didn't have any semantics at that time – it was very weak. So I moved consciously in that direction, and I was saying, I'm not ready to take further the notion of language in relation to social processes until I feel more confident of what I can say about language itself. So in that period, particularly in the sixties, I spent a lot of time, first of all, exploring Chomsky's work. And I found it didn't really answer my questions, it didn't help me to explore the right kind of issues. So I moved back to what I had been doing before, originally on Chinese. I shifted over into English; and in the sixties I worked with teachers at all levels, so I became involved with the context of developing a grammar for educational purposes. Now I still saw that as a part of what I sometimes call the social accountability of the linguist – although it wasn't directly political, it was, as I saw it, trying to make a contribution to society. And also, of course, we learn a lot about language from being involved in practical applications like this. I had this group in London, which I think must have been about the only time that somebody had got a research and development project where there were primary and secondary and tertiary teachers all in the same room, all doing the same job and working together. We spent about two years learning to talk to each other, finding out what each other was on about. That was immensely valuable.

By that time, of course, what I was doing in the core areas of language had very little value among linguists: it wasn't recognized. So I thought, OK, now in any case is it time to turn back to the social? And I tried to develop this notion of social semiotics. I did a lot of work in the seventies where I was moving away from the grammar and other core areas and saying, right, now let's look again at what is outside language and see if I can make contact there, but in a different perspective.

And then in the eighties I centred my writing again on the grammar. I thought, right, let's see how far we can make explicit a system-based grammar, but now with the semantics in it. By that time there were a number of people who were working in systemic computational linguistics. Up to about 1980, I had got involved a few times trying to test bits of the grammar computationally, but we didn't learn anything from it. We hadn't got to that stage yet; but from about 1980, with fifth generation computers, the computer became a real research tool. There was Bill Mann's project in California (Mann 1984) that I wrote the grammar for first, and then Christian [Matthiessen] was taken on. He was doing his Ph.D. in UCLA at the time and they took him on part-time. He extended the grammar, developed it, learnt the basic skills required for text generation, working with a computer (Matthiessen & Bateman 1991); and that fed back immensely, both through him as a person and as a great grammarian, but also through the experience of learning how to write grammars so that they could be processed in the machine. So all the time we've moved out into new directions, new kinds of application, but there's always been a significant feeding back into the theory.

GT: *One thing that constantly emerged last week [in the Systemic Linguistics Summer School run by Halliday] were references back to your early work, showing a continuity which seems to me to have been quite marked. There seems to be a constant thread in your thinking: one can go back to the early papers and find things in which the details may have changed, but the basic ideas remain. Would you say that you have essentially been working out ideas that were there in embryonic form from the start?*

MAKH: In a certain sense, yes. That's not to say, obviously, that there haven't been shifts. I'll give you one example. One important input was the political one, when I was working with a group of Marxist linguists who were trying to develop a Marxist theory of language. I learnt a lot from them, because we were very concerned to work out a theory that would give value to varieties of language that were traditionally neglected. I mean dialects as opposed to standards, spoken language as opposed to written, and learners' languages – children and non-native speakers, emerging languages from ex-colonies, unwritten vernaculars, all these kind of things. We didn't see ourselves as doing something terribly revolutionary; we saw this essentially as being present in European thinking, but needing to be brought together. Now, one example of where I've changed is that I had at that time what you might call a classical Marxist view, which was very much technology driven and therefore seeing language as a kind of second-order phenomenon, where essentially it was reflecting rather than construing.[2] But there has been a shift, generally, towards what has been characterized as neo-Marxist (I never liked these 'neo' labels, but it's certainly not 'post-Marxist'). I now want a better account of the balance between the material and the semiotic in human history. And so, instead of seeing language as essentially technology-driven, I would want to see it as a product of the dialectic between material processes and semiotic processes, so the semiotic become constructive – constitutive, if you like. That, I would say, is a fairly important shift (cf. Rosenau 1992).

SFL and other schools of linguistics

GT: *Very broadly, would it seem to you to be fair to characterize the two main streams of linguistics as isolating and integrating, with yours very firmly in the integrating camp?*

MAKH: Yes; if what you had in mind with 'isolating' was the mainstream tradition from Bloomfield via Chomsky in North America, with its insistence on autonomous syntax, with the way that they took language as a thing in itself, rather than as some element in a wider social system and process, then I think that's fair enough.

GT: *In the isolating tradition, socio-linguistics and pragmatics, for example, become things you can push aside if you're not interested in them, whereas, within the systemic-functional approach, you can't.*

MAKH: That's absolutely it. In a sense, the only reason why that tradition created sociolinguistics and pragmatics was because these weren't in the theory of language in the first place, where they should have been. And I always said that we didn't need a concept of sociolinguistics, because our concept of linguistics always was 'socio'. And similarly with pragmatics: to me this has always been simply the instantial end of the semantics. We don't need a separate discipline. Another dimension of the isolation, of course, is the isolation between system and text. If you're focusing on the system, the text is just data, which has no place in the theory. Then when somebody does want to come and study the text, they do it under a totally different disciplinary banner and both sides lose.

GT: *You mentioned earlier that you were outside 'mainstream' linguistics. Clearly there was a time during the 1960's when American structuralist linguistics was aggressively dominant. Did you ever feel like giving up linguistics?*

MAKH: Yes, there was indeed! About the mid-60's, when I wrote papers like 'Some notes on "deep" grammar' (1966) and 'Syntax and the consumer' (1964), I really did try to make contact with the mainstream. And the reaction was just: "Keep out!" I think if I'd been in the United States, I would have got out. I think it was only the luxury of not being in America that made it possible to survive, because so many good people in America were driven out: they just left the field. The work which should have been done, for example, on Native American languages was dropped for a whole decade or more. It was discouraging; but, as I say, the Atlantic was between us, so it wasn't quite that bad. And I've always enjoyed the teaching – we always had students who were interested.

But, on the other hand, I wasn't so bothered, in the sense that it never occurred to me that I had to persuade other people. I was never a missionary; I just wanted to get on with my own work. That was what became more difficult. Just to give you an example, I said just now that in the 60's data were out: the worst thing you could be called was data oriented. It was the really bad word of that decade. If you were data-oriented you were no linguist at all.[3] But you see, on the other hand, there was [Randolph] Quirk in the next department building up the Survey of English Usage, and he wasn't going to stand for any of that nonsense. I enjoyed working with him and Geoffrey Leech, David Crystal and so on. You weren't completely isolated, but you were shut out from the mainstream of linguistics. My feeling was that it didn't do me much harm but it did a lot of harm to the subject.

HC: *But presumably you are happier that you are mainstream now!*

MAKH: Well, yes. Although somebody once said to me later on: "Doesn't it worry you, always being out of fashion?" And I said: "There's only one thing that would worry me more, that's being in fashion." In a sense, though, this is a serious point. We all know political parties that do very well as long as they're in opposition!

Critical linguistics

HC: *Earlier you talked about the political aspects of your theory. It seems to me that, among modern linguists within the functional tradition, the one who shows that he is really on your side from the political point of view, not to mention the other aspects, is Gunther Kress (e.g. Kress & Hodge 1979). His work has evolved towards a very critical, political, interpretation of the linguistic analysis. How do you see this sort of step towards this more political preoccupation?*

MAKH: I see it very positively: I have a lot of interest in and respect for this work. There is a range of work that varies in the extent to which it actually engages with language; and I think that the sort of work that Gunther does, and other critical discourse analysts – Norman Fairclough (e.g. 1995/2010) and colleagues on the European continent and elsewhere – is outstanding in the way it does engage with language. There is a tradition which doesn't really engage with language, which is more like a kind of literary criticism where you make your commentary on the text but there's no way in which someone else coming along will get the same result. Now, I think critical discourse analysis stands out in the fact that they do consider language issues seriously. I have argued – and my wife [Ruqaiya Hasan] has done so more strongly because she feels very strongly about this – that they don't do it enough (e.g. Hasan 2009). They still need to locate what they say about language more clearly within a general framework, so that you really see to what extent a text is using the resources of the system, of the potential, in what sort of context of alternatives and so forth. So I think they could go further – and I'm not saying they all have to be systemicists – but in some way making really clear how they are seeing the system. This is the context of that remark I made once: "If you are really interested in the language of power, you must take seriously the power of language." Those are, if you like, the critical observations I would make. But on the other hand

I see them very positively. And there are other questions which are not specifically linguistic, which are not necessarily relevant here, but I think it is interesting to ask: What is the underlying social theory? What is the underlying socio-political base of the work? But that's a different question, and it's one that one asks not from the point of view of linguistics, but just from a more general political background.

HC: *I should add that the reason for my question was that in Brazil, together with the core of theoretical studies in SFL, there is a big development of research in the area of critical linguistics, and our effort has been to systematically ground research always on language and then go forward with the critical side after that; and so people will welcome your words of support in that respect.*

Future perspectives: Linguistics and cognition

GT: *Let me take you to the next question. How do you see Systemic Functional Linguistics as likely to develop in the next couple of decades? How would you like it to develop? What sort of issues do you think it should be addressing?*

MAKH: I hope it will continue to provide a resource for people who are asking all kinds of different questions about language. That seems to me important. What I hope will happen is that, just as the collaboration with educators took place over the last quarter century, a similar development will take place in relation to clinical work, to medical practice, to studies of language pathology, language disorders and so forth. That's much further behind, but it's beginning. I think collaboration between linguists and medical researchers would be very valuable. Another area related to that, which I think now is a tremendous source of inspiration and insight, is neuroscience. I mean the work which is being done on the evolution and development of the brain, since the leading edge is no longer simply the neurology, that is the pathology of the brain, but neuroscience, the actual evolution and operation of the brain. I think that a lot of ideas have been coming in which resonate very well with both our overall model of language and also the model of language development. That now seems to me to make very good sense, but we need to learn a lot more about it. We need people going into modern studies of the brain to see how we can interpret our linguistic findings.

GT: *Do you think that at the end through a combination of systemic linguistics with neuroscience you might show that, actually, Chomsky is wrong in his view of how language is learned?*

MAKH: Well, I think it depends on which version you take. I think he was wrong, in the first place, in his assessment of the data. He set up a pseudo-problem, by saying: "How can a child learn language with such impoverished data?" But when you actually record what goes on around the child, it's far from impoverished.

So that was just not a real question. There's another input from learning theory now: "What makes a language learnable?" I think we can now talk about various features, including quantitative features in our corpus, all kinds of patterns which we didn't see before, which relate to this question of how the child learns, because the child is able to recognize such patterns and build on them. I think we get a sense of at least what some of these patterns are. We are certainly programmed to learn: as Jay [Lemke] once remarked (cf. Lemke 1984, 1995), if children are predisposed to learn, adults are predisposed to teach. But you don't have to postulate built-in structural rules: I don't think there is any need for it and I don't think there is any evidence for it – I think Chomsky was wrong there too. And I hope that we'll continue to interact with educators – partly because many of them still have very primitive notions about language, at least in the countries that I know!

GT: *Would you say, very broadly, that cognition is perhaps the major new area for SFL, and that in a sense you're finally going below the skin?*[4]

MAKH: The question of cognition, I think, is a different one, because nobody has ever denied cognitive processes take place, processes of consciousness which are essentially part of the production and understanding of language. There's no doubt about that. I think the question which interests me is, how do you model these? The reason I don't talk about cognitive modelling is because there seem to me to be two problems with it. What Christian [Matthiessen] has done is to show (1998), very interestingly, how the model of mind and cognition which tends to be foregrounded in much research now is one that is simply based on folk linguistic concepts, mainly deriving from mental processes in the grammar. And I would add the further point that, if you try to use cognition as a way of explaining language, you tend to be going round in a viciously small circle, because the only evidence you've got for it is linguistic evidence in the first place. So I would say rather that we should take some model of language and use that to explain cognition. That's what the new book by Christian and me (Halliday & Matthiessen 1999) is all about: we are talking about "cognition", but we call it meaning. These are not contradictory; they're complementary. We want to say that somebody should explore the power of grammatics, as we call it, to push "upwards" and interpret cognitive processes as semantic, or (more broadly) semiotic.

GT: *Within Chomskian grammar from very early on there was a lot of commentary on his ambiguous use of 'grammar' – whether it was purely a way of describing structures for the linguist, or whether it reflected how language was processed. Is it right, perhaps, to say that we're coming to the point where, with a very well-developed model and with more information about the brain, it's possible to start blurring that line?*

MAKH: I think it is. I think it's a question of what you put there in the middle or on the other side of the line. Let me put it this way: I would feel that we could go straight from language to the brain, that we don't need to interpose an intermediate level of cognitive processing. I would say that our strongest, our most powerful methodology and theoretical resource is the one that we've developed in relation to language. Essentially language is more accessible and is better explored; therefore let's use the power of the linguistic theory to move in that direction. Maybe we don't need to postulate a mind, or cognitive processes, on the way.

HC: *By learning more about language, one learns more about the brain, then. And how about the mind?*

MAKH: Yes, and by learning more about the brain one learns more about language. The two then meet in the language-brain. The mind disappears – though consciousness remains. The critical concept to me is consciousness, because that is clearly defined evolutionarily. Part of the problem of the mind is: what are you claiming in evolutionary terms? This is why I often quote Edelman (1992), who follows Darwin. Darwin always said, there's no mysterious entity called mind; as we know more about evolutionary processes, it will fall into place. Now what Edelman is saying is, yes, it has fallen into place. If you do talk about mind in the folk linguistic sense, what is the status of it in terms of the evolution of the brain? It's like entropy, if you like: it's not a thing, it's something you postulate in an explanatory chain. Now I'm not sure we need it. We do need entropy, of course! But mind may be misleading rather than helpful.

Register

GT: *The next question concerns the current focus on patterning at text level. Many people have come into Systemics through text analysis, because they've found it beautifully adapted for that. At that level, you've worked with the concept of register,[5] but there has been a lot of discussion about the usefulness of the concept of genre. What's your position?*

MAKH: The kind of stratal modelling which Jim Martin has introduced involves saying that we have a separate stratum we call genre (Martin 1992). First, on a purely terminological point, I think he slightly misunderstood the notion of register as I originally meant to define it. That's as much my fault as his. But apart from that he's making the point that we need two strata here, above the linguistic system; and he relates this to notions of connotative semiotics – that is, language as the realization of other semiotic systems and processes.[6] I think it is very powerful, but it's partly a matter of what you are using the model for. I haven't found it necessary; but I'm not doing the sort of work in education that Jim is doing. It's particularly in the educational context that he has found this stratal model useful, and I'm happy with that. These are the sort of arguments that go on between colleagues: some people are comfortable with intention as a theoretical concept and find it helpful, but I'm suspicious of it as something that seems to lead to a circularity in the reasoning. But the overall framework is very close, and I have no problem with the genre model as Jim has developed it: it's extraordinarily powerful, and it's something which teachers have found useful, and which he and his colleagues have found useful both in working with teachers and also in preparing and designing materials and programs.

HC: *Would you agree with the association between genre and the level of the context of culture? If one wants to think about genre, not only as an adequate and acceptable tool if one is working in education, but thinking about it in terms of the theory, would you agree that it could be mapped against the context of culture?*

MAKH: Yes, I would. And I suppose that highlights the kind of difference, because to me the context of culture is the system end of the context of situation. I mean these are a single stratum related by instantiation.[7] Therefore that's the way I would see genre and register, rather than as two strata. But this is something we need to explore, because these are alternative ways of interpreting this phenomenon. But I agree that it is the context of culture that is the environment for genre – that's not in dispute. I think it is a question of whether you see genre as a separate stratum or as sub-system on the stratum of (discourse-) semantics.

GT: *But then if we take a more practical angle, the term genre is sometimes used when you are looking at the text as a whole, without necessarily projecting right up onto the culture. Do you find a need for a term to talk about how texts utilize register resources but within a particular overall organisation or patterning?*

MAKH: I've always seen that as a part of the notion of register. Let me put it this way. Suppose you collect instances: if you stand at that end, then you will arrive at groupings of text types, bodies of texts that are in certain respects like each other and different from others. If you then shift your observer position to the system end, then that text type becomes a subsystem, and that's what we call register. That's the way I would see it: it's the semantic analogue of what in the context of culture would be an institution of some kind, a recognized body of cultural practice, or institutionalized cultural forms; and that semantic entity, to me, would fall within the concept of register.[8]

GT: *You have made extensive use of the concept of marked versus unmarked choices,[9] more recently using computational means to arrive at a new perspective in terms of probabilities. In what ways do you feel that this changes our view of language? More particularly, does the fact that probabilities and therefore markedness vary within different registers (and across languages) raise problems with the idea of a functional grammar for a language: should we be thinking rather in terms of functional grammars?*

MAKH: Let me join up the notion of marked and unmarked, probabilities and the corpus. They are really all related, and I see the corpus as fundamental in shifting the whole orientation of linguistics, because for the first time linguists have data.

They haven't had data before; and this will enable them, I hope, to leap over a few centuries and move into the 21st century as a true science. This includes the quantitative dimension, which to me is important. The quantitative basis of language is a fundamental feature of language: I think that a grammatical system is not just a choice between a or b or c but a or b or c with certain probabilities attached – and you get these probabilities out of the corpus.[10] I think there is some misunderstanding here. People have sometimes said, well, any text is in some register or other, some genre or other, so it doesn't make sense to talk about the global probabilities of language. This is total nonsense. It makes perfect sense: that argument is rather like saying that just because every place on the earth is in some climatic zone or other, it doesn't make sense to talk about global climate; but of course it does. Global climate is global climate, it has certain features, certain probabilities, which we then look at more delicately when we get to the climate of Brazil or Britain or whatever. It is the same with language: it is essential to be aware of the notion of global probabilities in language. Now that the corpus is big enough, we can get at them, because the corpuses now range across lots of different registers, spoken and written discourse and so forth. So we need those global probabilities, but we need them as the kind of baseline against which we match probabilities in particular sets of texts, different registers. Indeed, I would define a register as being a skewing or shifting of the probabilities, because not many registers actually close off bits of the system. What they tend to do is to shift the probabilities, so it is the same system but with a different set of probabilities, not only in the vocabulary but also in the grammar.

Now, with marked and unmarked the problem is that we tend to define it in half a dozen different ways, and we need to get clear what we mean when we talk about marked and unmarked terms in systems. You can relate this to probabilities, and it may even turn out in the long run that we can define it in terms of probabilities; but I don't think we should do that yet. I think we should be thinking of it in semantic terms. Of course, we have the concept of formally marked, by morphological means: that's important, but it's easy to recognize and it doesn't necessarily go with semantic marking. The real concept that we can use is that of the unmarked choice, or unmarked option, in a grammatical system, which is a kind of default choice. I used to find this very useful in language teaching, because I could say to the students: "This is what you do, unless you have a good reason for doing something else". For example, you find out what the language does with its unmarked Theme, if it has a Theme, and you say, right, that is your basic option, but here are the conditions which would lead you to do something else.[11] I think it is a useful concept: it is linked to probabilities but I wouldn't want yet – or maybe ever – to define it in probabilistic terms.

GT: *Within a register you would use what otherwise would be a marked Theme, not as a choice open to an individual writer – in a sense there's very little choice, you've got to use this kind of Theme – but because of that register's conventions, which have evolved in response to a particular communicative need. I think that's an issue that worries some people: they're finding that in a particular register, you take a certain* option when there is no good reason not to, even though in the language as a whole that would be otherwise be a marked choice.

MAKH: That's exactly what I would say. They ought not to be worried about it; it is just a point that needs to be made explicit. There are two steps: one is to say that, in this register, what would in general be a marked Theme, or MOOD or whatever, becomes the unmarked option here. They shouldn't have a problem with that. The second step is to say: "Can we explain this?" What happens in general is that if you go back into the history you can, but things get ritualized, so that you may have to say, look, in terms of contemporary uses it doesn't really have any function. That's the way it evolved, and we can see why it evolved that way. It's best to do that if possible because adult language learners like explanations – they're not satisfied just with the idea of ritual. But you may have to say that, just as you have to learn there are irregular verbs in Portuguese or English or whatever, so you have to learn that there are funny things that go on and we can't explain them all. But in cases like these which are clearly semantic choices you can usually see where the unmarked option came from.

HC: *As you say, this is especially useful in the context of learning languages. When people raise these issues back home in Brazil, they usually have this sort of issue in the background. We do a lot of teaching of languages for specific purposes, and of course if you are doing LSP you are often dealing with very specific registers. For example, you may have to teach Brazilians how to interact successfully in discussion groups on the Internet, which involves informal interaction in writing. A student of mine found that the vast majority of requests for information will be in the declarative form introduced by expressions of politeness, like "I would appreciate it if you could tell me", or "I would be specially thankful if you let me know". The frequency of this marked use of the declarative is very high in that specific type of communication, and if you're teaching your students that kind of language you want an explanation for it.*

GT: *Yes, there are two levels. You can simply say: "This is what you do"; or you can talk through it, raising their language awareness, getting them to think about what it is in this new medium or mode of communication which means that that use is going to occur. I very often find students respond well to that approach and they remember because it makes sense.*

MAKH: I agree, it is much more memorable if you can make it make sense. I mean, we all know that as language teachers we sometimes invent explanations!

Practical issues of analysis

HC: *The recognition criteria for Theme are one of the few practical issues within Systemic Functional Grammar that have aroused disagreement. Do you see any reason for* *changing your view that Theme extends as far as the first experiential constituent of the clause, and no further?*

MAKH: I'm interested in this question, and I know that some people have preferred to take the Theme beyond what I would: to include the Subject, for example. Now I think this is worth exploring further. There are various reasons why I did what I did, one being intonational. It is generally true in our early recordings that in cases when a clause is broken into two information units, the break typically comes – in well over 50% of cases – at the point where the break between Theme and Rheme as I defined it comes: in other words, it would not include the Subject that follows a Complement or Adjunct. I have also said that I don't see the point of extending it to the following Subject because the Subject's got to come there anyway. Once you've chosen a marked Theme, you've got no more choice in the order, so you don't need to explain the Subject. So I'm not convinced by the motivation for extending the Theme; but it is something to explore, especially now that we've got the corpus: let's look at what happens in terms of the function of Theme in discourse. We need discourse reasons for claiming that Theme extends further, and I think that the issue is still open. But I admit that I have not yet been convinced of the need for it.[12]

HC: *In your Introduction to Functional Grammar (Halliday 1985a) you argue that transitivity and ergativity are alternative perspectives on processes.[13] Would you want to say that this applies to any clause?*

MAKH: I think this is a very interesting point. It is a typical kind of complementarity (cf. Halliday 2008a). I used to cite the old controversy from Newton's time about the nature of light: was it particle or wave? You could say that there is a single set of phenomena which range along a cline, and the phenomena at one end of the cline are better explained in terms of an ergative model, and the phenomena at the other end are better explained in terms of a transitive model. That after all applies to grammar and lexis. It's a cline, but there's one end where you do better using grammatical theory, and the other end where you do better writing a thesaurus or a dictionary. Now the next step could be to say, OK, but if that is the case, aren't these essentially different phenomena? Here of course I'm thinking of Kristin Davidse's work (1992): she has taken that step and I thoroughly applaud it. I had just said that there is one set of phenomena here, and there are reasons for looking at it from two different ends. I didn't take it further and say that I want to set up transitive and ergative as different classes of process. She took it that far, and I think it's quite fair to do that. It's a normal situation in complementarities of this kind. There are many of them in language – for example, tense and aspect, which are essentially complementary models of time. In some language systems, like Russian and other Slavonic languages, it's clear that they are both there, and it's clear which is which. In English, on the other hand, they are more problematic. I personally think that to talk about what people call perfective and continuous as aspect is not very helpful, because there is a much better model for these – secondary tense; and the aspect just comes in the non-finites. But you have to see which gives you a more powerful picture – and again thanks to the corpus we now have a lot more evidence we can look at.

In principle, coming to the level of structure, I like to do both, to give one interpretation in terms of TRANSITIVITY and one in terms of ERGATIVITY; but that's because in the way I developed it it seemed to me you were making different kinds of generalizations: the ergative perspective helps you in seeing where all the process types are alike, whereas the transitive perspective helps you in seeing the differences.

Complexity and computer-aided analysis

HC: *Just one last question about the complexity of the theory. I see a paradox between the theory being so complex and the vast amount of data we have access to these days. We want to be able to deal with all this data with the help of computers, but there is a kind of mismatch: the theory is good because it's complex, but on the other hand it is difficult to use it, because computers ...*

MAKH: ... are very simple!

HC: *Yes, too simple for the theory.*

MAKH: As you know, I defend the complexity of the theory, because we are talking about a very complex phenomenon, and it doesn't help anyone if you pretend it's simple. We have to build that complexity in, and what you're trying to do is to manage it. We hear a lot about this today, complexity management, and this is what we're dealing with. Five or six years ago I was working with Zoe James on the computer at Birmingham (Halliday & James 1993). We looked at the tagger, but we didn't use it because it was precisely the things we needed to know that it was very bad at. The parsers were still too slow: we were working with a million and a half clauses, so there was no way that we could rely on a parser. What we were looking for – and Zoe was brilliant at thinking in these terms – was a kind of pattern matcher, which could give us just enough evidence to identify the features we were interested in. Zoe got it to the right level of accuracy for polarity, tense and modality; but we never cracked the voice code – we were working on active and passive, and we never got it to quite the level where we thought that we had enough accuracy for our results to be valid. But that is just a matter of work. I had to leave, and she had to leave too, and so far no-one else has taken it up. Of course, the new parsers are a lot quicker and more accurate now; but in any case you need to identify your task closely and then see what part of the theory you need and use this for pattern matching. It's a question of deciding which area you're interested in, and then thinking, let's see what tools I need in order to get this out of the corpus. It may involve a total parse, or it may be something in between. It may be something that the tagger will help you with, but usually I'm looking at larger chunks, so word tagging hasn't been terribly helpful. Strategically you do need to define your task very precisely.

In a sense, this goes for text analysis generally, whether it is human or machine aided: you can't survey a text completely, because you'd be there until the end of the year working on one sentence. What you try to do is familiarize yourself with the text and the possibilities. This is something that is hard to teach students, because there is no algorithm for it: you need to get a sense of how you take in a text, then you say, I think that modality would be interesting here, or we really need to look at process types in this text, or whatever. You keep all the resources of the grammar in front of your eyes, and select those you think will be most revealing. You're not always right, of course! But otherwise you could have an endless task.

HC: *Well, thank you very much for your time.*

Cardiff University
July 1998

Notes

1 As Halliday points out, Basil Bernstein has had an important influence on the way in which systemic-functional linguists view the relationships between language and society. The aspect of his theory which led to the attacks on him that Halliday mentions was the idea of restricted and elaborated codes. A restricted code is the kind of language that we typically use in informal conversation with friends and family. For example, one of the features of our language in such contexts is that we do not need to make things explicit, because we can rely on the other person understanding when we talk about 'that thing over there' etc. An elaborated code is the kind of language that is used in more formal contexts (such as writing), when we need to make things more explicit – and we typically talk and write about more complex topics than in informal conversation. Bernstein argued that middle-class children had an advantage at school because they were more likely to be exposed at home not only to restricted codes but also to elaborated codes; whereas working-class children were more likely to be exposed only to restricted codes at home, and therefore faced greater difficulties in coping with the language of education. Bernstein emphasized that both codes were equally good at serving their intended function, and saw his work as providing a basis for more enlightened and effective approaches to education (cf. what Halliday says later about 'giving value to varieties of language that were traditionally neglected'). However, his views were mistakenly or maliciously interpreted by many critics as being a snobbish claim that working- class children were less intelligent and inherently unable to master the elaborated codes required for advancement in the society (cf. Atkinson 1985, Chapter 6: 'Bernstein and the linguists').
2 The fact that language does not simply 'reflect' social structures but 'construes' them is a fundamental tenet of systemic functional linguistics. The 'reflecting' view assumes that social structures exist and language use merely mirrors them: to take a simple example, we have different ways of talking to social inferiors and superiors because

society is organized in such a way that there is often a difference in rank between people who talk to each other. The 'construal' view, on the other hand, assumes that language use not only mirrors social structure but also constructs and maintains it: thus every time someone uses language 'appropriate' for a social superior, they are both showing their awareness of their status and simultaneously reinforcing the hierarchical social system. If people begin using less formal language when talking to social superiors (as has happened, for example, with the near disappearance of 'Sir' as a term of respectful address to men in Britain), they are in effect changing the social structure.

3 For example, Chomsky, in a paper published in 1964 (Chomsky 1964a), dismisses the study of language in use as 'mere data arranging', and makes the claim that a corpus 'is almost useless as it stands, for linguistic analysis of any but the most superficial kind'.

4 Halliday has frequently said that he only goes 'as far as the skin' in exploring language. That is, he sees no useful function in speculating separately about cognitive processes that might be involved, since – as he goes on to say – the only evidence we have for them is linguistic in the first place (see his later comments about the concept of the mind being 'misleading rather than helpful').

5 Register is 'linguistic variation according to use'. In different contexts of situation, people use language in ways that are recognizably different: for example, the language of a news report is different from that of a recipe. This is not just a question of the subject matter (though that is part of it): a whole range of lexicogrammatical choices will be different, often in subtle ways. Most registers do not use 'special' grammar (although there are a few marginal examples, such as newspaper headlines in English, which use some structures that are not used in any other registers). What changes is the whole configuration of choices: in any particular register, there is the likelihood that particular combinations of structures will occur (or will not occur), in a pattern of choices that is not exactly like any other register. As Halliday says later, the probabilities are skewed. To take some simple examples: imperatives are highly unlikely to occur in news reports, but highly likely to occur in recipes; past tense forms are highly likely to occur throughout narratives, whereas scientific articles are more likely to have a high incidence of present tense forms except in the 'Methods' section; and so on.

6 Systemic linguistics relies on a stratal model: that is, language is seen as a semiotic system that works at different 'levels' or strata. In Halliday's model, there are three strata, which we can see as going from the most abstract to the most concrete. The semantic stratum (the sets of meanings that we want to express) is realized by the lexicogrammatical stratum (the sets of wordings we use to express those meanings), which in turn is realized by the phonological (or graphological) stratum (the sets of physical sounds and marks that we use to express those wordings). Martin argues that the model should include a fourth and fifth stratum above semantics, namely register and genre, which are then realized by the semantics (in oversimple terms, people have generic sets of purposes to carry out when they use language, and those purposes are carried out by choosing certain combinations of register variables – field, tenor and mode – which implicate certain kinds of meanings).

7 Instantiation is a key concept in systemic linguistics. Any actual text (an 'instance' of language) is an instantiation of the language system (the 'lexicogrammar'). What this means is that the system does not exist independently of use (although people often talk as though the grammar of the language were a set of 'external' fixed rules). Each time someone uses language, they are both activating the system (or rather,

part of it) and, to an infinitesimal degree, changing it. Halliday has explained this relationship between instance and system by comparing it to that between weather and climate. What people are most conscious of is usually the day-to-day weather; but if we look at the patterns of weather from a long-term perspective over a number of years or centuries, we no longer talk of weather but of climate. These are the same phenomenon, but seen in different time-scales. Another way of putting this is that the weather 'instantiates' the climate.

Here Halliday is applying the same concept to contexts. A context of situation is an instance: every individual text arises in (and 'construes' – see note 2) a specific context of situation. But contexts of situation tend to recur: we recognize that there are close similarities between, say, one classroom lesson and another, or between one television news broadcast and another. When we get recognizable groupings of similar contexts of situation, those correspond to different registers: we can easily recognize the register of classroom interaction, for example ('Okay, so what does "diffraction" mean? Tim? ... Yes, that's right.'). Halliday is arguing that when we put together all the groupings of contexts of situation that we recognize as actually or potentially occurring in our culture, we have the context of culture – the system of contexts that operates in and constitutes our culture.

8 For an overview of register and genre, see C. M. I. M. Matthiessen (1993) 'Register in the round', in M. Ghadessy (ed.) *Register Analysis: Theory and practice* London: Pinter. For a critique of Martin's position, see R. Hasan 'The conception of context in text', in Fries & Gregory 1995. For attempts at clarification of his position by Martin see Martin 1999, 2001.

9 As Halliday goes on to explain, an 'unmarked' choice in the grammar is the one that is taken if there is no particular reason for doing anything else. A 'marked' choice is one that is taken when there is a particular contextual reason. For example, 'I went to London on Friday' has the unmarked word order (Subject first), and it is hard to predict what the surrounding sentences will be like. On the other hand, 'On Friday, I went to London' has a marked word order, and would most likely occur in a context where at least one of the other sentences started 'On Monday/The following day/etc. ...'. In other words, the speaker or writer is setting up a particular framework based on time sequence, which is signalled by highlighting the phrases of time by moving them to the front of the sentence.

10 For example, one system of grammatical choices is the choice between present, past and future tense. Traditional grammars simply record the fact that these three basic options exist. A corpus, however, can reveal that, if we look at the whole range of language use (the 'system'), people actually choose present tense more often than past tense, and past tense more often than future tense. This is as important a fact about the grammar as the existence of the three options. It is against this background, for example, that we can look at the skewing of the probabilities that Halliday mentions. To return to an example in note 8 above, the fact that past tense forms are the most likely choice in narrative is one of the features that make narrative distinctive, precisely because this does not follow the overall pattern of tense choices across all the uses of language. This issue is discussed in Halliday & James (1993).

11 In Systemic Functional Linguistics, Theme is the first 'content' element in the clause. It represents the 'starting point' of the clause, and serves to establish the framework within which the clause is to be understood. The examples in note 12 above are in fact to do with the Themes: the use of a marked Theme such as '<u>On Friday</u>, I went to London' signals to the hearer that the speaker is moving to the next frame in the time sequence. If the following Theme is then unmarked ('<u>I</u> visited the National Gallery'), it signals (amongst other things) that we are still in the same time frame of 'On Friday'.

12 For a fuller discussion of Theme, see Hasan and Fries (1995).
13 Transitivity in SFL refers not just to the verb, but to the way the experiential 'content' of the clause is expressed. It is a way of describing the processes and the participants being talked about. So, in a clause like 'He boiled the water rapidly', we have a material (physical action) process of boiling, involving an Actor 'he' (the entity doing the process) and a Goal 'the water' (the entity affected by the process), plus a circumstance 'rapidly'. This analysis brings out the similarities between this clause and a clause like 'She chopped the carrots finely'. But we can also look at the clause from a different perspective, the ergative one. If we compare the clause with 'The water boiled rapidly', we have the same verb but in a different transitivity structure – 'the water' is now the Actor. However, it is clear that in both cases the water is the 'location' of the boiling; the difference is that in the original clause 'he' is represented as causing the boiling to happen in that location. We can bring out the underlying similarity by using ergative labels: in both cases 'the water' is Medium (the entity in or through which the process comes into being), while in the first clause 'he' is the Agent (the entity causing a process to happen). For a full discussion, see Chapter 5 of M. A. K. Halliday (1994).

With Anne Burns (2006)

AB: *Michael, I might start off by asking you a very general question about perspectives one might take as a linguist on the notion of Applied Linguistics. Some people see themselves as using linguistic and applied linguistic theory to 'problem solve' real issues in the world – an enabling cast of mind as it were. On the other hand, there can be a starting point which is more 'practice-based', or is a proactive platform from which Applied Linguistics can be viewed. In a sense this is the essence of a conversation between David Crystal and Christopher Brumfit which was published in this journal in 2004. Where would you place yourself? What would be your response to these starting points?*

MAKH: I'm not sure how different they are. But to take the question as you put it, then I think I'd put myself closer to the first perspective. I do see Applied Linguistics as a problem-solving form of activity. In fact, I would say that generally about all theories if you like. I tend to have a problem-solving approach to theory in general – theories are a way of getting on with dealing with something, and that may be a highly abstract research problem or it may be something very practical. So I think the two notions in that sense are very complementary. Because the problems that need to be addressed, to be solved, range from those which are other forms of research at one end, to things which we would all see as pretty practical forms of activity, and of course, language teaching would be one of the central ones. But I think I would say I never have seen a very clear distinction between Linguistics and Applied Linguistics. I think we suffered from this a lot in perhaps the second half of the twentieth century – of the kind of polarisation between those two as separate domains.

AB: *Which has not been helpful…*

MAKH: And I don't think it's helpful.

AB: *In 2002, in your inaugural keynote address at the International Association of Applied Linguistics (AILA) in Singapore, you spoke about 'Applied Linguistics as an Evolving Theme' (later published as Halliday 2007b). You focused in that talk on the ways in which we should begin to envisage the role of Applied Linguistics at the beginning of the twenty-first century. Can you revisit some of the concepts you spoke about in that paper? For instance, it would be intriguing to know how you see the differences between Applied Linguistics as a discipline and a theme.*

MAKH: Yes, in that paper I did suggest that the notion of Applied Linguistics as a theme seems more appropriate, in the sense that the discipline, at least in the twentieth century, which is in a sense the century of disciplines, was very much defined by what you were looking at, what you were actually focusing on. And, in a sense this was a way of achieving a level of specialisation, which was necessary at that point in order for things to advance. I see that now as something which started off as being enabling and has become constraining, and we've got to break out of it. So I would say Applied Linguistics would be a good example of something that isn't tied to a kind of disciplinary base. It seems to me that it is much more a theme in the sense that it is a way of going about a whole number of different spheres of activity in which language plays some central part.

AB: *So you are envisaging its potential in being applied across disciplines and therefore this comes very much into play.*

MAKH: I think so, and I have tried to use the term 'transdisciplinary'. In a sense it was my reaction to interdisciplinary, because 20 to 25 years ago in the universities we were all being told we've got to be interdisciplinary. And I said, fine, but that usually turned out to be what Basil Bernstein (1991) used to call a 'collection code'. You know, a little bit of this, a little bit of that, a little bit of the other and I wanted to say what we need is something more transdisciplinary that redefines the structure of knowledge. What I mean is, you don't just leave the fields of knowledge as they are, and package a little bit from each like a mesclun salad in the supermarket. You rethink the whole plan of cultivation: not by constantly devising new formal structures, departments, schools, faculties, divisions or whatever, as is being done now on the 'shake-em-up' principle imported from business management, but by noting what ideas are emerging from the leading edges of contemporary scholarship – in things like complexity theory, systems thinking (really 'systems-and-processes') and so on. Our semiotics, which is the study of meaning in all its modes and manifestations, is itself an exploration along these lines.

AB: *So you viewed the notion of 'interdisciplinary' as leading to fragmentation rather than integration?*

MAKH: Exactly, and I think that is a very important point. The theme to me is a kind of unifying concept. Yes, there is a unity and people sometimes say, well Applied Linguistics is just a collection of different things. You're doing education or you're doing law, or you're doing medicine, or whatever, but I don't think it is. As I say, I think it is unified by this broader sense that most of the professional and, indeed, the daily forms of activity that we find ourselves in involve meaning in some way or another. Now we may not do anything about it, fine. But if we do, then it's Applied Linguistics.

AB: *I guess that brings us to the idea of whether we can say the study of all languages is Applied Linguistics. Or should we be talking more in terms of a sociolinguistics that is transdisciplinary?*

MAKH: Well, it rather depends on what you mean by sociolinguistics, doesn't it? Sociolinguistics, in the classic sense of the study of the inter-relation between language and society, language and social structure or whatever, is a definable field or fields, and, indeed, one in which there has been a lot of very important work in the last 50 years or so. I had a problem with it at the start in that from where I came, from the background of European linguistics and in particular the work of my own teacher, J. R. Firth, language was a social phenomenon anyway. So they would never have seen the need to separate out something called sociolinguistics from linguistics as a whole. But if you define linguistics more in terms of the formal study of linguistic structures, then it becomes a different operation where you, as it were, explore how these are embedded and activated in society. So I would take that as something that got itself defined in that period and achieved a lot of results. Now let me come back to what you said: would the study of all languages be Applied Linguistics? Well, no, I don't think so. I think here I made a comparison with applied mathematics, which was the application of mathematics to certain specific problems – physics, engineering, statistics and so on – so it's a highly theoretical discipline. You call it applied because you're not looking at it as the object but rather as an instrument for exploring something else. If you're looking at language as your object, still it's a largely theoretical pursuit. But if you're looking at it more as an instrument for intervening in something else, then that is what I think I would call Applied Linguistics.

AB: *Yes, because some would see Applied Linguistics as encompassing even things beyond language such as various cultures or various ways of looking at culture.*

MAKH: I feel that the more you push terms out like that, the more empty they become. If everything is Applied Linguistics then it doesn't say anything. So I think I wouldn't, I would say, no. You see, I have always been interested in other people's questions about language. And this is why, in a way, mainstream linguists don't regard me as a linguist because I don't ask linguists' questions. I tend to ask other people's questions about language, and everyone has questions about language – some are very important. So in a sense from that point of view my perspective has always tended to be applied. But I don't really see a big distance between that and the theory.

AB: *My own background and interests, and taking a lead from your work, have been very much in the field of educational linguistics, language in education and in literacy. Can you talk about what you feel have been some of the major contributions your work has made in the educational field?*

MAKH: Well, mine plus colleagues' work, for as you know there have been some among my own colleagues who have really opened up this field, such as Jim Martin here in Sydney, in the last 20 years or so (cf. Rose & Martin 2012). I think in a sense, going back to earlier stages in my own history, we had to define the very notion of language in education and language education. I mean, it wasn't there.

AB: *Yes, it wasn't a recognisable concept for many people. A sort of invisible underpinning to what goes on in everyday life.*

MAKH: Yes, absolutely, and because invisible, not attended to. And I remember in the late 1950s, early 1960s, and in particular when I moved to University College London in 1963, I pût up a project to the Nuffield Foundation for research and development. And this went through and they brought in the Department of Education Inspectorate as they always did for educational projects. We had some very useful and interesting discussions and decided to try and move into curriculum development, as it was in those days, at a number of different levels in the school system. Now, none of those concerned really had a clear conceptualisation of language in the primary school system, particularly in the first few years of what we used to call 'the infants'.

AB: *Yes, which is where, importantly, literacy skills are emerging and developing.*

MAKH: They were very clear about the target of literacy – there was no question about that. And David Mackay, who was in charge of that section of the project, was very clear that this was a linguistic operation, and that not only the teachers had to be able to understand about language but they also had to give the children ways of talking about language. They had to be able to talk about everything they wanted to learn. But language wasn't there as a concept. Literacy was. When you got into the secondary school, it wasn't there either. There, it was English or foreign languages. Each of them had its grammar bit and its vocabulary and what have you, but again no general concept of language. In the 1960s, at that time back in the University of London with the Programme in Linguistics and English Teaching (see Pearce, Thornton & Mackay 1989), what I felt we were trying to do was to work towards some sort of modelling, some sort of understanding of language which would be relevant throughout the educational process. And it was also at the time that Language Across the Curriculum (cf. Bullock 1975) came in as a concept. And again, I think, for the first time, teachers and others began looking at problems of science learning, maths learning, history learning and so on as problems of language. So I think the main contribution of that stage, and particularly through my colleagues in that project at University College London, was to establish a concept of language in the educational process.

AB: *Well, that was a significant breakthrough, and indeed the project was called 'Breakthrough to Literacy' and I remember working with these concepts myself at the time as a teacher in the UK. I don't think that previously there had been any particular training for teachers going into either primary school or high school. Certainly from my own recollection of the way I was taught at university when I was studying for an English literature degree, there was very little linkage with linguistic theory which would allow you to unpack some of the meanings or to look at how works of literature were expressed through language. It was almost unknown in the kind of training or education that people had available to them at that time.*

MAKH: Yes, I'm sure that was true. When we started working with the group of secondary teachers under Peter Doughty, who was the leader in that project (cf. Doughty, Pearce & Thornton 1971), this was very much the point that he was aware of. There was a concept of grammar, but the idea that you could actually use it to ask questions about why this particular poem could be understood in the way that it is – it just wasn't there.

AB: *You mentioned before your work with J. R. Firth and your own early work. It would be really valuable for readers to know what critical moments or movements there have been in your own career as an applied linguist. And also what have been the movements from outside the field from other disciplines that have had an impact on your own work and work that you have seen more recently in the field of Applied Linguistics?*

MAKH: That's a huge lot of questions!

AB: *Let's break them down a bit. Let's start with your own earlier work and the critical movements in your career.*

MAKH: I go back to my own experience in school, where I really enjoyed the study of literature. I loved it, particularly drama and poetry, and the teachers were keen, and of course were enormously well informed. But when they started talking about language, which they occasionally did, I thought they were talking nonsense. I mean, I couldn't even have formulated this, but it just didn't seem to make sense, to make any contact with what I could see there. And that started me wandering around, trying to find out if there was somebody who did talk about language sensibly. I remember burrowing around in the school library and finding a book by Leonard Bloomfield, but I didn't very much understand it. So if you go right back there, that was one kind of impetus for exploring language. And I have to say that both my parents were linguistically aware. My father was a teacher of English and Latin in the old secondary system. He loved language, he had the traditional grammar, but he made very intelligent use of it. And my mother was a teacher of French and a good speaker of French. So the interest in language was around in the home, which was a great privilege.

But then the British army took a group of us out of school at the end of 1941, beginning of 1942, to be trained in various Asian languages for intelligence work of different kinds. And I volunteered for that and got my first choice of language, which was Chinese. So my next set of problems, queries if you like, arose, not so much as a learner – as a learner you don't even know what questions to ask at that stage – but as a teacher, because after a couple of years of service in the Far East, I was one of those brought back to England to be an instructor in the later language courses. And this was still just before the end of the Japanese war, which everyone thought would go on for years. Then questions really started arising, because here I was teaching people Chinese, and that's when I started to think 'I can't explain this'. So that was another source that pushed me, and so Applied Linguistics in the educational sense comes from my own experience as a foreign language teacher.

Then, I got into very early investigation in machine translation with a group in Cambridge in the mid-1950s. The question arose, how do we get translation into the computer? We were just getting beyond the very early attempts where they thought all they had to do was to put a dictionary in and run the thing through the machine and it would come up with a beautiful translation (Halliday 1962). So that was a third way into questions which forced you to be very explicit about what you tried to represent and how you represented it.

AB: *And movements from other disciplines? How have they influenced or impacted on your work?*

MAKH: Well, I came out of the army after the war and went off to China to continue studies where again I had a brilliant set of teachers. One in particular was Wang Li, a fine scholar who not only taught me grammar and phonology, and the history of Chinese linguistics, but also trained me in dialectology and field work. I really enjoyed the Chinese dialect studies, investigating language as it was in ordinary daily life in different sections of the community. Then back in England, under my other great teacher J. R. Firth (see Firth 1957a, Palmer 1968 1970), I learnt about another kind of variation, which we came to call 'register' variation, variation according to use; and this was something we also got into in the 1950s from another angle where I was working with a little linguistics group in the English Communist Party. Here we were very interested in the problem of post-colonial society, decolonization, development of national languages, and that raised questions about register, functional variation in language and the problems of newly emerging national languages which had to develop technical registers for legal, administrative purposes, and so on. So I suppose in that period, in the 1950s, from these two angles I was getting a sense of language as a variable system, which was very important. Then when I moved out of teaching Chinese into linguistics, which was essentially in the 1960s, I was much influenced by the work of Basil Bernstein (see Bernstein 1971, 1973). I was always interested in society, social processes, social structures. I thought, and I still do think, that Basil Bernstein was one of the great minds of that time and he forced us to attend to all kinds of questions about language.

AB: *Variation?*

MAKH: Variation, yes exactly, with his notion of code...

AB: *Yes, codes and framing.*

MAKH: ... you know what I mean. With the push from the teachers on one side, and Basil Bernstein's sociological research unit on the other side, I had to look at the way language variation was relevant in the school, to education. These were the two main pressures coming through in the 1960s I would say.

AB: *Hence your concept of Applied Linguistics as a theme rather than as something which is narrowly defined as a discipline?*

MAKH: Yes, it very much comes from there.

AB: *And you must have thought through some of these critical movements for the recent ten volume collection of papers edited by Jonathan Webster for Continuum, trying to shape and bring together your contributions over the years. Apart from what you have already mentioned, was there any particular rationale for the way you structured or saw that work being structured?*

MAKH: Yes, the initiative came from Robin Fawcett who pressed me over the years, and I spent at least five to seven years trying to organise some of the papers into what I thought would be one or maybe two volumes. I realised I would need some further help; and then a mutual friend, Edwin Thumboo, suggested that I ask Jonathan Webster who was in Singapore when I first knew him. The next time I went to Hong Kong, where Jonathan had moved by then, I approached him about Edwin's suggestion and he just jumped at it. To cut things short, he took all my writing and sorted them into ten headings. Now he did that, and his groupings are of course thematic, so in a sense the titles of those books do represent the major themes. He suggested we start with one on grammar and I said fine, because I do think of myself as a grammarian primarily. It's a useful label, by the way, because when people ask you what you do for a living, you say you're a linguist, then they say, 'Oh how many languages do you speak?'

AB: *Yes, a typical reaction.*

MAKH: So I worked out a long time ago that there was a much better answer. I would say 'I'm a grammarian' and that stopped the discourse altogether! Anyway, after the volume on grammar, he suggested text/discourse analysis as the next, which is fine because a lot of the areas of application of linguistics involve discourse analysis. And again that was something we were always keen to do insofar as that was what grammar was all about, enabling you to analyse texts. So that itself becomes a theme that runs through a lot of applications. He noticed there were lots of examples of text analysis and selected these next; and then he made a general volume on language which is a general reflection on the nature and functions of language and structure. Then Ruqaiya [Hasan], my wife, who has been pushing me to get this done for years, said that the work on child language should come in next. So that was another theme.

AB: *That's been a very important aspect of the work you have done.*

MAKH: Because I love doing it. That again came in because of the teachers. You see, we used to do a lot of workshopping with primary teachers back in that time in London. And they kept saying, 'Okay we get these children from five years old, we know what they can do; we want to know what they've done before that'. And that was when we had our own child, so I said, 'Well, I'll find out', because there wasn't much written about it. There were a number of classic studies on the old style diary approach, where you did intensive studies of one child, from the late eighteenth century onwards. In fact, some of them were very good, but it had gone rather out of fashion. And I thought this approach was important and I had the advantage of having learned to do dialect fieldwork, so I could transcribe very quickly. So it was all natural data, and as I say, the impetus for that came from the teachers. So that was another theme coming from that time, the work with the primary school teachers. Then there was a volume on computational and quantitative studies. The computational one came out of the early, initial machine translation work, and then from working with Bill Mann in southern California (Mann 1984), in the 1980s, in text generation. The kind of natural language processing at that time was mainly foregrounding parsing, but he wanted to do text generation and he'd read some of my work, and said he'd like to use systemic grammar for this, so I worked with him for a couple of months and then Christian Matthiessen became resident linguist for the project (Matthiessen & Bateman 1992). The quantitative work was based on my conception of grammar as systemic and probabilistic. Then came two volumes of descriptive studies, one on English and one on Chinese; and then the last two are the ones on educational linguistics and sociolinguistics.

AB: *Just to move on from there, increasingly there is a need to analyse language multimodally. Where are the relevancies, the connections with your theoretical and semiotic approaches to language? How do you conceptualise the major influences that are occurring in multimodal analysis?*

MAKH: What we have to use is the word that Clifford Geertz (1973) uses, to 'thicken' our understanding, 'thick description'. This means we have to introduce further dimensions to our understanding. I think the notion of multimodality helps to do that. It is very important. It enables us to put the concept of meaning into the centre of attention because what all the modalities share is that they are semiotic modes.

AB: *They are meaning-making systems.*

MAKH: Exactly, important from that point of view of being meaning-making systems, together with the fact of bringing new technologies in language use.

AB: *Which is pushing the boundaries of the meaning-making systems both in literacy and in oral language.*

MAKH: And at all levels, I think. People are exploring very seriously the notion of what aspects of a learning process are more effectively presented in what kind of modality. So I think it's very important. My only reservation is that there is always a lot of pressure to get away from language. It's hard work focusing on language, so people want to do something else. So there is always a danger of people seeing other modalities as an easy option.

AB: *Going beyond language and text and paying attention to the visual, let's talk about images, here.*

MAKH: Images are very central! But I think that it is important to bear in mind that all those who make use of these other modalities, both as production and reception, also already know language. And that is a critical point in understanding how they work. So I think that you have to still maintain language itself at the centre of attention, as being in some way the key. I don't go so far as to say that everything that can be meant in any other modality can also be meant in language, because I think that would be an act of faith and I don't think it's demonstrated. Maybe, maybe not. That I think is not the point. But all the users of the other modalities are themselves language users and that is essential to their ability to control these other modalities.

AB: *Yes, because otherwise people see them as interchangeable and not with a linguistic semiotic system as the basis.*

MAKH: I think that some work Bernie Mohan (see Mohan, 1986) was doing some years ago with language and content was useful here. The people in intelligent computing refer to this now as data fusion. So there's a sense that all these modalities can be seen as sources that have to be fused together in some way, in some coherent body of information, or meaning.

AB: *This raises the interesting question of the extent you think your work in systemic functional linguistics is applicable to non-linguistic systems such as images and architecture as some have recently been arguing.*

MAKH: This is very interesting. I value very highly the sort of work started by Theo van Leeuwen in images and music (Kress & van Leeuwen 1996/2006, van Leeuwen 1999), and by Michael O'Toole (1994/2010) in visual arts, the language of displayed art and so on. What I understand by it is that we're not saying all these other modalities, these other semiotic modes, have the same properties as language. What we're saying is that we have a coherent model/theory of language, so let's use it to explore these other forms of modalities. It may need to be extended, but we will in turn learn from that experience and it will feed back to our understanding of language. Michael O'Toole's work on painting, architecture and sculpture is a classic case. We apply the notion of metafunction; we apply the notion of rank, and let's see. What he has come out with I think is brilliant because it has given people a non-technical, non-academic way of talking about their experiences of visual art. This is a way of exploring these other systems. It's not saying they are all isomorphic, that they all have these same properties. No, this is a way of looking at them and seeing where we get to. And my notion, as I was suggesting earlier, is to use the word 'appliable'

(Halliday 2008b). I have always been interested in trying to find an appliable form of linguistics, something that can be used to explore other things.

AB: *Yes, recently people have tended to play with such terms. We also have the term applicable linguistics. Is it applicable linguistics? Is it appliable linguistics? Are there differences in your view?*

MAKH: 'Applicable' to me has a difference. If I say applicable then it's with a sense of applicable to something. I'm not making a big issue of this! But there is a significant difference. If I say something is 'applicable', then it refers specifically to some task or at least some particular sphere of action. I want a more general sense, that of 'capable of and designed for being applied'. This has arisen out of the features we were talking about earlier, that even within my own experience there had been a range of different problems to be tackled, all in some way resolving themselves into problems of language; I wanted an account of language which would be serviceable in these contexts (and in other problem areas that I hadn't faced myself but that other people were facing, such as the clinical and the forensic), but which would be robust enough to learn from these challenges and to continue to evolve while taking on board new findings.

AB: *And continuing the theme of 'appliable' linguistics, one of the areas we haven't explored where the account of language is increasingly being applied is in work in translation. Some of this means bringing together theories of systemic functional linguistics and their implications for practice in the translation field, for instance in Korean. And of course there is also the work that's been done in descriptions of French, Vietnamese, Japanese, for example.*

MAKH: Well, this is another point. In my work from the early days in the 1960s, for example, I had to focus again on English, and one of the problems for anyone trying to work in a systemic framework is that you have to know the language very well. So we tended to focus on English first, and then a small number of other languages. Now, I'm glad to say this sense of systemic functional typology (cf. Caffarel et al. 2004) providing a lens through which you move into the exploration of other languages is being very much extended. And because I have had particular contact with China I know there's a lot of work going on there. Our early Chinese colleagues typically were specialists in English, but even when they were with us back in the 1980s they started working on Chinese, and there's now a good lot of work going on in the field of Chinese language studies.

AB: *Yes, it's really exciting to see this work being extended to so many different languages. I'd like to turn now to a final question. Your career coincided, if I can use that term, with the work of Chomsky. And obviously there have been very different paradigms of research and linguistic theory that have emanated from your work and Chomsky's. The question I'd like to ask is: what do you think Applied Linguistics would have been like today if there had been no Michael Halliday?*

MAKH: Well, there were plenty of others at work! I think there are two aspects to this. If you look at since, say, the 1950s when the term Applied Linguistics started being used, it's moved around. In my experience back in the 1950s, working with people like Peter Strevens and Ian Catford and our colleagues on the French side working on français fondamental and so on, it was mainly in the teaching of English or the teaching of French as a second language. It was interesting that language teaching was a minor theme when AILA was founded. It wasn't seen as a major field for the application of linguistics, though it soon became one. There was a political-historical context for this, that of the decolonization of British and French colonies, which led to a big industry in the teaching of these two languages, English and French. Then the gradual spread of English across the global scene made this particular aspect of language education a dominant theme in Applied Linguistics. I don't think I have played any part in the way this motif has evolved – my own concern has been more with mother tongue education, and especially language moving up the age range and across the curriculum.

I think the problem with the linguistics that has derived from Chomsky's work is that it has tended to distance itself from any form of application. Chomsky was quite clear himself about this: he said his theory had nothing to do with education. I tried always to keep theory and practice together, to say that theoretical Linguistics and Applied Linguistics are not two separate linguistic universes. Whether this has had any major effect in the educational field I rather doubt!

AB: *Well, in the field of second language education, there was obviously a period in which Chomsky's work in linguistics had a major impact – I guess in cognitive approaches to second language education. But my sense is that practitioners teaching in that field struggled to make linkages from the theories of Chomsky to what you actually did in the classroom.*

MAKH: I think that was true right from the early days of transformational theory. But, you just mentioned the work in cognitive linguistics and I see things generally moving together, in the sense that I would say for 'cognitive' read 'semantic'. In other words, 'cognitive linguistics' is a way of making meaning central again, the way it always should have been. I think the problem is precisely with the label 'cognitive', in the sense that meaning is seen as something outside language, which of course it isn't. Which is why practitioners in the field find 'cognition' a little difficult to manipulate and to manage.

AB: *Yes, the applications to language teaching are not easily identifiable. Michael, are there any final comments you'd wish to make about issues we've raised in this conversation?*

MAKH: I do feel that the range of areas to which we can and need to apply our understanding of language is very broad, and is getting broader all the time (for an overview of new directions see Hasan et al. 2005, 2007). So I think that moving into this century, that's the way we are going. Take as an example, the developments in clinical linguistics: the medical context is so important, but it takes time for the work to get off the ground. I think applied linguists are getting much more of a profile, being recognised as people who may have something to offer. In the last ten to fifteen years, perhaps the most important source of insight has been from brain science. I could never myself make much contact with the dominant psycholinguistics of the previous period of the 1970s and so forth. I read some work with interest but it wasn't adding any explanation. Now, in a way, everything has changed with the understanding of the evolution and development of the brain (cf. Halliday 1994). The place of language in that process is much more central than I think was recognised before. There's more of a sign of maturity now in the field, bringing in different theories which were maybe not linked in the past. You have to reach a certain level of theoretical understanding before they can be brought in. You know, right at the beginning of our conversation you mentioned the term proactive. I would say of myself, I have always been reactive rather than proactive. Maybe now is the time one should encourage those who are of the other more proactive type, and there are plenty of those around!

AB: *Becoming proactive is perhaps a good message for the future for Applied Linguistics! Michael, thank you for agreeing to be part of this conversation – I'm sure readers of JAL will find it of great value and interest.*

MAKH: Thanks for the opportunity! I think this is a great time for someone to be embarking on the study of linguistics; if I was just moving into this field I would be thrilled by the possibilities it offers. There's so much work waiting to be done!

Macquarie University
21 December 2005

About the authors

M. A. K. Halliday was born in Yorkshire in 1925. He was trained in Chinese for war service with the British army, studied in China, taught Chinese in Britain for a number of years, then moved into linguistics, becoming in 1965 Professor of General Linguistics at University College London. In 1975 he was appointed Foundation Professor of Linguistics at the University of Sydney, where he remained until his retirement.

Anne Burns is a Professor in the Department of Linguistics at Macquarie University, Sydney. She holds a BA (Hons) from the University of Wales (Cardiff) and a PhD from Macquarie University. Her research interests are in educational linguistics spanning second language literacy development, discourse analysis for the teaching of speaking, and more recently professional communication. She has authored a number of books on research and pedagogy in adult immigrant programs and is currently co-editing a book on second language teacher education for CUP.

12

With Hu Zhuanglin and Zhu Yongsheng (2010)

Introduction

The 36th International Systemic Functional Congress was held in Tsinghua University in Beijing in July, 2009, during which Professor M. A. K. Halliday of the University of Sydney was interviewed by Professor Hu Zhuanglin of Peking University and Professor Zhu Yongsheng of Fudan University. This is the transcript based on the interview. Questions asked and discussed during the interview include issues concerning developments of Systemic Functional Linguistics (SFL), the concept of appliable linguistics, SFL studies in the Chinese context, grammatical metaphor, and language generation and machine translation.

HZ: *I would like to express my gratitude to Professor Fang Yan and the organizers of this conference for giving Professor Zhu and me the chance to interview Professor Michael Halliday this morning. To speak frankly, we have some questions and problems in the course of our research that we would like to put to Professor Halliday. I will first invite my friend Professor Zhu Yongsheng to ask the questions.*

ZY: *The first question I am going to ask is actually the last question I should ask. As everybody sees, in the past 50 or more years a lot of achievements have been made by the school of Systemic Functional Linguistics. My question is: In what directions will SFL go in the future?*

MAKH: As you said, in a sense, that first question should come last! The future directions simply emerge as the work evolves. I see them in the topics people raise, the questions they ask of me, and of each other, and these seem very hard to summarize. I suspect that there will be a constant broadening of the areas in which we find ourselves working, and which we increasingly find ourselves called on to work in as people gradually come to recognize the central role of language in so many of their professional activities and interests. I think one of the things we've been trying to do is to say to people "Well, look: you've got a problem. Do try to think about it linguistically. The language element in what you're doing may be where the problems have arisen." Sometimes we do get called on; sometimes perhaps we should interfere on our own. I think the broadening of our activities is likely to continue, and it will go on making demands on the resources of the theory. As Jim Martin said in his plenary address, it is already complex; and no doubt it will get still more complex. It takes a long time to work through every aspect of the theory – though you can be applying it at the same time. But please do recognize that language is one of the most complex phenomena in the universe; so don't expect a theory to make it simple! If it is simplified, it is distorted. This does not mean that every user has to explore every part of the theory; but at least you should know where you are locating yourself in the total picture. That's how I see the future.

HZ: *OK, in connection to Professor Zhu's question, my question is somewhat related. In the past few years, you proposed a new term, "Appliable Linguistics". From memory (Halliday 2008b), and after checking with Professor Zhu, I believe the first time you mentioned this term was when you gave some lectures at Fudan University in 2004. The reason for me to raise the question is that not all Systemic Functional linguists can understand why you want to use this term. For instance, when I talked to Jim Martin [probably at the 10th Functional Linguistics Conference at Jiangxi Normal University in 2004; JRM], his answer was that he had never heard of Appliable Linguistics. It seems that even among Systemic Functional linguists some of our colleagues are not familiar with this term. So, why do you want to use this term since we already have Systemic Functional Linguistics? Further, when I heard this term, I tried to look it up in the dictionary. You can't find this word in most contemporary dictionaries. The word appliable can only be found in the Third Edition of Webster's Dictionary, which says it is obsolete. I'm curious why you choose this term instead of applicable.*

MAKH: Yes, I'm sorry to hear that it is obsolete – I thought I had invented it! I notice that you all have problems with it. It did not come out on your monitor; you wanted to type "appliable", but the system printed it as "applicable". Did you notice that?

HZ: *Yes.*

MAKH: The problem lies with the spell checks. The manual says you don't have to disable the spell check; you just add new words to its vocabulary. But watch it, because that is exactly what I want to say: appliable. It's not the name for the theory. It's not something new. It's just a description. It's a descriptive term, for which I can't use "applicable". You can't say an "applicable theory"; it doesn't make any sense. "Applicable" means applicable to certain specific uses; it's nearly always collocated with "to" this or the other. I need a general term, and "applicable" does not serve the purpose, whereas "appliable" does. I'm pleased to be told by Chinese scholars that there is no problem in Chinese. Instead of *yingyong* (应用) you say *shiyong* (适用), meaning something which is suitable for being applied. So that's the real difference: "applicable" focuses you on some particular issue – whenever I say "applicable", I always have in mind something that can be applied to some particular situation. But by "appliable" I don't mean that; I mean something which has evolved in contexts in which it can be applied, and what is guiding its evolution is this effect of being used in a wide range of different contexts. It's not a new name; it's a description.

HZ: *I have to cut in to add one more question. I can still remember about 30 years ago, I asked you a question "Within the Systemic Functional Linguistics, who is the* leader? Who is the head?" Halliday was very polite, saying "in Systemic Functional Linguistics, this group, everyone can say what he wants to say." So we follow this principle. I also had a chance to visit UC Santa Barbara. I asked Sandy Thompson, the head, "In the US, do you have Functionalism? Who is the head?" Her answer was "Yes, for the first question; for the second, no". That is, there is no school or association which tries to group all the functionalists together in the U.S. Now, can we expect that sometime in the future, within the Systemic Functional group, someone may try to influence the whole group, or take the lead? How can we solve the problem? Are we going to follow the American pattern? Everyone can have their own theory and everyone can have their own conference, or something like this. The reason for me to ask this question is that, by appliable linguistics, you want to set up a criterion, or a principle, of what we should be doing in the future. So long as one's theory is appliable, it is OK.

MAKH: No, you are forcing me to make a rule. I don't say something is okay or not okay. It's not my business. No. No, no.

HZ: *No, I'm not forcing you to answer this question. Thank you.*

MAKH: We are not imposing structure or looking for boundaries; it's not like that. This is an evolving system; I have no desire to control its evolution.

HZ: *Now we come to the second part of question.*

ZY: *I remember in the functional linguistics conference held in Xiamen at this time last year (2008), you said something about the "attitude". You referred to it in linguistic studies. You said that you yourself preferred the "both-and" attitude to "either-or" attitude in linguistic research. And my question is, by saying this, do you mean that you take this "attitude" not only to different branches within the Systemic Functional School, but also to other schools of linguistics, such as TG, cognitive linguistics and other theories? Furthermore, do you take this attitude as well towards human life in general?*

MAKH: That might help! No, it's not about linguistics; it's about language. You could apply the same principle at the meta-level if you like, to think about the schools of linguistics; but that's not what I mean. It's really in your ways of thinking about language. One example is the terms "grammatical/ungrammatical". It is said that a sentence has to be either grammatical or ungrammatical; syntax consistently draws a strict line between them. I don't agree with that; I think there is no clear opposition between grammatical/ungrammatical, because what appears grammatical depends so much on the context – the register, or the context of situation, and this notion of grammaticality will not draw a line for us between what we can interpret and what we cannot. I tend to think in terms of complementarities rather than exclusives. An example from descriptive grammar is that of Subject and Topic: it is said that there are Subject-Predicate languages and there are Topic-Comment languages, and every language will be either one or the other. But every language is both of these. Every language has an interpersonal structure as a form of exchange between speaker and listener, and a particular role in this structure is what we call the "Subject"; and every language has a textual structure as a contextualized message, and a particular role in this structure is often called the "Topic" (though this term is rather ill-defined; we need a more focused concept such as the "Theme"). In other words, both Subject and Theme, not either/or.

There are many other such examples, where different descriptions are set up in opposition but in fact both are part of the picture; for example, it is said that prominence must be either initial or final, whereas it is more likely to be both initial and final – they are just different kinds of prominence. So what I'm referring to, when I say "both + and" rather than "either/or", is the way of thinking about the language. But if we apply it to linguistic theory, we could consider "formal" versus "functional". There is a difference between these two approaches: ours is functional in a number of different senses, especially in the nature of what we think of as explanations. We explain the way that language is by reference to what language does – the functions in which language evolved. But of course we have to describe linguistic forms, although we don't go on to represent a language as a formal system.

HZ: *OK. As the second question is about the relation between "either-or" and "both-and", it is quite clear that our system is a system of "either-or", which is primary in our theory. It is the paradigmatic relation. When we are talking about the language system, I would like to add some questions. In our group, do we have some people doing their research after they have made the selection "either-or", and then try to put them together to realize the selection by way of "both ... and"?*

MAKH: Yes, the system is the theoretical representation of choice in language. That is a totally different issue – nothing to do with "either/or" as an intellectual stance, a strategy for thinking with.

HZ: *OK. Let's still talk about this question. As for linguistic studies or research, sometimes I think maybe "both-and" can also work. Actually, recently I wrote a paper about linguistic research, in which I argued for cross-disciplinary research when one sector is related to another sector; then, in SFL, can we benefit from the research findings from Cognitive Linguistics? I'm asking because language is a kind of thing; on the one hand it is individual, physiological and psychological; on the other hand it is social and conventional. Can we combine the two factors?*

MAKH: Yes. The cognitive approach, from my point of view, is another way of doing semantics – looking at it from outside language. The problem with making use of their findings is that they are rather short of realization rules. In other words, the categories they set up are interesting as ways of thinking about meaning. But, when it comes to asking how these categories will actually be realized in the lexicogrammar, it's very hard to know. We are always seeing language in what I call a "trinocular" perspective: we are looking from above, from roundabout, and from below. The cognitive linguists are typically just looking from above. Let's by all means look at some of these ideas coming up under the heading of cognitive linguistics and see whether they can map into an explicit model of language which also includes both the environment within semantics itself and the stratum below – can they also be interpreted in terms of realization in the lexicogrammar? The reason that Christian and I called our book, about 10 years ago now, *Construing Experience Through Meaning* (Halliday & Matthiessen 1999) was what we added in the subtitle *a language-based approach to cognition*. In other words, what the cognitive theorists are doing is looking into meaning from outside language; what we are doing is to say we can handle this by treating cognition as a form of language.

HZ: *OK. Now we will move on to the third question. As we know, this conference was held in Beijing, China, and so many of the papers were contributed by Chinese participants. So, in this case, Professor Zhu has questions in mind.*

ZY: *Many Chinese students, many followers of other schools of linguistics and scholars like Professor Hu and others have been working hard to do something for the improvement of the theory and its application. We are not satisfied with what we have done in the past decades. My question is: could you please give us some advice on what we should do, or what we can do in the future?*

MAKH: Well, I don't think my advice will be different in China than from anywhere else! Get more data, do more description, think more theory. I can expand on any one of these. We are still short of data; you are beginning to get very useful corpora in China, and we need to get access to these as fundamental sources of data for linguistic research. This means not simply corpus as used by lexicographers for instances of patterns in wording, but the corpus as repository of texts, because our work should be as far as possible text-based. So data is one thing.

Description, yes: I was listening to some excellent papers yesterday on descriptive work on Chinese. We need more of that – but not just on Chinese. Go out and work on more languages! It is not the case that Chinese and English are the only two languages in the world. (They may be the biggest, but that's not necessarily a virtue!) What you need is for people to be trained as linguists – not "English linguists" or "Chinese linguists": you need people to be trained as linguists who regard it as part of their work to explore any languages anywhere in the world, either as research data for linguistics or because there's some other reason for studying them. For linguists in China it might be suggested that they should study some of the regional languages, like Thai, Vietnamese, Cambodian, or minority languages within China itself. So there is a need for a great extension of descriptive work.

The third point is to encourage you to think theoretically. You express your question with a tone of modesty; but, as I said yesterday, Chinese throughout history have been the most theoretically minded people on earth. The great virtue of Chinese thinkers has been that they were often socially-oriented, and that is just the perspective within which SFL has evolved and flourished. So, as well as data and description, also theory.

HZ: *Actually we have many forums concerned with research on the Chinese language. Things are much more complex than you have covered in your answer. The first thing is, as a linguist, of course we should analyze the data. For Chinese linguists, then, we should analyze Chinese language. The problem is: I had many chances to attend international conferences, and they were divided into several sessions. When I tried to deliver a paper about Chinese language years ago not so many participants turned up, because many participants didn't know Chinese. Only those overseas who had attended the conference came to my paper. That's the reason why I lost interest in attending international conferences. What's the point for me to go there?*

MAKH: They obviously were not conferences on linguistics! Because a linguistics conference is one in which you talk about any language; it doesn't depend at all on what languages anyone knows. You are trained as a linguist to make your material intelligible to all the listeners. If it was a congress in some subject like psychology, I don't know; but if it's a congress of linguistics, then you talk about whatever language you are working on; that's an essential principle. And it is this principle that you use both in publications and conferences. You make your material intelligible to the audience on the assumption that they don't know the language. (Of course they must know the language in which you are giving the paper. If you're talking to them in Chinese, then they must understand Chinese! But that's an entirely different issue.)

I'm going to add another point here, which is this. Professor Huang Guowen and his colleague, Professor Chang Chenguang have taken seriously a complaint that I have been making for a number of years, that in China you read all the materials published (at least those that are in English, not necessarily in other languages); but outside China people are not trained to read the materials in Chinese. So we need a digest of publications which tells outsiders, in English, what work has been published in Chinese in SFL during the year, with email addresses showing how you get access to it – and this is now in hand, which is fantastic (see the *Annual Review of Functional Linguistics*, which the Higher Education Press began publishing in 2009). So this will solve one problem: at least the material written in Chinese will be accessible to those outside, who can follow up what seems to them to be interesting in one way or another. In the longer term, of course, more foreigners will learn Chinese; but most of them are not going to learn characters; so you would have to devise a system whereby any Chinese text is immediately transcribed from characters into pinyin. Until that happens, don't expect foreign adults are going to learn Chinese to the extent they can read your papers in characters. They can read the language all right, but you have to produce it in some form of roman script.

HZ: *My other concern is related to the fact that I tried to look at the history of the development of SFL. Actually you started from doing research of Chinese language. But* *later I noticed you put more emphasis on analyses of English. If you had stayed in the analyses of the Chinese language, maybe SFL would not have developed so fast. Do you think so?*

MAKH: Only in the sense that I was trying to push linguistics further. I had no ambitions in life; but I was enormously helped by my teachers of Chinese and so was able to explore the language for myself. That was a wonderful opportunity, for which I shall always be grateful. But circumstances changed; I became involved in language education work, which meant that I had to work on English. That probably speeded up the development of my ideas and also the spread of the number of people who were interested in the work. But it has nothing to do with the nature of the language. Any language will make the same demands on a linguistic theory. So it was an institutional factor, not a systemic factor, that lay behind what you were saying. At that time, it would not have been possible to develop the institutional resources needed to enable many people to work on Chinese.

HZ: *Still concerning the study of the Chinese language, I want to know your attitude toward iconicity. So far as Chinese is concerned, iconicity plays a very important role. But Saussure didn't agree with this. He thought arbitrariness is the chief matter.*

MAKH: A very good example of where we need "both-and", not "either-or"! Both are equally fundamental principles in language studies. A little caution here: are you talking about the Chinese language or about the Chinese script? Because these are very different things.

HZ: *Even including sound, I gave you my paper, right?*

MAKH: Saussure was right: in every language, the relationship between sound and meaning is basically "arbitrary" (a better word for this in English is "conventional"). There is then a minor motif of iconicity; more of it in some languages than in others, perhaps – Chinese seems to have very little; English maybe a little more, in the form of "phonaesthesia", or sound symbolism. But the principle, and the balance between the conventional and the iconic, are probably pretty constant across all languages.

As far as the writing system is concerned, since the Chinese script has retained the features of a morphemic system, not phonemic or syllabic, you can see its iconic origins. But nearly all scripts were pictorial in origin. Whenever I write the word <u>man</u> in English I am drawing three pictures. The letter <u>m</u> was a picture of running water, just like "shui", except that in Egypt the water was flat and calm, like ᴍᴍ whereas in ancient China some of the water was flowing much more steeply downhill, so it looked like 〝. Similarly when I write the letter <u>a</u> I am drawing a picture of an ox head; and every time I write the letter <u>n</u> I'm drawing a snake – because these were the initial sounds of words in ancient Phoenician, where these symbols were first used phonologically. So the iconic principle is present in all, or nearly all, writing systems; it is just more obvious in Chinese.

HZ: *The next question is also mine. We have discussed this question time and again. From the very beginning, Professor Zhu, Yan Shiqing and I have had some questions about grammatical metaphor, and we discussed this in Shanghai, and also at the Singapore conference. But I still want you to clarify some points. There are, for instance, lexical metaphor and grammatical metaphor, from below or from above, the same signifier with different signifieds, the same signified with different signifiers. These principles, do you think, still hold true?*

MAKH: They're not principles, I think; they are simply practices in the way people have looked at metaphor. The metaphoric quality, whether lexical or grammatical, is the same. What happened historically is that, in studying lexical metaphor, people have always tended to look at it from below, "same lexical item, different meanings" – that's just the way they looked at it. You can look at lexical metaphor just as well from above, but typically they didn't. Whereas I want to say, in order to understand grammatical metaphor it helps if you look at it from above. These are simply different ways of looking at metaphor of either kind. In lexical metaphor, as we all know, what is being transferred is lexical items – one lexical item shifting to another; whereas in grammatical metaphor, the move is in grammatical class, or grammatical rank, or both. Something shifts in class, from verb to noun or conjunction to verb, and so on; and typically something shifts in rank, from clause complex to clause, or clause to group. So in grammatical metaphor, the metaphoric shift is in grammatical categories; in lexical metaphor, the metaphoric shift is in lexical items.

These two kinds of metaphor play very different parts in the overall construction of meaning in the language. We may try to see if there's any pattern in the way the two interact; I don't know whether there is or not. Perhaps there is a tendency that, when people are adopting a certain particular stance and they don't know much about what they are talking about, or else they try to persuade you by pretending to know some kind of scientific authority, then they may mix up some lexical and grammatical metaphor all in one as if it carried an extra punch – but that's a very informal observation! Lexical and grammatical metaphor don't really reinforce each other. They are very different in the way they are incorporated into the text.

HZ: *So "on the fifth day they arrived at the summit" and "the fifth day saw them at the summit" are on the same level; they are still grammatical metaphor?*

MAKH: Yes.

HZ: *You don't have to make two clauses into one clause through nominalization. They don't have to follow this principle.*

MAKH: What you are doing then is switching around the categories within the same clause. So there is a change of class, and therefore of grammatical function, but in that instance there is no drop in rank.

HZ: *The next question is to do with the relation between text and discourse. I think at Beijing Normal University earlier this month, one participant asked the question "what is the difference between cohesion and coherence"; actually they are related to each other. At that time when we tried to translate the word "text" it could be translated as "pianzhang" (篇章) and discourse as "huayu" (话语). But in my memory, I read the version of translation by the late Professor Xu Guozhang, who used the term "yupian" (语篇). It combines both "pianzhang" (篇章) and "huayu" (话语). Do you agree with this?*

MAKH: This is Xu Guozhang's version?

HZ: *I couldn't find the original, but in my memory, it is his translation.*

MAKH: I can't remember now. I gave a definition to this in my book on complementarities – I forgot what it was, but I can tell you roughly what it was like. I found it useful myself to have the two terms "text" and "discourse": I tend to talk about "text" if I am looking at a piece of discourse as a linguistic object, a piece of language; whereas if I talk about "discourse" I am thinking of text which is being looked at more from the outside, probably in one of the various forms of "discourse analysis", where they are looking at the language but they are not primarily concerned with it as a linguistic object. So for me it's simply a difference of focus – of orientation if you like, which I use to separate the two terms. I have never seen any systematic study of how the two terms are used.

HZ: *Let me try to repeat what you have said in order to check whether I understand it. By "text", we try to concentrate on the language, within the language; by "discourse", outside the language. Because in the past, I used to think that "text" is related to language, whereas discourse is related to meaning.*

MAKH: But that's a relation of both-and, not either-or! You cannot put language on one side and meaning on the other; both are related to both. I think it's a matter of orientation and focus.

HZ: *Some people from literary criticism also use the term "text", but when it is translated into Chinese, it becomes "wenben" (文本) instead of "yupian" (语篇). So I want to find out whether they are two different things, or about the same thing.*

MAKH: Well, I'm not very sure how the term is used by scholars in other fields, such as literary criticism, I don't know.

HZ: *But for translation, it does not matter. I mean the contents. When they are talking about the text, do they mean the same thing as we linguists do?*

MAKH: Who are "they"?

HZ: *Literary critics.*

MAKH: Oh I see. I don't know. Probably they are not, on the whole, looking at the text as a linguistic object; sometimes they feel their approach is categorically different from that.

HZ: *This is a problem for us Chinese linguists. Sometimes we use different terms to the degree that at one of the conferences, we had to ask the participants to vote: "Do you advocate "yupian" (语篇) or do you advocate "huayu" (话语)?*

MAKH: I guess you are using "yupian" more; "huayu" doesn't seem to me so much used now – or is it?

HZ: *You can find more people use the term "huayu" (话语) today. Especially, when people talk about "huayuquan" (话语权), discursive power.*

HZ: *My next question is, in 1980, you were in Stanford on study leave, right? After you came back from the States in 1981, you talked about your research, about what you had done in the US. And you talked about clause generation, sentence generation. At that time you mentioned if you tried to generate a clause or a sentence by computer and if you used Chomsky's TG grammar, you would have different kinds of outputs, but you simply couldn't understand. But if you used SF approach, you could produce some clauses or sentences, which were somewhat intelligible. Thirty years have passed, have you got some new information about this kind of research, especially by Systemic Functional linguists, because you have mentioned different kinds of approaches, say, the Nigel Project, the Penman Project, and so on, three or four projects (cf. Mann 1984, Matthiessen & Bateman 1991, O'Donnell & Bateman, 2005, Teich 2009)? Can you tell us something about this?*

MAKH: I am not the best person to talk about what current work is going on. We have to go to Robin Fawcett on the one hand (e.g. Fawcett 2008, Tucker 2007), with his long-term project at Cardiff, to Christian Matthiessen and his collaborators, such as Wu Canzhong (e.g. 2009), in Sydney, to John Bateman in Germany, where Yang Guowen has been working, to Kay O'Halloran in Singapore, and so on. There are a lot of people now concerned with this; they know much better than I do. Look at a new book that has also come out, published by Continuum, called the *Continuum Companion to Systemic Functional Linguistics* (Halliday & Webster 2009). But just to fill in the background: this wasn't anything to do with Stanford (in Stanford I was in a very different environment, and only for a very short time). As I have said, I have been in and out of computational linguistics since the 1950s. I first worked in a machine translation unit in Cambridge in 1956–58; then in our work at University College London in the 1960s I came back to it; but at that time the technical resources were just not developed enough to make the computer really of interest as a linguistic research tool. It was from the 1980s onwards, with what was then called the fifth generation of computers, that this changed. The main thing of interest to me in the computer as a research tool for linguistics was: how could we actually use the resources of the computer to increase and deepen our understanding of language? For example, once you draw a system network, it generates a certain number of selection expressions, and that number soon gets very large indeed. You need a computer to process it: you need to be able to test a system network by going through all these selection expressions, and so on. So the computer as research tool for linguistics – that's one question.

But then from the other side, it was linguistics as research tool for the computational specialist. The work in the 1980s, when Christian Matthiessen was first becoming involved, was not at Stanford; I was at Irvine, but the work was being done in the University of Southern California. Bill Mann, who had started his "Penman" project there, came to me and said "I'm starting a text generation project, and I want to use your Systemic Functional Grammar. Would you please work with my programmer on a grammar to get us started?" So I drew up a clause system network for English. I think it had 81 systems in it; and I worked very intensively with the programmer for two or three months, in order to find out how to make our grammar programmable, how to make it explicit enough to be used. And from then on, when Christian Matthiessen was appointed to the project, they developed this text generation program. And as I said, simultaneously, Robin Fawcett working in Cardiff was developing another one. Now if you take a highly formalized grammar, like some variant of Chomskian or post-Chomskian grammar, you can get it airborne very quickly with a small dedicated system; but every time you want to move to a new task, you have to do the whole thing again. What we wanted was a system with a general capability which could be exported to other contexts. That work is still going on, and being expanded in Sydney to include multimodal and multilingual text generation (Matthiessen 2007a, Teruya et al. 2007); but now, as I said there are many more people involved in these projects – as well as important extensions like Michio Sugeno's research in brain science in Japan.

HZ: *The reason for me to ask the question is that I am curious about whether Systemic Functional linguists can play some role in developing machine translation. Today if you try to google, you find articles in English or in Spanish, and if you try to click a certain button, you get the article translated into Chinese quickly. Fifty or sixty percent are readable. Anyway, I am not certain about the latest developments.*

My last question is: since we are moving to an electronic period, digital period in which people today start to talk about hypertext, do you think that some day we will redefine the term "language"? That is to say, 6000 years ago, we only had speech; we only learned to hear and to say something. But beginning from about 6000 years ago, we have the writing system; we have both speech and writing. So language means the two things. Right? Actually, after the liberation of China, we emphasize literacy – the teaching of reading and writing. But today it's not enough. We encourage multi-literacies. That is, you have to learn other things. So do you think some day in the future, we are moving toward that direction?

MAKH: Yes. People have always wanted to extend the scope to other languages, and to other modalities, or other semiotic systems. For example, mathematics: you often read that mathematics is a language. But there is a distinction – there are certain properties belonging only to what is traditionally called language, such as its manifestation both as speaking and as writing; so I think it is useful for us linguists to confine the use of the word "language" to this, and to talk rather about "semiotic systems other than language". We need the general concept of semiotic systems, which would include a large number of systems other than language. If you start using "language" in this wider sense, you'll have to have a new name for language, because you've got to be able to talk about language in contrast to other semiotic systems. There will always be these centrifugal pressures; but I think probably the core sense of "language" will remain, and we will develop new vocabulary as we develop our understandings of the other semiotic systems, and the extent to which they can be modelled as if they were kinds of language. They differ from language partly because, in general, all those who use these other modalities also use language, and this has an effect on the way they evolve. I like Christian's term – he uses "multisemiotic" rather than just "multimodal" (Matthiessen 2007a, Bateman 2008), which allows the possibility that they are different semiotic systems – different ways of meaning with their own meaning potential. But I think we probably will not extend the term "language" to try to include all of these.

HZ: *I think Christian also uses the term multi systemic.*

MAKH: No. Multisemiotic. We also use Firth's term "polysystemic"; but that has quite a different sense: it is an important concept in the description of language, but it does not refer particularly to other modalities.

HZ: *Time is short. Actually I have a lot of questions. Anyway, Professor Zhu and I are very glad to have Professor Michael Halliday answer our questions. Dear Michael, thank you!*

MAKH: Thank you.

Tsinghua University
July 2009
Note: This interview was transcribed, according to the recording, by Xia Dengshan.
作者简介：
M. A. K. Halliday（韩礼德），澳大利亚悉尼大学（The University of Sydney）荣休教授，系统功能语言学理论创始人。
胡壮麟，北京大学外国语学院资深教授、博士生导师，研究方向：普通语言学、系统功能语言学、语篇分析、外语教育。Email: yyhzl@pku.edu.cn。
朱永生，复旦大学外文学院教授、博士生导师，研究方向：系统功能语言学、话语分析。Email: zhuyongsheng8@hotmail.com。

With Bilal Ibne Rasheed (aka Mushtaq ur Rasool Bilal) (2010)

Born in 1925 in England Michael Alexander Kirkwood Halliday received his BA Honours in Modern Chinese language and literature from the University of London. He lived in China for three years to study the Chinese language before returning to Cambridge where he completed his PhD in 1954 in Chinese linguistics. He taught Chinese for a number of years at Cambridge, and then taught linguistics at the University of Edinburgh, University College London and the University of Illinois. In 1965 he became the Professor of Linguistics at the University of London, and in 1976 he moved to Australia as the Foundation Professor of Linguistics at the University of Sydney where he remained until his retirement in 1987. Since then he has held numerous visiting appointments in various countries the latest being at the Hong Kong Polytechnic University. In 2006, the Halliday Centre for Intelligent Applications of Language Studies was established at the City University of Hong Kong. Halliday's collected works, compiled and edited by Jonathan Webster, have been published in ten volumes.

In the early 1960s Halliday developed an influential grammar model Systemic Functional Grammar, or Systemic Functional Linguistics, elaborating on the foundations laid by his teacher John Rupert Firth. He has worked in both theoretical and applied regions of the language study and is especially concerned with the application of basic principles of language in pedagogical practices. He was in Karachi last year for a conference where I caught up with him for an interview.

BIR: *Very nice to see you in Pakistan.*

MAKH: I am very happy to be here.

BIR: *Do you keep aware of the political climate while visiting Pakistan?*

MAKH: That's an interesting question, not specifically having anything to do with language. Everywhere I go I try to be aware of the political situation; that is part of one's knowledge of the world.

BIR: *Linguists like Noam Chomsky and, to an extent, Tariq Rahman are politically very active. Do you think there is any relationship between language and politics?*

MAKH: Oh yes, there certainly is, but it doesn't mean all linguists will be politically active or even politically aware. But of course there is this relationship, and on many levels. Political discourse after all is very important in the life of any community; it is conducted in language and it has been examined in studies by linguists of how politicians and others, for example the media, organize their language to get the message across and also in the wider sense how the language conveys what I call the general ideology of the culture.

BIR: *In recent years there has been considerable research in the field of linguistics, but when you were studying, more than half-a-century back, was the research being done in this field as actively as it is being done now?*

MAKH: I would say, in one sense, no, because there were fewer people involved. It was a very small community generally, but those who were involved did a great deal of very important research which remains the foundation of much that is being done today.

BIR: *How did you come to know that you have a linguist in you?*

MAKH: Oh a mixture of reasons; I was always interested in language. My parents were teachers – my father was a teacher of English and Latin, both language and literature, and my mother was a teacher of French, so the household was aware of language. And I was trained in a foreign language for service in the British Army in the Second World War. It was Chinese, which I found fascinating and so I went to study in China. I got involved in very early work in machine translation in the 1950s, and I was fond of literature and literature is made of language, so I wanted to study language.

BIR: *Language and literature are closely related, yet these are distinct fields of study. Do you think a deeper study of language can provide us with a better understanding of literature?*

MAKH: I do, but of course that is the question you should ask Ruqaiya Hasan, my wife (e.g. Hasan 1985b). She is the person to ask, and she has in my view made a major contribution to a language based theory of literature. Now there are literary specialists who are aware that literature is made of language; others feel that they want to pursue literature and not undertake an explicit analysis of the language of which it is composed – I don't agree with them.

BIR: *You mentioned that you were engaged in World War II. Were you an interpreter or a teacher?*

MAKH: Not exactly either. It was intelligence work, military intelligence. Our job was to find out what was happening in China, which was of course a close ally with Britain in the Second World War, and make sure that the information was accurate and transmitted to authorities in Britain, and to try to prevent misinformation.

BIR: *You are often termed as an applied linguist. Do you agree?*

MAKH: Well, I don't make a distinction between applied and theoretical linguistics. It is something which is much more a feature of American linguistics, which has always drawn a sharp line between theory and application. We never have. So I will say yes, in one sense, I am very much concerned with what linguistics can contribute towards answering other people's questions and solving other people's problems. But I feel that it will only succeed if we have a powerful linguistic theory as a basis for what we are doing.

BIR: *Please tell us about your experiences of learning and teaching Chinese.*

MAKH: I had been a learner of Chinese, though I didn't start it until my seventeenth birthday, and while teaching others I knew very well what were the problems of a native English speaker when faced with Chinese. So I think the advantage was, having been through the process of learning Chinese, I could bring the experience to my students in my approach to teaching the language. But I also found it a very great challenge to work on the language; especially as the grammar of Chinese was not very much studied at that time. I should say that my own early work was entirely focused on Chinese.

BIR: *Was Chinese not taken very seriously by the Chinese or the Europeans?*

MAKH: By both of them. There were of course Chinese linguists including my teacher, Luo Changpei, and there were European and American linguists as well who studied Chinese, but not a lot, and still on a relatively small scale with many problems unresolved.

BIR: *During your time the famous Sapir-Whorf hypothesis had been put forward. Did that influence the direction of research you were engaged in?*

MAKH: Yes, I think it did. I have to say that my main background was from two or three other sources, but I came to know about this work of Sapir and Whorf particularly at quite an early stage. Although clearly there is a great deal common in all languages, each language has its own way of seeing the world and interpreting it, and you have to try and understand what it is. Whorf was really the first to make it explicit.

BIR: *So would it be safe to assume that you subscribe to the Whorfian hypothesis that our thought is shaped by our language?*

MAKH: Yes, the problem is that their work has widely been misunderstood. For example some people say that you cannot transcend the limits of your language, which is simply not true. Language provides the best way in to understanding the conceptual framework of any science.

BIR: *Any science?*

MAKH: We have done a lot of work in different regions of education and one area that I have been particularly interested in is the teaching of science. Now it was clear many years ago that many of the problems that typical high school students have are in the language in which science is constructed (I am not sure about the teaching of science in a foreign language as it is in Pakistan). The genre-based pedagogy developed in Australia (Rose & Martin 2012) includes giving access to the language in which a subject is constructed.

BIR: *How did you manage to get a London degree while remaining at China?*

MAKH: Well it was an external degree, because we were not students in the normal sense of the word. My first degree was from London, but I was actually already studying at Peking University. I did three years postgraduate studies in China and then got a scholarship from Britain, so I went back to Cambridge to do my PhD.

BIR: *While you were engaged in research in China the war broke out. Were you affected?*

MAKH: Well everyone was affected, but it didn't stop my work!

BIR: *After returning to London you ran into some problems when you were asked to get enlisted in the Communist Party. How did you react to that?*

MAKH: First, of course, to clarify, I enlisted myself, thinking what happened in China was very necessary for the development of China and I wanted to see if my views were applicable in the UK. I spent several years very active in the Party. The trouble was that I found it too much to be both politically active and a scholar. I couldn't do both, and I thought I will do better and will make more of a contribution as a linguist than as a politician.

BIR: *Did that affect your career?*

MAKH: Well, it did in one sense. It was what they now call the McCarthy period, when the American Senator McCarthy succeeded in essentially establishing a cold war mentality – mainly in the United States but it crept into Europe as well. I was supposed to be given a job at London University, but I didn't get it because I had refused to say that I wouldn't join the Communist Party. So I went to Cambridge.

BIR: *But you wanted to work with J.R. Firth who was in London.*

MAKH: Well, Firth was one of the really great men of the last century and I wanted to be supervised by him.

BIR: *But you were at Cambridge and he was in London.*

MAKH: Well they are not far apart.

BIR: *But how did you manage?*

MAKH: It took a bit of organizing, and that's when I found that you could work on trains. I like trains for their very good environment for study. I took a year full time in London during my course because there was no supervisor of linguistics at Cambridge.

BIR: *How did you find Firth as a supervisor?*

MAKH: Firth was wonderful. Politically he was very right wing, on the opposite end of the spectrum; but it didn't matter, mainly because we both come from the same part of the country. We are both Yorkshiremen. Firth was very tough but he liked people to stand up to him.

BIR: *Tough in the sense?*

MAKH: I mean intellectually. He could be quite bullying too but he was a wonderful man. At times he would say things very firmly but if you said to him, 'Hang on, I don't think I agree with you' and he would say 'Oh yes, you might be right.'

BIR: *So it must have been great getting along?*

MAKH: Oh yes, it was. It was a wonderful experience. This is what you have to say to people if they are doing something like PhD research. Your relationship with the supervisor is so important. You don't have to agree with them, but you must be able to interact with them to exchange ideas.

BIR: *When we disagree many of us become disagreeable. So, how to disagree without becoming disagreeable?*

MAKH: (With a big laughter) A very good question and I don't think I am going to offer an answer to this.

BIR: *Allow me to be a little frank; was there any arm-twisting involved between Firth and you?*

MAKH: No, I don't think so. I am not trying to evade the question; it's a very reasonable question. When I did my PhD and when it was published I said to him, 'May I dedicate it you?' and he said, 'Yes.' He was very pleased. I then wrote a very long article after a couple of years which I knew he would have disagreed with. I contacted him and said, 'Can I send it you?' He said, 'Look I'm coming to this conference, you are coming too, so we'll talk about it there.' He died that very night, the night before. So I never got to listen to him about what he thought of it.

BIR: *Did you have anything in common with Firth in terms of ideas and framework?*

MAKH: Oh yes, we had a great deal in common. I was called a Firthian by my friends. I took an enormous number of his ideas and developed them. He didn't want me to stand still and liked his students to move on. I did move on but the foundation of his ideas is very much there. But it was not just him; I was also influenced by one professor in China in particular. His name was Wang Li.

BIR: *You have done a lot of research on the Systemic Functional Grammar. How would you explain it to an ordinary student of linguistics?*

MAKH: You can imagine it takes a very long time, so I am not trying to do that now. Essentially what we are saying is when we explain linguistic features of any kind we explain them by reference to their function, maybe the function of language as a whole or functions of small parts within the grammatical and phonological systems. Our approach emphasizes language from a functional point of view and we're strongly oriented towards meaning rather than form. We have a strong orientation towards applications, and are trying to develop a theory which is useful for people who are not just linguists but people with other problems where language is involved.

BIR: *You have done a lot of research in the Chinese language; which part of Chinese fascinates you the most?*

MAKH: Well, its grammar, the grammar of Mandarin. I did some dialect research with (Professor) Wang Li, but I suppose my main interest is in the grammar of modern Chinese.

BIR: *What do you think of Chomsky's Transformational Generative Grammar (TG) and the Language Acquisition Device (LAD)?*

MAKH: I disagree with the Language Acquisition Device, which is simply wrong, and it has been shown to be wrong by recent work on the brain (e.g. Edelman 1992). As far as Transformational Generative Grammar is concerned Chomsky has moved a long way step by step. He is a great man, but his orientation is strongly formal and mine is functional. I studied his works very intensively quite some years ago and I found he did not answer any of my questions, so I gave it up.

BIR: *Your work has greatly changed the role of linguistics, which now plays a major role in our understanding of various social sciences. What do you think are the limitations in this regard?*

MAKH: In case of my work and that of most of my colleagues we would have a stronger link to sociology. We have our interests very much in language in its social context, language in interpersonal activities and so on. We have a strong link with sociology, in particular with the work of the great sociologist Basil Bernstein. A sociologist looks at the problem from a sociological point of view and we look from a linguistic point of view. We have had less contact over the years with psychology, because the dominant trends in psychology were not compatible with what we were doing. We have much more contact with the neuroscience than with psychology, but it doesn't mean we have no contact with psychology.

BIR: *Is there any chance of one field of knowledge dominating the other?*

MAKH: Chomsky says that linguistics is a branch of psychology, but I don't think I agree with him. I think they complement each other; they have to.

BIR: *And the last question: how do you stay fit at the age of eighty-five? Is there any strict physical routine which you follow?*

MAKH: Well, I'm just lucky. I am not quite eighty-five, I'm eighty-four. I have to say I don't know how one tries to keep brain and body active. I like mountain walking; I love long walks in the hills and mountains. So I try to do that whenever possible; if I can't I walk in the streets in the city. I don't drive a car, that's one good thing.

Karachi
July 2010
http://impressionsnthoughts.blogspot.com/2010_07_01_archive.html

14

With J. R. Martin and Paul Thibault (2011)

PJT: *The first question basically has a research focus, about you as a linguist over the years. From the perspective of discourse analysis or phonology the majority of your work appears to focus on grammar, and you have positioned yourself as primarily a grammarian on many occasions. But in the 70s, your gaze seemed to shift outwards beyond the clause to cohesion (Halliday & Hasan 1976) and social context in relation to your work on language as a social semiotic (Halliday 1978b). So what prompted this movement from grammar to social semiotics and then back to the grammar again (Halliday 1985a), and more recently, your return to work on English intonation with Bill Greaves (Halliday & Greaves 2008)?*

MAKH: OK, two questions. In relation to the first one, because I tried throughout the 1960s to sort of, how should I say, integrate myself and my thinking into what was then the dominant establishment, (and it was very dominant – the Chomskian paradigm had just washed right over), and I tried to come to terms with this and even in my publications (like 'Some notes of deep grammar' – Halliday 1966) to make contact with it in some way or another, and that was a total failure. So by the end of the 60s, when I'd left University College, I just saw 'Well nobody's interested in that anyway, so I'll go back to my other love, which was language in society'. So the 70s was I think entirely, as you rightly say here, working on language and social context, and so forth, and work on cohesion which had already started. But that again was, as it were, beyond the normal bounds of grammar. So that explains that move. Then coming back again was essentially to find that there were actually people like Jim here, who were interested in looking at language in that kind of a way, and Ruqaiya comes very much into the picture with the sort of work she was starting to do. So when I came over here (to Sydney) and started the new department I thought at least we will give courses – it's going to be a mixed department, as it always was, but we will include some of my work on grammar, and so it started again.

Intonation, well, I never lost that interest but just didn't get to work on it in between, and came back simply because Bill Greaves came to me one day and said 'I'm going to write a book on intonation, will you help me?' And so I said, 'Well, yeah, anything you want to know', but of course finally I got drawn in. Maybe I pushed my way in, but I don't think I did. I didn't mean to. So I got drawn into that and shared the work; and of course the whole technology was so different that it really was a new task as far as I was concerned, so that brought me back into it.

PJT: *In the retirement interview that Jim, Ruqaiya and Gunther organised back in 1987 (Interview 6, this volume), they covered several phases of your career from a* *biographical perspective – but they missed out on the period between leaving the University of London and taking up a Chair at Essex and then Sydney. Can you fill us in a little on your movements and research in that period?*

MAKH: Well the movements – you know at least the first part because I had left University College with the intention of taking up an appointment at the University of British Columbia, which I already had.

But the Canadian government decided otherwise, and took a long time to decide anything at all. But finally they said 'No no no, you can't come into Canada'. And this time, of course, as I often pointed out, was really very helpful because that was precisely when Nigel was born, so I spent an awful lot of time studying his language, thanks to the Canadian government. So from retiring from University College for more than a year in fact, I was just at home, in London.

In 1971 we left London. We went first to Brown University, where I was a visiting professor for one semester; that was the second half of 1971, thanks to Nelson Francis. Essentially what I was doing was picking up on invitations that I'd had but never been able to pick up. From Brown I went to the University of Nairobi, courtesy of Mohammed Abdulaziz, who was the Head of the English Department there; that was the first half of 1972. Then 1972/73 I took up the fellowship at what they call the 'ThinkTank', the Centre for Advanced Study in the Behavioural Sciences, which was on the Stanford campus in California, although nothing to do with that university. So that was that year.

You had to be proposed for those fellowships. And Sydney Lamb had been there in the year before. He proposed my name, and that's how I got there. But of course he wasn't there the year when I was.

From the Centre in Stanford, the next year was at the University of Illinois, at that time called Chicago Circle (now just UIC, University of Illinois Chicago). That was a new campus, an urban campus, and a very interesting place to work because there were a lot of people there who were definitely first generation college students – a lot of African American students. So a very nice environment to work in. Except that although Chicago is a wonderful city it has a horrible climate.

And then I had accepted this position at the University of Essex, though I had already told them by then I wasn't going to stay. By then I had got the offer from Sydney so we went to Essex just for a year.

JRM: *And the cohesion and the social semiotics, this was all happening through this period?*

MAKH: Yes, but together with the work on child language (Halliday 1975).

PJT: *And Adam Makkai was in Illinois?*

MAKH: It was Adam Makkai that got me to Illinois, yes. We could have stayed there; that was a permanent employment. But we just didn't enjoy living in the United States. This is the simple answer.

PJT: *How do you see the notion 'language as social semiotic' at this particular stage? In a way the idea harks back to the relevance of Malinowski's 'context of culture'. It seems that up to this point, so far anyway, a theory of language and culture remains a sketch still waiting to be filled out, in SFL and probably in any theory of language for that matter. What do you think needs to be done to overcome what I perceive as a gap? Do you think that Malinowski's very different ideas concerning context of situation and context of culture with respect to the way Firth's re-inflected them can still provide valuable touchstones for tackling these problems?*

MAKH: I think you have to separate here the situation and the culture, as far as context is concerned. I mean Firth never mentioned context of culture; of course it's there in Malinowski (1935). And I think that Firth (1957a, Palmer 1968) would have no place for any of kind of overarching generalizations of that kind. For the context of situation, on the other hand, he was simply concerned to make it more theoretical – turning it into something that you could integrate with the remainder of linguistic theory essentially. What he called the exterior relations of language were one part of his spectrum, so that I think needs to be preserved. I think we have to try to do that.

Moving out, I brought back the context of culture notion because I simply wanted to say: here we have an analogy – we are talking about the move between the system and the instance. In terms of language this is the system versus the text; in terms of culture, the social semiotic if you like, you would have the culture as the system and the situation as the instance. So I simply wanted to draw that analogy. But I am not sure how I would try to go about theorizing any integrated notions of language and culture. I think this is too far away from me. My notion of social semiotics is simply to say, all right, we recognize language as a semiotic meaning-creating system, but we have to see it always in its social context.

PJT: *Earlier attempts involve people like Whorf (1956); he was pretty sketchy too. But it was the same general problem, wasn't it, on the cultural level?*

MAKH: Yes. Part of the problem has been that so many attempts ever since the 18th century have been made to link the features of language with features of culture, and they are all rather absurd because they're far too concrete, and too compartmentalised. You just pick out one bit of language and say 'Hey, that resonates with that particular feature of culture.' It soon falls down. So I think we are not nearly enough at a sufficiently abstract level; it may be possible ...

PJT: *Would that mean that the notion of language system itself could be made even more abstract than it currently is?*

MAKH: Well, possibly yes. There's another question later on related to this. Well yes, if what you are saying is we must get up to a level where we are thinking in terms of concepts and categories that can be applied both to culture and to language.

JRM: *Do you think for Malinowski that context of culture and context of situation are in a kind of instantiation relationship or that would be your inflection of the terms?*

MAKH: Well he wouldn't have put it that way, I think, but I don't think that's that far off from what you were thinking about – speaking in terms of the way in which he used the terms in *Coral Gardens and their Magic* (1935) – via translation … problems raised by translation.

PJT: *Firth schematised it for the kind of reasons you said earlier, and it seems to me that Malinowski is much more interested in what later anthropologists were interested in, because that's what he was – an anthropologist.*

MAKH: Yeah, that's right.

PJT: *That thick description, incredible things, the way he described things; it's most amazing.*

MAKH: I agree. And as he said, you know, we forget this, but he just happened to be one of those people who could learn languages very quickly. So he was very soon on the inside of the culture that he was working on; that's how he was able to do it.

PJT: *Yeah, he developed a lot of insights about the activities; in modern terms, it was very multimodal, the way he describes things.*

MAKH: Yes.

PJT: *Like Hjelmslev (1961), you model levels of abstraction within language and between language and social context through a hierarchy of stratification with lower levels realising the higher ones. And realisation's been explored here and there in terms of notions like metaredundancy, emergent complexity, interlocking diversification and others too. How do you presently conceive the relation? And do you feel the same conceptualisation is possible for all borders, for example phonology realising grammar, grammar realising semantics, language realising social context? And is arbitrariness still a helpful concept in thinking about these borders? And can you clarify whether you see realisation as an encoding/decoding relation, or something different?*

MAKH: So first of all I think you just need two levels of thinking about this double articulation if you like. In other words you have to see realization as in one sense the same relationship throughout. And it means this is at a very abstract level. The reason I did at one time use the term decoding/encoding was because it just happens that one of the critical systemized areas of language is that of relational processes of the identifying kind, where the relation between the two parts is essentially that of realization. Using the functional labels from the grammar, say the Token and Value, then Token realizes Value, and Value is realized by Token. And the grammar actually sorted it all out beautifully between the voices (active/passive) in English. But at the same time I think you need to make the distinction between different kinds of realizations, different things between different strata. Ruqaiya Hasan has different terms for these, for example activated for the higher levels. I think arbitrariness is an essential concept – because critically the line between the content and the expression is different, in the sense that prototypically that has to be arbitrary otherwise you couldn't have language; there's no way that languages could construe experience if that was not the case. So you have to say that it is typically arbitrary although there are as we know non-arbitrary aspects to it. And then the other way round, if you then stratify within the content or within the expression, what you get is typically non-arbitrary, although there will be arbitrary features which creep in. That I think is the fundamental distinction that has to be made.

So you have that cut versus the rest, and then you have a different relationship in the two content strata from that in the two expression ones. So I think on the one hand you have to say yes, it is a single relationship throughout. I wouldn't tend to use the term encoding/decoding now; I changed it largely in the context of writing the grammar, simply because there's too many meanings associated with code, too much baggage associated with the term. But essentially it is that; I don't think there's anything wrong with that.

Okay, the reason I like Jay Lemke's metaredundancy (1995) is that did seem to me one way of capturing what was common to all these relationships throughout. The interlocking diversification, that was Syd Lamb's term (Lockwood 1972), or coined by Gleason maybe, I'm not sure.

But they, I think they don't contradict each other; they are just looking at it from different angles.

JRM: *And the language and context border, different again?*

MAKH: Yes. And the language and context border different again, although again, that's a question of saying 'Can we actually model and represent and interpret context within the framework of what is generally involved as a theory of language?' Firth thought you could and I think so too if only because it's the best chance you've got.

PJT: *If you assume that language is about context, then there would be something very odd if it couldn't be modelled in some way like that.*

MAKH: Yes, but then I mean the same applies to the phonetics end – can we model that environment in an analogous way?

PJT: *Yeah, and so it goes down both ends in different ways – the phonetics, body, brain end and through the situational contextual ...*

JRM: *A question on stratification and metafunctions.*

The realisation relation between semantics and grammar as far as interpersonal meaning is concerned seems clearer than for ideational meaning. We're thinking here of speech function and exchange structure vs mood; appraisal vs the range of resources expressing, grading and sourcing attitude compared with the essential re-labelling of grammatical systems as ideational semantics in your work with Christian Matthiessen (Construing Experience through Meaning 1999). Why have clearly stratified descriptions, with distinctive valeur been easier to develop for interpersonal than for ideational meaning?

MAKH: Yes, right, well I suppose they have, although ... I mean, in the work with Christian on *Construing Experience* ... we deliberately set out to move in from the grammar, which means that it was as it were ... built on what you're calling relabelling; but I think it's a little more than that. I think the concept of metaphor is itself an answer to that. I mean, it's not a relabelling; the very fact that there is metaphor in language, whether grammatical or lexical, means that you have a stratification there.

Now the question of how you move in to the ... how you traverse the gap between the grammar and the semantics. I think this is difficult, because you could move the boundary between the two around more or less where you want; and I think we need a lot more thinking about it. But I don't think it is just a relabelling. I think there are ... I mean, let us consider the area of TRANSITIVITY and process types. I think there is a lot more that we need to do to understand such things as transitive and ergative, and the way in which processes are in fact construed. But I suppose I would've said if we're essentially moving up but in terms of the same framework, then it doesn't matter to me – you can keep the same labels if you like. Only it helps to have different terms simply because people get lost otherwise; they don't know when they're moving up and down ...

JRM: *OK ... a question on grammatical metaphor.*

It seems that your work on grammatical metaphor has involved two different conceptions of the relation between semantics and grammar. One for example, Construing Experience through Meaning (1999), involves semantic junction, so that two meanings come together in the semantics and are then realised in grammar; the other, which I have tended to employ (e.g. Rose & Martin 2012), involves stratal tension, with semantics and grammar each contributing a layer of meaning but with incongruent coding between the strata. If we think of metaphor as involving two meanings, in some kind of figure/ground relation, one symbolising the other, the latter conception seems more apt. How do you currently see grammatical metaphor in relation to realisation?

MAKH: Yes ... well, I don't think these two are very different, are they? Looking at grammatical metaphor in terms of traditional metaphor theory, but from above (so to speak) rather than from below: the junction is between the meaning of the class to which the transferred form is assigned (so *motion* as noun, congruently an entity) and the class meaning of the non-transferred term (so *move*, verb, congruently a process). Or it could be between the meaning of two structures, like nominal group and clause. So there is incongruent coding between the two strata. I'm not so sure about seeing this as a relation of figure to ground; but I would stress that the relationship is the same as it is in lexical metaphor, which I would also treat as a kind of semantic junction.

JRM: *With semantic junction, how do you capture the layering then, when there is something literally there on the surface, but we need to read through it.*

MAKH: Well, is it "literally there on the surface"? – except in the general sense that all wording is "on the surface" of meaning. The ordering, in metaphor, is historical, in all the dimensions of linguistic history: the congruent is the meaning in which the word, or the grammatical category, first appeared – first evolved in the language, and first develops in the child. Then there's a recoupling between the semantics and the grammar – which could I think be thought of as a kind of stratal tension.

JRM: *OK... a question on stratification.*

In recent publications with Christian Matthiessen (e.g. the revised 3rd edition of Introduction to Functional Grammar, 2004), alongside a stratified content plane, as grammar and semantics, images of stratification include a stratified expression plane as well, as phonology and phonetics. Why is phonetics now considered a stratum of language rather than an interface between meaning and matter, or simply as matter, outside language, as language substance or whatever?

MAKH: Well language substance will be inside language, I think. And the answer is, phonetics always should have been there; I just didn't work on it, focusing essentially on stratification within the content plane. I know in early work I just left phonology sitting out there on its own. There might have been some influence there from Firth's notion of exponence. I'm not sure. But I would see phonetics as expression substance (in the Hjelmslevian framework). So I would like, definitely, to see it inside the expression plane; it should have been there all along.

JRM: *So is it resisting the emic/etic kind of distinction that you would be brought up with the American structuralism, or is it just a different kind of proportionality to what we found between semantics and grammar?*

MAKH: Well it's ...

JRM: *I guess I've been trained to chuck out the etics and try to keep the phonology to emic patterns...*

MAKH: Yes, it is emic/etic if you like, isn't it? The phonology is the organisation, which is systemicised in my terms. I think there is an analogy here between the grammar and semantics relation (as Hjelmslev saw it) and the phonology and phonetics one. Of course you can run the levels right through in a line, as W. S. Allen would have done – with semantics realised by grammar realised by phonology realised by phonetics. Or you can see it in Hjelmslev's terms as a matrix – with content/expression cross-classified by form/substance (with semantics as content substance, grammar as content form; and with phonology as expression form, and phonetics as expression substance).

JRM: *OK, a question on phonology.*

With reference to phonology, do you think that phonology as currently conceived misses too many of the dynamical aspects of the expressivity of the body, and do these paralinguistic features need to be brought back into language as part of the expression plane – as phonology or perhaps as phonetics if we assume a stratified expression plane? What role would the notion of prosodic realisation play in such an endeavour?

MAKH: Yes, ah ... I think that we need here precisely to maintain the phonology/phonetics, so let's do it two parts. First the prosodic features. I've always made this distinction between the prosodic and the paralinguistic, the prosodic being systemized in the phonology, so that I would see prosodic features as systemic and thus as part of the phonology. I wouldn't draw the line phonetically here because essentially any sound feature, or almost any, perhaps not all, can function prosodically in a given language. I mean there are obvious examples, things like oral/nasal resonance or Firth's 'y' and 'w' prosodies, all these things which in some languages work as phoneme-like segments and in other languages work as prosodies (see Palmer 1970 for a collection of key papers in Firthian prosodic analysis). So that boundary is very fluid and very much depends on the language.

Now, I always maintained paralinguistics as something that didn't get into phonology, but as it were played its part from outside the linguistic system. I don't think I invented this distinction!

Features like voice quality for example can be paralinguistic or not, depending on the language. There are languages in which voice quality is in the phonology, where the breathy/creaky opposition is in fact phonological.

PJT: *Distinctive then.*

MAKH: Yes, distinctive, yeah. So the question is whether they need to be brought into language as part of the expression plane; as phonetics perhaps, or an expanded phonetics. Do you want to maintain phonetics as strictly focusing on speech sound, or do you want to extend it into paralinguistics, or even other modalities?

PJT: *Yeah ... I mean, I think there, I would tend to see it more in the phonetics, than the phonology, and because the border line,... I mean, take gesture, in the sense of hand gestures, and vocal gestures... there's some deep play-out in the way they're processed neurally as part of the common system; the evidence seems to point to that direction. So at some level there is a deep connection, suggesting they may be part of one larger system.*

MAKH: Yeah.

JRM: *What will we call it?*

MAKH: Yes, that's a good question, yes.

PJT: *It's more to do with some kind of full-body meaning making.*

MAKH: Yes, you want a combination of phonetics and kinesics, don't you?

PJT: *So we are onto a question about metafunctions and types of structure.*

In a lot of your writing, for example, the second edition of Introduction to Functional Grammar (1994), you associate constituency with experiential meaning and iteration with logical meaning, alongside prosodic structure for interpersonal meaning and culminative structure for textual meaning. But in the seminal paper 'Modes of meaning and modes of expression ...' (Halliday 1979) the imaging and discussion suggest more of an orbital/serial opposition for experiential and logical meaning. Which do you prefer, and if constituency for experiential meaning, how would SFL account for the nucleus, margin and periphery patterns you and others have noted for experiential meaning at both clause and group rank?

MAKH: Going back to the 'Modes of meaning ...' paper, which was a much earlier write up of this notion, I think we need a term which covers both the sense of constituency as configurations of different functions, and the orbital form of organization. So we need something that says, well, these are recognizable segments, and in some contexts, in some languages, or in some parts of a language, we are going to see them as configurations of separate functions, but in others, as in Jim's Tagalog work for example (e.g. Martin 1996a), you clearly want to see them as an orbital relation. So in fact that is another complementarity I think, within the more general notion which we need in order to capture both as typical of the experiential.

JRM: *So you've been using constituency as the general term, but...*

MAKH: Yeah.

JRM: *...but perhaps we need something more general.*

MAKH: Yeah, it does seem to exclude the orbital notion, which we shouldn't. So I think we need a more general term which would cover both ...

JRM: *I guess the term constituency also implies that there is a whole, what the formalists used to call a mother-node, or something you know, on top of the parts, a whole-part relation.*

MAKH: Well, yes, in terms of rank. The notion of a functional configuration seems to me means you are talking about something that has an existence as a whole.

And now it might be true in the long run we will in fact find it helpful to model all of these configurations in orbital terms, but I don't think so, at least not at this moment. I think we need something more general.

JRM: *It's just that I've been suspicious that constituency is actually a simplified conflation of the different kinds of structure, and wondering if the culminative pattern mapped onto the segmental one is what gives us that part/whole feeling, and that when we start factoring metafunctionally, we'd want to get away from it (e.g. Martin 1996b).*

MAKH: Right, no I don't see that. I suppose the point is that there are only certain basic forms of structure. So, you know, it's fun to play with these and say what you've got is a particle, a field, a wave... now we've got string theory, and that's the logical metafunction there as well. That's essentially a kind of complementarity, if you think about it. So they are just the possible forms of organization; there aren't that many.

JRM: *It was four in modes of meaning, modes of expression; that was 1979 wasn't it, that paper?*

MAKH: Was it already, I can't remember if I had the iteration.

JRM: *Well... almost.*

MAKH: Almost...

JRM: *There's a section at the end.*

MAKH: OK.

PJT: *OK, a question on lexis. Over time SFL has developed two traditions of analysis as far as lexical relations are concerned, one based on collocation (e.g. Sinclair 1966, 1987) and the other on lexis as delicate grammar (e.g. Hasan 1987b). Do you see these as being a complementarity? Or is a more integrated approach possible, using corpus evidence, for example to motivate delicate lexical systems? One concern we have got here is the problem of arguing for or against proposals for lexical systems. How for example can we go about justifying the classification of attitudinal lexis in appraisal theory as opposed to alternative categorisations?*

MAKH: Yes, I do see it, again, as a complementarity (Halliday 2008a). I think they are looking at lexis, lexical organization and the lexical item, in terms of the syntagmatic and paradigmatic environment. So I think it's the development of the corpus which makes it possible now to say 'well, can we go behind this, can we see something further...'.

I think the lexis as delicate grammar notion is important, because what you are able to do there is to isolate out, to separate out the features that go into the lexical items as was started long ago in componential analysis, the difference being that with the lexis as delicate grammar these are systemized. So in that case I think it becomes possible to motivate, in the sense that the lexical item is clearly seen as the realisation of a set of selections in different systems. And that then gives you – it must have been a conversation with Jim a very long time ago about the ... semantic relations which were involved in collocation – it gives you a way in to looking at that in much more detail and with much more accuracy, which would in turn then I think be the way of justifying your location of a lexical item, within its place in the frame.

Now the problem with APPRAISAL (Martin & White 2005) is simply that it's a lot harder in the interpersonal, because the boundaries are not there – because you're floating not only in a different type of space, but also in a rather uncertain area between the grammar and the lexis: that of essentially grammatical systems realized by lexical items. That in itself is not a problem, but to what extent can you actually as it were decompose these items that work in the APPRAISAL system into their different features? For that I think the lexis as delicate grammar notion is a possible way in.

JRM: *Still there's the challenge of how you motivate once you get to the delicate features in the grammar; it gets harder to motivate them, to argue for one particular feature rather than another, than for the general ones, I think.*

MAKH: Well, OK, but if you take – isn't it a question of simply teasing them all apart and saying, well, this item differs from this one in respect to this particular feature, and from that one in respect to that feature and so on, and these then become systemized ... while other features are not recognized in this language or this part of the vocabulary and so I mean it's just a lot of work!

JRM: *I'm hoping the translation and interpreting people can help us, having worked finally with one (Ladjane de Souza); they can bring the meaning of the lexical item to consciousness far more easily than I can, as a grammarian or a discourse analyst. I was so impressed; I lost every argument about the meaning of a word with her.*

MAKH: That is very true. I have also been arguing for the tremendous importance of translations and translators in expanding the meaning potential of a language.

PJT: *OK, on multimodality and language. It's been around the last ten or so years now (e.g. Martinec 2005, Dreyfus et al. 2011). There has been a transformation in discourse analysis, including most importantly in SFL inspired discourse analysis, from a relatively mono-modal linguistic perspective to a multimodal one. Here and there in your work, you have in a sense cautioned against privileging modalities other than language over language. In what senses do you feel language is a semiotic system unlike the others, and what concerns you about this multimodal turn?*

MAKH: One thing that concerns me is that language is seen by too many people as too hard. And the trouble is that the multimodal gives people a lovely excuse for running away, and saying, 'Oh look, there's something else we can do, you know'. So many times in the history of linguistics we've come across this sort of problem – any excuse to get away from language and study something else. But my sense is that we are still lacking in theoretical thinking about these other modalities. And we need to do this. We need to say 'How far can we get by using the concepts and categories of a linguistic theory, in relation to these other modalities'. That's a very important question to ask; this is why one of my favorite books, which is sitting there, the new edition of the Michael O'Toole's book, *The Language of Displayed Art* (1994/2010). There he quite clearly says, you know, I'm going to use the full power of linguistic theory and see where it takes me; and it takes him a long way, and it's beautiful.

I'm not saying it's the only way, or that it would take you the whole way. But the question is 'Have we yet got many alternatives?' There are those like Baldry and Thibault (2006) who have taken this up, but that is very much in an applied context. Then there is work on music, for example Theo van Leeuwen (1999), and now Ed McDonald who's got some more coming out (2011a).

JRM: *The Semiotics Margins (Dreyfus et al. 2011) book just come out yesterday and the paper by Ed is there – a very good one.*

MAKH: And I think it was in this book of yours (Bednarek & Martin 2010), *New Discourse on language*, David Caldwell (2010) has referred to Ed's work (McDonald 2005).

So we need to say: 'Remember there are these two ways in, they're both worth exploring; they don't exclude each other'. At the moment the linguistic theory is more powerful than the other, so use it. But you know, don't expect it to go all the way ... and beware of the dangers. This is why O'Toole is so good. I think he avoids the danger which is inherent in an effort like this – that you're going to use it too simplistically, too superficially, and too much, perhaps, in looking at the realizations of the linguistic values rather than their underlying meaning.

PJT: *And another issue there would be the issue of the modeling of these other system; we probably haven't covered anywhere near enough of that.*

MAKH: Well, I will say that too.

PJT: *And that's really a crucial thing to get developed.*

JRM: *To our chagrin, all of our really successful exports involve running away from language, running away from grammar. Cohesion, genre, appraisal, multimodality. If you've been at the UTS Multimodality conference in December 2010, exactly what you're saying was there. People show the text, and say 'This is sexy text', and then maybe they show a text of somebody who is talking, posting or writing about the sexy* text and say 'Here is a sexy text, talking about the sexy text'. With no analysis of any of the texts whatsoever.

MAKH: No, no, I know. So how do we combat this? It's not that I don't think these things need doing, they do. But there is a lot of sheepism; everyone will follow what everyone else is doing. This is what is happening, I'm afraid, at the moment.

But I do want to say one thing about language. I've always been very cautious about claiming uniqueness for language as against other semiotic systems. But I think one thing that is important in these multimodal contexts is that I think it's true that all those who've used these other multimodalities, who produce and understand them, also have language. And I think that's very important.

PJT: *Another thing that strikes me at least, in relation to talk as opposed to written text, is that many of the things people might be calling modalities are actually part of the contextualization of language. We need to think of it more in those terms, and have a more unified view on that.*

MAKH: Yes, that's very true, they are part of the contextualization of language.

JRM: *It's part of the polemic, setting a linguist up as logocentric, a monomodalist, as opposed to the good guys, who are multimodalists.*

MAKH: Yes, that's true. It's partly as you say, a response to that, you know – they want to call us logocentric, and I always say logocentric and proud of it!

JRM: *That's right, you can't blame a linguist for being logocentric! Really it's our job.*

PJT: *Another question on multimodality.*

Do you see language itself as a multimodal or multisemiotic system in the sense, say, that in writing, for instance, verbal and visual-spatial modes are in principle often difficult to distinguish in some respects... or in speaking, language and gesture share certain properties that suggest to some researchers that they are in fact part of one overall system? Do you think that 'language' itself is being reshaped by for example, computer technologies, just as it was by writing and print technologies? Is 'language' itself not only polysystemic but also multisemiotic?

MAKH: Yeah – to start in the middle, because I've been thinking about that in ... well it was a paper I gave in Vancouver on the history of meaning. Because I want to say that language, in some sense – that meaning potential is being reshaped each time by the expansions into writing, into print, and now into e-modes, the computer technology. This is certainly already happening, and I think people are beginning to recognize this.

Again, language and gesture etc. is part of one overall system; in a sense we've already touched on that, so I'd say, yes again; it's this question of always as it were pushing up a level and saying, well I may have to think somehow in more abstract terms to get something which covers both; I may try and import these over from language but I am then redefining them along the way.

Now is language itself not only polysystemic but also multisemiotic? That becomes, doesn't it, the old question of how far do you use the term language. And again I've been a little bit cautious on this, and said I don't mind extending the term language, except that then you have to find another term for language, because you do need to be able to talk about and to theorize language as polysystemic, but not in this specific sense, not in the sense that I would understand it as inherently multisemiotic.

JRM: *So, it's like the visual literacy problem; if you talk about visual literacy, then what you call literacy?*

MAKH: Then what do you call literacy, exactly, that problem, yes.

JRM: *Question on meaning and matter.*

Whatever your reservations about too strong a focus on modalities other than language, the push into multimodal discourse analysis raises the question of how far we can push a social semiotic perspective beyond language, including analyses of matter from a semiotic perspective – we're thinking here of some of Radan Martinec's (e.g. 2000, 2001) work on systems of action and Paul's interests in the signifying body for example (Thibault 2004). How do you see the limits of a semiotic perspective in relation to matter, and in general terms the complementarity of the meaning and matter (including the semiotic and the somatic if we want to narrow the question down a little to the interface as embodied in humans)?

MAKH: I recall the Russian semiotician Aleksandrov, who was with us at the Wenner-Gren conference back in 1972 (Fawcett et al. 1984a, 1984b include selected papers from this meeting); he started his paper by saying "whenever I look at any phenomenon from the point of view of what it means, I am doing semiotics".

I think you've got to set different parameters, for all the different scales of existence here. In one sense all organization is meaning, so you can say from the moment matter organizes itself after however many nano-seconds of the big bang or whatever, you have meaning. And that is quite a useful way of thinking about it ... matter, in a sense, needs meaning to organize itself. That's what in the broader sense this meaning is. However, being realistic in terms of research goals, we restrict the notion of semiotic; and there're different ways of doing this. One way is to say, well it is meaning as operated by conscious beings, and so you can take Edelman's (e.g. 1992) view that anything warm-blooded involves semiotic activities. Again that's reasonable. Or you can limit it to humans. So I'm just going to talk about meaning as understood and operated by human beings. But looking at these things beyond human language as forming systems of meaning is a viable way to do it; it enables you to integrate the strict linguistic concerns with these broader ones of different kinds. I think that the opposition of matter and meaning, which is just one of these things that's useful to think with, can be used throughout to look at complex ... another way to see it is as a way of managing complexity: let's look at a complex phenomenon in terms of the matter, the material component and the semiotic component.

So I think the limits of the semiotic perspective are really very variable in terms of your research goals, and scope.

PJT: *There are some physicists (e.g. John Collier) who believe all matter is intrinsically meaningful or semiotic in a process view of the Universe? So, is there an interface between meaning and matter conceived as a complementarity, or is it more a question of the different ways that matter gets organised across scales of time and space?*

MAKH: I don't know about John Collier, but I mean all matter is intrinsically meaningful in this sense of being organised; this is presumably similar to what I'm saying.

PJT: *When you said a bit earlier about so many nano-seconds after the big bang ... well of course none of us was around then ... presumably what you mean is there are certain patterns of organization there, that they in theory, if someone were there with the right equipment to do so, they in theory would be measureable patterns, material patterns in the universe, in some part of the universe ...*

MAKH: and we're getting at them now.

PJT: *We're getting at them now...*
and the fact that we are getting at them now so to speak raises the other question, I mean, that then we're able to turn them into meaning in some sense of that word.

MAKH: Okay, it's our operation on them that turns them into meaning.

PJT: *Yeah, and I mean, this is going a little beyond the question here, but those patterns ... as material things we can measure them, or in theory we can measure them ... but can we measure meaning?*

MAKH: Well then this is why I've cautioned against identifying meaning with information. Let us keep these apart. Information is measureable; it's the parts of meaning that can be measured, so, as George Williams said, it can be measured in bytes, or whatever. But I don't think that exhausts the whole of meaning. Now that's just the old question: is it a limit on our ability to measure or is it an inherent limit, I don't know. But certainly I think in real life at the moment we should recognize that there are forms of meaning that we can't measure, at least in any kind of quantum form. We may be able to scale them, with more or less organization ... I don't know.

PJT: *Some of that scaling's got to do with scaling up to observer perspectives, which of course could be us or maybe something else, that we don't know about either, you know, other beings, or forms of life ...*

Or even robots or something, and so on. But anyway, I mean, it seems to me, because, the idea of information, the Shannon/Weaver idea, that it's the probabilities in the system ... but meaning's dependent on the observers who do something to the information, from their particular perspective.

MAKH: In one sense it does depend on them, I mean ...

PJT: *Well I mean making meaning depends on having a perspective on the information, and doing something with it, integrating it to your perspective.*

MAKH: You are right; that's looking at it specifically from the point of what we recognize as meaning.

PJT: *Yeah, yeah that's right. And then the information becomes something else, which I guess we call meaning.*

MAKH: Yea, it's fine with me ... I've thought of meaning as the more inclusive term, that's the point, nearer to the perspective of John Collier ...

PJT: *It's interesting to clarify that ...*

JRM: *Easy one, on language, brain and mind.*

At the recent Connecting Paths conference in Hong Kong and Guangzhou, the relation of your work to Lamb's perspective on language and the mind was of course canvassed, but the relations between SFL and neo-Darwinian neuro-biology (e.g. Deacon, Edelman and so on) was scarcely mentioned. How do you feel your inter-organism perspective sits in relation to Deacon (e.g. 1997) and Edelman's (e.g. 1992) work and what directions do you see for potential collaboration?

MAKH: When I started with that 'inter-organism', that goes back to working with teachers back in the 60s and 70s; part of this focus was because most of educational discourse was in terms of educational psychology, and I found it profoundly unsatisfying, I couldn't see that it had anything to say that was of any interest. I tried to engage with it, but I couldn't. So what I wanted to say was look, let us instead focus on the inter-organism perspective on language; it came from working with teachers on the project.

Now, that all changed after what, roughly around the 1990s, with the evolution of real brain science, but my immediate reaction was Hah! that's it, that's what we've been waiting for, because that resonates beautifully with the sort of view of language that we've been working with and developing, and I think that is true now. So again, it's a complementarity; it doesn't exclude the intra-organism perspective but it's one I felt ... I really got very excited when I first read *Bright Air, Brilliant Fire*, by Edelman (1992), it was terrific ...

Now, so there should be directions for potential collaboration. When I was talking to Terrence Deacon in Vancouver, he's a very nice chap and we had a good chat; and I said do you know the work of Sydney Lamb? And of course he didn't. They know nothing about Sydney Lamb. So I want to say, at least first of all have a look at that. Tell us, does it make sense? Or not? Because I can't judge. It looks as though it does. And I don't see anything incompatible with what they're saying, but I don't know. So I feel that needs exploring and it's very important to get that bridge built as it were.

JRM: *Extending the question, neuro-biologists (Deacon and Edelman) are not strongly focused on the interpersonal/dialogical nature of the human brain whereas many recent developments in neurobiology, starting with mirror neurons, put the emphasis on the dialogical brain, if not in those terms. This suggests that SFL could enter into an interesting dialogue with these developments. How would you view this possibility?*

MAKH: I think that, again, the mirror-neurons and that whole development is again very exciting. I mean, let's go back some time ago, when it was Robin Dunbar that I came across first in the Scientific American (cf. Dunbar 2010), who was saying yes, alright: the evolution of human brain – people have begun to see this as part of the increasing complexity of the relations between the human organism and its environment, fine. But, he said (and I thought "hah!, you are absolutely right"), but they forget the social environment, and it is equally important to say, yes, but the environment includes the social relationships with other people. So there I think we got the beginning of this sense, because that was inherently moving in the dialogic direction. Then I read about the mirror-neurons so I thought that seems to fit in too. So I think it would be a fascinating dialogue. But can we get them interested in language? That's our problem. Because we see, I think, that language is the absolute key to exploring these things further; but they don't, so somehow or other we have to persuade them.

PJT: *Well, yeah, I mean, that was the thing, I talked to at the end that day last November, at City University; that was the thing missing in the discussion (the Connecting Paths conference at the Halliday Centre). But of course, there was no time then to do anything with it.*

JRM: *The third part of this question is my favourite trigger for dinner table arguments with colleagues.*

In relation to this theme, do you envisage that a robust model of meaning and matter (language and brain in this instance) can be constructed without involving a theory of mind? By extension, this question is of course related to how comprehensive your conception of a language-based theory of learning is for education.

MAKH: It's related, but it's not the same thing I think. I always avoided using the term mind, because, I didn't see I needed it for one thing, but also because it's one of these terms that just get thrown around without anybody asking what they are talking about. Consciousness ... Ruqaiya has read and thought much more in that area (Hasan 2005), particularly the work of Susan Greenfield (e.g. 1997), who was the first person I was aware of who provided a plausible definition of the mind. She said: well the mind is the personalised brain. We know now that the brain has to be built through interaction with the environment; it develops in the individual child and the mind is what results from that process. That's a good use of the term. Whether that would be a theory of mind in the sense you mean here, I'm not sure.

PJT: *It's a theory of brain, isn't it?*

MAKH: Yes ...

JRM: *I guess I'm thinking more ... I mean, the whole of linguistics is still wrapped up in a cognitive framework where there has to be cognition between language and the brain, and I'm asking do we need three things or two things.*

MAKH: I don't think we do need three things. I mean I'm not at all convinced that we do. I don't know how far to develop this, since I haven't been involved in the dinner table arguments ...

JRM: *Most people find it absolutely outrageous the idea that your brain and language or brain and semiosis would be enough; I mean that's seen as kind of crazy.*

MAKH: Now, how comprehensive is the theory in relation to education.

If this refers to the idea of a language-based theory of learning, what I was saying was that there are a whole lot of things to be learnt from looking at language development, and I think these need to be built in to our thinking about language education, and in fact into educational thinking in general. They offer another way in to looking at questions of learning.

PJT: *I don't want to go into this, but it's for another time, but it depends on your definition of mind.*

MAKH: It does.

PJT: *Yeah, actually, I mean you can see as, I mean you talk about personalized brain, in Susan Greenfield's sense, so that's the networks and meanings which are supported by ... that one's involved in over a life trajectory. But one that is supported by the physical brain, you know.*

MAKH: Yes, but then the question becomes, how do you get at these except through language?

PJT: *You probably don't; they're the semiotic processes, including of course, language.*

MAKH: No, I mean, leave it open, clearly; but what I want to say is 'explore the power of language to handle all the things we are concerned with here. And if we need something else, okay, fine.'

PJT: *I mean the brain generates semiosis, in interaction with others, but mind is the emergent social semiotic product of that. A dialogue between the human and life sciences.*

The distinction between an intra-organism view of language and an inter-organism one that you made in the 1970's (in the light of the very different questions Chomsky and colleagues posed about language) can now be re-thought in the light of the advances made in biology, neuro-biology, and complex systems theory (among other things). The biological evidence nowadays is that we just are social and cultural beings and this is reflected in both phylogenesis and in ontogenesis. So how do you see this relationship now, between the intra-organism and the inter-organism perspective, and what contribution might your theory make to the new dialogue between the human and life sciences?

MAKH: Well in a sense maybe just setting up that whole opposition is inappropriate now, because of the way the two perspectives aren't that different, in fact. So I was saying last time you asked the question, it was introduced with a particular function in that particular context, such as you say. As regards the contribution the theory might make to the new dialogue between the human and life sciences ... well, it is the whole notion of the human sciences that in itself is such an important collocation, because, as we know, the practical point of view is that whatever you do in linguistics in the university, the vice-chancellor always puts it in the wrong place, because they have no concept of the human sciences itself, let alone as linguistics as one of them. So I think one of the important things is to get linguistics put in the context of the human sciences and the whole area in the context of scientific endeavour generally; and one of the things that I think has been lacking is any general sense of population thinking in the human sciences.

And in linguistics ... this may be getting a little bit off the point, but I've been very much concerned with the apparent social disjunction within linguistics between those who are working on very detailed descriptions of individual languages, and particularly those who are motivated because the language may be threatened with extinction, and so it's their job to do this as quickly as possible – the actual description of a particular language, defined in the traditional sense, and the kind of gap between that and the thinking about language which has become possible through the corpus tool, for instance, so we can handle large volumes of data. One of the things that Ruqaiya did was that study in the 80s (Hasan 2009) where she studied the populations of mothers and children and used quantitative statistical methods to come up with results which led to her notions of semantic variation and so on. Just take it as an instance, and say that is scientific method applied to language, with the human species as a population in the more traditional sense.

So I think that the contribution that we have to make is to show that our approach to language can be called a human science, and there's a very real sense in which that is a science. Not because of the name, I don't care, but because of mapping it into knowledge in general.

PJT: *And, I mean, about population thinking then, it's a particular scale as compared to other scales that one might attend to scientifically. But it seems to be one of the important things here is that the mechanisms at work, at that therefore need both describing and explaining at that particular level, are basically statistical causality.*

MAKH: Yeah.

PJT: *And, that's what you are suggesting?*

MAKH: Yes, and it's so important in early language development. There's no question about it.

This is why I was very interested when I was working out the notion of bi-modal probability profiles (cf. Halliday & James 1993), where your grammatical systems, you get ... you don't get all, as it were, different probabilities all over the possible scale; you get some systems which are essentially equal (equi as I call them) – so roughly speaking, 'past and present', 50% each, and you get some which are skew, like 'positive/negative', roughly speaking, 9 to 1, something like that. These pictures obviously get modified over time as you learn more about it, but that sort of thing makes sense from the point of view of learning a language, and it gives a basis for our concept of markedness. We don't define it in this way, we just say, the child grows up right from the start with the notion that there are marked systems in language; typically you find they will learn the unmarked first. If it's a system with a skew probability then they will learn the unmarked form long before the marked one, so it gives you an insight into markedness. But then going back to the information theory of Shannon and Weaver (1949), this is very interesting from the point of view of information, because the equi- kind of distribution, so past 50% present 50%, corresponds to a system with no redundancy, so maximum information, no redundancy. What about the 9 to 1? That is also very interesting because that is exactly the point at which redundancy and information balance out. The two are equal. It's not exactly .9 .1, but very very close to it. So I think it's something that is actually built into our sensibilities beyond language, our sense that we sort things out, and we tend to look at them in this way: either they're kind of equi-probable, or they're clearly skew on this kind of scale.

I found that a very interesting way of thinking about the statistical properties of our linguistic system.

PJT: *Yeah, I mean I think children, young children, how they learn about object continuity, and things like that – there's certain work done in more recent psychology which is all in the same line; it's based on probability, it's statistical learning.*

MAKH: I didn't know that.

PJT: *So ... because language and experience of the world in general are completely enmeshed with each other then obviously there's some basis that's common to all these things ...*

I think population dynamics is a actually key thing; I've been writing about that in some of my more recent stuff (e.g. Thibault 2004), thinking about it in those terms ...

MAKH: Yeah, I think you are right.

PJT: *Okay we have a question on ontogenesis and the dispositions to teach and learn.*

In Learning How to Mean (1975), partly as a reaction to Chomskyan innatist perspectives on language development (they called it acquisition anyway), you emphasised the active role of the child in building semiosis – arguably backgrounding the role of mentoring caregivers. And this work has been cited by progressivist/constructivist educators in support of their position (i.e. strident advocacy of 'benevolent inertia' on the part of classroom teachers). On the other hand you've quoted Jay Lemke's work (1995) on the complementarity of adults' disposition to teach in relation to children's disposition to learn. Would you write differently if you were writing it now, giving more prominence to the mentoring role of caregivers?

MAKH: Another very good question, yes. You are right, I was emphasising the active role of the child in that context of the Chomskyan notions of innatism. And so it will have had the effect, I accept this, of backgrounding the role of mentoring caregivers, which I feel very strongly about; as you say I quoted Jay Lemke on this. But partly it was a factor in the way that I was actually conducting the study, because as you know this was ... I have a few recorded texts but I didn't use them very much except as a final check; almost everything that I have there was simply from a notebook and pencil, with me sort of hiding behind the furniture or even just remembering. Remember I had had the great good fortune to be trained, by Wang Li in fact, in Canton, in dialect fieldwork; and I had a very good short term memory, I could recall exactly something that was said including the intonation and rhythm, and then within the short time go and write it down. I also found a very interesting thing that you had to re-read it within 3 to 5 days, the short-term memory span; otherwise you couldn't work out what it meant – you'd forgotten, with the very early stuff.

Now in all my notes there is always the other person in the conversation – always there, but with a different level of confidence. In other words I guarantee that what I wrote for the child's discourse was accurate; I didn't bother with that for the adults. So the adults' could be a paraphrase, or something like that, I couldn't do both. Now this meant that the focus in the material itself was strongly directed towards the child's performance. Now I was aware that we need to know just as much about what the child can understand, and about the interactive process. It wasn't that I was not concerned about the interactive, with the nature of dialogue essentially as the basic medium of learning. But that the way I was doing it forced me to pay attention, and this was a deliberate decision – to focus on what the child is able to say, and understand because he can say it; you also show up where there's a gap or inconsistency, or failure to understand; but you don't try to incorporate the whole of the adult discourse into it, or the caregiver discourse.

JRM: *We need much more tape recording as with Clare Painter's work (see Painter 1984, 1998, 2009)…*

MAKH: But then Clare Painter will use more tape recording. The technology had changed. To get that kind of unobtrusive tape recording when I was studying Nigel was impossible.

If I was writing it now I would give more prominence to the other interactants' discourse.

PJT: *Some of what we are talking about now leads quite naturally into the next one, which is on ontogenesis, scaffolding and the micro-functions.*

Your theory of language development is strongly interpersonal or dialogical, and you sometimes make links to the complementary work of Trevarthen (e.g. 1974; in fact he also makes links to you), who is one of the great pioneers in the field. Trevarthen assigned an important role to the flow of emotion or affect between the infant and caregiver, and he saw this as the driver of the system, of the whole dyad, particularly in that first year.

It would seem to us that the scaffolding role of caregivers is no less crucial, as characterised in embryonic form by the early work of Vygotsky (1962, 1978). This would suggest that adult and child participate in many forms of co-agency and co-regulation. So it would be interesting to see how this might prompt us to rethink some of the early micro functions of language that you described. How do you see this now?

MAKH: Well, I as you know as I just said, I agree with that suggestion. And I was very much influenced by what Trevarthen was doing; he was working on it at that time … through his work with the newborn, the neonate, actually filming side by side, with a split image of the baby and the mother both in the space, but simultaneous, and totally correlated. So you can see this pattern of exchange of attention; but once a movement of some kind was set up, you could see that the child is fractionally ahead. So the child is actually leading the dance, and the mother immediately picking it up, responding, developing it and so forth. There was quite a number of papers coming out by that time; there was one very good book, a collection by Andrew Lock, which was picking up on some of this work. But that's talking now about back in the 70s.

Now just a comment on the last point, rethinking some of the early micro-functions: yes, that started me thinking when I read this, but I haven't thought it through. Clare's was already doing that, rethinking these micro-functions in terms more of the mother's exchange of attention together with, say, affect (Painter 2003). So all I can say is I haven't thought further about that.

JRM: *She did try to re-read them, and did a relabeling as an exchange of feeling rather than in more speech functional terms.*

MAKH: Yes, she did.

PJT: *The thing you mentioned early about the baby being a little ahead, in the mother-infant dialogue, shows the anticipatory dynamic at work there.*

MAKH: Yes, what was at issue at the time, in relation to both these last two questions, was that people commented on my analysis and said that the infant doesn't really have these meanings, the meanings are kind of attached by the mother or the caregiver to some gestures or noise made by the child and the child picks it up. And I thought well, alright, it is of course an adjustment, there's no doubt about that. But I think it's overdoing it to say that you cannot attribute any meaning to the child's initial performance.

When I glossed the child's utterances, as for example "Oh nice to see you, and let's look at this picture together", that kind of thing, this was based on very careful observation of the context in which these things came out. And there I stick to my opinion that the child is leading the dance. Yes, sure, the mother or whoever then comes in, the meaning gets adjusted in relation to this, that and the other; she responds and so on. So it is negotiated. But I still think the initiator …

JRM: *People doubting you must not have had children or never have interacted with them, because when you do, it's obvious. I used to be really impressed by you and Clare until I had children; then I thought, hey, this is so clear (laughing).*

PJT: *But, I mean, the other thing to say on that is, it seems to me part of the whole dynamic anyway, you represented it at the level of the glossing, so in a sense the metalinguistic level of the analysis, but what you are doing is also mirroring the fact that, that's part of the natural dynamic, that say, caregivers and infants, they are attributing meanings to each together.*

MAKH: Yeah, I mean the critical thing is that the adult treats the child as a meaning making being; we often see that not happening across the life around us, sadly.

PJT: *A question on hierarchies and complementarities.*

Your recent book Complementarities in Language (2008a) focuses on the complementarities of grammar and lexis, system and text, speaking and writing. Alongside these linguistic concerns the metalanguage of SFL itself involves a number of complementarities (e.g. metafunctions, system and structure, typology and topology) alongside several hierarchies (e.g. delicacy, rank, stratification). It seems to us that the notion of metalinguistic complementarity (heterarchy if you will) is not very well understood (and may be unsettling to some theorists). Could you comment on what it means to build the notion of complementarity (alongside hierarchy) into a linguistic theory? Do you think language itself is a complementarity of hierarchical and heterarchical, or in other words, non-hierarchical, principles of organisation, and that one or the other may hold sway at any given moment, or on any particular time-scale?

MAKH: Yes, there's a lot in this; it is very complex. Let's start at the end. Take for example one of the matrices, or matrixes I've used as one model representation for a long time – the rank/metafunction matrix (e.g. Halliday 1973: 141). You can locate grammatical systems in every language in one cell in a matrix of that kind, and it's clear that there you have a combination of the two: you have the metafunctions, so non-hierarchic, a heterarchic one, but you also have rank, which is hierarchical; obviously there are other variables you could bring in, any pair of them you can turn it into a matrix, but the issue – I always used to say to students, 'Where are you locating yourself, in your language, in what you're doing?', and it's very important to be able to say, 'Well, I am at this point.' and it's very often an intersection between things of this kind, and so yes I do.

Now building the notion of complementarity into a linguistic theory. I think the point is how far are you going to extend the notion of complementarity beyond the sense in which I originally borrowed it, starting with things like transitive and ergative, or tense and aspect, where I was saying these are truly complementary. These are in the language, not in the metalanguage; they contradict each other but you must have both perspectives in order to understand what's going on. Take the two models that are present in, say, tense and aspect, with tense being location, the point of reference, to which there is attached a past, present or future, and time is like that, it ... sort of flows through from future to present and into past – or is it really aspectual? Is it something that is kind of latent and then emerging into being? They can't both be true, but they are, and you won't understand the linguistic construction of time if you don't have both. But that I would call a complementarity in the classical sense, well the Bohr sense; and there are others.

Now then I extended this, and it then doesn't have a clear boundary, because talking about the things in that book, about speaking and writing, okay, you could say language is fluid, unfolds in time, or it is static, as an organization of bits and pieces; they can't both be true, but of course we know they are. They are because one is speaking and the other is writing. So I was thinking well these could be thought of as complementarities, and this is one of these places where the accidents of history led me into it because I got this invitation from England to lecture in these three places, Birmingham, Nottingham and Liverpool. And I knew the bosses in each place; they were good friends of mine; they had all specialized in different areas. John Sinclair has always been keen on this interaction of grammar and lexis, and Mike Hoey was always interested in the relation of between system and text, and Ron Carter has been counterposing written and spoken in relation to his notions of creativity – you know all this; so it just seemed to me, I wanted to fit in with my own context there, and this seemed to be the underlying theme which could essentially relate all of them, at least by extension.

The question then is, what are we doing if we try to apply this system, this notion of complementary to metalanguage. Well in terms of the hierarchies, and heterarchies, yes, in a sense we could say these form a complementarity in that they are contradictory ways of organizing matter or meaning.

Now the metafunctions themselves, I don't, at the moment see that I would prefer thinking of those as in the complementary relations to each other ...

JRM: *But aren't they alternative, contradictory, all true, ways of looking at the sentence?*

MAKH: Well it's a question of are they contradictory; I don't see that they are.

JRM: *But isn't there in a sense in which clauses are used for interacting, and for construing reality and for organizing text?*

MAKH: I don't see the kind of inherent contradiction; it's just doing two different things ... but okay, that's the sort of issue that one can raise because if there is a sense in which complementarity is useful as a generalized notion, then there's the usual problem, let's be careful to remember what it originally meant; where it clearly was that, you know, light cannot be both wave and particle, but it is, you've got to see it as both. So it is open; but certainly I found it useful; it's one of these things which are good to think with.

PJT: *So it is tied up for you with the both/and.*

MAKH: Yes, yes it is.

PJT: *It's discussed in that interview, the Chinese interview [Interview 12, this volume].*

MAKH: Yes.

JRM: *Heterarchy implies what, just different hierarchies; but I think the metafunctions are interlocking.*

Things like typology and topology, system and structure (syntagmatic/paradigmatic) seem to me like classic complementarities.

MAKH: Yes, but in an already somewhat extended sense.

PJT: *But I didn't see heterarchy as different hierarchies, but rather different principles, competing with one another; maybe one principle comes to the fore for a certain amount and...*

MAKH: Yes, they're different principles; a heterarchy doesn't have to be a hierarchy, absolutely not. But this was an interesting point you made right at the end ... one or the other may hold sway at any given moment, on any particular time-scale ... I hadn't thought of that ... hm ... I mean it's that "hold sway"? But yes, I suppose in some forms of organization it could be the case, but I'm not sure about in language, I just don't know.

JRM: *If you set up the function/rank matrix, the ranks are organised by one kind of principle, the metafunctions by another; I'm saying the theory has a lot of that kind of 'twoness' in it – what do we call it? And I think it actually is a metalinguistic reflection of complementarity in here.*

MAKH: Well, yes, I'm certainly not rejecting that.

JRM: *And it's, one of the things that people would find particularly disturbing, all of these complementarities, because people like hierarchies.*

MAKH: Yes, they like hierarchy, you are right.

JRM: *Especially the constituency one.*
Instantiation and logogenesis.
One way to think about instantiation is in terms of the bundle of features selected from system networks and their actualisation as specific structure. When we move from grammar to discourse (or grammar to phonology for that matter) we seem to need a more dynamic conception of the actualisation process, taking time and co-textual contingency into account. Do you see logogenesis as an essential part of the (process of) instantiation?

MAKH: Let's just take instantiation – the term makes it sound like a process. Do I see logogenesis as an essential part of ... let me take your term here, actualization, because actualization always means more than instantiation; it's instantiation plus realization.

Let me come back to my well-worn favourite analogy, the climate and weather; the climate is instantiated in the weather (e.g. Halliday & Matthiessen 1999). So any instance of weather, any particular situation in the weather is an instance of climate; the climate is the theory, in other words. So yes, the weather is a process, but I think of instantiation as the relationship between the two, as we see it as investigators, in our metalanguage as it were. And I would myself always want to say that when you're talking about the process, you are always talking about instantiation plus something else; now in language typically that would mean realization. So you can take any particular instance of language, and can look at it as instantiation, on any particular strata. They'll all be different in the instances, the selection from grammar networks, phonology networks and so on. But when it becomes text, then it is not just a product of a process of instantiation. It's rather a process of realization, or exponence. So that's where the logogenesis comes in rather than in the relationship of instantiation itself.

JRM: *So when you say realization now, you are meaning more than the relationship between the strata?*

MAKH: No, no, I mean with exponence, it's ... come back to Firth, who wanted to make the point the exponence is different; he didn't like the generalized stratal hierarchy. Long back in history when we were students, there was a very interesting argument going on between Firth and Allen; Sydney Allen had a much more hierarchical view of the strata. But Firth, as you know, didn't use those analogies – he used a spectrum. So when Allen drew his diagram, it would be a linear sequence as used by Sydney Lamb, where you have semantics, grammar etc., in a linear sequence. But when Firth drew it, these were all different blobs; there was grammar, lexis, phonology – all leading directly down to exponents. So for Firth these were not an ordered hierarchy but a set of things which formed a spectrum, and where exponence meant the final output which involved all of them, but not ordered.

PJT: *Taking that back a bit to what you said just before ... so if you put it in other terms, the actualization in text is where you bring realization and instantiation together, cos instantiation on its own is just a logical reconstruction from a particular observer perspective, say the climate one in your analogy, or the weather one – whereas realization is like the relation of grammar and phonology, going back to an earlier question. Materialized, embodied ... you need the actualization, because the system is virtual, okay, a virtual entity, that's its status. It gets actualized in text, and text brings together all these things.*

JRM: *You're technicalizing actualization then ...*

MAKH: Actually yes, we probably should.

JRM: *Because I've been using instantiation for this.*

MAKH: Or we could bring back Firth's exponence.

JRM: *Users and uses.*
The overall cartography of SFL theory is often mapped as a matrix, with stratification along one axis and instantiation along another (e.g. Matthiessen 2007b). This is an effective way of modelling the system of language in relation to its uses, but backgrounds language variation in relation to users. Recently Jim's students (Bednarek & Martin 2010) have been pushing towards a third dimension concerned with identity issues (involving terms such as individuation, allocation, affiliation). In spite of the work on coding orientation (Hasan 2009), do you think SFL needs to give more attention to modelling variation according to users alongside variation according to use? In this regard, is the traditional distinction between dialectal variation and coding orientation still a useful one?

MAKH: Yes, another excellent question. Let me go back to the original Basil Bernstein codes (1971) – you must remember that coding orientation is the term into which he retreated, after he'd been slaughtered and his notion of code misunderstood (cf. Labov 1969, 1972a, 1972b) ... because I saw the code as squarely on the user dimension, but very abstract, way above dialect, in the sense that the speaker who, whatever the use, maintained a location in one of the original pair, elaborated and restricted code, and was in fact selecting within the total meaning potential. You will get people switching between one and the other, in typical register-like contexts of situation, as seen in Gumperz's old work (1964) – that was also switching dialects, but it doesn't have to be like that. Thus the enormous care that

Basil Bernstein and others had to take during the original 1960's work, in saying this is nothing to do with dialect. Because as soon as people saw this work they immediately mapped elaborated code onto standard English and restricted code onto dialects and Basil had to get out of that one. So it seemed to me that code belonged near the system end, but still along the user dimension rather than that of use. But I am not too sure the extent to which it is a third dimension rather than a sub-category of the users. I would stick by this, in the sense that I don't see coding orientation as alongside dialectal variation, although one might argue – your question set me thinking about this – that in coding orientation you are actually on these two scales together. You are very near the system end, certainly in terms of uses, maybe also in terms of users.

JRM: *So the users dimension for you is the dialect one?*

MAKH: Yes.

JRM: *So dimensions that carry the implication of only formal variation; but you wouldn't hold to that, you would allow for semantic variation along the dialectal...*

MAKH: Yeah, there can be.

JRM: *OK.*

MAKH: I mean ... you know.

JRM: *Because some of the Christian Matthiessen's matrixes* (e.g. 2007b), *it seems he has the dialectal variation down as holding the semantics constant...*

MAKH: Well, I think that's the prototypical. I started from that definition and took it as a way of thinking about it (e.g. Halliday et al. 1964). Dialect is variation according to the user, so you have your own dialect. Many people have more than one and they will switch according to use (that's where Gumperz's 1964 work came in) and that of course also can accommodate semantic variation. But, take Ruqaiya's work (Hasan 2009): her notions on semantic variation came out precisely in studying the codal variation she found among her mother-child dyads.

JRM: *If you treat the concept of coding orientation as different kinds of use, they give rise to different kinds of consciousness, identity, or whatever; so how do we model the distribution of identity, the different forms of consciousness, semiotically in SFL? It seems to be a missing ...*

MAKH: Yeah, it wasn't there. But maybe your identity dimension has to be incorporated with both. It has to be somehow some confluence of the user variation and use.

JRM: *Sure, sure, maybe that's why we have them as a third wheel and can't articulate how they are related to the other two.*

Okay, a question on appliable linguistics.

Recently you've proposed the notion of an appliable linguistics in relation to a linguistic theory that takes responsibility for language problems and develops theory in relation to such issues. In some respect this seems to be just another way of talking about your ongoing conception of linguistics as an ideologically committed form of social action. Why did you feel the need to re-focus attention on the idea of linguistic theorising and social responsibility? And what do you consider the social responsibilities of the linguist to be?

MAKH: Why did I, it's a good question, yes … I think it partly came with experience in China, where I wanted to get across … to get around a bit through the networks there, to get across the notion of what motivates the theory in the first place, and I wanted to get across to them the notion of a theory as problem driven, task driven if you like, and I was constantly meeting in China this comment that you get fed up of, you know 'We Chinese are practical people, we don't think in theoretical terms' when in fact they're the most theoretically minded nation on earth.

And so I wanted to say 'Well let us try and contextualize this approach to linguistics, approach to language, in that sort of framework of thinking'; and it happens that in Chinese you can make a clear distinction between applicable and appliable, so the yingyong and shiyong, and the shiyong (适用) means as it were 'suitable for or capable of being applied', whereas yingyong (应用) means 'actually applied to something'. So I thought, you know, that will work here, to get those terms across. As so often in these things it is driven by a particular conjunction of situational features. But whether it is in any sense a kind of redefining of the social accountability notion, I think it's also trying to say 'Well look, we've been so dominated by the notion that applied linguistics means education – it has meant language education, for a generation at least; we do want to get away from this'. Now the two volume *Continuing Discourse on Language* (Hasan et al. 2005, 2007), which is a brilliant collection, it is one thing the Chinese won't publish for some reason. I mean everything else we do, they publish in China. I cannot get them to take that.

So the second point in this was … applied linguistics has in a sense been hijacked to mean language in educational contexts, particularly second language learning.

JRM: *I think in China applied very commonly means just text analysis; they say, 'We like SFL because it's applied, because we can use it to analyse text', not addressing a problem at all.*

MAKH: That is another point, Jim, you are absolutely right, because I want to say text linguistics is not applied linguistics at all; it's linguistics. So yes, that has to be also part of the picture.

So it's just part of the discourse, trying to clarify what are the ranges of application and what we mean when we talk about text in discourse analysis.

PJT: *Oh, something occurred to me there, given the critique you just made of the educational linguistics connection. One thing that's often missed here that the notion of education obtains in work places and so many other domains outside schools, outside the university.*

MAKH: You see this is the context of what Christian Matthiessen is doing; they got him over to the Polytechnic University Hong Kong saying very clearly we are a technical institution basically, technical and scientific. But we recognize the need for a humanities section and that has to include linguistics. But when you say what do they mean by this, it's 'Communication is important.' That's all they know. So Christian took it right from the start; there's this challenge to get across a much broader sense of learning so that you know that language is involved in all the things that are going on around you.

PJT: *Learning happens everywhere.*

MAKH: Exactly, and language is a part of it. So in a sense that is one way of broadening it out, still in an educational context because at the Polytechnic University there is, as always, a base in terms of some real problems: how students can get their English level to the point where it should be, as well as at the same time getting them to learn their chemistry and their physics and all the rest of it. The whole notion of language and learning, or language in learning I'd rather say, just has to be brought into the picture.

JRM: *The next one really extends this in terms of sites of intervention.*

As far as engagement with language problems is concerned, education has been a special focus of your own work and of SFL in general, although of course many sites of engagement have emerged (clinical linguistics, forensic linguistics, translation so on). Do you think education is a site unlike the others? And are there other sites of intervention which you would like SFL to explore more fully?

MAKH: Relating to what we just said, yes it is unlike all the others – or it should be, in the sense that if you at least broaden the understanding of education and what learning is, and what teaching is that forms part of it, it will be unlike all the others; but again it just got so specifically focused.

JRM: *I wish we had a teaching/learning verb.*

MAKH: Yes, well you see, *learn* in our dialect, in Yorkshire dialect means teach as well.

JRM: *Well, you're all set. I think in my native southeastern Canadian dialect too.*

MAKH: I don't know if you remember, you may not have seen it, but many years ago I did a little paper called "The teacher taught the student English: an essay in applied linguistics" (Halliday 1976c) where I did a grammatical analysis of teaching; but that needs to be extended. Ruqaiya did one on the context of teaching/learning, an analysis in linguistics terms of this process as a social institution.

PJT: *That was in a Hong Kong publication, as I recall, her article. I think I have seen a version of it there.*

MAKH: Yes, yes, maybe it was. So I think one needs to look more deeply into teaching and learning from the standpoint of an appliable linguistics.

I'm glad you mentioned translation; translation has been underexplored until recently. My way into it originally of course was through early attempts in machine translation (Halliday 1962). It was exciting work, which now appears in histories of machine translation! This was in the 1950s, with a very brilliant philosopher Margaret Masterman. I was trying to get over the idea that the machine translation project had to be not simply about computerizing linguistic structures; it had to be system based. I didn't get very far.

But, obviously linguistic evaluation of translations is a very high level of demand to make; but also translation is a very important process in human life, in part because it is typically expanding the meaning potential of the target language, by bringing in things from outside. And also because there's been so much work done on unwritten languages, but as far as I know very little on the question of those people, many of whom will speak three, four, or five different languages – what does that actually do for their own meaning potential? How can we model the language system of someone like that who has grown up without any writing, but in a community where he has to learn say two languages – two versions of his mother tongue, one to talk to everyone around him, another to talk to the in-laws, and then he's got to learn a third language because he marries out to the next village or whatever, and I don't think we've got much understanding of that yet.

PJT: *A question on stylistics now.*

Now and again in your career you've demonstrated the potential of applying SFL analysis to highly valued literary texts. Do you believe that the language and semiosis of such texts is distinctive? And how much progress do you think we have made in understanding this difference (in relation to and pushing beyond theories of foregrounding/deautomatisation, for example)?

One problem here is that we know little about the semiosis of very large texts such as novels and drama? You have worked a bit on the Priestley play (Halliday 1982) *and on a novel by Golding* (Halliday 1971), *for instance, yet we still seem to be in the dark when it comes to very large-scale semiotic processes/products? Do you have any specific ideas on the way forward here, or is it a problem at all?*

MAKH: Yes, let me make two points there. As you say the problem is that we know little about semiosis in very large texts; one way into that which I was in fact using, in a way, in all four of those things that I've done, the Priestley, the novel by Golding, on the Tennyson, part of *In Memoriam* (Halliday 1988), and also on the last paragraphs in *The Origin of Species* (Halliday 1990b), and it is a point that was made in literary semiotics (by – who was it? – an Italian scholar), that typically in a long, large scale work, let me use Ruqaiya's terms here from her *Linguistics, Language and Verbal Art* (Hasan 1985b), there's a kind of double articulation within the semantics that's characteristic of a literary work: there's what she calls the symbiotic articulation, which is the meaning you get out of the wording as it is, and then there's a level of theme, in very much the traditional sense of theme in literary studies, where you are saying in all this is in fact encapsulated some further concern of the writer, so you talk about, you know, Shakespeare's history plays are about order in the universe, that kind of thing. Now how do you actually get at that. One way that was suggested, I'm sure you will know about it ... was that typically in a longer work you will find some sections where you get a dense concentration of language which in some way presents this underlying meaning in a more accessible, almost a more surface type of form, and that prominence may be at some critical location in the work. So for example, in Priestley, the passages that I looked at were right slap in the middle, as also in Tennyson, and in both cases there's a kind of hinge in the play or in the poem, just at this point where you get this highly dense concentration of meanings which as it were give you the message. It might be foregrounded in other ways: the Golding was interesting because it was a transition point, where suddenly we flip from one universe to another, but nine tenths of the way through.

And you know the first word, after a full stop and a gap on the text, was "It". Now "It" was Lok; we had been with him for all the rest of the novel, as a participant, interactant, and "he" suddenly became a thing, "a strange creatures, smallish, and bowed". It's another way of foregrounding a particular section, and saying, 'Well look here, you can see what's happening'. And in the Darwin, of course, it's famous, that passage at the end; those last few paragraphs just slam the message home. So this was one way which I used and found helpful for thinking with. But there's also again the statistical; if you go back to Ruqaiya's PhD thesis, she compared a Golding novel with one by Angus Wilson, but she did it simply by analysing samples of clauses right throughout the whole text and showing tendencies – the first six clauses on every even numbered page or something like that, randomising in that sense. So I think we need to do a lot more in that second way, of large scale processing of these texts. We've been focusing on certain parts to get a detailed picture but we also need to try to get the picture of the whole, in essentially quantitative terms.

JRM: *Interesting what you say about the longer texts in some sense, in an overdetermined way, telling you what the theme is in concentrated sections; because in apprenticing high school stories it seems not quite that, but you get the narrator or a character explicitly announcing the theme at a critical point* (cf. Martin 1996c). *So some of the kids learn to ask 'Where's the theme? Who's saying it at what point of the story?'*

MAKH: Yes, in a lot of literacy criticism, that kind of explicitness was viewed with disfavour; the poet or the writer should not suddenly give the message clearly, we want to have to dig it out ourselves. Priestley in fact is an example, someone who was often criticised for sort of announcing the theme. I always said 'Well why the hell shouldn't they?' – because, you know, I'm one who ... David Butt did so much work on Wallace Stevens (e.g. Butt 1988) but I can't work on Wallace Stevens because it's too hard to get a theme out of it.

JRM: *You ought to try postmodern texts.*

MAKH: Yeah.

PJT: *That point you made a little earlier about quantitative analysis of say a novel, of course that goes counter to the usual humanistic tradition when dealing with literary texts, but actually adds a new tool which I think it is complementary to this.*

JRM: *A question on languages other than English.*
Slowly but surely SFL descriptions of languages other than English, and language families other than Indo-European are emerging. But many of these still suffer from taking IFG descriptions of English structure as a starting point and not moving on enough from there. It seems to us that beginning with system rather than structure, with higher ranks rather than lower ones, with discourse rather than grammar and with instances of language use (texts) rather than Introduction to Functional Grammar (second edition 1994) function structures is the way forward. Have you any thoughts on how we can foster a less Anglo-centric IFG perspective?

MAKH: Yeah, it's so important this; you're absolutely right. It always used to amuse me in China (because all my early work was on Chinese grammar) that they simply borrowed the English from *IFG* and transferred that onto Chinese. One thing that seems to me tremendously important is work in comparative and typological studies; the typology book did a lot (Caffarel et al. 2004) – that I think is a tremendous work, and I hope we get more of those, because comparison and typology help to stop this Anglo-centric bias of so much of the work.

We need to make sure that descriptions are theorized in terms of the theoretical categories, so perhaps more noise about the distinction between the theoretical and the descriptive, even though we know they can get blurred, and there's nothing wrong with using descriptive categories from language A as the way in of thinking about language B, that's fine, as long as you know what you are doing.

JRM: *That's in fact what I did in Tagalog (cf. Martin 2004), I just went through IFG, trying to see what I could see using those descriptive categories for Tagalog, and then feeling miserable, and trying to change it.*

MAKH: Yes, you don't pretend you don't know things, cos you do, that's fine. But realize the distinction because it forces you to back off and think of the language in its own terms.

JRM: *It's tough Michael; I've been working with a group, Mira Kim and various students in Sydney now, for three years, and they still find Christian's chapter at the end of the LOTE book* (Caffarel et al. 2004) *incredibly challenging* (Matthiessen 2004); *so when they are working on their language, to get up above that, and think about how half a dozen languages might be working in the same area, it just seems overwhelming. Slowly it happens, but you know, it's really really tough.*

MAKH: Because this is one of these places where we need much more of the 'how to' kind of work, how to ...

JRM: *Proceduralise it ...*

MAKH: It is hard, I know. I think that the metafunctional base of the analysis is a strong point to start with, because you can say yes, you can be sure that this language you're dealing with will operate on metafunctional principles; they will come together, probably there will be something you can call a clause and there will certainly be something you can start off with calling a clause. Bear in mind the different types of structure that we don't want to be locked into, but it is hard ...

JRM: *Then of course they come interpersonally expecting to find the Subject, textually expecting Theme to come first, you know...*

MAKH: Well I tried to do this in a little paper published in China, about how do you, what are the questions that you ask (Halliday 1992b)? You don't say 'Is there a Subject in this language?' You say 'Is there a system which does this, or something like it, and if so, is there a role within that structure, that does something like that?' Okay, then maybe you want to call it by the same name.

JRM: *The systems are more challenging for people than we realize, perhaps having worked with the theory for some decades; the structures are easy for them to bring into consciousness, and use; but when you say let's start from mood systems, let's start from speech function, it's tough.*

MAKH: Yeah, that's why I wrote *IFG* the way I did, entirely structurally, because that's how I've always taught. It was actually Christian Matthiessen who blasted that out of me. He said to me 'Why? We can use these systems from the start.' His way into that had been when he was exporting the Nigel grammar, because they had to package it – this was in the computational linguistics project that Christian had worked in many years ago in the University of South California (Matthiessen & Bateman 1991). And they developed this text generation by computer, and they wanted to export it to other people. So Christian wrote a whole lot of material to accompany it, because some other body of researchers who had no background in systemics was going to use it. And it was out of that that he developed the notion 'Well that was presenting systems, first of all, based on system networks; why can't we teach it that way?'

JRM: *But you were right, because in a sense the third edition of IFG (2004) then becomes a reference book; you can't really use it as textbook.*

MAKH: Yea, no no.

PJT: *I have the experience of using the third edition in Norway in the MA course, and it's impossible to use it in teaching book for those students ...*

JRM: *We don't know how to write a textbook that starts with systems.*

MAKH: That's true.

PJT: *I had to go back to IFG 2nd edition for those students.*

MAKH: You're not the only one, I mean a number of people have said this ...

JRM: *And it's out of print in the English speaking world; in China they still have it.*

MAKH: I've tried, but they wouldn't keep it in print as the Chinese have done in Chinese; *IFG* 2 is now out in China in Chinese translation. But *IFG* 3 is out in China, in English.

JRM: *You can't buy IFG 2 in English, even in China?*

MAKH: Er ... in China I don't know

CELIA PUN: *In some places they do have some stock, but not too many left.*

MAKH: They are probably not printing any more; it's probably part of the agreement ...

MAKH: It's a good point to make, that we don't yet know how to start people off with systems.

PJT: *A question now on socio-cognitive dynamics and language systems, which also raises interesting questions about the socio-cognitive dynamics of different non-Anglo communities and the embeddedness of the language system in these? Now the Saussurean legacy, at least if you go by the received view of Saussure, has tended to separate the language system from these. However, it could be argued that the two are intrinsically related to each other and that a language system constitutes a historically evolving solution or response to those sorts of dynamical issues. Do you think we can bring these together more than has so far been the case?*

MAKH: Hm ... I don't know. This notion is not one I'm used to thinking with, the socio-cognitive dynamics. So I think I have nothing too useful to say about it!

PJT: Alright, it might go back to when we were talking about language and culture earlier; in part, it's another level of abstraction, and we just haven't got there.

MAKH: So, let me put it this way, in what terms do we talk about socio-cognitive dynamics?

PJT: *Well it's deliberately hyphenated.*

In a typical North American perspective, cognition is thought of something going on in an individual way, inside the individual; but I mean, going back to the Russian tradition, Vygotsky, it's not seen like that at all. It's social, it's cultural, but it's also biological. All these things are of course complex, and interrelated to each other. So if cognition is meaning, how do beings get on doing the things they do in the world?

MAKH: I suppose, you know, being logocentric, let us at least use language as a way in.

JRM: *Okay, SFL in China.*

As we know there are probably more SFL scholars in China now than the rest of the world combined, and the first generation of Chinese SFL scholars with PhD training are now becoming supervising professors. How do you see the strengths and weaknesses of current work on SFL in China and what are your hopes for its future?

And then do you think we can learn more from the Chinese tradition of linguistics and can Chinese SFL scholars help us here? Do the Chinese have different thinking, in some respects, concerning what language is and how to theorise it? Do you see this as an interesting area of future development? No doubt your own thinking about language has been importantly influenced by this tradition, but can we take these issues further and open up new thinking about language?

MAKH: Yeah, not only the first generation, but the next generation, now have also got their students coming along; students of students, this is great. In certain places in particular where there has been some kind of direct transmission, they get a very solid well-rehearsed base, sometimes rather selective, but that's fine. The weaknesses, I think I would say, are 1, what I called 'sheepism', the tendency of the Chinese to follow each other in one direction; if one of them is going to work on this they're all going to work on this. That has been a problem a bit in the past, because the Chinese tradition was still there, whereby it was the supervisor told you what you're going to do, so your supervisor has to plan, you do this, you do this, you do this; I think that happens in natural sciences very often. But we were very encouraged by our last visit to Guangzhou; after the Connecting Paths conference in November (2010) we stayed around there. And there is a new generation there, and a younger dean, Head of School, Chang Chenguang. We found that their students were opening up a lot, so instead of saying "Well, I was told to do this." they had been selecting some of their own topics, they had their own questions, and we had very interesting discussions with some of them. So I think that is opening up there again with more sense of initiative – in the sense that a research job is a quest point of inquiry, it's not about your satisfying certain needs. So I think that that will continue, but I think there has to be, and this is number 2, in China, they have to be prepared to be more courageous in thinking theoretically. They tend at the moment to still take what's there, what's offered, whereas you move over to one of the hard sciences and there's masses of original work in China. So it's not a feature of the culture, and nonsense like that; but perhaps it's part of the tradition, in this human sciences area. So that's one thing that they have to overcome. And then 3, coming back to what we were saying before, they have to get more of a sense of what it means to say appliable linguistics; it means first of all that we recognize lots of different applications. These have hardly begun to be explored, but also that you must continue to back up application with theory, and feed between the two. I don't think that's yet happening on a good enough scale, but the basis is there, and the resources are there. So, I think there's a lot of hope for expanding there, and your time spent there Jim, and others in the international community, is very important; we do need to keep backing that up, and steering a little bit.

Now the Chinese tradition of linguistics – I of course learnt a lot from it, because my teacher Wang Li was a specialist, not only a phonologist and grammarian, but also in the history of Chinese linguistics, which he knew absolutely backwards and forwards. The scope of this was patchy of course, because it had no grammar, for the very simple and obvious reason that Chinese had no morphology. So they never asked grammatical questions, where the Indians did and the Greeks did. It was strong in lexicography, from a very early date, before 200 BC, they had a thesaurus type lexicon. And later on, more a kind of … it was not so much a dictionary tradition; it was almost an encyclopaedia, so a combination between a dictionary and encyclopaedia. It's a strong tradition in Chinese universities, and I have two of the standard reference works here.

But the real strength of course was in phonology (Halliday 1981b), I mean the real strength in the more core areas of the subject, which again goes back to two thousand years ago, gradually evolving in the few centuries, the first half of the first millennium, AD, then being impacted by scholarship from India, which de-stabilised it for a while. But once they absorbed what was there, that gave it a phonetic base. The Chinese phonology was totally abstract; it had no phonetics at all. It simply said 'classify syllables according to their initials and finals', what was like what, and how they were constructed, but it had no phonetics; imported from India, this came at the end. So that gave a different way in to thinking about language, and naturally that was reflected in Chinese schools, where a lot of the concepts are laid down.

Now Chinese schools then had an import of western traditional grammar for a while. I don't know in detail what they do now. I have had some sense of it from people I know who've worked in the schools in China. The Chinese language obviously has a prominent place in the educational process, but the schools I think still don't do very much in the way of analysis. They take the literary approach and also as I said the more traditional kind of encyclopaedic approach.

So probably a big input came in right from the start in my own thinking, from the phonology, which coincidentally Firth knew quite a lot about, because he worked with Chinese scholars, and he approved of them very much. He once said to me, if only we'd got our modern phonology from China, we would never heard of the phoneme, and that (he implied) would have been a very good thing – I've told that story before.

But the question of different thinking concerning what language is and how to theorize it is blocked in China to a certain extent by the obsession with Chinese characters. They are a thorough nuisance; they get into the way of clear thinking about language so often; and this absolute tie up which Chinese following their education find very hard to unpack, to even think about, because you know the same word means (the junction of) a morpheme and a syllable and a character, and that is to my mind one of big hurdles that one has to get over, to deconstruct the language away from its script, which also of course services those who are determined to prove the uniqueness of the language and the culture. Ed McDonald's written about that in a very interesting way (2011b).

So that I think has to be taken apart; but on the other hand, I think that you get to really interesting questions, like how did the development of the Chinese script influence not only their thinking about language, but also their experience of language, which it clearly did because there's no explicit relationship to units of speech sound. And on our part, we can ask questions like, what about the place of scripts in general, with the Chinese as one example, on the development of meaning potential. So the challenge is different, in a language with that kind of writing, once the thinking becomes dependent on those who are literate, which is quite a recent thing, in fact, in history altogether. And it also raises issues like the relative weight carried by different language users in expanding the meaning potential of languages. So one must bring the history of Chinese into the picture, both Chinese thinking about language and Chinese experience of language, each in its own context.

JRM: *Okay, SFL as a neo-Marxist linguistics. At various times you've positioned your SFL as appliable linguistics, as an endeavour oriented to the development of a neo-Marxist linguistics. How successful do you feel you and similarly engaged colleagues have been in developing such a perspective? Do you think a specifically Marxist or (neo-) Marxist perspective is the way to go nowadays, or do you think that we need to develop a new kind of materialist approach to language?*

MAKH: I don't know; I haven't kept up with recent work in these areas. I think that we were in those early days, when we had the Communist Party linguistics group, successful to the extent of asking questions about languages and aspects of language which just weren't seeing the light most of the time. We were trying to think about things like spoken rather than written language, about dialects rather than standard, about development of new national languages, and social stratification in language – all these kinds of things which were not on the agenda generally in linguistics. I think we developed some quite interesting thoughts about that; this was particularly Jeff Ellis, who was brilliant, and Dennis Berg, Jean Ure, Trevor Hill, Peter Wexler, a little group of us, with those four at the core, and I suspect that somewhere buried under heaps of paper is actually some of the things we wrote at that time, which we passed on up to the party; but I don't know that anyone did very much with them. Maybe they got in some way put into things like party programs concerning decolonization, the need for development of national languages, because otherwise there were still lot of the people around who said let them all learn English, or French or whatever. But, beyond that, I got separated from it; partly we got separated off from each other, but I got sidetracked into almost a different career, not just teaching linguistics, that was alright, but working with the teachers and the research groups in London in particular, and so didn't specifically develop this Marxist theme.

You and I once had a discussion Jim, I think, about 1985 before I retired, touching in on this kind of thing, and I think you were saying, and I agree with you, that we lacked the semiotic component in the Marxist's tradition about language, or rather perhaps the constructivism component, because Marx was always on about the importance of ideas, but in his whole scheme of things, language doesn't really get mentioned. We were trying to develop a Marxist perspective. But things have changed now, and people are suddenly saying, well there was this bloke in the 19th century called Karl Marx, you know he got a lot of it right. Sure he did.

I never used the term "neo" but it's fair enough; it was Marxist type materialism, but reinforced with a more discursive approach, an approach which gave more value to the semiotic component, seeing it as not just as some body of ideology in the strictly Marxist sense.

JRM: *I always saw it as taking language out of superstructure and bringing it down to be more a base for things ...*

MAKH: Well the superstructure idea was – now did you ever read about the Soviet linguistics controversy? I have a very interesting book about this, *Stalin and the Soviet Science Wars* written quite recently by an American, Ethan Pollock (2008). Stalin worked with these things and then pronounced, and of course once he'd pronounced, that was the end, and everyone else had to shut up. One of the things that he did was a general denunciation of Marrist thinking – work based on N.Y. Marr; he was long dead by that time – which depended among other things on the notion of language as superstructure; it was part of the superstructure that evolved along with the social base. Stalin decided it was not too difficult to demolish that, and simply said 'Well you know, when people develop a class society, they don't all stop speaking to each other'. So this became the orthodox line, that language was not part of the superstructure; it was something separate, and had its own living and depended on ... the grammatical system and the basic lexical stock, which then got into Swadesh's work (e.g. 1972) – Swadesh was a Marxist; so Swadesh's notion about, what's the term ... glottochronology, this constant time frame for linguistic change, so that if you wanted to measure affinity between languages in countries where you don't have the evidence, like say North American first languages, then you take the basic word stock, the hundred or so words that you could reasonably consider belong in this, and you see to what extent, what percentage of them are the same with each; that came out of Stalin. But that's a side issue now, so yes, I think we do need to continue trying to develop it; I think that has to remain part of our thinking. Sorry for that rather long winded answer ...

JRM: *No no, that's interesting. We're being very prognostic now, aren't we! A question on the future of the language sciences.*

Now that the economic hegemony of the western world is over, its academic hegemony will similarly erode. In the language sciences, the hegemony of Chomskyan formalism has waned, but not the general cognitivist episteme in which it was situated. How do you see, or hope to see, the language sciences evolving over the next generation or beyond? What kind of 'revolution' might be possible if computing meaning becomes possible?

MAKH: Well we touched on this earlier, so I don't think I want to try and say much about this. But this notion earlier on of the human sciences – I think we've got to relocate language sciences in the total structure of knowledge. Now that is partly a matter of revising that total structure anyway, and we're all aware of attempts to do under labels like inter-disciplinary and trans-disciplinary, the idea that there are themes like complexity which unite scholars from all the different disciplines which share common problems. If that is allowed to happen – because at present, at least here, the authorities are totally conservative and just want to preserve everything the way it is – if that is allowed to happen, then I think we'll get to see the true notion of the human sciences with linguistics as one. I would like to say linguistics has to be at the base of it; that's obviously my prejudice, but I think there are reasons for saying that, because the next step after that is to say, right, but language is actually the unifying factor in all knowledge, and the way in which we integrate human knowledge is through language and an understanding of language. I think there are two steps to this; there's that of relocating language studies themselves, in a better, broader and restructured knowledge framework, but then there is also that of redefining the place of language in the whole of the structure of knowledge, which we have ... which we may think about quite a bit but haven't got very far in persuading anyone else.

Now the computing meaning is, yes, it should make a difference but we're up against this problem you all know about, you know, we can spend years as we have done working away in research teams on things like text generation and machine translation, but there are all these companies putting things out, as products of trial and error, and they'll work up to a point and people are very happy with them. So there's not much encouragement then to say, yes, but we think there's still an important component that comes from academic projects and academically organized research. I think there is, but I think we haven't been integrating these two ways into our thinking.

JRM: *It just seems what you and Paul are talking about, this population quantitative orientation to the human sciences, can't depend on manual analysis, text analysis; it has to be automated.*

MAKH: Now that I also agree, but I was interpreting your computing meanings in, how shall I say, a higher more theoretical sense of actually to being able to model not just the grammar, but also the semantics ...

JRM: *Yeah, I meant something quite mundane there; I meant to be able analyse lots of data.*

MAKH: No, I would have no doubt about that.

JRM: *Who would our partners be in the human sciences? I mean there's so much erosion of knowledge in anthropology, sociology, and even linguistics, if you think of discourse analysis, as French critical theory moves in and turns everything into very weakly classified humanities. I mean you lose the science; we've had a generation at least of this.*

So there's something that has to be reclaimed, which Joe Muller (e.g. 2000), Karl Maton (e.g. Maton & Moore 2010) are very concerned about in sociology. I recall talking to Bernstein, late in his life, about the moves from culture studies into sociology, which drove him absolutely crazy.

MAKH: Karl is very interesting, I don't know much about his semantic gravity, semantic density – something to think about it. But yes, it's a very good question now who are the natural allies here. I would hope the sociologists would be around, but it's rather, again, a matter of identifying themes, isn't it? Because take students of literature, among those there are certainly some who should be central to this exercise; talk to David Butt who is so well read in philosophy, as well as literature, and linguistics. David goes to those symposia with people discussing complexity theory, which he finds very helpful. So it seems to me we're going to have to look not in terms of the established disciplines so much as in terms of common themes.

JRM: *I think Karl puts it as "allegiance to a common problem."*

MAKH: Yes, I'm, you know, too old to go into these things now, but complexity theory is clearly important because so much of our activities concern the management of complexity and there's a lot in common from the highest theoretical level down to practical techniques.

JRM: *Okay, the next one's from Fran Christie actually, concerning the overdetermined negative reactions to your work on grammar, and other things.*

Over the decades a small number of well-positioned linguists have tended to react very negatively to your work on grammar, a reaction that seems to us too negative – in some sense overdetermined. Objectively speaking, you privilege system over structure, and use function labels alongside class ones, in order to capture a wider set of systemic relations; what is it do you think that makes these re-orientations to grammar so provocative?

MAKH: Yeah, some people almost behave as if they are threatened by that somehow. I think part of it is related to everyone's sense that they know all about language because they have been depending on language since they were born, and they have been taught about it in their primary school, and it's very hard to go back and rethink things that could be the foundations of your thinking from a very early age. But complaints about too many different terms, I don't really believe in those, because every discipline has its terms. I think that's just an excuse for not thinking them through. But it's never really bothered me a lot; it should have done, I accept that ...

JRM: *It's curious.*

MAKH: Now I don't know in your list of interviews whether you are including that one which is in fact in writing, 'Mark these linguists' (Interview 3 this volume); there is something in there about this. I mean there's simply something about having to reflect on language itself before you start doing it in any kind of a technical framework, which some people do find threatening.

JRM: *You think that's general across cultures or a particularly English problem?*

MAKH: I wonder ... I don't know.

JRM: *Oh well, okay, these are getting smaller points. In the biographical interviews we've done with you, you do mention your war work in India, where you were involved in counter-intelligence. Can you just tell us about your knowledge of Chinese, what role that played there?*

MAKH: Early on in the war, some people from SOAS, and I think Firth was undoubtedly one of them, approached the War Office, and said "There is undoubtedly going to be a war in the far East, it's time we trained more people in Far Eastern languages". And they kind of put it in a drawer and forgot about it and then suddenly somebody remembered how about doing this, and so they developed this program for intensive language teaching in one of four languages, Chinese, Japanese, Turkish, Persian, and we were taken up to London, just within a particular window of one year of age from high school. And we were given these elaborate tests, which again had been worked out by Firth I think, on language aptitude, and which were specific to the different languages – very clever, I wish I had a copy of it. I was in the Chinese group, but also by choice, and then we were parceled out among the three services, so army, navy, air force, which had specifically different requirements – but most of the Chinese group I think were in the army. Others were different; I mean in the Japanese group people were particularly wanted for the air force. The Chinese group had a variety of different jobs, but a number of us were sent to this Chinese Intelligence Wing, which was in Calcutta, and it was a counter-intelligence unit which had to do things like censoring all the mail going in and out of China, getting reports from people in Japanese-occupied China about what the situation was there, writing it up, passing it on to London, getting reports about the fighting at the front, and who was fighting who, how it was going on – we knew, far better than many, what was going on at that time. And then typical sorts of intelligence work, a mixture of really genuine knowledge gathering with playing at being spies, like taking little cameras around and photographing odd suspicious-looking Chinese on the street; but you know, it didn't do any harm. And I think it did play an important part in the sense that there was a very effective gathering of information via the British military attaché in Chungking, coming in from China, then channeled through us, and eventually up to the foreign secretary in London. And so that was really the main thing, plus preventing security leaks.

JRM: *So Chinese were coming back and forth, that you were interviewing and working with?*

MAKH: Yes, but there were others who were doing that. There was another group who was actually stationed at the airport in a place called Dinjan. There was only one flight between India and free China, through to a place whose name I know in Yunnan, I've forgotten it for the moment ... it's a historical site now; it's the airport where all these planes landed, somewhere near Baoshan, in Yunnan in China. Those stationed in Dinjan airport would be interviewing Chinese who came there, checking all the security and that kind of thing.

JRM: *How were you using your Chinese?*

MAKH: Partly in reading, because we read the mail and stuff that came in, and we had a group of Chinese working with us doing that job. They consulted about problems, should we censor this, what shall we do with this and so on. So that was involving talking in Chinese; but we also had been trained in writing, so we were of course able to read the documents. There was a certain amount of interviewing individuals around the place.

JRM: *Hmm, interesting. Okay, then the next one has to do with Paul and me, our age (around 60). So you've been productively retired now for almost 25 years. How would you weigh up the pros and cons of retirement versus a life of teaching/supervision and administration?*

MAKH: I found always that teaching and supervision were very positively related to research; so I never saw that as any kind of competition. I like teaching, I like supervising and I found I got as much out of it as I gave. Administration was quite the opposite; I'm very bad at it and I find it quite stultifying and definitely getting in the way. We were talking about China earlier; one of the sad things in China up till now has been that as soon as a scholar really establishes himself as a good scholar he was taken away to become a dean or something and that was the end of it, no more research; I hope that's changing now. And I have been very lucky, in being able to go around to places, take part in conferences, do visiting slots in quite a few places over the years, which I have always very much enjoyed; so as long as I've been healthy and able to think, and to talk, I've enjoyed it. I was lucky, especially in today's world where the burdens of quote 'administration' are horrendous, much worse than they were in my time – it was starting in my time, as you know Jim cos you took over [as Head of the Linguistics Department, 1986–1987: JRM], and it was already getting to the point where you spend most of the time justifying what you are doing rather than actually doing it; it's got ten times worse now, so I think in that situation, sadly because you're needed as a teacher, but I wouldn't blame anyone for saying I'm going to take retirement, because that doesn't mean you are stopping; on the contrary, I mean, not at all.

JRM: *That's what worries us, we'll have to work too hard if we retire.*

MAKH: You will! I'm sorry about that. But you're not getting out of that!

JRM: *Also we are wondering what it is that keeps you working, in spite of career turns stemming from your political beliefs, hostile intellectual climes, and the compelling attractions of life by the sea in Fairlight or Urunga? What keeps you doing linguistics?*

MAKH: Yeah, it's a good question. I suppose it's simply feeling the challenge of wanting answers. I think I've mentioned somewhere – I don't think it was any interview, I can't remember, but I had a number of different ways in which were driving me towards thinking about language, and one was literature in fact, from school days, when I really enjoyed reading English literature, but felt I wanted to know something about language and my teachers either didn't say anything about language or if they did it was nonsense, and I said, well you know, somebody somewhere must be able to say sensible things about language. And my father, definitely, he was very helpful; he was a secondary school teacher, well versed in traditional grammar but very intelligent, so I never actually had any courses in traditional grammar in school, but I knew about it from my father in the home, watching him mark examination papers and so on.

JRM: *Just as Ruqaiya learned her cooking, not from being taught to cook but from her observing her mother in the kitchen.*

MAKH: Yeah, yeah, exactly. And then I think, secondly, it was being forced to become a foreign language teacher at the age of 20, with no training whatever, and suddenly being faced with classes of adult students who wanted to learn Chinese, and this was a real challenge because I wanted to be able to explain things to them. That's where the Theme notion came from. I've always been happy to acknowledge that I got it from the Prague School (e.g. Halliday 1970a), but actually I didn't. At the time I didn't know anything about the Prague School or its works, but I simply had to face the question, how to know what to put first in the Chinese clause. That led eventually into the notion of Theme; luckily Chinese is rather like English in that respect (Halliday 1959). Then there was the Marxist challenge, the challenge of trying to find things to say about language which would actually lead us into the largely invisible aspects, or varieties of language, which we talked about earlier, so the Marxist background was there.

And then machine translation (Halliday 1962), how to get language into the computer and my failed attempts to persuade the little group that we needed to implement the concepts of system and system networks; they were all for doing it structurally, but it was good fun. So there were already questions from outside from which were pushing me. When I was doing the Chinese course, I never heard of Firth, although he was in the next building; but when I was posted back to London, after a year in India, as an instructor in a Chinese course that I started teaching, then I got to know about Firth, and his work, and sat in on his lectures. I wasn't yet his research student obviously, I was there still in the army, but was able to get some idea of what he was on about: here is someone who really thinks about language and what is more thinks about non-European languages, that was another important factor. Later, with my political views, well I lost various jobs, sure, but there were others. I was sorry about one thing: I would have been quite happy doing what I was doing in China which was studying Chinese dialects; I'd have been quite happy to spend a life doing that, but you couldn't, and then I was witchhunted out of SOAS and that's the only place where I could have done it, anyway, so all that changed. But it's fine, you know, other things happened.

As far as the life by the sea is concerned, yes, but it's, you know, a good working environment.

My problem is that since we both retired, we've been able to go over to Europe much more often than we could before. Both of us love visiting in England and so of course we go over there, and we just have great fun with family and friends, and then we don't get to work. And I'm free of it now pretty well, I'm not doing the work anymore; but Ruqaiya's still hard at it, with her collected works, which is great (e.g. Hasan 2005, 2009).

JRM: *Okay, finally, we are wondering where you think you get your feel for English from? I think as linguists we all develop a sense of when someone has brought a description home, and your mapping of English grammar is an especially sensitive one. How did you come to so insightfully describe English as she is writ or spoke?*

MAKH: I think that, again, both my parents were involved; my mother was a teacher of French, until she had to give up because in those days once a woman was married she couldn't go on being a teacher; the idea was that you were keeping a job away from the menfolk, but she kept in the business, examining and so on. My father was a teacher of English and Latin, and a dialect scholar, a dialectologist, so there was a great sense of the value of language and including the value of dialect – he was a great dialect enthusiast. His work was recognised recently in a book that David Butt is telling me about (Joseph & Janda 2003) which has, he says, a very good account of the dialect survey. Just one other point. I have this ability, and I don't know why particularly, but I can actually construct real genuine spoken discourse out of my head. I've had to do this once or twice so I know; once it was with the teachers in London, and we were asked would we put on a scripted sort of conversation. And I said, "Yes, we'd love to do that about the project and what we were doing." And I just wrote it, as conversation, and we recorded it and I was struck by people saying, this is wonderful, it's just how we talk. Well I didn't know if there's anything special to be being able to do this, maybe there is, I don't know. But I was always as it were sensitive to what spoken language is like; where that comes from, I really don't know.

But we sent it in the BBC, who said the Third Programme, which was a kind of intellectual program, maybe still is, I don't know, and they rejected it on the grounds that the job of the Third Program was to stimulate but not to inform. We told them too much I'm afraid! It was a pity.

JRM: *So you've been able to reflect on spoken English then, without having to transcribe and tape record and all that sort of thing. You can bring it up, so to speak, and listen to it.*

MAKH: Well yes, in a way I could. That was also reinforced by the training from Wang Li. Because what I was doing with him was going to a lot of classes of course, but I was also in his little research project on Cantonese dialects, and I'd learnt enough Cantonese by then to join. I've forgotten my Cantonese now, it's a pity, I was quite fluent then. And so what we did was we got speakers all around Guangdong, a typical Chinese province, and an absolute forest of different varieties, different dialects. But they all knew standard Cantonese so that we interacted in Cantonese. And I helped with the phonology where I did the tones, I was very good at that. But I also wrote my own grammatical questionnaire, which I think was the first, because recently somebody claimed to have been the first person to do that about 30 years later, so I have that; did Jonathan publish it in that Chinese volume (Halliday 2005)? I don't think he did … So I had this ability to focus in, listening to spoken language, recall it in chunks with all the intonation, and analyse it so to speak because we didn't have a tape recorder. Well, we had a wire recorder, but it wasn't that good because the wire used to break and you got a cloud of the stuff you clean pans with in every corner of the room. So to a certain extent for some reason I don't know, I had this sense. Also I always loved the sounds of verse; my favourite poets from early on were those like Tennyson and Milton who make music out of words, that kind of combination of wording and sound.

JRM: *Thank you Michael, beautiful.*

Sydney
3 February 2011

Bibliography

Allen, W. S. (1956) System and structure in the Abaza verbal complex. *Transactions of the Philological Society*, 127–76.

Armstrong, E., A. Ferguson, L. Mortensen and L. Tougher (2005) Acquired language disorders: some functional insights. R. Hasan, C. M. I. M. Matthiessen & J. Webster (2005) (eds) *Continuing Discourse on Language. Vol. 1.* London: Equinox. 383–412.

Atkinson, P. (1985) *Language Structure and Reproduction: an introduction to the sociology of Basil Bernstein.* London: Methuen

Bakhtin, M. M. (1981) *The Dialogic Imagination* (translated by C. Emerson & M. Holquist) Austin: University of Texas Press.

Baldry, A. and P. Thibault (2006) *Multimodal Transcription and Text Analysis: a multimedia toolkit and course book with associated on-line course.* London: Equinox.

Bateman, J. (2008) *Multimodality and Genre: a foundation for the systematic analysis of multimodal documents.* London: Palgrave Macmillan

Bednarek, M. and J. R. Martin (eds) (2010) *New Discourse on Language: functional perspectives on multimodality, identity, and affiliation.* London: Continuum.

Berger, P. and T. Luckman (1967) *The Social Construction of Reality: a treatise in the sociology of knowledge.* Garden City, NY: Anchor Books.

Bernstein, B. (1971) *Class, Codes and Control 1: theoretical studies towards a sociology of language.* London: Routledge & Kegan Paul (Primary Socialisation, Language and Education). (Republished with an Appendix added by Paladin, 1974).

—(ed.) (1973) *Class, Codes and Control 2: applied studies towards a sociology of language.* London: Routledge & Kegan Paul (Primary Socialisation, Language and Education).

—(1975) *Class, Codes and Control 3: towards a theory of educational transmissions.* London: Routledge & Kegan Paul (Primary Socialisation, Language and Education).

—(1990) *Class, Codes and Control 4: the structuring of pedagogic discourse.* London: Routledge.

Birch, D. and M. O'Toole (eds) (1988) *The Functions of Style.* London: Pinter.

Brown, R. (1973) *A First Language: the early stages.* London: Allen & Unwin.

Bühler, K. (1934) *Sprachtheorie: die darsellungfunktion der sprache.* Jena: G. Fischer.

Bullock, A. (1975) *A Language for Life* (The Bullock Report). London: Her Majesty's Stationery Office.

Butt, D. (1988) Randomness, order and the latent patterning of text. London: Birch & O'Toole (eds), London: 74–97.

Caffarel, A., J. R. Martin and C. M. I. M. Matthiessen (eds) (2004) *Language Typology: a functional perspective*: Amsterdam: Benjamins.

Caldwell, D. (2010) Making metre mean: identity and affiliation in the Rap music of Kanye West. Bednarek & Martin (eds), 59–79.

Chomsky, N. (1964a) Formal discussion: the development of grammar in child language. U. Bellugi & R. Brown (eds) *The Acquisition of Language.* West Lafayette, IN: Purdue

University (Monographs of the Society for Research in Child Development 29.1), 35–9.
—(1964b) *Current Issues in Linguistic Theory*. The Hague: Mouton. (Reprinted in J. A. Fodor & J. J. Katz (eds) (1964) *The Structure of Language: readings in the philosophy of language*. Englewood Cliffs, NJ: Prentice-Hall, 50–116).
—(1966) *Topics in the Theory of Generative Grammar*. The Hague: Mouton.
Crystal, D. and C. Brumfit (2004) Coping with change in applied linguistics. *Journal of Applied Linguistics* 1.3, 383–98.
Davidse, K. (1992) Transitive/ergative: the Janus-headed grammar of actions and events. M. Davies and L. Ravelli (eds) *Advances in Systemic Linguistics*. London: Pinter, 105–35.
Deacon, T. (1997) *The Symbolic Species: the co-evolution of language and the brain*. New York: W. W. Norton & Company.
Dore, J. (1976) Review of *Learning How to Mean* by M. A. K. Halliday. *Language and Society* 6, 268–77.
Doughty, P., J. Pearce and G. Thornton (1971) *Language in Use*. London: Edward Arnold.
Dreyfus, S., S. Hood and M. Stenglin (eds) (2011) *Semiotic Margins: reclaiming meaning*. London: Continuum.
Dunbar, R. (1992) Why gossip is good for you. *New Scientist* 1848.
—(2010) *How Many Friends does one Person Need? Dunbar's number and other evolutionary quirks*. Cambridge, MA: Harvard University Press.
Edelman, G. (1992) *Bright Air, Brilliant Fire: on the matter of the mind*. New York: Basic Books.
Ervin-Tripp, S. (1973) *Language acquisition and communicative choice: essays by Susan Ervin-Tripp*. Stanford, CA: Stanford University Press.
Fairclough, N. (1995) *Critical Discourse Analysis: the critical study of language*. London: Longman (Longman Applied Linguistics). (2nd revised edition 2010).
Fardon, R. (1999) *Mary Douglas*. London: Routledge.
Fawcett, R. P. (1980) *Cognitive Linguistics and Social Interaction: towards an integrated model of a systemic functional grammar and the other components of an interacting mind*. Heidelberg: Julius Gross.
—(1988a) The English personal pronouns: an exercise in linguistic theory. J. D. Benson, M. J. Cummings & W. S. Greaves (eds) *Linguistics in a Systemic Perspective*. Amsterdam: Benjamins (Current Issues in Linguistics Theory 39), 185–220.
—(1988b) What makes a 'good' system network good? – Four pairs of concepts for such evaluation. J. D. Benson & W. S. Greaves (eds) *Systemic Functional Approaches to Discourse*. Norwood, NJ: Ablex, 1–28.
—(2008) *Invitation to Systemic Functional Linguistics through the Cardiff Grammar*. London: Equinox.
Fawcett, R. P., M. A. K. Halliday, S. M. Lamb and A. Makkai (eds) (1984a) *The Semiotics of Language and Culture: Vol 1: language as social semiotic*. London: Pinter.
—(1984b) *The Semiotics of Language and Culture: Vol 2: language and other semiotic systems of culture*. London: Pinter.
Fillmore, C. (1968) The case for case. E. Bach & R. T. Harms (eds) *Universals in Linguistic Theory*. New York: Holt, Rinehart & Winston, 1–88.
Fine, J. (2006) *Language in Psychiatry: a handbook of clinical practice*. London. Equinox.
Firth, J. R. (1950) Personality and language in society. *Sociological Review* 42, 37–52. (Reprinted in Firth 1957, 177–89).
—(1957a) *Papers in Linguistics 1934–1951*. London: Oxford University Press.

—(1957b) A Synopsis of Linguistic Theory, 1930–1955. *Studies in Linguistic Analysis* (Special volume of the Philological Society). London: Blackwell, 1–31. (reprinted in Palmer 1968, 168–205).

Fishman, J. (1970) *Sociolinguistics: a brief introduction*. Rowley, MA: Newbury House.

Forsyth, I. and K. Wood (1977) *Language and Communication*. London: Longman.

Geertz, C. (1973) *The Interpretation of Cultures*. New York: Basic Books.

Gerot, L., J. Oldenburg and T. van Leeuwen (eds) (1988) *Language and Socialisation: home and school* (Proceedings from the Working Conference on Language in Education, Macquarie University, 17–21 November 1986). Sydney: Macquarie University.

Giblett, R. and J. O'Carroll (1990) *Discipline, Dialogue, Difference: proceedings of the Language in Education Conference, Murdoch University,* December 1989. Murdoch: 4D Duration Publications.

Gray, B. (1985) Helping children to become language learners in the classroom. M. Christie (ed.) *Aboriginal Perspectives on Experience and Learning: the role of language in Aboriginal education*. Geelong: Deakin University Press. (Sociocultural Aspects of Language and Education), 87–104.

—(1986) Aboriginal education: some implications of genre for literacy development. Painter, C. & J. R. Martin (eds) *Writing to Mean: teaching genres across the curriculum*. Applied Linguistics Association of Australia (Occasional Papers 9), 188–208.

—(1987) How natural is 'natural' language teaching: employing wholistic methodology in the classroom. *Australian Journal of Early Childhood* 12.4, 3–19.

—(1990) Natural language learning in Aboriginal classrooms: reflections on teaching and learning. C. Walton & W. Eggington (eds) *Language: maintenance, power and education in Australian Aboriginal contexts*. Darwin, NT: Northern Territory University Press, 105–39.

Greenberg, J. H. (1963) *Essays in Linguistics*. Chicago: University of Chicago Press.

Greenfield, S. (1997) *The Human Brain: a guided tour*. London: Weidenfield & Nicholson.

Greimas, A. J. (1966a) *Sémantique Structurale*. Paris: Larousse.

—(1966b) Éléments pour une théorie de l'interprétation du récit mythique. Roland Barthes (ed.) *Communications 8: L'Analyse structurale du récit*. Paris: Seuil, 34–65.

—(1969) Des modèles théoriques en socio-linguistique. International Days of Sociolinguistics Conference, Istituto Luigi Sturzo, Rome. (Reprinted in A. J. Greimas. 1976. *Sémiotique et Sciences Sociales*. Paris: Seuil, 61–76).

—(1983) *Du Sens II: essais sémiotiques*. Paris: Seuil.

Gumperz, J. J. (1964) Linguistic and social interaction in two communities. *American Anthropologist* 66.S3, 137–53.

Halliday, M. A. K. (1956) Grammatical categories in modern Chinese. *Transactions of the Philological Society,* 177–224.

—(1959) *The Language of the Chinese "Secret History of the Monguls"*. Oxford: Blackwell (Publications of the Philological Society 17). (Collected Works 8, 5–171).

—(1962) Linguistics and machine translation. *Zeitschrift für Phonetik, Sprachwissenschaft und Kommunikationsforschung.* 15.1/2, 145–58. (republished in M. A. K. Halliday & A. McIntosh. 1966. *Patterns of Language: papers in general, descriptive and applied linguistics*. London: Longman (Longman Linguistics Library), 134–50). (Collected Works 6, 20–36).

—(1964) Syntax and the consumer. C. I. J. M. Stuart (ed.) *Report of the Fifteenth Annual (First International) Round Table Meeting on Linguistics and Language Teaching.*

Washington, DC: Georgetown University Press. (Monograph Series on Languaes and Linguistics 17), 11–24. (Edited version republished in Halliday & Martin, 21–8). (Collected Works 3, 36–49).

—(1966) Some notes on 'deep' grammar. *Journal of Linguistics* 2.1, 57–67. (Collected Works 1, 106–17).

—(1967a) *Intonation and Grammar in British English.* The Hague: Mouton.

—(1967b) Notes in transitivity and theme in English: Part 1. *Journal of Linguistics* 3.1. 37–81. (Collected Works 7, 5–54).

—(1967c) Notes on transitivity and theme in English: Part 2. *Journal of Linguistics* 3.2, 199–244. (Collected Works 7, 55–109).

—(1968) Notes on transitivity and theme in English: Part 3. *Journal of Linguistics* 4.2, 179–215. (Collected Works 7, 110–53).

—(1970a) Language structure and language function. J. Lyons (ed.) *New Horizons in Linguistics.* Harmondsworth: Penguin, 140–65. (Collected Works 1, 173–95).

—(1970b) *A Course in Spoken English: intonation.* London: Oxford University Press.

—(1971) Linguistic function and literary style: an inquiry into the language of William Golding's 'The Inheritors'. S. Chatman (ed.) *Literary Style: a symposium.* New York: Oxford University Press, 362–400. (Collected Works 2, 88–125).

—(1973) *Explorations in the Functions of Language.* London: Edward Arnold.

—(1974) *Language and Social Man.* London: Longman. (Collected Works 10, 65–130).

—(1975) *Learning how to Mean: explorations in the development of language.* London: Edward Arnold (Explorations in Language Study).

—(1976a) Anti-languages. *American Anthropologist* 78.3, 570–84. (Reprinted in M. A. K. Halliday 2007 *Language and Society.* London: Continuum). (Collected Works 10, 265–86).

—(1976b) *Halliday: system and function in language* G. Kress (ed.). London: Oxford University Press.

—(1976c) The teacher taught the student English: an essay in applied linguistics. P. A. Reich (ed.) The Second LACUS Forum. Columbia, SC: Hornbeam Press, 344–9. (Collected Works 7, 197–305).

—(1977a) Ideas about language. M. A. K. Halliday *Aims and Perspectives in Linguistics.* Applied Linguistics Association of Australia (Occasional Papers 1), 32–49. (Collected Works 3, 92–115).

—(1977b) The context of linguistics. M. A. K. Halliday *Aims and Perspectives in Linguistics.* Applied Linguistics Association of Australia (Occasional Papers 1), 19–31. (Collected Works 3, 74–91).

—(1978a) An interpretation of the functional relationship between language and social structure. U. Quasthoff (ed.) *Sprachstruktur - Sozialstruktur: zur linguistischen theorienbildung.* Konigstein: Scriptor, 3–42. (Reprinted in M. A. K. Halliday 2007 *Language and Society.* London: Continuum). (Collected Works 10, 251–64).

—(1978b) *Language as Social Semiotic: the social interpretation of language and meaning.* London: Edward Arnold.

—(1979) Modes of meaning and modes of expression: types of grammatical structure, and their determination by different semantic functions. D. J. Allerton, E. Carney, D. Holcroft (eds) *Function and Context in Linguistic Analysis: essays offered to William Haas.* Cambridge: Cambridge University Press, 57–79. (Collected Works 1, 196–218).

—(1981a) Structure. M. A. K. Halliday & J. R. Martin (eds) *Readings in Systemic Linguistics.* London: Batsford, 122–31.

—(1981b) The origin and development of Chinese phonological theory. R. E. Asher & E. J. A. Henderson (eds) *Towards a History of Phonetics*. Edinburgh: Edinburgh University Press, 123–39. (Collected Works 8, 275–93).
—(1982) The de-automatization of grammar: from Priestley's 'An Inspector Calls'. J. M. Anderson (ed.) *Language Form and Linguistic Variation: papers dedicated to Angus McIntosh*. Amsterdam: Benjamins, 129–59. (Collected Works 2, 126–48).
—(1984) Language as code and language as behaviour: a systemic-functional interpretation of the nature and ontogenesis of dialogue. R. Fawcett, M. A. K. Halliday, S. M. Lamb & A. Makkai (eds) *The Semiotics of Language and Culture: Vol 1: Language as Social Semiotic*. London: Pinter, 3–35. (Collected Works 4, 226–49).
—(1985a) *An Introduction to Functional Grammar.* London: Edward Arnold. (Revised 2nd edition 1994, revised 3rd edition, with C. M. I. M. Matthiessen 2004).
—(1985b) *Spoken and Written Language.* Geelong: Deakin University Press (Republished by Oxford University Press 1989).
—(1987) Language and the order of nature. N. Fabb, D. Attridge, A. Durant & C. MacCabe (eds) *The Linguistics of Writing: arguments between language and literature.* Manchester: Manchester University Press, 135–54. (Collected Works 3, 116–38).
—(1988) Poetry as scientific discourse: the nuclear sections of Tennyson's *In Memoriam*. Birch & O'Toole, 31–44. (Collected Works 2, 149–67).
—(1990a) New ways of meaning: a challenge to applied linguistics. *Journal of Applied Linguistics* 6 (Ninth World Congress of Applied Linguistics, Special issue). The Greek Applied Linguistics Association (GALA), 7–36. (Collected Works 1, 139–74).
—(1990b) The construction of knowledge and value in the grammar of scientific discourse: with reference to Charles Darwin's *The Origin of Species*. C. de Stasio, M. Gotti & R. Bonaderi (eds) *Atti del XI Congresso Nazionale dell'Associazione Italiana di Anglistica, Bergamo,* 24 e 25 Ottobre 1988. Milano: Guerini Studio. (Collected Works 3, 168–92).
—(1991) Towards probabilistic interpretations. E. Ventola (ed.) *Functional and Systemic Linguistics: approaches and uses*. Berlin: Mouton de Gruyter, 39–62. (Collected Works 6, 42–62).
—(1992a) How do you mean? M. Davies & L. Ravelli (eds) *Papers from the Seventeenth International Systemic Congress, University of Stirling, July 1990.* London: Pinter. 20–35. (Collected Works 1, 352–68).
—(1992b) Systemic grammar and the concept of a "science of language". In Waiguoyu (Journal of Foreign Languages), 2 (General Series No. 78), 1–9. (Collected Works 3, 199–212).
—(1993) Towards a language-based theory of learning. *Linguistics and Education* 5.2, 93–116. (Collected Works 4, 327–52).
—(1994) On language in relation to the evolution of human consciousness. S. Allén (ed.) *Of Thoughts and Words. The relation between language and mind*. London: Imperial College Press, 45–84. 9 (Collected Works 3, 390–432).
—(1995) Language and the theory of codes. A. Sadovnik (ed.) *Knowledge and Pedagogy: the sociology of Basil Bernstein*. Norwood, NJ: Ablex, 127–44. (Collected Works 10, 231–46).
—(1998) Grammar and daily life: concurrence and complementarity. T. A. van Dijk (ed.) *Functional Approaches to Language, Culture and Cognition*. Amsterdam: Benjamins, 221–37. (Collected Works 1, 369–83).
—(2005) *Studies in Chinese Language.* London: Continuum. (Volume 8 in the Collected Works of M. A. K. Halliday, edited by Jonathon Webster).

—(2007a) *Language and Education.* London: Continuum. (Volume 9 in the Collected Works of M. A. K. Halliday, edited by Jonathon Webster).
—(2007b) Applied linguistics as an evolving theme. Halliday 2007a, 1–19. (Collected Works 9, 1–24).
—(2008a) *Complementarities in Language.* Beijing: Commercial Press.
—(2008b) Working with meaning: towards an appliable linguistics. J. Webster (ed.) (2008) *Meaning in Context: strategies for implementing intelligent applications of language studies.* London: Continuum, 7–23.
Halliday, M. A. K. and W. S. Greaves (2008) *Intonation in the Grammar of English.* London: Equinox.
Halliday M. A. K. and R. Hasan (1976) *Cohesion in English.* London: Longman (English Language Series 9).
—(1985) *Language, context, and text: aspects of language in a social-semiotic perspective.* Geelong: Deakin University Press. (republished by Oxford University Press 1989).
Halliday, M. A. K. and Z. L. James (1993) A quantitative study of polarity and primary tense in the English finite clause. J. M. Sinclair, M. P. Hoey & G. Fox (eds) *Techniques of Description: spoken and written discourse.* London: Routledge, 32–66. (Collected Works 6, 93–129).
Halliday, M. A. K. and J. R. Martin (eds) (1981) *Readings in Systemic Linguistics.* London: Batsford.
—(1993) *Writing Science: literacy and discursive power.* London: Falmer (Critical perspectives on literacy and education) & Pittsburg: University of Pittsburg Press. (Pittsburg Series in Composition, Literacy, and Culture), 1993. (Greek translation Athens: Metaixmio 2004).
Halliday, M. A. K. and C. M. I. M. Matthiessen (1999) *Construing Experience Through Meaning: a language-based approach to cognition.* London: Cassell.
Halliday, M. A. K., A. McIntosh and P. Strevens (1964) *The Linguistic Sciences and Language Teaching.* London: Longman (Longmans' Linguistics Library).
Halliday, M. A. K. and J. Webster (ed.) (2009) *Continuum Companion to Systemic Functional Linguistics.* London: Continuum.
Hardaker, D. (1982) *Language in a Regulative Context.* Honours Thesis, Department of Linguistics, University of Sydney.
Hasan, R. (1985a) Meaning, context and text: fifty years after Malinowski. J. D. Benson & W. S. Greaves (eds) *Systemic Perspectives on Discourse,* Vol. 1. Norwood, NJ: Ablex (Advances in Discourse Processes XV), 16–49.
—(1985b) *Linguistics, Language and Verbal Art.* Geelong: Deakin University Press (Reprinted by Oxford University Press 1989).
—(1987a) The grammarian's dream: lexis as most delicate grammar. M. A. K. Halliday & R. P. Fawcett (eds) *New Developments in Systemic Linguistics Vol. 1: theory and description.* London: Pinter, 184–211.
—(1987b) Directions from structuralism. N. Fabb, D. Attridge, A. Durant & C. MacCabe (eds) *The Linguistics of Writing: arguments between language and literature.* Manchester: Manchester University Press, 103–22.
—(1995) The conception of context in text. P. Fries and M. Gregory (eds) *Discourse in Society: systemic-functional perspectives.* Norwood, NJ: Ablex, 183–283.
—(2005) *Language, Society and Consciousness.* London: Equinox (Vol. 1 of The Collected Works of Ruqaiya Hasan, edited by Jonathan Webster).
—(2009a) *Semantic Variation: meaning in society and sociolinguistics.* London: Equinox (Vol. 2 of The Collected Works of Ruqaiya Hasan, edited by Jonathan Webster).

—(2009b) A view of pragmatics in a social semiotic perspective. *Linguistics and the Human Sciences,* 5.3, 251–79.
Hasan, R. and P. Fries (eds) (1995) *On Subject and Theme: a discourse functional perspective.* Amsterdam & Philadelphia: Benjamins.
Hasan, R., C. M. I. M. Matthiessen and J. Webster (eds) (2005) *Continuing Discourse on Language: a functional perspective,* Vol. 1. London: Continuum.
—(2007) *Continuing Discourse on Language: a functional perspective.* Vol. 2. London: Continuum.
Henrici, A. (1981) Some notes on the systemic generation of a paradigm of the English clause. London: Halliday & Martin, 74–98.
Hill, C. (1974) *Change and Continuity in Seventeenth Century England.* London: Weidenfeld & Nicholson.
Hjelmslev, L. (1961) *Prolegomena to a Theory of Language.* Madison, WI: University of Wisconsin Press.
Hodge, R. (1998) Halliday and the stylistics of creativity. *Functions of Style.* D. Birch and M. OToole (eds). London: Pinter, 142–56.
Horvath, B. (1985) *Variation in Australian English: the sociolects of Sydney.* Cambridge: Cambridge University Press (Cambridge Studies in Linguistics 45).
Huddleston, R. D. (1971) *The Sentence in Written English: a syntactic study based on an analysis of scientific texts.* Cambridge: Cambridge University Press.
Huddleston, R. D., R. A. Hudson, E. O. Winter and A. Henrici (1968) *Sentence and Clause in Scientific English.* London: Communication Research Centre, University College London.
Hudson, R. A. (1971) *English Complex Sentences: an introduction to systemic grammar* (North Holland Linguistic Series 4) Amsterdam: North-Holland (North Holland Linguistic Series 4).
Hymes, D. H. (1971) Competence and performance in linguistic theory. R. Huxley & E. Ingram (eds) *Language Acquisition: Models and Methods.* New York: Academic Press.
—(1974) Linguistic theory and functions in speech. *Foundations in Scoiolinguistics: an ethnographic approach.* London: Tavistock, 145–78.
Hymes, D. H. and J. Fought (1975) *American Structuralism,* T. Sebeok (ed.) *Current Trends in Linguistics* 13. The Hague: Mouton, 903–1176. (republished in 1981 as *American Structuralism*). The Hague: Mouton (Janua Linguarum, Series Maior 102).
Joseph, B. D. and R. D. Janda (2003) *Handbook of Historical Linguistics.* Oxford: Blackwell.
Kress, G. and R. Hodge (1979) *Language as Ideology.* London: Routledge & Kegan Paul.
Kress, G. and T. van Leeuwen (1996) *Reading Images: the grammar of visual design.* London: Routledge (Revised 2nd edition 2006).
Labov, W. (1968) *The Social Stratification of English in New York City.* Washington, DC: Center for Applied Linguistics.
—(1969) The logic of non-standard English. G*eorgetown Monographs on Language and Linguistics* 22. Washington, DC: Georgetown University Press (Reprinted in Labov 1972a, 201–40).
—(1970) The study of language in its social context. *Studium Generale* 23, 30–87
—(1972a) *Language in the Inner City: studies in the Black English vernacular.* Philadelphia: University of Pennsylvania Press.
—(1972b) Letter to the Atlantic. *The Atlantic* 230, 5 November, 45.
Lakoff, G. (1971) Presupposition and relative well-formedness. D. D. Steinberg & L. A. Jakobovits (eds) *Semantics: an interdisciplinary reader in philosophy, linguistics and psychology.* Cambridge: Cambridge University Press, 329–40.

Lamb, S. M. (1966) Epilegomena to a theory of language. *Romance Philology* 19, 531–73.

—(1970) Linguistic and cognitive networks. Paul Garvin (ed.) *Cognition: a multiple view.* New York: Spartan, 195–222.

van Leeuwen, T. (1999) *Speech, Music, Sound.* London: Macmillan.

Lemke, J. (1984) *Semiotics and education.* Toronto, Toronto Semiotic Circle Monograph 1984, 2.

—(1985) Ideology, intertextuality and the notion of register. J. D. Benson & W. S. Greaves (eds) *Systemic Perspectives on Discourse vol. 1: selected theoretical papers from the 9th International Systemic Workshop.* Norwood, NJ: Ablex, 275–94.

—(1995) *Textual Politics: discourse and social dynamics.* London: Taylor & Francis.

Lévi-Strauss, C. (1966) *The Savage Mind.* London: Weidenfeld & Nicholson.

Lock, A. and E. Fisher (eds) (1984) *Language Development: a reader.* London: Croom Helm.

Lockwood, D. G. (1972) *Introduction to Stratificational Linguistics.* New York: Harcourt, Brace, Jovanovich.

Mackay, D., B. Thompson and P. Schaub (1970) *Breakthrough to Literacy, Teacher's Manual: the theory and practice of teaching initial reading and writing.* London: Longman.

Maling-Keepes, J. and B. D. Keepes (eds) (1979) *Language in Education: the language development project, phase 1.* Canberra: Curriculum Development Centre.

Malinowski, B. (1923) The problem of meaning in primitive languages. Supplement I to C. K. Ogden & I. A. Richards *The Meaning of Meaning.* New York: Harcourt Brace & World, 296–336.

—(1935) *Coral Gardens and their Magic.* London: Allen & Unwin.

Mann, W. (1984) A linguistic overview of the Nigel text generation grammar. *The Tenth LACUS Forum 1983.* A. Manning, P. Martin & K. McCalla (eds.). Columbia, SC: Hornbeam Press, 255–65.

Martin, J. R. (1985) Process and text: two aspects of semiosis. J. D. Benson & W. S. Greaves (eds) *Systemic Perspectives on Discourse vol. 1: selected theoretical papers from the 9th International Systemic Workshop.* Norwood, NJ: Ablex, 248–74.

—(1987) The meaning of features in systemic linguistics. M. A. K. Halliday & R. P. Fawcett (eds) *New Developments in Systemic Linguistics Vol. 1: theory and description.* London: Pinter, 14–40.

—(1992) *English text: system and structure.* Amsterdam: Benjamins.

—(1993) Genre and literacy – modelling context in educational linguistics. *Annual Review of Applied Linguistics* 13, 1993, 141–72.

—(1996a) Transitivity in Tagalog: a functional interpretation of case. M. Berry, C. Butler, R. Fawcett & G. Huang (eds) *Meaning and Form: systemic functional interpretations.* Norwood, NJ: Ablex (Meaning and Choice in Language: studies for Michael Halliday), 229–96.

—(1996b) Types of structure: deconstructing notions of constituency in clause and text. E. H. Hovy & D. R. Scott (ed.) *Computational and Conversational Discourse: burning issues – an interdisciplinary account.* Heidelberg: Springer (NATO Advanced Science Institute Series F – Computer and Systems Sciences, Vol. 151), 39–66.

—(1996c) Evaluating disruption: symbolising theme in junior secondary narrative. R. Hasan & G. Williams (eds) *Literacy in Society.* London: Longman (Applied Linguistics and Language Study), 124–71.

—(1999) Modelling context: the crooked path of progress in contextual linguistics (Sydney SFL). M. Ghadessy (ed.) *Text and Context in Functional Linguistics.* Amsterdam: Benjamins (CILT Series IV), 25–61.

—(2000) Design and practice: enacting functional linguistics in Australia. *Annual Review of Applied Linguistics* 20 (20th Anniversary Volume 'Applied Linguistics as an Emerging Discipline'), 116–26.
—(2001) A context for genre: modelling social processes in functional linguistics. J. Devilliers & R. Stainton (eds) *Communication in Linguistics: papers in honour of Michael Gregory*. Toronto: GREF (Theoria Series 10), 287–328.
—(2004) Metafunctional profile: Tagalog. Caffarel et al. (eds), 255–304.
Martin, J. R., C. M. I. M. Matthiessen and C. Painter (1997) *Working with Functional Grammar*: Arnold. (1997). (2nd revised edition *Deploying Functional Grammar*. Commercial Press: Beijing. (The Halliday Centre Series in Appliable Linguistics) 2010).
Martin, J. R. and P. R. R. White (2005) *The Language of Evaluation: appraisal in English*. London: Palgrave.
Martinec, R. (2000) Types of process in action. *Semiotica* 130–3/4, 243–68.
—(2001) Interpersonal resources in action. *Semiotica*, 135–1/4, 117–45.
—(2005) Topics in multimodality. Hasan et al. (eds), 157–81.
Mathesius, V. (1964) On the potentiality of the phenomena of language. J. Vachek (ed.) *A Prague School Reader in Linguistics*. Bloomington, IN: Indiana University Press.
Maton, K. and R. Moore (eds) (2010) *Social Realism, Knowledge and the Sociology of Education: coalitions of the mind*. London: Continuum.
Matthiessen, C. M. I. M. (1993) Register in the round. M. Ghadessy (ed.) *Register Analysis: theory and practice* London: Pinter, 221–92.
—(1998) Construing processes of consciousness: from the commonsense model to the uncommonsense model of cognitive science. J. R. Martin and R. Veel (eds) *Reading Science: critical and functional perspectives on discourses of science*. London and New York: Routledge, 327–56.
—(2004) Descriptive motifs and generalisations. Caffarel et al. (eds), 537–673.
—(2007a) The multimodal page: a systemic functional exploration. T. Royce & W. Bowcher (eds) *New Directions in the Analysis of Multimodal Discourse*. Mahwah, NJ: Lawrence Erlbaum, 1–62.
—(2007b) The 'architecture' of language according to systemic functional theory: developments since the 1970s. R. Hasan, C. M. I. M. Matthiessen & J. Webster (eds) *Continuing Discourse on Language: a functional perspective* Vol. 2, 505–62.
Matthiessen, C. M. I. M. and J. A. Bateman (1991) *Text Generation and Systemic-functional Linguistics: experiences from English and Japanese*. London: Pinter.
Matthiessen, C. M. I. M., K. Teruya and M. Lam (2010) *Key Terms in Systemic Functional Linguistics*. London: Continuum.
McDonald, E. (2005) Through a glass darkly: a critique of the influence of linguistics on theories of music. *Linguistics and the Human Sciences* 1.3, 463–88.
—(2011a) Dealing with musical meaning: towards an embodied model of music. Dreyfus et al. (eds), 101–21.
—(2011b) *Learning Chinese, Turning Chinese: challenges to becoming sinophone in a globalised world*. Abingdon: Routledge.
McKellar, G. B. (1987) The place of socio-semantics in contemporary thought. R. Steele & T. Threadgold (eds) *Language Topics: essays in honour of Michael Halliday*. Amsterdam: Benjamins. 523–48.
Mohan, B. A. (1986) *Language and Content*. Reading: Addison-Wesley.
Muller, J. (2000) *Reclaiming Knowledge: Social theory, curriculum and education policy*. London: Routledge.

O'Donnell, M. and J. Bateman (2005) SFL in computational contexts: a contemporary history. Hasan et al. (eds), 343–82.
O'Toole, M. (1994) *The Language of Displayed Art*. London: Leicester University Press (a division of Pinter). (Revised 2nd edition. London: Routledge 2010).
Painter, C. (1984) *Into the Mother Tongue: a case study of early language development*. London: Pinter.
—(1998) *Learning through Language in Early Childhood*. London: Cassell
—(2003) Developing attitude: an ontogenetic perspective on appraisal. *Text* 23, 2, 183–210.
—(2009) Language development. M. A. K. Halliday & J. Webster (eds) *Continuum Companion to Systemic Functional Linguistics*. London: Continuum, 87–103.
Palmer, F. R. (1968) *Selected Papers of J R Firth 1952–1959*. London: Longman.
—(ed.) (1970) *Prosodic Analysis*. London: Oxford (Language and Language Learning).
Parret, H. (1974) *Discussing Language*. The Hague: Mouton.
Parsons, T. (1964) *Social Structure and Personality*. Chicago: Free Press.
Pearce, J., G. Thornton and D. Mackay (1989) The Programme in Linguistics and English Teaching, University College, London, 1964–1971. R. Hasan & J. R. Martin (eds) *Language Development: learning language, learning culture*. Norwood, NJ: Ablex (Meaning and Choice in Language: studies for Michael Halliday, Advances in Discourse Processes XXVII), 329–68.
Pike, K. L. (1967) *Language in Relation to a Unified Theory of the Structure of Human Behaviour* (2nd edition). The Hague: Mouton.
Pollock, E. (2008) *Stalin and the Soviet Science Wars*. Princeton, NJ: Princeton University Press.
Reich, P. A. (1970) Relational networks. *Canadian Journal of Linguistics* 15, 18–50
Reid, T. B. W. (1956) Linguistics, structuralism, philology. *Archivum Linguisticum* 8, 28–37.
Rose, D. and J. R. Martin (2012) *Learning to Write, Reading to Learn: genre, knowledge and pedagogy in the Sydney School*. London: Equinox.
Rosenau, P. (1992) *Postmodernism and the Social Sciences*. Princeton, NJ: Princeton University Press.
Sampson, G. (1921) *English for the English: a chapter on national education* (1970 edition). Cambridge: Cambridge University Press.
Sankoff, D. (1978) *Linguistic Variation: models and methods*. New York: Academic Press.
Saussure, F. de (1959) *Course in General Linguistics* (C. Bally & A. Sechehaye (eds), translated with an introduction and notes by W Baskin). New York: McGraw-Hill.
Schegloff, E. (1971) Notes on a conversational practice: formulating place. D. Sudnow (ed.) *Studies in Social Interaction*. Glencoe, IL: Free Press, 75–119.
Shannon, C. E. and W. Weaver (1949) *The Mathematical Theory of Communication*. Champaign, IL: University of Illinois Press.
Sinclair, J. McH. (1966) Beginning the study of lexis. C. E. Bazell, J. C. Catford, M. A. K. Halliday & R. H. Robins (eds) *In Memory of J R Firth*. London: Longman, 410–30.
—(1987) Collocation: a progress report. R. Steele & T. Threadgold (eds) *Language Topics: essays in honour of Michael Halliday. Vol. II*. Amsterdam: Benjamins, 319–32.
Sinclair, J. McH. and R. M. Coulthard (1975) *Towards an Analysis of Discourse: the English used by teachers and pupils*. London: Oxford University Press.
Souza, L. M. F. de (2010) *Interlingual Re-Instantiation: A Model for a New and More Comprehensive Systemic Functional Perspective on Translation*. PhD thesis. University of Sydney: Australia, and Universidade Federal de Santa Catarina: Brazil.

—(2011) A tradução de termos de recentes desenvolvimentos da linguística sistêmico-funcional para o português brasileiro. Tradução e Comunicação, 22, 73–90, Available at: http://sare.unianhanguera.edu.br/index.php/rtcom/issue/ view/79/showToc. [accessed 3 September 2012].
—(forthcoming) Translation as interlingual re-instantiation. *Text & Talk*, special issue in honour of Michael Halliday, edited by Geoff Thompson.
Swadesh, M. (1972) *The Origin and Diversification of Languages*. London: Routledge & Kegan Paul.
Teich, E. (2009) Linguistic computing. M. A. K. Halliday & J. Webster (eds) *Continuum Companion to Systemic Functional Linguistics*. London: Continuum.
Teruya, K., E. Akerejola, T. Anderson, A. Caffarel, J. Lavid, C. M. I. M. Matthiessen, U. Petersen, P. Patpong and F. Smedegaard (2007) Typology of MOOD: a text-based and system-based view. Hasan et al. (eds), 859–920.
Thibault, P. (2004) *Brain, Mind and the Signifying Body: an ecosocial semiotic theory*. London: Continuum (Open Linguistics Series).
Threadgold, T., E. A. Grosz, G. Kress and M. A. K. Halliday (1986) *Semiotics, Ideology Language*. Sydney: Sydney Association for Studies in Society and Culture (Sydney Studies in Society and Culture 3).
Tickoo, M. L. (1985) *Language across the Curriculum: selected papers from the RELC seminar in Language across the Curriculum*. Singapore: SEAMEO Regional Language Centre.
Trevarthen, C. (1974) Conversation with a two-month-old. *New Scientist* 62, 230–5.
Tucker, G. (2007) Between lexis and grammar: towards a systemic functional approach to phraseology. Hasan et al. (eds), 953–78.
Turner, G. J. (1973) Social class and children's language of control. B. Bernstein (ed.)1973 *Class, Codes and Control 2: applied studies towards a sociology of language*. London: Routledge & Kegan Paul (Primary Socialisation, Language and Education), 135–201.
Vachek, J. (1966) *The Linguistic School of Prague: An introduction to its theory and practice*. Bloomington, IN: Indiana University Press.
Vygotsky, L. S. (1962) *Thought and Language*. Cambridge, MA: MIT Press.
—(1978) *Mind in Society: the development of higher psychological processes*. M. Cole, V. John Steiner, S. Scribner & E. Souberman (eds) Cambridge, MA: Harvard University Press.
Whorf, B. L. (1956) *Language, Thought and Reality: selected writings*. Cambridge, MA: MIT Press.
Winograd, T. (1983) *Language as a Cognitive Process. Vol. 1: syntax*. Reading, MA: Addison-Wesley.
Wu, C. (2009) Corpus-based research. Hasan et al. (eds), 128–42.
Zumthor, P. (1972) *Essai de Poétique Médiévale*. Paris: Seuil

Index

Allen 106–7, 108, 236–7
anti-language 50–1
appliable linguistics 187–8, 192, 239–40, 247
applied linguistics 65, 91, 97–8, 118–19, 179–90, 204–5, 239
appraisal 221
arbitrariness 11, 83, 197, 215

Bakhtin 83
Barthes 127
behaviourism 45
Berger and Luckman 152
Bernstein 3–4, 36, 37, 69, 77, 119, 123, 124–5, 126, 152, 153–4, 161–2, 174, 180, 184, 208, 237–8, 251
Bloomfield 33, 34–5, 55, 151, 161, 164
Boas 54, 123
Bourdieu 126, 155
brain 190, 228–9
Breakthrough to Literacy 52, 62, 116, 119, 121, 154, 162, 182–3
British Council 122
Bühler 14, 17, 79, 156

Cambridge 104–5, 130, 200, 206
Catford 116, 119, 188
China (Halliday's work and study there 1947–50) 99–104, 206, 255
Chinese 96–9, 113–15, 149, 183–4, 188, 197, 204, 205, 208, 256
Chinese linguistics 149–50, 161, 195–7, 246–8, 253–4
Chinese phonology 91–2, 101, 149–50, 161, 247
Chomsky 1, 4, 5, 31, 33, 34–5, 37, 41–2, 44, 45, 46, 51, 53–4, 55, 62, 117, 122, 151, 162, 164, 166–7, 188–9, 200, 203, 208, 209, 211
class (vs function) 78, 143
clinical linguistics 132, 166, 189–90

code 238 *see also* Bernstein, Hasan
cognition 167–8, 227–8
cognitive linguistics 189, 194–5
cohesion 154, 157, 211
communicative language teaching 70
Communist Party 117, 184, 206, 248–9
complementarity 193–4, 233–6
complexity theory 251
computational linguistics 92–3, 130–1, 132, 163, 184, 186, 200–1, 250–1
connotative semiotic 82, 129
constituency 7, 33, 34, 82
content plane 83, 215
context 122–32, 144, 157, 211, 215–16
   of culture 69, 213–14
   of situation 80, 87–8, 132, 169, 213–14
   see also field, mode, tenor
contextual configuration 88
Copenhagen School 74 *see also* Hjelmslev
corpus linguistics 195
covert categories *see* cryptotype
creativity 36, 86 *see also* stylistics
critical linguistics 166
cryptotype 123

de-automatization 84
Deacon 227
deep structure 34
delicacy 46, 75
Derrida 126, 127
diachronic 19
dialect 80, 82, 150, 161, 238
diatypic variety *see* register
discourse 83, 84, 199
Dore 47
Doughty see *Language in Use*
Douglas 128, 154
dynamic open systems 110, 129

Eco 84, 85
Edelman 168, 208, 224, 227

Edinburgh 117
ergative 87, 172–3
Ervin-Tripp 49
ESL 119, 128
experiential 14, 15, 24, 82
exponence 76, 108, 217, 236–7
expression plane 83, 216

Fairclough 165
Fawcett 43, 46, 158, 185, 200, 201
field 80–1, 87–8, 145
Fillmore 42
Firth 1, 5, 7, 20, 29, 33, 37, 45, 74, 75, 76, 83, 87, 91, 96, 105–8, 109–10, 118, 120, 123, 125, 144, 149, 150, 151, 161, 181, 183, 184, 206–8, 213–14, 217, 236–7, 255
Fishman 91, 161
function (vs class) 12, 13–14, 78, 112, 143

Geertz 186
generative semantics 33
genre 72, 88, 168–9, 206
grammar (top-down approach) 108, 150
grammatical metaphor 128, 198, 216–17
Gray 120
Greaves 121, 211
Gregory 151, 159
Greimas 34, 84–5, 126
Gumperz 237

Harris 34, 44, 55
Hasan 88, 119, 153, 154–5, 158, 162, 165, 185, 204, 211, 215, 255
heteroglossia 83
hierarchies 233–6
Hjelmslev 5, 6–7, 11, 14, 20, 33, 34, 38, 61, 74, 82, 85, 125, 151, 214, 217–18
Huddleston 45–6
Hudson 43
human sciences 229, 250
Hymes 1, 4–5, 17, 91

ideational 12, 14, 15–16, 17, 144, 156, 216
    see also experiential, logical
individuation 237–8
information 24, 157

Information Sciences Institute (I.S.I) 130–2
instantiation 74–5, 81, 169, 175–6, 236–7
inter-organism 1, 3–5, 16, 31, 34, 226, 229
interdisciplinary 180, 250
interpersonal 12, 14, 17, 82, 89–90, 144, 156, 216
intonation 26–7, 121, 211
intra-organism 1, 4, 16, 31, 226, 229
Introduction to Functional Grammar 157, 172, 217, 219, 243

Jakobson 79

knowledge about language 65–6
Kress 165, 187

Labov 1, 5, 29, 51–2, 91, 125, 155, 161, 162, 237
Lakoff 33
Lamb 5, 10, 18, 33, 34, 151, 212, 215, 226–7, 236–7
language across the curriculum 67, 182
Language and Communication 63, 162
language and education 31–2, 52–3, 62–3, 64, 67–72, 116–22, 135–6, 151, 162, 168, 197, 206, 240–1
language development *see* ontogenesis
Language Development Project 63, 64, 119, 128, 136
Language in Use 52, 63, 64, 121, 154, 162, 182–3
language-based theory of learning 70, 128, 227
language teaching 97–9, 149, 254–5
language typology 188, 243–4
langue 18, 75, 100, 125, 156
learning about language 64
learning language 64–5
learning through language 64
van Leeuwen 187, 222
Lemke 80, 110, 129, 167, 231
Levi-Strauss 34, 37, 77
lexicogrammar 5–6, 8, 9
lexis 9, 220–1
literacy 32, 71
logical 14, 15
logogenesis 236–7
London School 33, 74, 79
Luo Changpei 100–1, 103, 205

machine translation 201–2, 241, 255 *see also* Cambridge, computational linguistics
Mackay see *Breakthrough to Literacy*
macrofunction 28, 29, 111 *see also* ontogenesis
Malinowski 11, 14, 34, 47, 74, 79, 80, 87, 125, 144, 151, 152, 156, 213–14
Mann 73, 93, 131, 163, 186, 200–1
Martin 46, 71, 84, 88, 89, 128, 157–8, 168, 181, 191, 211, 221, 243, 249, 254
Martinet 34, 151
Marxist linguistics 117–18, 150, 152, 157, 163, 248–50, 254–5
materialist linguistics 130
Mathesius 44, 156
Maton 251
Matthiessen 131, 158, 163, 167, 195, 201, 240, 244
McCawley 33
McKellar 92, 132
meaning potential 6, 9, 62, 75–6, 109
metafunctions 77, 78–9, 81–2, 111, 143–4, 156–7, 216, 219–20 *see also* ideational; interpersonal; textual
metaredundancy 214–15
microfunction 29–30
mode 80–1, 87–8, 127–8, 145
Mohan 154, 162, 187
mood 13, 16, 26, 77, 81, 156
multimodality 186–7, 221–4

neurobiology 227
nominalization 25

O'Toole 187, 222
ontogenesis 13, 19–20, 27–31, 47–50, 52, 65, 69, 71, 83, 89, 121, 137–8, 157, 166–7, 185–6, 212, 231–3

painter 57, 158, 232–3
paradigmatic relations 7, 20, 21, 76, 79–80, 109
paralinguistics 218
parole 18, 75, 100, 125, 156
particulate 82
Peking University 99, 100
Penman Project *see* Mann
periodic 82

phonetics 218
phonology 218, 256
phylogenesis 20, 110
Pike 5, 33, 151
post-structuralism 110, 125, 127
pragmatics 81, 164
Prague School 5, 13, 33, 34, 74, 79, 151, 156
probabilities 80, 109–10, 115–16, 169–70, 173–4, 230
process (instantiating system) 20, 61–2, 74–5, 81
prosodic 82
proto-language 30–1, 50, 89, 111

rank 21, 220
realization 6, 9, 10–11, 20–1, 33, 81–2, 108, 112–13, 214–15
register 72, 80, 82, 88, 120, 132, 150–1, 168–71
Reid 150
restricted languages 120, 150
Robins 106–7
Rothery 71

Sankoff 51
Sapir 54, 86, 123, 151 161, 205
Saussure 5, 11, 18, 44, 61, 74, 75, 100, 125, 197, 245
scale and category grammar 158
School of Oriental and African Studies (SOAS) 97, 104–5, 118, 123, 255
scientific English 130, 206
semiotics 125–6, 140–1, 180, 224–5
Sinclair 21
social semiotics 84–5, 153, 162–3, 212, 213
sociolinguistics 91, 164, 180–1
sociosemantics 1, 29, 85
Steiner 159
stratification 5, 20–1, 81–2, 83–4, 108, 125, 175, 212–15, 216, 217–18, 236–7
Strevens 116, 188
structure 7, 8, 13–14, 76, 77, 108
structure (vs system) 20
stylistics 32, 36, 61, 74, 85–96, 204, 241–3
subject (vs topic) 193–4
Swadesh 249–50
synchronic 19
syntagmatic relations 8, 21, 76, 109

system 7, 76, 88, 108, 143
system (vs process) 20, 61–2, 74–5, 81
system network 7, 75, 76–7, 109, 130–1, 143

tenor 80–1, 87–8, 145
text (as process) 20, 61–2, 74–5, 81
text (as semantic unit) 20–1, 82–3, 199
textlinguistics 56
textual 12, 14–15, 17, 24, 82, 144, 156
theme 24, 81, 157, 170–2
thick description 186
Thornton see *Language in Use*
tone 26
tonicity 26
topic (vs subject) 193–4
traditional (school) grammar 64
transdisciplinary 180, 250
transformational (generative) grammar 42–5, 53–4, 55, 86, 122, 189
transitive 87, 172–3

transitivity 13, 22–4, 32, 77, 81, 84, 87, 172, 177, 216
translation 221, 241
Trevarthen 50, 232
Troubetzkoy 33
types of structure 219–20

universals 36–8, 39, 41–2

verbal art *see* stylistics
Vygotsky 71, 232, 246

Wang Li 101–4, 106, 149–50, 208, 231, 247
Webster 185
West Coast functionalism 159
Whorf 36, 37, 54, 55, 85–6, 114, 123–4, 152, 161, 205, 213
Winograd 43, 57
World War II service 99, 149, 150, 204, 252–3